Contents

4.0 Consumption

5.0 Contexts

Notes on Contributors

Michael Allen is Lecturer in Film, Television and Electronic Media at Birkbeck College, University of London. Previously, he spent three years as Research Officer at the British Film Institute, where he developed multimedia programs to aid the academic study of film and television. He has also taught Film and Television Studies at the University of East Anglia, University of North London, and Royal Holloway College. His areas of research include: the history of media technologies, early cinema, modern American cinema, and digitalisation and digital culture. Publications include *Family Secrets: The Feature Films of D.W. Griffith* (BFI, 1999) and *Contemporary US Cinema* (McLean Press, 2002).

William Boddy is a Professor in the Department of Communication Arts at Baruch College and in the Certificate Program in Film Studies at the Graduate Center, both of the City University of New York. He is the author of *Fifties Television: The Industry and Its Critics* and of numerous articles and book chapters on media history and is currently completing a social history of twentieth-century electronic media.

Scott Bukatman is Assistant Professor of Media Studies in the Department of Art and Art History, Stanford University. He is author of Terminal Identity: The Virtual Subject of Postmodern Science Fiction (Duke University Press), Blade Runner (British Film Institute) and *Matters of Gravity: Special Effects and Supermen in the 20th Century* (Duke, forthcoming).

Jeremy G. Butler is Associate Professor in Telecommunication and Film at The University of Alabama. Creator of *ScreenSite* (the Web's first site for film/TV studies), his current research interests include television genres and the crossover between television and the Internet. He has published a number of articles on film, television, and new media, including 'VR in the ER: *ER's* Use of E-Media' (*Screen*). He has also written *Television: Critical Methods and Applications* (Lawrence Erlbaum Associates, 2001) and edited *Star Texts: Image and Performance in Film and Television* (Wayne State University Press, 1991).

John T. Caldwell is producer/director of the films *Rancho California (por favor)* (2002) and *Freak Street to Goa: Immigrants on the Rajpath* (1989), and Associate Professor of Film, Television, and Digital Media at UCLA. His media studies books include *Televisuality: Style, Crisis, and Authority in American Television* (Rutgers, 1995) and *Electronic Media and Technoculture* (Rutgers, 2000), and a special volume of *Emergences* on 'Globalism, Convergence, and Identity' (Vol. 11, 2001). Recipient of NEA and Regional Fellowships awards, his productions have been televised in Australia and the U.S., and screened in Amsterdam, Paris, Berlin, New York, Chicago, and Sundance.

Sean Cubitt is Professor of Screen and Media Studies at the University of Waikato, Aotearoa, New Zealand. A Web-poet and media/arts journalist, he has published widely on contemporary arts, media and culture. Among his publications are *Timeshift: On Video Culture*, *Videography: Video Media as Art and Culture*, *Digital Aesthetics*, *Simulation and Social Theory*, and two co-edited anthologies in press, *Aliens R Us: Postcolonial Science Fictions* and *The Third Text Reader*. He is currently completing a book on time and special effects for MIT Press.

Anne Friedberg is Associate Professor of Film Studies at the University of California, Irvine. She is the author of *Window Shopping: Cinema and the Postmodern* (University of California Press, 1993) and co-editor of an anthology of critical and theoretical writing about film, *Close Up 1927–1933: Cinema and Modernism* (Cassell U.K./Princeton University Press, 1998). Her current book project, *The Virtual Window: From Alberti to Microsoft* situates the convergence of cinema, television and the computer screens within a cultural history of the window as an architectural and figurative trope.

Ben Goldsmith is a Research Fellow at the Australian Key Centre for Cultural and Media Policy, Griffith University, Brisbane. He has published articles on Australian cinema and media regulation, and co-authored (with Julian Thomas, Tom O'Regan and Stuart Cunningham) *The Future of Local Content: Options for Emerging Technologies*.

Dan Harries is Senior Lecturer in Film and Visual Culture at Middlesex University, London. Formerly Director of Online Media at the American Film Institute in Los Angeles and creator of *CineMedia* <www.cinemedia.org> – the Internet's largest film and media directory. His current research focuses on intertextuality, media spectatorship, and digital culture. He has published a number of articles on film and media theory, co-authored (with Bert Deivert) *Film and Video on the Internet* (Wiese, 1996), and wrote *Film Parody* (BFI, 2000).

Michele Hilmes is Professor of Media and Cultural Studies at the University of Wisconsin-Madison. She is the author of *Hollywood and Broadcasting: From Radio to Cable* (Illinois, 1990), *Radio Voices: American Broadcasting 1922–1952* (Minnesota, 1997), *Only Connect: A Cultural History of Broadcasting in the United States* (Wadsworth, 2001), and co-editor (with Jason Lovigio) of *The Radio Reader: Essays in the Cultural History of Radio* (Routledge, 2001). She is currently editing *The Television History Book* (BFI, 2003) and working on a history of the mutual influence between the United States and Great Britain in the development of broadcasting.

Henry Jenkins is the Director of MIT's Comparative Media Studies Program. He is the author, editor, or co-editor of nine books, including *Textual Poachers: Television Fans and Participatory Culture*, *From Barbie to Mortal Kombat: Gender and Computer Games*, *Hop on Pop: The Politics and Pleasures of Popular Culture, Rethinking New Media*, and *New Media and Democracy*. His column, 'Digital Renaissance', appears monthly in *Technology Review*. He regularly consults about the social and cultural impact of media change with organizations ranging from the Federal Communications Commission, the Interactive Digital Software Association, and the World Economic Forum.

Marsha Kinder chairs Critical Studies in the School of Cinema-Television at the University of Southern California. Since 1997 she has directed the Labyrinth Project at USC's Annenberg Center for Communication, producing interactive documentaries in collaboration with filmmakers Pat O'Neill, Peter Forgacs, Nina Menkes, Carroll Parrott Blue, and Mark Jonathan Harris and writers John Rechy and Norman Klein. She also edits a series of scholarly CD-ROMs, including her own 'Blood Cinema' and Yuri Tsivian's 'Immaterial Bodies', and is developing an e-learning course on 'The International Legacy of Russian Modernism'. A member of *Film Quarterly*'s editorial board since 1977, she has published over 100 essays and 10 books.

Peter Lunenfeld teaches in the graduate Media Design Program at Art Center College of Design, Pasadena, CA. He is the author of *Snap to Grid: A User's Guide to Digital Arts, Media and Cultures* (MIT, 2000), editor of *The Digital Dialectic: New Essays in New Media* (MIT, 1999) and editorial director of the highly designed Mediawork pamphlet series for the MIT Press on the intersections of art, design, technology and market culture. The first, *Utopian Entrepreneur*, written by Brenda Laurel and designed by Denise Gonzales Crisp, was published in September 2001.

Lev Manovich <www.manovich.net> is an Associate Professor at the Visual Arts Department, University of California, San Diego where he teaches courses in new media art and theory. He is the author of *The Language of New Media* (The MIT Press, 2001), *Tekstura: Russian Essays on Visual Culture* (Chicago University Press, 1993) as well as over 50 articles which have been published in more than 20 countries. Currently he is working on a new book, *Info-aesthetics*, and a digital film project, 'Soft Cinema'.

P. David Marshall is chair of the Department of Communication Studies at Northeastern University in Boston. He is the author of *Celebrity and Power* (Minnesota, 1997) and co-author of *Fame Games* (Cambridge, 2000/01, with Graeme Turner and Frances Bonner). His current research has focused on new media and he has two other books currently in production and writing: *Web Theory* (Routledge, 2002, with Robert Burnett) and *New Media Cultures* (Edward Arnold). He is also the founder of *m/c: a journal of media and culture* <www.media-culture.org.au>.

Tara McPherson is an Assistant Professor of Gender Studies and Critical Studies in USC's School of Cinema-TV, where she teaches courses in television, new media, and contemporary popular culture. Her writing has appeared in numerous journals and edited anthologies. She is co-editor, along with Henry Jenkins and Jane Shattuc, of *Hop on Pop: The Politics and Pleasures of Popular Culture* and author of *Reconstructing Dixie: Race, Place and Femininity in the Deep South*, both forthcoming from Duke. She is also currently co-editing two anthologies on new technology, was co-organizer of the 1999 conference, *Interactive Frictions*, and is a founder and co-organizer of the *Race in Digital Space* conferences.

Tom O'Regan is Professor in the School of Film, Media and Cultural Studies and Director of the Australian Key Centre for Cultural and Media Policy at Griffith University, Brisbane. He co-founded the cultural and media studies journal *Continuum* (1987–1995). His books include *Australian Television Culture* (Allen & Unwin, 1993) and *Australian National Cinema* (Routledge, 1996). He is a co-author of the recent report *The Future for Local Content* (Australian Broadcasting Authority, 2001). He is currently researching arts and media audience development strategies, contemporary film studios and trajectories for cultural policy.

Jan Simons is lecturer Film and New Media Studies at the University of Amsterdam. Former chief editor of Dutch film magazine, *Skrien*, his current research interests include cognitive approaches of audio-visual media, European cinema, new media and new narrative formats, and digital cultures. He has also published *Zwevende Kiezers & Zappende Kijkers. Politiek en Beeld* – a study of political communication through television, and a forthcoming introduction to new media.

Douglas Thomas is Associate Professor in the Annenberg School for Communication at the University of Southern California. His research focuses on the social and cultural impacts of new media and technology. He co-edited (with Brian D. Loader) *Cybercrime: Law Enforcement, Security and Surveillance in the Information Age* (Routledge, 2000) and wrote *Hacker Culture* (University of Minnesota Press, 2002).

William Uricchio is Professor of Comparative Media Studies at the Massachusetts Institute of Technology (MIT), Cambridge, USA and Professor of Comparative Media History in the Institute for Media and Representation at Utrecht University in the Netherlands. His research focuses on the emergence of media technologies, media practices, and the construction of audiences and knowledge. He has written extensively on early technologies of representation such as the camera obscura and nineteenth century photography, on the regulation of taste and social space in early cinema, and on the historiographic implications of today's new media.

Janet Wasko is a Professor in Communication Studies at the University of Oregon, Eugene, Oregon. She is the author of *Movies and Money* (Ablex, 1982), *Hollywood in the Information Age* (Polity, 1994), and *Understanding Disney: The Manufacture of Fantasy* (Polity, 2001).

Plate 01
Still from *The Matrix* (1999)
See page 24

Plate 02
Advertisement for the Philips FlatTV
See page 32

Plate 03
Screen shot from *Jimmy Neutron: Boy Genuis* Web site
See page 66

Plate 04

Screen shot of the Napster browser

See page 86

Plate 05

Screen shot from *Zot!* Online

See page 139

Plate 06
Screen shot of *The Blair Witch Project* (1999) DVD interface
See page 150

Plate 07
Screen shot from *Big Brother* (CBS, 2001) Web site
See page 179

Plate 08
Still from *Timecode* (2000)
See page 216

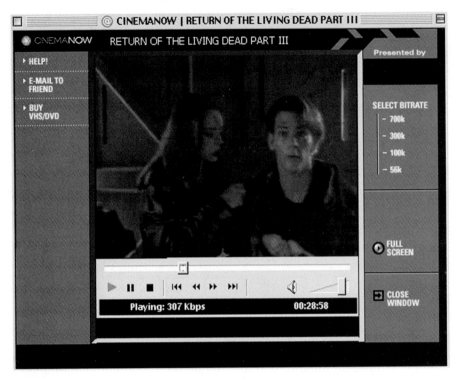

Plate 09

Screen shot of CinemaNow Web site screening *Return of the Living Dead Part III* (1993)

See page 197

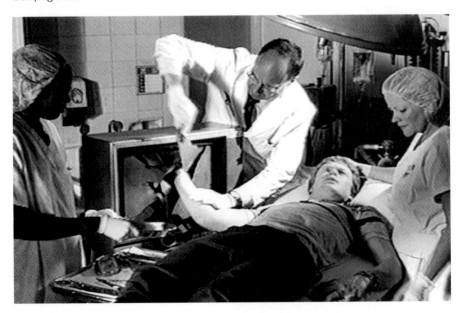

Plate 10

Still from TiVo television commerical

See page 246

Preface

The term 'new media' has become an effective catchword both as a description of the digital delivery of media via the Internet, DVD and digital television and as a reference to the 'newness' such technologies have brought to media more generally. But what makes new media 'new'? Is it the new ways in which we interact with media? Is it the new convergences (and bundling) of media technologies? Or is it the increasing interdependence (and overlap) of various media products? In short, the answer is that the 'newness' of new media can be attributed to all of these factors and more.

The interaction, augmentation and interdependence arising between what can be roughly deemed as 'old' media and 'new' media producers are some of the most prominent aspects of contemporary media. Films are now modelled after successful computer games, Web sites are leveraging popular television programmes and DVD titles are combining movies with a host of digitised paraphernalia. While movie 'tie-ins' may not be a new phenomenon, the lines between the original and the 'tied' text are becoming blurred as one text may be produced simultaneously and equally across various platforms. This synergistic relationship among media has become a necessary feature within the new media market paradigms and the growing global production and marketing ecologies. Traditional media producers are keeping a cautious finger in the digital media pie, while new media producers are more than eager to bring on board traditional entertainment brands, titles and talent.

Similarly, changes in media distribution and consumption are evident on a number of fronts. Hollywood studios and national television networks have actively expanded the reach of their products by simply 'inserting' their movies and television programmes into a digital platform, such as the viewing of material on the Internet or the production of feature film DVDs. Others have attempted to create new and innovative ways to make the viewer a more interactive participant in the viewing process. Venues for media exhibition are also changing with e-cinema and video-on-demand now competing with more traditional modes of exhibition such as the cinema or broadcast television. Such shifts signal the return of vertical integration within Hollywood, as well as the move to horizontally leverage products across the media spectrum – all in the name of creating the next successful 'integrated media experience'.

Since the early 1990s, many of us teaching and researching in the areas of film, media and communication studies have been both bemused and intrigued by the potentialities and eventual realities of new media (also referred to by a variety of terms including multimedia, interactive media, online media and digital media). We began to modify existing media courses, as well as to devise specific courses, to consider new and emerging forms of media. At the same time, scholars expanded their existing research areas to investigate the relationships between 'new' and 'old' media.

This book brings together many of these scholars, from a variety of academic disciplines including film, media and communication studies, to document, analyse and forecast the shifting parameters of the 'new' media. These scholars share the view that these developments have arisen not out of some sort of cultural, historical or technological vacuum, but instead have developed within and have been conditioned, pre-empted and influenced by a broader context and array of existing media technologies, production strategies, narratives, aesthetics, spectatorships and patterns of consumption.

The book is divided into five sections that represent areas of analysis typically conducted in the study of media: Technologies, Production, Texts, Consumption and Contexts. Of course, the very nature of new media makes such division into discrete sections a fairly difficult task, and, while each chapter makes a solid contribution to its designated section, it also makes pertinent connections across the sections and highlights the dynamic and fluid nature of the 'new' media.

1.0

TECHNOLOGIES

We begin this book with a discussion of the different technologies that characterise new and emerging media and the charting of their developments within a broader historical dimension of media technologies, particularly film and television.

Writings about new media quite often focus exclusively on the 'wow factor' of emerging media technologies, highlighting the 'magnitude' of the Internet, the 'interactive speed' of DVD or the 'amazing resolution' of digital television. Although the authors of the following chapters share this enthusiasm for the potential of new media technologies, they are also cognisant of the complexities inherent in these developments which go beyond scientific breakthroughs, including the tendency of certain forms of new media to lag behind touted potential and to fail (sometimes remarkably) to materialise into viable media platforms. By placing the successes and failures of new media technologies into a broader context of both analogue and digital media technologies, the following discussions expose and explore the circuitous relationship that exists between media technologies, production methods, texts and spectatorships.

These relationships are particularly evident when one analyses how the digitisation of media creates content that is highly 'portable', making the distribution and exhibition of such content across platforms and technologies increasingly easy. In fact, this makes it quite difficult to discuss specifically one type of emerging media technology without acknowledging a host of other technologies that utilise and harness digitisation's versatility.

The chapters in this section (and in the book as a whole) consider a wide range of new media technologies, including digital video, cable television, digital special effects, DVD, satellite television, nonlinear video editing, electronic games, digital television, CD-ROM, e-cinema, and the Internet. As many of the following chapters point out, the material differences between media technologies have been increasingly eroded and subsequently converged), and any discussion of a particular media technology will almost certainly rub up against other forms of technology. The following section, therefore, investigates both the promises and the failures of recent technological developments and situates them within the larger historical and cultural contexts of media technology.

1.1

Cable, Satellite and Digital Technologies

Michele Hilmes

New technologies come into the world not in a pristine state, but deeply embedded in social context.[1] For broadcasting, and for film to a certain extent, one of the most significant and powerful forces is that of *nation*. From its inception, radio and then television broadcasting developed in a deeply nationalistic context, guided by the twentieth-century imperatives of national definition, unification and defence. Broadcasting, though ideally suited as a technology to transgressing borders, defying social and political boundaries, and addressing audiences as private individuals in their homes rather than as public citizens of a nation, was from the beginning drawn under tight national control. Carefully kept from crossing national lines, crafted to address only its own citizens and no others, shaped and regulated by national governments, broadcasting history reflects this nationalistic bias.

While the impact of cable, satellite and digital technologies on the media universe encompasses many aspects, within the context of nation their most salient and disruptive characteristic centres on their function as modes of *transmission*. Cable, though in many ways a far more localised medium than broadcasting, was able to break through the limitations enforced by regulated broadcasting systems and eventually open up the national media universe, not least by more tightly integrating film into televisual content. When linked with satellite transmission in the late 1970s, cable television's channel capacity soared, along with its ability to escape restrictive national regulations. During this process cable and satellites exceeded their initial function as primarily transmitters of existing media and became an arena for innovative production of new modes of creative expression and expansion of access to a greater diversity of cultural products and meanings. Digital technology has accomplished much, and promises much more, along these lines. This chapter will examine each technology in turn, assessing its ability to extend and disrupt the national restrictions and functions of film and broadcast media, and looking at their convergence in the early years of this new century.[2]

CABLE TELEVISION

Cable transmission did not begin with television. Various countries experimented with wired transmission of radio, most significantly perhaps in the UK, where so-called 'relay exchanges' allowed subscribers to save the cost of buying individual radio sets (and paying the licence fee) by simply installing a loudspeaker hooked up to the central exchange, for a few pence a month. Later, the wired services brought in commercial stations broadcasting from Luxembourg and Normandy, much to the BBC's displeasure.[3] A few US cities experimented with subscription radio sent over wires into customers' homes. Yet the expense of laying wires where few limitations on reception then existed, due to US radio's abundant and relatively wide-ranging signals, made such experiments short-lived.

It was not until the late 1940s, as television's reach spread much more slowly than the immense hype surrounding it, that a few remote localities in the US began to set up high-ground antennae (community antennae, hence the acronym CATV) and run wires down into homes and businesses below. Picking up signals available from nearby cities' TV stations, the earliest cable operators (often the local appliance store owner, whose interest was in selling television sets) charged subscribers a dollar or two a month. Thus cable began as a re-transmission medium, encouraged at this point by broadcasters as it widened their audience base and raised their advertising rates. This was particularly true during the licence 'freeze' of 1948 to 1952. However, once the freeze was lifted and new stations began to spring up in previously underserved areas, it did not take long for broadcasters to perceive cable as a threat as it could pull in distant rival stations or even offer special programming on available channels, such as films, syndicated programmes and local productions.

In other countries where television began as a state-sponsored public service monopoly (the far more common model, especially in Europe), great effort was expended to ensure that broadcast reception was available nationwide from the beginning. Competition with state broadcasters was not allowed. After the early 1950s, in areas where reception difficulties abounded, for example, within large apartment buildings in major cities or in mountainous areas, cable was used much as it was in the US, as a re-transmission device. However, until satellite transmission promised an outside source of programming, cable was limited in most public-service based systems to the two or three state services available. Few incentives for expansion existed. In some countries, however, particularly Belgium, Luxembourg, Switzerland and the Netherlands, cable was used more extensively to relay multiple public service stations into areas outside their reach.[4] In Canada, with its mix of public and commercial broadcasting, cable expanded much more rapidly, mostly as a vehicle for bringing American programming into Canadian homes, by microwave.[5]

During this early period in the US, another possibility, later to become highly significant for cable, reared its head, much to the dismay of certain sectors of the industry. In the late 1940s and early 1950s, several methods for bypassing broadcast networks by bringing uncut and uninterrupted feature films to television audiences made their debut. Subscription television, transmitted either via unused UHF frequencies or via cable, would allow customers to receive additional channels of film entertainment either for a monthly fee or on a pay-per-view basis. A few ambitious entrepreneurs, allied with Hollywood studio interests, attempted to test the technology in both the US and Canada. Although reviled by struggling cinema owners, and ultimately shut down by regulators who saw their duty as protecting broadcasters from competition, cable seemed to promise a means for breaking the bottleneck of the solidifying three-network oligopoly in the US and allowing the film industry a foothold in television that had been denied it by regulatory decisions. However, the Federal Communications Commission (FCC) ruled against pay-TV experimentation as it began to crack down on the importation of distant signals in the early 1960s.[6]

Opposed by broadcasters and regulators, limited to twelve or fewer channels, faced by high system construction costs, cable might have remained forever a secondary medium were it not for two technological developments of the late 1970s: satellite broadcasting and fibre optics. Yet even before these technologies expanded cable's abilities, the early 1970s in the US, Canada, Europe and other leading television nations began to witness a rise in perceptions of cable's social potential. Pressure was building to break free of broadcast television's limitations, whether commercial or public, and expand the number and types of service available. In the US, commercial network television was increasingly perceived as a 'vast wasteland' dominated by greedy sponsors and a 'lowest common denominator' programming mentality. Cable promised the 'narrowcasting' of more specialised minority programming, local access channels that could pick up the community television function that local commercial stations had long since dropped, and commercial-free film channels: a television of abundance rather than scarcity. The fact that the UHF band remained largely empty, and might have provided many of these same services, went unexamined in the rush to embrace the 'new' technology.

In Europe, where some countries had begun to privatise broadcasting and expand the number of public channels, the promise of cable's interactivity proved compelling, evoking visions of public participation in civic decision-making. Cable was seen as the potential backbone of the burgeoning deployment of information technology. It also allowed the growing pressure towards expansion of media systems to bypass the difficult battles over terrestrial broadcasting and move into a new, promising arena uncolonised by established interests. A 'blue skies' scenario developed, whereby cable would solve the myriad problems that seemed so deeply embedded in current broadcasting systems.[7] This was avidly encouraged by the burgeoning cable industry in the US and by some public broadcasters and state agencies elsewhere. The FCC began to make cable's way a little smoother, marked by cable regulations passed in 1972. In Canada, regulators' attempts to limit cable to communities that already had two or more Canadian stations available, and to allow only one commercial and one public US channel on those that met that standard, sparked general outrage and the proposal was dropped. In the UK, cable began to be studied for its potential, and in 1983 a few companies would begin to offer regional services. Yet cable was expensive to install and still depended largely on broadcast programmes for its material. In 1975 cable subscription rates stood at only 12 per cent of homes in the US. Struggling local franchisees began to sell out to larger companies, creating the first multiple systems operators (MSOs).

However, in 1975 Time Inc.'s subsidiary Home Box Office (HBO) launched the first service to take advantage of satellite distribution of unique, film-based programming to local cable franchises nationwide. Leasing a commercial satellite transponder and using it to beam its signal across the satellite footprint, HBO was only the first of cable's rapidly expanding specialised services that began to find a niche. Simultaneously, fibre-optic technology, which sends data through bundled glass fibres in place of the old copper wire, allowed cable systems to expand their channel capacity exponentially in the 1980s. From 12 channels, cable grew to the 'Bruce Springsteen phase' ('52 channels and nothing on') and beyond. Now cable came into its own. Atlanta station owner Ted Turner beamed his WTBS, with its exclusive franchise over the Atlanta Braves (also owned by Turner), up onto a satellite transponder, founding the first cable 'superstation'.

Other channels appeared quickly, from Turner's second effort, the Cable News Network (CNN, often derided during its early years as the Chicken Noodle Network, due to its low production values), to music video-dominated MTV, all sports all the time on ESPN, and other more varied offerings such as CSPAN (televising Congress and other governmental activities), USA (a varied-format channel owned mostly by movie studios), the Christian Broadcasting Network (CBN), Black Entertainment Television (BET), various home shopping channels, and pay-TV services such as Showtime and The Movie Channel. Rules imposed by the FCC meant that cable operators were obliged to carry all 'significantly viewed' local stations in each franchise area, giving a boost to independent stations that would eventually lead to the inception of new, movie-studio networks Fox, United Paramount Network (UPN) and Warner Bros. (WB).[8] The demand for programming created by this surge in venues sparked the growth of independent production in Hollywood and elsewhere, and created new television outlets for such marginalised forms as independent films, documentaries, children's programmes and ethnic/foreign language film and television. Eventually, the film and television industries would become so tightly intertwined through cross-investment and production that they could hardly be separated any longer. Original production for cable would, in the 1990s, begin to rival both network television and film for audience and critical acclaim, as with HBO's series The Sopranos. By 2001, the number of television channels available in the average US home had reached 55, an increase from 39 only eight years before.[9]

Cable expanded across the globe. Canada's subscription rates had exceeded 80 per cent by the early 1990s.[10] In Europe, as a wave of privatisation and commercialisation transformed the public service environment, cable was envisioned as playing a key role in the new telecommunications infrastructure. It could be used to open up limited national systems to the new, combined public and commercial multi-channel service now prevalent in most countries. By 1992, cable reached as many as 92 per cent of homes with televisions in Belgium and 87 per cent in the Netherlands, with most nations above the 30 per cent mark. Only France and the UK resisted the trend. Both had attempted to launch cable services; both had run into unforeseen difficulties resulting from a late start, cumbersome regulatory restrictions and the unexpected rise of direct satellite competition.[11] In order to continue the story of cable's development, and to address some of the cultural and political issues it raises, we must first turn to a history of the development of satellite technology.

SATELLITES

By the mid-1980s satellite broadcasting and cable had become deeply intertwined. Cable as we know it could not exist without the national and international distribution that satellites make possible. On the other hand, as direct broadcast satellite (DBS) becomes a medium in its own right, it promises the first real competition to cable television services. Both media depend on the vital technology of the geostationary satellite. The first satellites used for communication purposes were launched in the early 1960s by US telecommunications companies such as AT&T, Hughes and RCA. The Communications Satellite Corporation (COMSAT) was formed in the US in 1962 with the encouragement and participation of the US government, much as RCA had been formed earlier, to co-ordinate American satellite development, investment and use. In 1964 the International Telecommunications Satellite Organization (INTELSAT) brought together a consortium of countries to serve a similar purpose for international satellite operation. At first managed by COMSAT, it became an independent corporation in 1973, with shares owned by over 100 member nations (the US, through COMSAT, owns 25 per cent).

Television networks and telecommunications companies began using satellites to distribute their signals in the 1970s. With the success of HBO and other cable channels, the demand for commercial transponder space, usually leased from the satellite operator, soon rose to such an extent that the aerospace industry could hardly keep up. Not only cable, but also network and syndicated programming are distributed via satellite, as are radio, data and voice communications, all vying for transponder space. Live coverage of events across the globe depends on it. Add to this most nations' use of satellite communications for defence and information-gathering operations, not to mention the burgeoning cellular phone industry and, increasingly, wireless Internet transmission, and the demand for satellite capacity seems infinite. The geostationary band is becoming full. (Digital technology may save the day here, as discussed below.)

The half-hemisphere-sized footprint of the typical satellite signal began to change the rules of the national media game radically. In the early stages of satellite television transmission, dishes were so large and expensive to install that most satellite reception was done through cable channels: cable systems provided the middleman between service providers and the home audience. This fact alone helped to slow the development of cable in some European countries, such as France and the UK, as so much of the early television material available via satellite consisted of US-based entertainment and news programming. State broadcasters and agencies (particularly those who already produced the bulk of programmes viewed in their home countries) saw no need to invest public dollars to bring American programming to their national audiences, and would-be commercial providers needed government permission to operate, usually meeting with opposition from state broadcasting interests. However, in more heavily cabled countries, the importation of distant signals via satellite, both from the US and from other European broadcasting systems, became a widespread practice.

In the US, DBS became a small but thriving industry in the 1980s, sending satellite signals directly to receivers in people's homes. It was subscribed to mostly by residents of rural areas with no access to cable (creating the 'double-wide and dish' set-up so prevalent across the nation's heartland) and by some city dwellers through SMATV (satellite master antenna television) systems that wired apartment buildings, dormitories and hotels with a dish on the roof and wires running to the units within. It did not yet present much of a challenge to the expanding cable industry. However, by the mid-1990s, with the deregulation of cable television and with most local franchises remaining monopolies in their areas, dissatisfaction with rising subscription rates, limitations on channels carried and the less-than-perfect service that monopolies tend to provide began to encourage DBS ownership. Here digital technology becomes key to DBS's current stage, and we will pick up this story in the next section. Yet in the US, satellite broadcasting's role up until now has been primarily linked to the cable television revolution. In an already commercial and fairly diverse environment, DBS presented simply one more option for delivery of the same kinds of entertainment, news and speciality channels that American audiences have regarded as normal since the 1980s. The US's large landmass, nearly the size of a satellite footprint, meant that the importation of other countries' signals was not an immediate challenge, although Canadian and Mexican channels should certainly be receiving more widespread distribution in the US than they currently are.

In Europe and across the globe, however, the impact of satellite broadcasting has been profound. Coming at a time in the late 1980s when deregulation and commercialisation of broadcasting systems were taking place in most countries, as one author puts it, 'the rapid expansion of satellite channels had a tremendous impact. It removed, effectively, all practical constraints on the prompt development of private commercial channels.'[12] For many countries, one of the primary cultural effects of satellite broadcasting was an influx of American films and series, as well as entire channels of American programming, offered by satellite services that crossed many borders. It is also significant that the late 1980s saw the collapse of the Soviet Union and renewed movements towards political reorganisation and liberalisation across the globe. Satellite broadcasting played a significant role in the liberalising and globalising of media systems that went along with this process.

The first commercial satellite to debut in Europe was the Astra satellite operated out of Luxembourg, launched in 1988 with 16 channels. In the UK, the Independent Broadcasting Authority in 1986 had authorised British Sky Broadcasting, a consortium composed mostly of UK commercial television providers, to introduce satellite television to Britain in a regulated, public service context. However, due both to technical and administrative problems, its launch was delayed until 1990; in 1989 Rupert Murdoch's Sky Channel beat it to the punch, broadcasting into Britain from the Astra satellite, outside British regulatory control. By 1991, Murdoch had bought out the struggling BSB operation and renamed it BSkyB.[13]

Offering a mix of music videos, news, popular films and television series (many of them American), and sports, BSkyB's success in Great Britain and across Europe demonstrates not only the influx of American programming that satellite broadcasting brought, but also its inability to be controlled by the regulations of individual nations. The European Community

Directive on Television attempted to impose some order on satellite channels, including a vague ruling that 'a majority proportion of their transmission time, excluding the time appointed to news, sports events, games, advertising and teletext services' be reserved for European-produced programmes. Yet it simultaneously confirmed the fact, now raised to a principle, that if a satellite service launched from one member country passed its own local regulations, it could not be screened out by any other member nation.[14] By 1991, a host of pan-European satellite services were on offer: 21 English language services, ten German, 11 French and 29 others. Some of the most popular channels were SkyOne, Eurosport, MTV, CNN, Euronews, Canal Plus and the TNT Cartoon Network. In Quebec, satellite channels became an important source of French-language programming.

Of course the impact of satellite television was not confined to North America and Europe. Satellites drove the movement towards globalisation in the 1990s as the primary vehicle of international communication. The whole world was soon watching US-based channels such as CNN, MTV and HBO, along with competitors from other nations such as the BBC World News, the European ARTE, India's Zee-TV and Mexico's Telemundo, among a host of others. In countries such as India, the first major competitors to state broadcasters emerged, often based around regional cultures and languages.[15] In Taiwan, pirate cable systems began to spring up, bringing in foreign television channels via satellite, but also providing one of the few spaces for oppositional political programmes.[16] In mainland China, illegal home dishes picked up Murdoch's STAR TV signals from Hong Kong, breaking the communications isolation that had for so long prevailed in that country. However, it remained for the digital revolution to shatter national boundaries conclusively.

DIGITAL CONVERGENCE

In the US, by 2001 DBS (satellite broadcasting directly to the home; sometimes called DTH in Europe) was growing at a rate faster than cable television. The US's two major satellite distributors, EchoStar and DirecTV, ranked in the top ten of subscriber television services, right up there with cable MSOs such as AT&T, Time Warner, and Comcast. DirecTV was number three.[17] This development had everything to do with the stunning proliferation of digital technology in the 1990s. Digital transmission technologies primarily led to the unprecedented rate of convergence between cable, satellites and broadcast television and film, along with newer technologies such as the Internet and its myriad applications.

Digital media begins with the advent of the computer: data broken down into a series of 1s and 0s so that it can be handled, stored and transmitted by the microchips at the heart of modern technology. By the mid-1980s, computers had been developed that were able to convert more complex data – pictures, graphics, music and sounds – into digital formats. But for the most part this was happening in discrete, specialised environments: the video editing suite, the design departments of architectural firms, the sound studios of recording companies and the production facilities of print media companies. The technology that brought sophisticated digital applications together in a way that exponentially multiplied their uses was the Internet, beginning in the early 1990s. The Internet's rapid colonisation of other media and spread into all areas of modern life helped to accelerate the transition from analogue to digital media, as it began to seem clear that digital modes of creation and transmission would dominate the coming decade and probably the century. Cable television regained something of its former cachet as media and information industries looked around for high-speed routes into consumer homes. It seemed as though the television set would no longer function as just a visual entertainment device any longer: hooked up to the home computer, television would deliver telephone and Internet service and possibly invade household privacy by collecting data on its users as well. However, a struggle was taking place in the world of broadcasting that would transform the medium, even though its parameters were not at all clear when the process began.

In the mid-1980s, high-definition television (HDTV) technology, developed in Japan, threw American broadcasters into disarray. HDTV promised to deliver much higher quality pictures and sound, along with an improved screen aspect ratio (a CinemaScope-like 16:9 versus television's boxy 4:3), by increasing the definition, or number of scanning lines, used to compose a televisual image. The US had always had a poorer quality television image than most European and Asian countries, the result of the 525 scanning line NTSC standard as opposed to the 650 scanning line PAL system used elsewhere. As cable, satellites and the new broadcast channels brought film and television closer together than ever, improvement of picture quality seemed an important goal.

However, HDTV, with up to 1080 scanning lines, required a much greater bandwidth to broadcast than standard American television. To make this technology feasible, broadcasters would need additional, broader spectrum space, operating in tandem with their current assignments as they made the change to HDTV. Just as the broadcasting industry was coming to terms with this fact, the FCC began to look into repossessing and auctioning off some of the mostly empty UHF band frequencies formerly reserved for broadcasting. US broadcasters determined to ward this off, along with the prospect of becoming dependent on a Japanese technology, by promising Congress that, if it would leave the UHF bands in place for future HDTV use, American electronics manufacturers, broadcasters, and filmmakers would embark on a campaign to develop their own brand of HDTV.

At this point, however, the digital revolution intervened. With digital technology, a much higher definition television picture could be produced, as good or better than the Japanese MUSE technology (an analogue/digital hybrid) that had started the drive. By 1993, US manufacturers had come up with a strategic 'Grand Alliance' standard for digital transmission of television signals, representing a technical compromise between the competing needs of different industry segments, that could handle a variety of digital high-definition formats with varying degrees of resolution, pixel density, frame rates and scanning methods. Digital technology also possessed another advantage: not only could it be used to broadcast a high quality picture, but it could also be used to compress signals in such a way that four or five standard quality channels could be transmitted on bandwidth previously adequate for only one; a single cable channel could carry 12 or more. This is called *multiplexing*.

In a very clever manoeuvre, US broadcasters managed to win an astonishing victory in the Telecommunications Act of 1996, not only keeping their current analogue frequencies, but also receiving, gratis, billions of dollars worth of higher frequencies on the UHF spectrum. They achieved this by keeping Congress confused about the two competing capacities of digital transmission: high definition and multiplexing. Multiplexing would allow each broadcaster to turn one channel into several, multiplying not only the number of potential channels available, but also the advertising revenue obtainable from them. Or such additional channels could be used for Internet services or leased to corporate customers for other types of data transmission. US broadcasters saw dollar signs. Meanwhile Congress continued to think of digital television as a way of ensuring that American television picture quality emerged as second to none, certainly not to the Japanese. Broadcasters managed to convince Congress that they still needed the additional bandwidth in order to provide this high-quality image, while making plans for more profitable multiplexing. Congress's generous decision to award an additional frequency to each licenced US station provided an enormous windfall for the broadcasting industry.

However, the rules did stipulate that all VHF frequencies would have to be returned to the Federal government by 2006 or by the time that digital television ownership had reached 85 per cent penetration of the US market. Most major networks began digital broadcasting during 2000. Yet by 2001, even among those willing to invest more than $2000 for a digital television set, few were able to experience this new technology, as 80 per cent of Americans receive their television via cable. Cable systems were under no such regulatory pressure to convert to digital broadcasting, although many had already begun the process for reasons of their own – largely to compete with DBS. Digital cable allowed not only more channel capacity, but also enhanced ability for two-way communication, providing interactive guides to the increasingly complex programmes on the 100 or more channels now made available, as well as more pay-per-view services. It also increased prices for cable service to consumers already disenchanted with cable franchises' forays into Internet connection and unimpressed with cable's service record. DBS began to benefit from the digital revolution as well.

The main factor holding DBS back from greater market penetration in the mid-1990s was its inability to deliver local television stations to its customers. Instead, the two dominant US companies, DirecTV and EchoStar, had begun to import distant station signals into markets across the country, forming contracts with one affiliate from each network (usually in a major urban location) and purveying its signal to DBS subscribers: a network affiliate superstation. Local station owners resented the competition within their own markets, and DBS subscribers missed the local news and sports, which were only available to them if they switched over to their broadcast antennae (or, in rural areas, not available at all). To remedy this situation, in 1999, the FCC passed the Satellite Home Viewer Improvement Act, effectively extending cable's regulations to DBS. By January 2002, satellite providers were required to begin carrying local station signals in each local market served. DBS companies objected on the same first amendment grounds long argued by cable operators, but the rule remains in place today. This, too, is made possible by digital technology's ability to split the satellite signal, permitting local signals to crowd onto an existing satellite channel, usually via microwave. However, one sector of television that DBS's spread threatens is cable's role in local communities. Most cable franchises pay a fee of 5 per cent of gross revenues to their local municipalities, besides providing channels space and some funding for local access channels. Satellite broadcasters are under no such obligation. And once again the Internet promises to play a key role in DBS use, since a new type of two-way high-speed wireless Internet access called VSAT technology debuted in November 2000 through a coalition of EchoStar and Microsoft.[18]

In Europe, the convergence of digital telecommunications and cable, and digital technology and satellites, has produced a boom in those industries, particularly in the UK, now Europe's largest pay-TV market. According to *The Economist*, 'Digital technology has transformed the economics of multi-channel television, enabling independent operators to cater to market niches, and the big pay-TV companies to offer hundreds of channels.'[19] Movie channels account for a substantial proportion of satellite-distributed digital fare, especially in their 'nearly-on-demand' manifestations, where staggered 15-minute showtimes allow almost continuous availability of individual films. By 2001, digital pay television channels, delivered either by DBS or cable, had reached 44 per cent of UK households and accounted for 20 per cent of all television viewing.[20] The BBC announced plans to roll out digital television, but had run into delays by Summer 2001. Australia's five terrestrial public channels debuted in digital multiplex in January 2001, with regulations that prevented commercial networks from following suit until 2008. Japan rolled out fully digital television on NHK in 2000, with plans for expansion. China announced elaborate plans for a national digital service in the Summer of 2001.

However, in light of the developed world's embrace of these new wonder technologies, it seems necessary to emphasise that the vast bulk of the world's population has yet to experience regular and reliable telephone service, much less encounter even a distant echo of the digital revolution. Yet clearly the tide of new media cannot be rolled back, especially as wireless Internet applications join news and entertainment in the cable/satellite/digital interface. New applications arise faster than our ability to understand or control them.

OUTLOOK

The convergence of cable, satellite and digital technologies has transformed the basic arena of film and television distribution from the national to the global. Escaping from the geographical, cultural and regulatory boundaries that formerly played such a crucial role in the production, circulation and reception of media, global convergence means that, even while opportunities for new kinds of creativity and cultural hybridity exist and expand, threats emerge over which existing systems of control have little sway. I end this chapter with mention of only a few of the major areas of revolution and renegotiation.

One prominent factor is the dominance of US media. According to Greg Dyke, Director General of the BBC, 'We are told the world is globalising – that's not true: it is

Americanising. It is essential that TV, radio and online should reflect the cultures of particular countries'.[21] The fact that so many of the integrated media companies distributing channels worldwide are American-owned, and that their content is heavily US-oriented, threatens the cultural integrity of nations adopting new media. While theories of cultural hybridity point to the many examples of local adaptation, experimentation and cultural growth spurred by the opening up of sometimes repressive and restrictive national media regimes, the pre-eminence of channels such as CNN in world news coverage and American domination of the Internet point in the other direction. However, it is precisely the disenfranchising of popular culture (and cultures) in many state public service systems that left the field open for American products to enter; new media promise a corrective to their exclusivity that is not necessarily American. And some would argue that the film, television, video and music produced in sites such as Hollywood, Hong Kong and Bombay represent less the culture of those nations than a new world popular culture, emanating from world production centres.[22] It is certain that the boundaries of the national – imagined, after all – will continue to erode and blur, culturally as well as technologically.

As national regulations lose their grip over multinational conglomerates, little remains to halt the monopolising tendencies of some of the biggest corporations in their march across the globe. A new form of 'global lawlessness' could be the result. If Rubert Murdoch's 2001 proposed merger with DirecTV goes through, his Sky Global satellite service would have reached 300 million homes across North and South America, Asia, Europe and Australia. Teamed up with Hughes/GM, DirecTV's owners, Sky Global under Murdoch's management would have made him 'the only global TV gatekeeper with control of both the programming and the platform that funnels that programming into homes around the world'.[23] Although the US continues to exercise some limited anti-trust supervision of major media mergers in that country, and the European Union monitors those that affect its member markets, for example denying the proposed Internet merger of MCI/Worldcom and Sprint in 2000, little authority exists to block the spread or to direct the operations of mega-corporations such as Murdoch's or others such as AOL Time Warner and Bertelsmann.

One area of particularly contentious 'lawlessness', or the attempt to assert too-aggressive legal rights, is that of intellectual property and copyright. The Napster saga of 1999–2000 brought the world's attention to the threat posed by new digital technologies to the legal concepts currently used to contain culture, define ownership and channel profits in the Internet age, pitting adamant copyright holders against resistant users. For the past few decades, Hollywood has fought to maintain its control over illegal copying and distribution of videocassettes and faces further challenges with the more perfect reproducibility of DVDs. Satellite channels beaming programmes into areas where competitors have already purchased exclusive rights to their exhibition have caused problems in Canada. Recently a consortium of film studios has announced plans for digital distribution of films over the Internet, in a pre-emptive move to ward off both Napster-like file-sharing technologies and the threat posed by smart recorders such as Tivo and Recall-TV. As one studio representative put it, 'We want to give honest people an honest alternative.'[24]

'Honesty', as defined by an industry rarely associated with that quality itself, is only one of the defences of the legal status quo that may be put seriously to the test as digital invasion of national, cultural and industrial territories continues.

Finally, new media convergence seems certain to result in a redefinition, not only of the national, but also of the local. The concept of 'nation' has been, as I have argued, one primary way of drawing boundaries around a certain community of interest and structuring media products and systems within its terms. In the context of twentieth-century nationalisms, this seems so obvious as to be 'natural' and inevitable. Yet other organising ideas have also operated. In countries such as Germany, sub-national *regional* identities shaped the *Lander* structure of broadcasting, influencing film production as well. In the Netherlands, the 'pillarised' broadcasting system that divided control between dominant social groups – Protestants, Catholics, conservatives, liberals – produced a different way of 'locating' culture and distributing power. In the US, the concept of 'local broadcasting' has mostly been defined by urban areas, not by states or regions; one innovation of the public broadcasting system was to allow the emergence of statewide networks.

The digital era, offering instant communication across all these largely geographical types of communities, promises a redefinition of 'the local' based on affinities, interests, language, politics or other cultural identities that supercedes or at least complements other definitions, particularly the national. Thus hip-hop music fans in Japan, England, Poland and the US may represent one kind of 'local' identity, while Web sites and satellite television channels aimed at Indian diasporic communities in South America, Canada, Africa and Greece create another type of locality. Non-governmental organisations (NGOs) concerned with environmental or women's issues can now connect worldwide, creating political entities and pressures that are both global and local. Theorists have barely begun to explore these nation-defying collectivities, and indeed many of our leading media theories, such as those grounded in the public sphere or political economy, will have a very hard time incorporating their challenges in that context. Yet it is vital that we do so, approaching new media convergence neither with blue sky Utopianism nor its equally technologically deterministic converse, dystopian gloom, that has marked so much twentieth-century theory.

Culture, rather than nation, promises to define the media of the twenty-first century and to present the battleground on which most of its struggles will be waged. Yet the means of culture still fall under the sway of nationalised organisations at present or of commercial concerns that threaten to replace the flawed power distribution of national governments with the often even less scrutable mechanisms of marketplace and profits. While technology, inseparably allied with culture, the market and the state, does occasionally hand us ways to redistribute communicative power in a more equitable manner, the forces of containment and control just as rapidly move in. This chapter is an attempt to point at both the promises and the betrayals of recent developments in cable, satellite and digital transmission and to indicate new ways of thinking that may prove helpful in re-imagining their potential and actual use.

Notes

1. For theorisation of this principle, see Raymond Williams, *Television: Technology as Cultural Form* (London: Oxford University Press, 1978) and Brian Winston, 'How Are Media Born?', in John Downing, Ali Mohammadi and Annabelle Sreberny-Mohammadi (eds), *Questioning the Media: A Critical Introduction* (London: Sage, 1990).

2. It is difficult to escape the national bias in which so much scholarship, including my own, has been based. Thus my primary focus here is on the US, UK and other English-speaking nations, though these developments have occurred throughout the globe and certainly deserve a wider focus.

3. Asa Briggs, *The History of Broadcasting in the United Kingdom, Vol. II: The Golden Age of Wireless* (London: Oxford University Press, 1965), pp. 356–60.

4. Peter J. Humphreys, *Mass Media and Media Policy in Western Europe* (Manchester: Manchester University Press, 1996), pp. 164–5.

5. Paul Rutherford, *When Television Was Young: Primetime Canada, 1952–1967* (Toronto: University of Toronto Press, 1990), pp. 137–40.

6. Michele Hilmes, *Hollywood and Broadcasting: From Radio to Cable* (Urbana: University of Illinois Press, 1990), pp. 116–37.

7. See Thomas Streeter, 'The Cable Fable Revisited: Discourse, Policy, and the Making of Cable Television', *Critical Studies in Mass Communication* 4.2, June 1987, and Thomas R. Eisenmann, 'The U.S. Cable Industry, 1948–1995: Managerial Capitalism in Eclipse', *Business History Review*, vol. 47, Spring 2000.

8. Michele Hilmes, *Only Connect: A Cultural History of Broadcasting in the US* (Belmont, CA: Wadsworth, 2001).

9. Jim Rutenberg, 'Much in a Name', *New York Times*, 15 July 2001, p. B4.

10. Richard Collins, *Culture, Communication, & National Identity* (Toronto: University of Toronto Press, 1990), pp. 45–6.

11. Peter J. Humphreys, *Mass Media and Media Policy in Western Europe*, p. 165.

12. Ibid., p. 169.

13. Andrew Crisell, *An Introductory History of British Broadcasting* (London: Routledge, 1997), pp. 221–3.

14. Ralph Negrine, *Politics and the Mass Media in Britain*, 2nd edn (London: Routledge, 1994), pp. 188–207.

15. Shanti Kumar, 'An Indian Personality for Television?', *Jump Cut*, no. 43, July 2000.

16. Szu-ping Lin, 'Prime Time Television Drama and Taiwanese Women' (PhD dissertation, University of Wisconsin-Madison, 2000); Lori Thompson, 'Illegal Cable Thriving in Taiwan', *San Francisco Chronicle*, 3 April 1991, p. 4.

17. John M. Higgins and Gerard Flynn, 'Cable Slows, DBS Sprints', *Broadcasting and Cable*, 4 June 2001, p. 30.

18. Ken Terry, 'Can DBS Deliver the Internet?', *Cablevision*, 28 May 2001.

19. 'Outgrowing Auntie', *The Economist*, 18 August 2001.

20. Ibid.

21. Ibid.

22. Michael Curtin, 'Media Capitals: Cultural Geographies of Global Television', in Lynn Spigel and Jan
     Olsson (eds), *The Persistence of Television: Critical Approaches to Television Studies* (Durham, NC:
     Duke University Press, 2002); Frederick Wasser, 'Is Hollywood America? The Trans-Nationalization of
     the American Film Industry', *Critical Studies in Mass Communication* 12:4 (1995), pp. 423–37.

23. 'Sky Is No Longer the Limit', *Variety*, 21 February 2001, p. 27.

24. Rick Lyman, 'Hollywood, An Eye on Piracy, Moves to Rent Movies Online', *New York Times*,
     17 August 2001, pp. A1, C3.

1.2

Digital Filming and Special Effects

Sean Cubitt

ANALYTICAL AND SYNTHETIC

It is curious that digital photography should have spawned a respectable critical literature,[1] while digital cinematography has, as yet, generated very little theoretical work that deals specifically with film.[2] Two possible reasons come to mind. First, digital cinema approaches more closely the culture of animation than lens-based cinematography. And second, the darkroom has always been a key factor in photographic practice, whereas in cinema, post-production has traditionally been understood as the editing process, rather than the developing and printing of the film strip. I raise this curiosity, which in all likelihood will be a brief and passing phase, only because it raises another conundrum. Traditionally, studies of cinema history have always devoted a chapter to pre-cinematic devices (phenakisto-scopes, thaumatropes and so on) and especially to the chronophotography of Eadweard Muybridge, Etienne-Jules Marey and their contemporaries (the most influential, although now controversial, account is Ceram, 1965).[3] Like other contemporary scholars, I rather dis-trust this continuity model of cinematic development. The quickest way to describe the difference between chronophotography and cinematography is to point out that the unit of chronophotography is the still frame, but that of cinema is three frames: the one just past, the current one and the one coming up. Crudely put, chronophotography was an analyti-cal medium: cinema is synthetic. This is why chronophotography rather than cinema became the tool of choice for Taylorism and 'scientific management'.

A neat enough argument. My attention was caught, however, by a slide projected in a lecture by my colleague Anne Kennedy showing Marey's experiment with an assistant in a black bodysuit marked with white lines for the major limbs, allowing Marey to make a multiple exposure plate of the movement of the lines. An image of the assistant in the experimental regalia was captioned 'Marey's motion capture suit'. After arguing for some time the discontinuity between photographic and cinematic histories, I found myself having to agree: motion capture does hark back to Marey. The immediate thought that followed was: 'Isn't Muybridge's trip-wire operated array of cameras for capturing the motion of a horse the basis for John Gaeta's "bullet time" digital camera array as used in *Blade* (1998) and *The Matrix* (1999)?' Has digital cinema rewritten the history of the medium by assimilating chronophotography, in the same way that it has subsumed into its composite imaging the techniques of animation? And is my neat pedagogical antithesis between analytical and synthetic imaging thus promptly outdated and possibly quite wrong? To get to the heart of this puzzle we need two things: some history and some technology. First, though, we need to define what we mean by special effects and to single out those that are securely and indubitably digital.

THE POLITICAL ECONOMY OF SPECIAL EFFECTS

Special effects come in several varieties, and many are only marginally affected by the transition to digital technologies. Sound effects are still largely produced by the established analogue means of Foley editing, although there are specific examples in which the effect is dependent on digital equipment. Enhancing recordings – for example, to emphasise the lower register – merely expands on analogue techniques. However, Ben Burtt's design of the sound for the laser swords in *Star Wars* (1977) is dependent on the capabilities of digital mixing, even though many of the elements that make up the sword (for example, a Porsche backfiring) derive from real-world sources.[4] One telling example: the gloopy sound of the liquid metal enforcer in *Terminator 2: Judgment Day* (1991) is a faithful reproduction of the sound produced by turning an open can of dog food upside down. The digital production of music is becoming more significant, especially for lower budget productions such as Daniel Aronovsky's *Pi* (1999). The continuing difficulties that the music industry has with the MP3 sound compression format and its use in pirating recordings mean that the full impact of digital music has yet to be felt in the cinema, although virtually all recording now entails the use of digital machinery, if only at the mastering stage, as is notoriously the case with *Pulp Fiction* (1994). It is also the case that Hollywood's continuing love affair with the live orchestra is now backed up by the use of timecoded prints to facilitate synchronisation of score and image in the recording process. Meanwhile the digital control of theatre acoustics has become increasingly significant with the development of Dolby and THX systems. However, digital sound as a whole is still dependent on analogue and imitates it even more closely than visual effects. Thus there are no plans in hand for digitally synthesised voices, even though synthespians, virtual actors existing only in computers, are being developed as a commercial proposition.

Some fields of visual effects are likewise still very close to their analogue counterparts. Stunts, while often enhanced digitally, are pretty much analogue phenomena. The same is true for pyrotechnics and demolition, including miniature pyrotechnics and model work. Prosthetics and make-up, as for example the severed limbs, wounds and piercings with burning arrows in the opening battle sequence of *Gladiator* (2000), are done using time-honoured techniques. New technologies of latex and other modelling materials have changed the craft of make-up, but the fundamentals still apply, and the impact of digital technologies has been minimal. Modelling has, however, been deeply affected by the rise of digitally controlled animatronics. The difference between *The Muppet Movie* (1979) and *The Lost World: Jurassic Park II* (1997) is more than generic. The earlier film relied heavily on human operators working inside the life-size puppets, with only a modicum of wire- and hydraulically controlled mechanical movement. The animatronics for *The Lost World* involved the control of machines of up to nine tons with multiple axes of movement including such nuances as sniffing and flaring nostrils and apparent heartbeats. One significant advance in that film was the successful waterproofing of the circuitry, allowing the creatures to move through a waterfall, for example. To some extent, however, these dinosaurs are the direct heirs of the saurians in *King Kong* (1933), with the major differences that they can be filmed in real time rather than using stop-motion and that they are far easier to combine with the live action, especially in emotive scenes with actors.

Equally intriguing is the transition from painted backdrops, painted mattes and rear projection to chromakey and green-screen technologies, in which action is played out in front of a screen the colour of which acts as a reference tone, allowing all elements of the image which are that colour to be replaced with either a different piece of film footage (effectively rear-projection) or a digital still or moving panorama. Optical printing offered, from the 1930s onwards, a variety of complex and rich effects, such as the flamboyant wipes in *Flying Down to Rio* (1933) and the transformations of Tara in *Gone with the Wind* (1939), where the matte work was likewise outstanding. Rear projection was a major strength of the Ufa studios, where Hitchcock learnt his trade. It is a tricky effect to pull off, as the levels of illumination have to be very finely balanced and the focus adjusted to preserve the sense of depth in harmony with surrounding scenes. Moreover, synchronisation is a permanent problem: every film buff has noted the disparity between jauntily swung steering wheels and back-projected straight roads: there is a fine example of this in Hitchcock's own *Notorious* (1946). The replacement of these techniques with blue- and green-screen technologies was not without its hiccups. The log-line for the first *Superman* movie (1978), 'You will believe a man can fly', no longer convinces us. The wire work with Christopher Reeves is fine, but the compositing of foreground and background produced a strong line around the superhero that now appears unacceptable. Wire work in general has spread rapidly from its home in Hong Kong, where King Hu's *Touch of Zen* (1969) introduced the combination of wire and slow motion that would fuel the New Wave directors Ringo Lam, John Woo, Samo Hung and, most of all, Tsui Hark. With *The Matrix* (1999) and *Crouching Tiger, Hidden Dragon* (2000), Hollywood has appropriated the spectacular stunt choreography tradition in the interests of a cosmopolitan cinema that, despite the failure of *Crouching Tiger* to impress audiences in the Peoples' Republic, augurs a renewed effort to ensure that the American entertainment industry achieves a solid share of the rapidly expanding Asian market.

This family of effects is driven first by the need for spectacle and second by the need to deliver it at reasonable cost. Even the swollen budget of *Gone with the Wind* would not permit the building and burning of a Southern mansion. Using painted mattes and optical printing techniques, though intrinsically expensive, saved huge amounts of money. Rear projection, even if specially shot by a second unit, is far cheaper than taking the whole cast and crew on location. Miniature pyrotechnics, such as those used in the first *Star Wars* trilogy (*Star Wars* 1977, *The Empire Strikes Back* 1980, *Return of the Jedi* 1983), are clearly going to be far less costly than blowing up full-size sets. By the same token, the principle behind building sets as flats and leaving out sections that will not be seen by cameras leads directly to the building of virtual sets. There is no specific gain in spectacle: Ford's Monument Valley or Welles's Xanadu are no less impressive than Cameron's *Titanic*, and all three exist solely as pro-filmic, solely in order to be cinema. That one is digital, one constructed and one framed and composed does not alter the fact that all three are specifically cinematic. So there is no specifiable gain in awe or beauty. What is gained is the economy with which these sets can be manufactured and used.

The earliest and most heavily computerised branch of the film industry, the Asian animation business based in Japan but with major studios throughout the Southeast Asian tiger economies and in India, follows the same logic. Few of the auteur animators in commercial cartoons are responsible for every frame. The lead animator sets the ground rules for characters, movements and environments, and supplies the artwork for key frames. The business of supplying the frames between key frames is 'in-betweening' and is laborious, repetitive, highly skilled, but at the same time not particularly creative. Mechanising this process was a natural place for economising on dull, repetitive work. Nonetheless, some aspects were slow to be fully mechanised. A human animator has no problem understanding how one part of a body moves in front of or behind another, but a computer needs to be instructed. This work on the z-axis (the depth axis of an image, at right angles to the picture plane) was for some time resistant to computerisation, and there are still several competing systems for sorting it out. A second problem was that of soft objects. A human animator knows that when a ball hits the floor, it compresses before rebounding. This observation became an absolute at the Disney studios in the 1930s, the law of constant volume: no matter how stretched, squeezed or battered, Mickey and Goofy were to keep the same apparent volume, unlike such competitors as Felix the Cat. Unfortunately, even in this quasi-mathematical form, a computer has difficulty understanding the problem, especially if it is instructed to work only in the two dimensions of cel animation. The result was balls that looked as if they were made of iron – hence the preponderance of billiard balls in early digital animations. The problem of making the objects soft and resilient was complex and took several years to resolve.

Once worked out, however, the results were highly successful. Katsuhiro Otomo's *Akira* (1987) became an international cult success, the subject of intensive use of computer animation for both in-betweening and for the creation of parallax effects, that is, the creation of an illusion of depth effected by making foregrounds move faster across the screen than backgrounds, as when nearby telegraph poles flash by, while distant trees and fields move more serenely past the window of a moving vehicle. *Akira* was not entirely original here: its parallax effect can be seen as a skilful computerised imitation of the rotoscope, a device based on multiple transparent layers of animation cells used to create foreground and background planes in the Disney studio from the late 1930s onwards. Animation studios also pioneered the use of digital extras. In *The Lion King* (1994), the wildebeest stampede was produced by supplying a small number of distinct behaviours and appearances for the wildebeest, replicating them digitally and controlling their stampede through the use of a flocking algorithm, one of the simple mathematical rules that gives a reasonable facsimile of natural behaviour (in this case the rule is 'always try to be surrounded by other wildebeest'). The carnival scene in *The Hunchback of Notre Dame* (1996) similarly employs a range of individual characters with specific appearances and behaviours, each of a slightly different duration, replicated in large numbers to give the sense of a turbulent and disordered crowd. Such digital extras become highly significant for both scale and cost-saving in Cameron's *Titanic* (1997).

Behind these technical and commercial successes lies again the importance of finance. Now that the global market for children's animation is largely supplied by the Tokyo-based studios, the demand far outstrips the number of skilled animators available. The availability of desktop computers with sufficient power and programs of sufficient sophistication for domestic level machines has driven the cost of computer animation rapidly downwards. In Thailand, even though wages have been kept very low, computerisation is now cheaper. This follows the proletarian model proposed in the 1970s by Harry Braverman.[5] The creative industries are imitating the retail and service industries by lowering the skills level of the workers by transferring those skills to machines. This process began in weaving in the eighteenth century, with the card-controlled Jacquard loom, one of the frequently cited ancestors of punch-card instruction storage systems. If the transfer of live skills to fixed capital began in one craft, it is not surprising that it should today return to assimilate another.

There remains a further area of digital cinema to consider: the use of computer programs such as Movie Magic to control budgets and schedules, and of scriptwriting software not only to format, but also to suggest plot structures and story twists. Even storyboarding has been altered by the arrival of packages capable of animating two-dimensional boards in rough but effective three-dimensional form. The pre-production arena has thus been carefully digitised, too. Inasmuch as the script has been, for almost 70 years, the central device for control of production expenditure in the North American film and television industries, its automation is a gain in efficiency through standardisation. Integrated script and production packages can be presumed to be in the pipeline. Pre-production is still then recognisably what it always has been, but with the additional control and economic efficiency given by digitisation.

DIGITAL TOOLS

Thus far we have suggested that digital cinema is a continuation of analogue media by cheaper means. However, it is in the nature of technological innovations to take on a life of their own. We all have desktop computers not because they increase our creativity, but because of a single software innovation: Lotus 1–2–3 and the spreadsheet. This permitted highly skilled accounting and arithmetical functions to be undertaken by unskilled office workers and made the devices needed to run the software economically viable. However, once the device was available in offices and swiftly afterwards in homes, the unused potential of the gadgets began to encourage the proliferation of new usages. Much the same can be said of the spread of digital film-making. At a certain point it becomes cheaper to buy the hardware to run Softimage than to hire animators. Just as the desktop computer became a cultural phenomenon, and in the same way that professional computer-mediated communication networks became the hacker paradise of the Internet, so the economically driven ubiquity of imaging software has opened up a new range of possibilities.

The first lesson for any student of computer graphics (CG) and computer-generated images (CGI) is the distinction between bitmap and vector graphics. The bitmap is the more familiar mode. In bitmap software, each pixel of the screen is ascribed a co-ordinate in a two-dimensional Cartesian grid known as a raster display the x and y axes of which cross at origin, which in most software programs is at the top left-hand side of the display. High-definition monitors approximate the density of 35mm frames (which contain about a million molecules of light-sensitive silver salts). Each pixel can now be given a specified set of qualities, notably colour. Areas of the screen can be selected and moved, copied and pasted, or given instructions ('filters', for example) to change in a specified way. These changes are governed by algorithms, mathematical formulae applied to the address and colour code of the pixels selected, and are familiar from Photoshop and AfterEffects, among many other programs. When a bitmapped image is magnified, the blocky, square shapes of the raster display are preserved, as is visible in some of the tornado effects in *Twister* (1996, a film rescued by stunning sound design). Bitmap images, however, do introduce layers to cinema. Analogue cinematography exposes a whole frame for a split second and stores the light coming in as a single, coherent image. Bitmap images permit operators to stack image elements over one another in layers and to perform various actions on each layer separately. Thus the digitally enhanced cracks in the glass window of the trailer dangling over the cliff in *The Lost World* could be laid into the image as a layer between live action and blue- or green-screen. The cracks themselves were rotated and stretched to fit the frame of the window, without altering any other component layers in the foreground or background. The effect of layering opens a new language for cinema, or perhaps reopens one of its least recognised: titling.[6] Peter Greenaway's *Prospero's Books* (1991) and *The Pillow Book* (1996) reveal how important these effects can be in reinvigorating the existing traditions.[7] Layers are not exclusive to bitmapped images and draw on the familiar technology of the rostrum camera used for laying graphics and text over cinematographic or video images. But layers are now intrinsic to digital cinema, unlocking new-found powers.[8]

Bitmap images are literally maps. Each point has a mathematical description which defines how it is displayed. Vector graphics, by contrast, instruct the computer to create virtual objects, which are only displayed at a later phase of their development. These vector objects may be very simple forms, such as a two-dimensional curve, or more complex three-dimensional objects. These shapes are not defined by the x and y co-ordinates of the raster display, but by algorithms that define their curvature and their volume. This means that a vector graphic can be expanded at will without becoming blocky. Vector effects have the added benefit of using less computer memory, as they describe curves, for example, according to algebraic principles, needing only the addresses of the end points, rather than storing the address and quality of each point along the way. For example, a circle might be described using formulae such as $2\pi r$, instead of a long list of addresses for every point on its circumference. This makes handling three-dimensional objects far simpler and allows for far more effects. In particular, vector 3D graphics can be viewed from any angle and at any magnification without losing detail. In addition, vector graphics tend to use polar co-ordinate systems (two quantities, angle from the pole and distance), rather than Cartesian (which requires three quantities, distance along x, y and z axes, to describe each point in three dimensions), allowing faster calculation of position in virtual space. The result is not digital 'painting', but digital 'sculpture', objects that have specific qualities in three virtual dimensions, rather than the two permitted by bitmapping. Three-dimensional vector pro-grams usually come with a library of surface textures that can be applied to objects, which usually begin life as bare wire frames. Ray-tracing technology allows these surfaces to be applied in the same vector-based way – that is, as algorithms – so that objects can be viewed at great magnification and yet maintain meticulous detail, not only in pattern, but in texture as well. Three-dimensional, sculptural objects in the computer can also be lit and viewed from anywhere in that space and the behaviour of virtual light traced as a vector, reflecting off one surface, absorbed by another, casting shadows on a third. Not only does this complex of possibilities once again ease the burden of labour-intensive drawing by hand, but also, in the case of *Toy Story* (1995), the vector-based 3D toys can be transferred to computer-aided design and manufacture (CADCAM) programs so that the toys can be manufactured as immediate spin-offs, and new scenarios can be created – for example, for television – at little extra cost.

It is at this point that a further example of continuities between old and new media can be observed. During the preparation of *Snow White and the Seven Dwarfs* (1937), Walt Disney employed an actress to model the heroine. Her movements were both the subject of life drawing and recorded on film as a reference point for the princess's movement in the film. This pursuit of naturalism in animation that was the hallmark of Disney recurs 60 years later in the use of motion capture technology. Here an actor's face or body is dotted with emitters that can be recognised by a computer: light-reflecting discs, for example, or less visible infrared devices. The actor is scanned in motion, playing out emotional states or action sequences. The data recovered can then be applied to a wireframe object in virtual space, such as Buzz Lightyear, to provide the synthespian with a wider and richer emotional naturalism and a more credible set of anthropomorphic movements. As already pointed out, this takes us back to Marey's chronophotographic techniques, while leading forwards to the notion popularised in a number of technical and consumer journals of wholly lifelike syn-thetic performers, the 'idoru' of Gibson's recent cyberpunk fictions.

Of course, these three-dimensional objects have to be transferred to two dimensions in order to be transferred to film. In some projects, the result is subjected to bitmap modifi-cations, such as the application of digital 'dirt' to add to the verisimilitude of the well-used toys on *Toy Story*. The opposite procedure is also an option. Bitmapped data of sufficiently high resolution can be imported into vector packages in order to be mapped onto virtual surfaces, for example, to support reflections of the live footage environment in the liquid metal body of *Terminator 2* or to supply the human features for Schwarzenegger's disguise as an overweight airline passenger in *Total Recall* (1990). This process is especially important to the field of morphing, where the ability to translate from live to virtual physiognomies is an important potentiality.[9] The four central tools – virtual objects, virtual surfaces, virtual lighting and virtual camera – can all be controlled with great precision, so that matching CGI and live-action footage can be achieved with the minimum disruption to cinematic illusion. Thus the virtual lighting can be rigged and calibrated to the same specification as the real lighting on the set with which the object is to be composited. Of particular significance is the fact that the virtual camera's movements around a virtual object or environment can be stored and applied to the digitally controlled movement of motion-control cameras capturing live footage, so that the two movements can be matched.

Motion control is, if anything can claim this distinction, the single most important aspect of the digital cinema. This is because, articulating layers with virtual vector space, it represents a hinge point between the analogue and the digital that is specific to the moving image. Motion control is a digital governor that recalls the movement made by a camera and repeats it. It is widely used in rostrum camerawork for titling and animation, and is now a key element of the new cinema. Critical to it is the treatment of the camera as if it were a virtual object on a par with the digital sculptures created in cyberspace. Because the single most delicate and precise task of the production process is compositing, the marrying of digital effects and live-action footage into a single frame, the ability to match camera movement in the two domains is critical. It has also led towards new conceptualisations of what a movie camera might look like, most impressively in John Gaeta's 'bullet-time' camera built for *The Matrix*. Here the traditional camera is replaced by an array of 70 still cameras and two motion cameras controlled digitally by a motion-control rig which itself is synched with an entirely digital mock-up of the whole scene. The entire array functions as a single device offering speeds of up to 500 frames per second in any shape including 360-degree circling of the image. This technique combines motion and still cameras. In addition, the post-production phase allows for the interpolation of new frames into the sequence. Interpolation works by the same process as in-betweening. Given two successive frames, the computer can be instructed to interpolate a third by averaging the differences between the initial two, thus extending the action and providing virtual slow-motion (see plate 01). Although this resembles step-printing, the traditional method for extending an action in the optical printer, the difference is that the new frame has never actually been exposed in a camera. It is instead a digital artefact.

The whole can now be assembled. Increasingly, after some awkward experiences, films are being edited on digital nonlinear suites. The term 'nonlinear' is a video expression. Analogue video editing demanded a linear style. Once the opening shot had been laid down and followed by a second shot, the only way to recut was to start again from the beginning, as each shot followed the next in linear progression on the tape. Random-access memory (RAM) storage means that any shot can be shortened or lengthened, or moved at any time during the edit. This was always true of film editing, which is why most programs draw on the language of the film editor's suite (using terms such as 'bins', for example). The major advantage of digital editing is that it allows compositing of live-action and digital components, and the mixing, in layers, of cinematographic, bitmapped and vector graphics.

The sand demon of *The Mummy* (1999) uses such vector effects when it disperses into flies or grains of silicate. Flocking behaviours guide the film's scarabs. This is a medium-budget film. Effects have emerged from the action and science-fiction genre to become central to films such as *What Dreams May Come* (1998) and *Magnolia* (1999). But now not only Hollywood and not only blockbusters benefit from CGI: the medium-budget *Space Truckers* (1997) had its effects largely completed in Ireland. Peter Jackson cut his effects teeth with *Heavenly Creatures* (1994), relying on the emerging effects industry of Wellington, New Zealand ('Wellywood'), and bringing back as a prize *The Lord of the Rings* (2001). Jeunet and Caro moved from festival animations to *Alien Resurrection* (1997) via their *Delicatessen* (1990) and *The City of Lost Children* (1995). Pioneering titles such as Tsui Hark's *Zu: Warriors of the Magic Mountain* (1983) give a sense of the power of Hong Kong cinema. Today Atom Films and other microcinema sites show large numbers of digital showreels and calling-card shorts. The sales drives of both Sony's Vaio and Apple's iMac depend on the attraction of running nonlinear editing and effects packages on home movie systems. The effects of 1982's *Tron* can already be performed on entry-level computers using freeware, partly because it is entirely bitmapped, partly because effects are only 'special' when they are also 'cutting edge'. There remains the stranglehold on distribution addressed elsewhere in this collection. However, the creative tools of the industry are being internationalised and democratised, as well as shifting into new creative directions.

TEMPORAL AND SPATIAL

Blue-screen technology refers to the layers of the image as plates: background plate, matte plate, and so on. Matching the various plates requires one more technical device. When a camera moves through space, objects close up appear to move more quickly than more distant objects. When compositing, the editor has to take account of this parallax effect, ensuring that the planes or layers move in relation to one another in such a way as to convince the spectator that they share a common spatial orientation to the camera. This final adjustment to composite images suggests a solution to the problem with which I started: is digital cinema analytic or synthetic? Frequently, when the answer to a classificatory or categorical question seems difficult to find, it is because the categories employed are wrong. Parallax describes relations in space through a relation in time, the relation of relative velocity. Perhaps our categories of space and time, analytic and synthetic, are what is really at issue.

Why was chronophotography considered 'analytic'? Because it fragmented time into discrete steps and used those steps to analyse movement. Historically, its major function would be in the design of workstations in industry. In other words, and despite its name, chronophotography was a spatial art, rather than a temporal one. However, the return of chronophotography in forms such as bullet time suggests the opposite: that chrono-photography has at last become an art or craft for the microscopic investigation of time. Cinematography, by contrast, first appeared as a purely temporal form, demanding the unit of three frames, rather than one. But the parallax effect gives away the true nature of cinema as it has developed over the intervening decades. Movement in cinema is not purely tem-poral, but is responsible for producing the illusion of depth. Deep-focus photography, for example, so widespread in contemporary Hollywood as to have become clichéd, used to depend on fast film stocks and extra lighting for more distant objects. Today, however, it rests on the audience presumption that large, fast-moving objects are closer than small, slower ones. In the neo-Hollywood of the 1990s and 2000s, space has usurped the privi-lege of time. Narrative is diminishing in importance (hence the ubiquity of the 'mythic quest'), while diegesis, the imaginary worlds created by films, becomes more significant. Gotham City is more important than the forgettable narratives of the Burton and Schumacher *Batman* films: *Batman* (1989), *Batman Returns* (1992), *Batman Forever* (1995), *Batman and Robin* (1997). This is why the most cited manual of Hollywood script writing today is Christopher Vogler's *The Hero's Journey* (1996), a spatial metaphor of travel which also introduced Hollywood to 'mythic structure', a second spatial metaphor, in place of the linear, temporal models of the past.

To some postmodern commentators, this shift towards spatialisation represents a tri-umph over linearity and is considered subversive of narrative form and therefore good. What such commentaries ignore is that the digital domain is governed not by the forms which dominate cinema, depiction and narrative, but by data arrays: databases, spreadsheets, catalogues, search engines, info-bots, geographic information systems, mapping and other fundamentally spatial organisations of knowledge. Whether digitisation is cause or effect of this cultural drift is beyond the scope of this chapter. What is clear, however, is that the most intensively digitised films offer us entry to fictional worlds which become zones in which, in fantasy, we can play out not only the narrative on offer, but also a hundred more. In this sense, the effect, and especially the imaginary world of a film or film cycle (Federation Space in the *Star Trek* series, for example), has taken over from the star, not just as a box-office draw, but also as the prime site of fantasy for audiences. The recycling of vector graphical objects in film-associated games and their applicability to CADCAM manufacture means that this fantasy can be played out directly with toys and other products that are direct descendants of the objects caught on-screen. And diegetic worlds can benefit not only from spin-off markets, but also from the fan-base built up by audiences who continue the narratives of *Star Trek*: *Star Trek: The Motion Picture* (1979), *Star Trek II: The Wrath of Khan* (1982), *Star Trek III: The Search for Spock* (1984), *The Voyage Home: Star Trek IV* (1986), *Star Trek V: The Final Frontier* (1989), *Star Trek VI: The Undiscovered Country* (1991), *Star Trek Generations* (1994), *Star Trek: First Contact* (1996), *Star Trek: Insurrection* (1999) and of course three television series; *Star Wars*: including *Star Wars: Episode I – The Phantom Menace* (1999), *Star Wars: Episode II – Attack of the Clones* (2001), and a series of tele-vision spin-offs; *Alien* (1979), *Aliens* (1986), *Alien 3* (1992) and *Alien Resurrection* (1997);

and other cult series, giving individual films, and more importantly the formats of fictional worlds, immense value, greater even than that of the biggest stars. Far from subverting the dominant media, such post-narrative spatialisation works hand-in-glove with it.

Rather than time-based narrative, we have entered the era of the cinema of effects. Such is the case with *Gladiator*, where battle after battle becomes more and more spectacular. The film's time is marked as an experience of a sequence of visual and auditory shocks, rather than as an unfolding plot. Certainly the protagonist is on a journey: his desire to return home. But that journey becomes a desire to die, and his death travels with him from the moment of his wife's death, a static and unchanging point around which the quest narrative is structured. The doomed love of *Titanic* serves a similar function. These and many such narratives ('Neo, you are the One') of recent years devolve upon the recognition and acceptance of fate, a fate that is entirely against the concept of history as open-ended evolution and change. Sophisticated crane and Steadicam work operates in the same direction: to remove the temporalities of classical editing, replacing it with a view of spaces within which audiences orient themselves without reference to the rules of continuity cutting. Instead, temporal units become elements of a spatial structure in films such as *Pulp Fiction* and *Magnolia*, as much as in more obviously effects-driven films. Thus in *Independence Day* (1996), we know from the narration that the big explosions occur simultaneously. However, we do not only see them one after another: each is shown a number of times, and the moment itself is announced visually by a laptop computer's clock, aurally by 'It's time', and musically through a crescendo in the rhythm, prior to the actual explosions. Time, therefore, is not merely distended: it is spatialised.

A great deal of time has been spent talking about the shift from cinematic depiction to digital fantasy, no longer burdened or defined by the task of representation. But media, and especially digital media, are not only representational, a task undertaken only in specific circumstances and within film only truly attempted in the documentary. Media mediate. They stand between people, as the material forms of our relationships. The more those relationships appear to us as the ineluctable relation between objects in space, the less we can feel at home in an historical sphere of action. Spatialisation of the effect may appear to save us from the linearity of narrative, but the two are, to paraphrase Adorno, the torn halves of an integral tyranny to which, however, they do not add up. Immanuel Kant is largely responsible for the division of space from time when, in the *Critique of Pure Reason*, he argued that these two dimensions exist a priori, that is, before human thought. This binarism haunts the aesthetics of representation, and it is at this level that digital cinema works, altering and reconstructing the relations between temporality and space. The true task of digital cinema is not simply to free itself of representation. There is too much at stake in the development of digital documentary for that to be an option. Nor is it to become entirely spatialised, the ideal of a user-navigable immersive virtual reality. Nor yet is it to return to the linear temporality of narrative cinema. It is rather to create a new temporal art, capable of mediating relationships between people as historical and therefore as evolving and open. This new art of time will also of necessity be a new spatial art, as it will have to address as a given that relationships between people are now global. Network technologies give us an inkling of where such a vast art form might come from and the lack of access to it a sense of why it is so important to develop: only those who cannot speak for themselves are condemned to be represented.

Meanwhile those who are audiences for increasingly breathtaking spectacles find themselves in a curious double bind. The protagonist of *The Matrix* has to learn to want escape from its illusions, but as audiences, we want to remain in them. *Gladiator* offers a moral judgment on the Roman games, but we go to see it in order to witness them, even though our identifications (and possibly those of the Romans, too) are at least as much, if not more, with the victims as with the perpetrators. Such diegetic worlds are self-contained and exclusive: only those who participate are inside the world. Spatial fiction depends upon spatial exclusion, much as free trade depends on the immobilisation of would-be migrants. The new spatialisation of special effects cinema is as illusory and as damaging as the linear temporality of the narrative cinema it replaces. Reconceptualising media history, we leave behind the analytic/synthetic distinction, and even the space/time distinction, in order to envisage a cinema that is inclusive and for the first time recognises its destiny not as representation or storytelling, but as mediation, and its destiny not as a binarism, but as a dialectic.

Notes

1. See Fred Ritchin, *In Our Own Image: The Coming Revolution in Photography* (New York: Aperture Foundation, 1990); Derek Bishton, Andy Cameron and Tim Druckery (eds), *Digital Dialogues: Photography in the Age of Cyberspace*, Ten: 8 Photo Paperback, vol. 2 no. 2, Autumn 1991; Paul Wombell (ed.), *Photovideo: Photography in the Age of the Computer* (London: Rivers Oram Press, 1991); William J. Mitchell, *The Reconfigured Eye: Visual Truth in the Post-Photographic Era* (Cambridge, MA: MIT Press, 1992); Martin Lister (ed.), *The Photographic Image in Digital Culture* (London: Routledge, 1995); Kevin Robins, *Into the Image: Culture and Politics in the Field of Vision* (London: Routledge, 1996).

2. But see Graham Weinbren (ed.), 'The Digital', special issue of *Millennium Film Journal*, no. 34, Autumn 1999; John Caughie and Sean Cubitt (eds), 'FX, CGI and the Question of Spectacle', special issue of *Screen*, vol. 44 no. 2, Summer 2000; Tim Murray (ed.), 'Digitality and the Memory of Cinema', special issue of *WideAngle*, vol. 21 no. 3, 2001; Vivian Sobchack (ed.), *Meta-morphing: Visual Transformation and the Culture of Quick-Change* (Minneapolis: University of Minnesota Press, 2000). See also, Andrew Darley, *Visual Digital Culture: Surface Play and Spectacle in New Media Genres* (London: Routledge, 2000).

3. C. W. Ceram, *Archeology of the Cinema*, trans. Richard Winston (London: Thames and Hudson, 1965).

4. Vincent LoBrutto, *Sound-on-Film: Interviews with Creators of Film Sound* (New York: Praeger, 1994), pp. 13–49.

5. Harry Braverman, *Labor and Monopoly Capital: The Degradation of Work in the Twentieth Century* (New York: Monthly Review Press, 1974).

6. See Margaret Morse, *Virtualities: Television, Media Art, And Cyberculture* (Bloomington: Indiana University Press, 1998), pp. 71–98.

7. See Yvonne Spielmann, *Intermedialität. Das System Peter Greenaway* (München: Wilhelm Fink Verlag, 1997); Alan Woods, *Being Naked Playing Dead: The Art of Peter Greenaway* (Manchester: Manchester University Press, 1996).

8. Yvonne Spielmann, 'Expanding Film into Digital Media', *Screen*, vol. 40, no. 2, Summer 1999, pp. 131–45.

9. See Vivian Sobchack (ed.), *Meta-morphing*.

1.3

CD and DVD

Anne Friedberg

> Just as water, gas, and electricity are brought into our houses from far off to satisfy our needs
> in response to a minimal effort, so we shall be supplied with visual and auditory images,
> which will appear and disappear at the simple movement of the hand, hardly more than a
> sign. . . . I don't know if a philosopher has ever dreamed of a company engaged in the home
> delivery of Sensory Reality.[1]

Paul Valéry's 1928 forecast provides a stunning augury of contemporary telecommunications: images and sounds have become a utility; each household has a supply that enters
the home via broadcast signals, cable wires, satellite reception, DSL lines, telephone
modem hook-ups, delivering 'Sensory Reality' at 'the simple movement of the hand'. As the
twentieth century ended, new systems of circulation and transmission began to replace
the cinema's projection screen and to link the screens of the computer and television
with the dialogic interactivity of the telephone. In this new media environment, the media of
telephone, radio, television, films and the Internet interact among themselves and their
cross-purposed interaction poses new questions about their technological specificities.
'Convergence', once merely a discursive buzzword, has become, by 2002, a literal description of the co-dependency of the movie screen, television screen and computer screen.
Now, a variety of screens – long and wide and square, large and small, composed of grains,
composed of pixels – competes for our attention without any convincing arguments about
hegemony. Screens have become a pervasive part of daily experience: laptops, personal
digital assistants (PDAs), GameBoys, cell phones add mobility to the screen's face. Desktop
computers, CRT, LCD, and PDP television and computer display screens,[2] multiplex cinema
screens, IMAX screens, Jumbotrons, expand the size and function of the fixed and im-
mobile screen. As screens multiply in a proliferation of 'display technologies', an equally
daunting number of 'delivery platforms' compete to supply images and sounds: videotapes,
CDs, CD-ROMs, DVDs, MP3, 'streaming' audio and video on the Web.

   The changes in screens and our 'interfaces' with them have occurred at the speed of
fast-forward. In an essay written only a few years ago (1997), 'The End of Cinema:
Multimedia and Technological Change', I explored the ways in which the then new

technologies challenged the discrete object of the 'film', placing 'the cinema' in an expanded field of screens, served by an expanded variety of production and delivery formats.[3] In that essay, I argued that a 'convergence' of film and television technology began without fibre-optic cable, occurred before the digitalisation of imagery and preceded the advent of the home computer. The VCR, I argued, was the first technology to begin to erode the historical differences between television and film, altering as it did the terms of electronic and cinematic viewing. In addition, the technologies which transformed the media environment of the 1980s – the VCR, cable television and the television remote – not only changed our concept of film-going and television-viewing, but also prepared us for another 'convergence': the television and computer screen.

But now, by 2002, the material differences between cinematic, televisual and computer media have been eroded beyond recognition by the digital technologies that have transformed them. Televisions have become more like computers: hard-disk video recorders (TiVo, ReplayTV) record television signals onto an auxiliary hard-drive;[4] HDTV-ready televisions use chips running mega-MIPS. Conversely, computers have become more like televisions: MPEG and QuickTime 'movies' and 'streaming' videos flash across and through Web browser pages. Multimedia home stations which combine the functions of telephone, television and gaming console (Microsoft's Xbox, Nintendo's Game Cube, Sony's PlayStation 2) further confound the technical differentiation of film, television and the computer.

The segregation of histories of telephony, moving image and computing technologies now appears – in post-millennial retrospect – as a set of arbitrary separations that disregard the inter-medial complexity of technological development.[5] To write a 'history' of these new media formations is to encounter many familiar historiographical challenges. As Stephen Heath warned, in an earlier historical moment (1978) when the 'cinematic apparatus' seemed a dominant technological form:

> Technological determinism substitutes for the social, the economic, the ideological, proposes
> the random autonomy of invention and development, coupled often with the vision of a
> fulfillment of an abstract human essence – and some of the wildest versions of this latter are
> to be found in accounts of the (then aptly named) 'media'. . . . [Cinema's] history is a history of
> the technological and social together, a history in which the determinations are not simple but
> multiple, interacting, in which the ideological is there from the start.[6]

While careful not to overstate the determinations of technological development, Heath and other 'apparatus' theorists attempted to provide a rigorous account of the technological and social specificities of the cinema as a single medium.

In this way, we may wish to regard Marshall McLuhan as the first 'apparatus' theorist. Back in 1964, when McLuhan proclaimed 'the medium is the message', his sound-bite aphorism drew attention not only to the *media*tion that the media implied, but also to the specificity of each separate medium. He inveighed against a content-based study of the media: 'The "content" of any medium,' McLuhan wrote, 'blinds us to the characteristics of the medium.'[7] Instead, he prescribed an analysis of the effects – 'the change of scale or pace or pattern' – that each particular medium might produce. While McLuhan analysed the interrelatedness of media in an evolutionary scheme ('The content of any medium is always another medium'),[8] he also insisted that each new medium would 'institute new ratios, not only among our private senses, but among themselves, when they interact among themselves'.[9] How then do we account for the 'new ratios' produced by the rapid and recent changes in the screens and interfaces of moving image media?

Another McLuhan-styled media-prognosticator, Nicholas Negroponte, has suggested a counter-polemical aphorism, turning McLuhan's 'the medium is the message' on its head. 'The medium is not the message in the digital world,' declares Negroponte. 'It is an embodiment of it. A message might have several embodiments automatically derivable from the same data.'[10] For Negroponte, digital technologies have dissolved the specificity of individual media: digital imaging, delivery and display effectively erase the messages implicit in the source medium. Negroponte imagines a media world of digital images making their way to digital display endpoints, with little or no difference in content, only a subtle 're-purposing' for display. Negroponte proclaims: 'The basic difference between today's TVs and PCs has nothing to do with location, social habits, or our need to relax. It has to do with how the bits arrive.'[11] If we follow Negroponte's axiom ('the medium is not the message in the digital world'), we arrive at a newfound determinism: digital technology inherently implies a convergence of all media forms.

German media theorist Friedrich Kittler anticipated this loss of media specificity when he wrote (in 1986): 'The general digitalization of information and channels erases the difference between individual media.'[12] Yet Kittler predicted that the installation of fibre-optic cable, and not the phone-wires of the Internet or the wireless future of the Web, would be the technology to turn film, television, music and phone calls into a single medium.

But have we arrived at a convergent 'single medium'? Have the screens of cinema, television and computer really lost their apparatical distinctions? One sales Web site for flat-screen monitors effectively conflates the multiple functions of the screen – television, film display, Internet browser – now displayed within the same electronic picture frame:

> Hanging on a wall they look more like art rather than a TV set. When you're not watching TV, DVD videos, surfing the net or reading your e-mail, there is no need to switch the plasma panel off. It can be used as an electronic picture frame, with a continuously changing selection of artworks of your choice: An endless art collection![13]

Another advertisement declares: 'He loves 19th century works, I prefer 20th. We agreed on a piece from the next century' (see plate 02). As the changing technologies of 'delivery' alter the effect of moving images in 'display', the histories here are all recent, in the cusp of the millennial turn. Whatever form a 'piece from the next century' will take, we still need to ask questions about the altered effects of screens that are mobile and fixed, that bring images and sounds in varied sizes and shapes, that permeate our public and private spaces, sit on our desktops, in our living rooms, on our laps, or are handheld, accompany us on airplanes, in automobiles, to desert islands. Are we inching towards the 'home delivery' of 'Sensory Reality'?

DELIVERY AND DISPLAY: THE NEXT NEW THING

> We need a book about the failures of media, the collapses of media, the supercessions of media, the strangulations of media, a book detailing all the freakish and hideous media mistakes that we should know enough now not to repeat, a book about media that have died on the barbed wire of technological advance, media that didn't make it, martyred media, dead media. THE HANDBOOK OF DEAD MEDIA. A naturalist's field guide for the communications paleontologist.[14]

In 1997, just as the VCR had nearly completed its 'penetration' of television households, the digital-video-disc (DVD) player was released into the consumer market. In 1997, there were 95 million VCRs in the US (89 per cent of households) and about 400 million world-wide (42 per cent of television-owning households). The first DVD players were released in Japan in November 1996 and introduced to the US market in March 1997. Players slowly trickled into other regions. By the end of 2000, there were 12 million DVD homes, 2.8 million of which have both DVD player and DVD-ROM computer.[15] Clearly, manufacturers hoped that the DVD player would replace the VCR and that, just as audio CDs supplanted vinyl records in the 1980s, this new digital format would condemn the videocassette to the 'barbed wire of technological advance' and the martyred heap of dead media. The following account forms a chapter in such communications paleontology. 'New' media implies that the 'old' is forever obsolete. As Gramsci put it, 'the old is dying and the new cannot be born; in the interregnum a great variety of morbid symptoms appear'.[16]

LASER DISCS:[17] CDs, LDs, CD-ROMs, CD-RW, DVDs, DVD-ROMs, DVD-RW

Audio compact discs (CDs) entered the consumer market in 1982. Relying on optical laser technology – a laser beam focuses on small spot of a non-magnetic disc to read digital information encoded in sub-micron 'pits' – the CD was thought to retain audio quality without degradation. As an initial CD promotional slogan, Philips proclaimed: 'perfect sound forever'. Despite early assurances to the contrary, sound quality is not forever: digital media can degrade. CDs can lose data as the foil substrate beneath the clear plastic coating oxidises when this happens; the disc becomes dull and unreadable by the CD player or drive. (Nor are CDs free from distortion: they have merely introduced new kinds of distortion, for example, digital 'jitter', time-based and phase anomalies.) Some experts estimate that the shelf life of the average retail music CD is no more than seven to ten years, after which some of the data on the disc will be lost. A 50-year-old vinyl disc may well be more playable than a 50-year-old CD.[18]

But CD users were drawn to the playback features made possible by optical laser technology; one could easily skip tracks and control the sequence of audio tracks with the touch of a remote. As the CD began to replace its analogue predecessors, consumers replaced their existing album collections with a 'new' digital version of what they already owned on vinyl or tape.[19]

Like their audio relatives (CDs), video laser-discs (LDs) allowed the user to access specific portions of the disc (in this case, a scene of a film) in a nonlinear fashion. This was a considerable advantage over the playback of a videocassette, which required rewinding at the end of each tape and fast-forwarding to locate a sequence. The 12-inch platter LD was available in two different formats: CAV (which allowed for freeze-frame and slow-motion on playback) and CLV (which allowed for scan, pause and search on playback). LDs were packaged with materials not available on videotape releases: original cinema trailers, deleted footage, alternative soundtracks, voiceovers by film-makers and scholars, displays of script pages and other production materials.[20] While a CLV laser-disc held one hour per side, a CAV disc only held half an hour. This meant that the user could not view an entire film without getting up to change discs. Despite some of the advantages of laser technology over magnetic tape, the video laser-disc and the dedicated laser-disc player, readily available throughout the 1980s, never took hold of the consumer market.[21] Pioneer Entertainment, the long-time champion of the laser-disc, finally abandoned it in June of 1999.

But the video laser-disc found a new format in the CD-ROM (compact disc with read-only memory). The CD-ROM did not require a dedicated player; it was readable in computers equipped with CD-ROM drives. Because they had the same size and format as audio CDs, CD-ROM drives were 'backward compatible' with CDs. The storage capacity of the CD-ROM (600MB) was large enough to hold video materials, but not large enough to hold an entire film on one disc. Hence, the CD-ROM replicated the same problem that may have doomed the laser-disc: the viewer could easily navigate the disc, but still had to 'change the record' mid-film. Yet, like other optical disc formats (CDs and CD-ROMs), laser-discs were marketed as 'read-only' for playback and did not offer recordable or re-writable features. But the important step here in a narrative film screen/computer screen convergence, was that the CD-ROM brought the display of films to the computer screen.

ENTER DVD

The DVD (digital versatile disc or digital video disc) expanded the storage capacity of the CD-ROM. With the help of MPEG compression technology, one DVD disk could hold hours of high-quality audiovisual content. This meant that an entire film could fit on one side of a DVD.[22] The DVD had many of the same basic features as the CLV laser-disc and the CAV laser-disc, and some DVDs offer branching, multiple camera angles and parental control features. As with the larger LD formats, the user could access a different section of the disc in a near instant, with no fast-forwarding or rewinding required.

Because DVDs adhere to the same physical dimensions as CDs and CD-ROMs, the DVD player, whether stand-alone or in a computer, is 'backward compatible', which may give it an edge in a consumer market wary of buying into the wrong format.[23] Yet, as the forking paths of product evolution would have it, the DVDs 'backward compatibility' for CDs and CD-ROMs does not extend to the videocassette or laser-disc, which seem destined for extinction.

The stand-alone DVD player was introduced to the consumer market as a successor to the VCR, a smaller more efficient laser-disc player to play back pre-recorded films. In this regard, its playback features were developed well before its recording capacities, the reverse of VCR development. When the VCR was first introduced as a consumer appliance in the early 1980s, it was marketed as a means for recording broadcast and cable television. Hence it was deemed a video cassette recorder (VCR), not a VCP (video cassette player). The sale and rental of pre-recorded films and the playback of home videos was a secondary development as film studios realised that the videocassette not only extended the shelf life and play time of the theatrically released film, but also provided a venue to re-market film titles that were already in their libraries.

In the four years since its introduction to the consumer market in 1997, some form of DVD technology, such as a stand-alone DVD player, DVD-enabled game console, PC-based DVD-ROM drive, can be found in one-third of American households.[24] In Europe, the statistics show an equivalent growth curve: in 2000, the 'DVD video player base' in Western Europe grew nearly four-fold to 5.4 million homes, while the number of VCR households increased by a further 4 per cent to 124 million.[25] The growth curve of DVD ownership has occurred more rapidly than the growth rate of VCR households in the 1980s, a rate which already occurred at an acceleration of the rate of television households in the 1950s. (I am not certain how to read this statistic, although it seems to suggest that the consumer appliance market has grown quicker to declare successors and dispose of dead media.)[26]

So where are we in a narrative of convergence of film, television and computer screens? As a delivery format, the DVD seems to be the golden disc that effectively transects the computer/television divide. The DVD can be played either on a dedicated DVD player or on a computer (many new PCs have DVD drives) and viewed on a television monitor – CRT, projection or plasma. In addition, as other appliances develop, the DVD may be playable on game consoles, Internet appliances, set-top boxes, car entertainment systems and portable players. New-generation gaming consoles such as XBox, PlayStation 2 and Game Cube offer features that include DVD players, output jacks for HDTV, broadband connections and hard drives for storing music and games.

Here there may be a wrinkle in the story. As the DVD was originally conceived as a playback device, it is only recently that manufacturers have begun to develop its recording functions. The warring formats, recordable (DVD-R) and rewritable (DVD-RAM, DVD-RW or DVD+RW), and resultant market confusion about recordable DVD may replay the VHS versus Beta 'format wars' of the 1980s. Perhaps if manufacturers had begun by exploiting and thinking about the possible computer interfaces of the DVD, these format wars would not take a toll on a technology that may be rendered obsolete as the streaming of images

and sound goes online and as PVRs (personal video recorders such as TiVo and Replay TV)
negotiate the set-top box acquisition of satellite and cable materials.

STREAMING: WIRED AND WIRELESS DELIVERY

What is the future of the DVD in a wired or wireless world? Once movies and video images
are available to home screens via satellite or Web streaming, the delivery format of DVD
joins the endangered species list. Wireless delivery via satellite to a home receiver con-
demns the format necessity of the DVD as a means of delivering moving images and
sounds. The future of wired delivery relies on diastolic changes in bandwidth and compression; as the bandwidth of the digital pipe expands, images and sounds will stream
through it slimmed down by ever-more efficient compression algorithms. The average user
with a dial-up connection accesses the Internet at 56 Kbps, while 128 Kbps are necessary
for fluid streaming media connections. At the time of writing, broadband access via cable,
DSL (digital subscriber line) or fibre-optic cable is still limited by coverage area and price.
Online game play requires high-bandwidth connections; movie files are still too large to be
sent across the Internet.

If audio-streaming formats in any way portend the fate of video streaming, the case of
Napster and its file-sharing protocols demonstrates how copyright and licensing become
pivotal issues once a consumer-durable – a disc – is no longer the means for registering
proprietary use or sale. Audio MP3 files are small and they can easily be transferred across
the Internet.[27] While MP3 technology could endanger the market hegemony of the pre-
recorded CD in the same way that the CD threatened the vinyl record in the early 1980s,
this may not be the case. Currently, MP3 users are legally allowed to stream (that is, listen
to songs online, but not download them to their hard drives). The survival of the MP3
format, still tangled in the courts, hangs in the balance.

BOX-TOPS AND THE CONSOLE-ATION PRIZE

> In the ultimate living room, TVs and music don't stand alone; they interact with each other,
> with the Internet, with the PC in the home office or the electronic game equipment in the
> family room.[28]

Auguries of convergence always suggest a teleology: some media are seen as transitional
and others seem destined to evolve into the next species. A media paleontologist could
examine the fossil remains: the VCR may have begun to erode the differences between televisual and cinematic viewing; the DVD may have served as the delivery format that serves
the displays of computers and televisions alike. New-generation gaming consoles such as
Xbox, PlayStation 2 and Game Cube offer features that include DVD players, output jacks
for HDTV, broadband connections and hard drives for storing music and games. While this
iteration of game console seems somehow poised to further bridge the gap between the
digital world of the PC and the analogue world of television, one cannot predict what

delivery or display format will survive the vicissitudes of the consumer market. And yet amid these morbid symptoms, the 'home delivery' of a digitised 'Sensory Reality' seems some-how assured.

Notes

1. Paul Valéry, 'La Conquête de l'ubiquité', first published in *De la Musique avant toute chose* (Paris: Editions du Tambourinaire, 1928); 'The Conquest of Ubiquity', *Aesthetics*, trans. Ralph Mannheim (New York: Pantheon Books, 1964).

2. PDP (plasma display panel) or 'flat-panel display' screens – which sandwich a neon/xenon gas mixture between two sealed glass plates and produce a crisp digital image – are about one-tenth the thickness and one-sixth the weight of CRT (cathode-ray tube) monitors.

3. See Anne Friedberg, 'The End of Cinema: Multimedia and Technological Change', in Christine Gledhill and Linda Williams (eds), *Reinventing Film Studies* (London: Arnold, 2000), pp. 438–52.

4. Alternatively called personal video recorders (PVRs), digital video recorders (DVRs) or hard-disk-drive (HDD) video recorders, these devices record television programmes onto a hard disk drive for playback.

5. For other recent accounts of an integrated history of media, see Siegfried Zielinski, *Audiovisions: Cinema and Television as Entr'actes in History* (Amsterdam: Amsterdam University Press, 1999); Jay David Bolter and Richard Grusin, *Remediation: Understanding New Media* (Cambridge, MA: MIT Press, 1999).

6. Stephen Heath, 'The Cinematic Apparatus: Technology as Historical and Cultural Form', in *Questions of Cinema* (London: Macmillian, 1981), pp. 221–35.

7. Marshall McLuhan, *Understanding Media* (Cambridge, MA: MIT Press, 1994), p. 9.

8. Ibid., p. 8.

9. Ibid., p. 53.

10. Nicholas Negroponte, *Being Digital* (New York: Alfred Knopf, 1995), p. 71.

11. Nicholas Negroponte, 'Bit by Bit, PCs are Becoming TVs. Or is It the Other Way Around?', *Wired.com*, 1 August 1995.

12. Friedrich Kittler, *Grammophon, Film, Typewriter* (Berlin: Brinkmann & Bose, 1986); 'Gramophone, Film, Typewriter', *October*, no. 41 (1986), pp. 101–18.

13. See <www.digitaldefinitions.co.uk/>.

14. Bruce Sterling, *The DEAD MEDIA Project: A Modest Proposal and a Public Appeal*, 1995, <www.deadmedia.org/modest-proposal.html>.

15. Statistics and their sources vary: these statistics are from London-based *Screen Digest*, July 1997; 'Digital America 2001', Report by Consumer Electronics <www.ce.org> and CENTRIS Research and Information Service.

16. Antonio Gramsci, *Selections from the Prison Notebooks*, Quintin Hoare and Geoffrey Nowell Smith (eds and trans.) (London: Lawrence and Wishart, 1971), pp. 275–6.

17. The term 'disc' – as in compact disc, laser-disc, video disc – refers to a 'read-only, optical-storage medium that is generally round and made of nonmagnetic metal, coated in plastic, and covered with small pits designed to be read from and written to by laser'. The term 'disk', on the other hand,

refers to 'small, flat, portable piece of plastic (a floppy disk) or a less-portable metal-encased storage disk (a hard disk) coated with a magnetic material'. Constance Hale (ed.) *WIRED STYLE: Principles of English Usage in the Digital Age* (San Francisco: Hard Wired Books, 1996), pp. 44–5.

18. Leah A. Lievrouw, 'New Media: Nonobvious Things About New Media: "Dead Media" and the Loss of Electronic Cultural Heritage', *ICA Newsletter*, vol. 28 no. 1, January 2000.

19. In the early 1980s, the pre-recorded audiocassette also vied with the vinyl LP as a delivery system for home audio. In 1983, sales of vinyl LPs were surpassed by the audio music cassette. Only ten years later, in 1992, CD sales surpassed audiocassettes.

20. Voyager's 'Criterion Collection' featured CLV laser-discs with letterboxed formats and ample amounts of additional material. In 1993, Criterion launched a series of CD-ROMs. In 1998, the Criterion Collection was launched on DVD.

21. Only 1 per cent of American households own them: 1.33 million units were sold between 1985 and 1993. When the DVD came out in 1997, there were about 3 million laser-disc players in the US.

22. MPEG (moving picture experts group) set standards for coding audiovisual information (films, music and video) in a digitally compressed format. A DVD holds a minimum of 4.7GB (gigabytes), enough for a full-length film and a maximum of 17GB, significantly higher than a CD-ROM which can hold 600MB. DVDs use MPEG–2 to compress video data. DVDs released in the US include Dolby Digital surround sound, which produces five discrete audio channels. This format allows software producers to include multiple language audio tracks, subtitling or multiple camera angles.

23. Backward compatibility is also a key issue in the current policy disputes about the introduction of high-definition television (HDTV). As a footnote to the early marketing history of DVD, Divx – the acronym for Digital Video Express – was a proprietary DVD format introduced by retailer Circuit City and a Los Angeles law firm. Divx discs required a special Divx player and could be viewed for one 48-hour period, beginning when the disc was first inserted into the player. If the disc were viewed again, the Divx player would automatically, via modem, phone into a billing office to bill the registered customer for another 48-hour period. While Divx players also played 'open' DVD movies, the format was the subject of strident criticism on the Internet and elsewhere. Divx officially stopped registering new customers in June 1999 and ceased all operations in June 2001.

24. This according to an August 2001 survey by the industry trade association Consumer Electronics Association (CEA): <www.ce.org>.

25. Statistics from London-based *Screen Digest*, <www.screendigest.com>.

26. Over two hundred models of DVD players are available from dozens of electronics companies. Prices for the first players were $1000 and more. By the end of 2000, players were available for under $100 at discount retailers. The price of DVDs is almost as low as its VHS counterparts and the demand for and availability of DVD rental films has increased exponentially. In 1997, in the US, 900 titles were available on DVD; in 1998, 3000. By the end of 2000, there were over 10,000 titles available on DVD in the US and over 15,000 worldwide.

27. MP3 is an abbreviation for the file extension for MPEG, audio layer 3. Layer 3 is one of three coding schemes (layer 1, layer 2 and layer 3) for the compression of audio signals. Layer 3 uses perceptual audio coding and psycho-acoustic compression to remove superfluous information. The result in

real terms is that layer 3 shrinks the original sound data from a CD with some sacrifice of sound quality.

28. Consumer Electronics Association (CEA), 'The Ultimate Living Room' *5 Technologies to Watch*, 2001, <www.ce.org/pdf/5TechnologiesToWatchOct.011.pdf>.

1.4

The Internet and the World Wide Web

Jeremy G. Butler

Computers began to find their way into the cinema in the 1950s, but these early computers were seldom connected to any others. It was not until 1983 and the release of *WarGames* that the networking abilities of computers insinuated their way into popular culture, resulting in a mixture of awe and dread. In that film, a young high school student connects his computer, via telephone, to what he believes to be a computer game company. In truth, he has unintentionally hacked into a military computer, which he almost provokes into starting World War III. *WarGames* distinguished itself from earlier films about computers in its emphasis on computer-to-computer communication for its narrative arc. This film and the 'cyberspace' of William Gibson's novel *Neuromancer* (1984) introduced computer networking into mainstream narrative texts.[1] Moreover, they roughly coincide with one of the various 'births' of the Internet. In 1982, the basic rules, the fundamental protocols, governing the networking of networks were finalised. Indeed, it is from these protocols that the name, 'the Internet', derives. In the early 1980s, however, the Internet was still the arcane province of inventors, government engineers and computer hobbyists.[2]

For many in the general public, the Internet remained a rather murky, ill-defined notion until the World Wide Web began popularising network access in 1993. However, the Web itself was actually invented two years before that rush of media and public attention. Furthermore, the principles that underly it can be traced back at least 50 years. To understand the origins of the Web, we must look at how its concept of interlinked documents evolved and how an interface for navigating through those links emerged.

TEXT BECOMES HYPER

The principal conceptual source for the Web is the work of Vannevar Bush in the 1930s and 1940s. Bush proposed a unique method of data storage and retrieval in the 1945 essay 'As We May Think', which appeared in *The Atlantic Monthly* and was disseminated widely through excerpts in *Life* magazine. At a time when the first fully electronic computers had barely materialised, Bush was envisioning the Memex, a radical data system. The Memex would contain *all* of one's books, letters, photographs, microfilm and so on, and facilitate access to them through a few flips of levers, resulting in material being projected onto a desktop screen. Moreover, Bush envisioned a unique method for creating 'trails' through these data. As one hopped from item to item, a record or 'trail' was kept of the route one took, connecting items to each other. The Memex was never actually built, but clearly it provides the conceptual framework for much of what we take for granted in today's Web browsing: links between text and images, bookmarks, the ability to move backwards through the Web pages you have already visited, and so on.

The Memex's principle of linked data bore fruit in 1960 when Ted Nelson began work on Project Xanadu, a largely unrealised effort to implement his concept of 'non-sequential writing'.[3] For Nelson, as for Bush, thinking is not sequential or linear. Instead, it jumps from one concept to another. It is associative and nonlinear. The computer, Nelson argued, could facilitate this associative and non-sequential logic. In 1963, he coined the terms 'hypertext' and 'hypermedia' to refer to this associative linking between words and images in Xanadu.[4] But Xanadu still remains mostly incomplete. Even though its proponents declare that the Web is a 'diabolical dumbdown of [their] original hypertext idea', until now it has proved to be the most successful 'non-sequential' phenomenon in the history of computers.[5]

The legacy of Memex may be observed in several important hypertext experiments in the decades after 1945, but none of them attracted much attention from the general public.[6] Hypertext would not become part of our lexicon until the early 1990s. At that time, Tim Berners-Lee, an English computer programmer, was working at CERN, the European Laboratory for Particle Physics near Geneva, Switzerland.[7] In March 1989, he circulated a proposal for a hypertext-based 'information mesh'. This mesh became identified as the 'World Wide Web' during 1990 while he was actually creating the program to run this system. Berners-Lee began demonstrating Web software in late 1990 and in summer 1991 it was installed on CERN's main computers, announced to the public via various Usenet newsgroups, and its software (both client and server) distributed freely via the Internet.[8] Berners-Lee had created the two basic building blocks of the Web: a protocol for exchanging files across the Internet and a set of conventions determining how text would appear in Web browsers. With the hypertext transfer protocol (HTTP) and the hypertext markup language (HTML), Bush's dream of the Memex was beginning to become a reality. And even though Nelson, who coined the term 'hypertext', dismisses the Web as a bastardisation of his Xanadu project, it is clear that HTTP and HTML brought hypertext navigation out of research laboratories and into homes and offices across the world.

ILLUMINATING THE WEB

It has become commonplace to remark upon the meteoric rise of the Web, but in 1991 it was essentially a text medium that seemed no more remarkable than other information-distribution systems such as the University of Minnesota's Gopher. In June 1993, two years after the Web's release to the Internet at large, there were approximately 130 Web servers worldwide and it was showing good but not outstanding growth. One year later, the number of servers rose to 2738, more than 20 times more than the previous year. During the next year, the number increased another eight-and-a-half times to 23,500 servers, a phenomenal 179,769 per cent growth rate over two years.[9] The impetus for this mid-1990s Web interest was a browser that could effectively handle images and position them on the screen. In 1993, the Web's first 'graphical user interface' (GUI) was introduced, which turned the Web into the Internet's 'killer app', an application that attracted millions to the Internet.

When CERN released Web software to the Internet in 1991, most personal computer users were accustomed to a graphical user interface. Berners-Lee's text-based Web seemed like a throwback to pre-Mac, pre-Windows computing. To succeed, the Web needed its own GUI and that was just what Marc Andreessen and a team of students at the University of Illinois at Urbana-Champaign provided. Andreessen was working as an undergraduate intern at the University's National Center for Supercomputer Applications (NCSA). In just three intense months, Andreessen and NCSA staff member Eric Bina generated 9000 lines of programming code and created a Web browser that wholly integrated images into the Web experience. They called their browser Mosaic and announced its release on Usenet newsgroups on 23 January 1993. The initial release of Mosaic was built for the Unix operating system, which runs on very few home computers, but Windows and Mac versions arrived later that year and requests for Mosaic soon swamped NCSA.[10] Its instantaneous success heralded the beginnings of a new, graphically oriented Web.

Andreessen did not remain long at NCSA once the popularity of Mosaic became obvious. He and the other key members of the Mosaic team were courted by Jim Clark, the founder of Silicon Graphics and a successful producer of high-end graphics computers. In April 1994, they incorporated a new company to create a Web browser similar to Mosaic. In fact, they initially intended to call the company Mosaic Communications, but when they found they did not have legal rights to the Mosaic trademark, they changed the company's name to Netscape and the browser they were to create became known as Navigator (though most people just referred to the browser itself as 'Netscape').[11] Tackling the programming job with the same mad enthusiasm that they had with Mosaic, Andreessen and his Netscape team released their first version of Navigator in December 1994, just eight months after the company's official incorporation. Navigator was a noticeably better browser than Mosaic. It was faster, crashed less and displayed images and text in new ways. Further, Navigator's success was nurtured by the free distribution of its fully functional 'beta' (test) versions, which were always available for download. Most of Navigator's sales were to corporate buyers; individuals tended to rely on the free beta versions. Moreover, Netscape's Web server (and not its client, Navigator) provided its principal revenue stream. Netscape was one of the most successful of the so-called 'dotcom' businesses (so named for the '.com' ending to their domain names), with an initial public offering on the stock market that placed its worth at $1 billion.

Netscape's success did not go unnoticed by Microsoft, which thus far did not even own a browser. In late 1994 and 1995, while preparing Windows' first major revamping in five years, Microsoft CEO Bill Gates was suddenly awakened to the Web's significance. Microsoft quickly bought the software code for the Spyglass browser, a commercial version of NCSA Mosaic, and dubbed it Internet Explorer 1.0, bundling it with Windows 95 when it was released in August. Windows 95 significantly improved Windows' networking capabilities and graphical interface (becoming a virtual clone of the Mac interface), but Internet Explorer was not as stable, efficient or fully featured as Navigator. Still, the call to arms had been sounded. Throughout 1995 and 1996, Microsoft and Netscape battled back and forth with new releases every few months. Microsoft integrated Internet Explorer deeper and deeper into Windows and did everything it could to discourage Windows' users from installing Navigator. Netscape joined in the chorus of voices claiming that Microsoft's actions were a monopolistic attempt to control the Web and an anti-trust suit was filed against Microsoft in 1997. The case would not go well for Microsoft, but by then Navigator's market share had decreased dangerously and it had gradually lost its technological advantage over Internet Explorer. In March 1999, AOL acquired Netscape and, even though Netscape remains as a separate entity today, the releases of Navigator have slowed to a crawl. There are even indications at this time (summer 2001) that Netscape may get out of browser business altogether.

LOOKING THROUGH THE WEB WINDOW

In a narrow sense, the Web could be thought of as only the text, images and sounds that are shared via the hypertext transfer protocol, such as those appearing on a simple Web page of text and still images. But that view of the Web is not true to Berners-Lee's original conception. He conceived the Web as a gateway to a broad spectrum of information sources. Thus, a remarkable variety of data has always been accessible through Web browsers. In other words, the browser–client has always been able to communicate with many different types of Internet servers (for example, Gopher and file transfer protocol). We view all manner of Internet resources through the windows that our Web browsers have become. Additionally, Microsoft and Netscape have bundled other Internet clients (principally e-mail and Usenet) with their browsers, blurring the distinctions among Web browsers and e-mail/Usenet readers. It is small wonder that novices do not comprehend the difference between the Web and the Internet.

The enormous variety of applications and services we routinely employ through our Web browsers makes it quite difficult to chart a comprehensive history of the post-1993 Internet. We will, however, sketch the evolution of a few key concepts and technologies, especially those pertaining to the convergence of the Web, television, cinema and other mass media.

AUDIO AND MOTION VIDEO

The introduction of audio and motion video to the Web has been slow, at least in comparison to the Web's normally hyperactive evolution. The graphics-centred Web that evolved in 1993 and 1994 was mostly silent and mostly still images, with some primitive animation. Soon after, however, audio/video add-ons or 'plug-ins' began to appear for Web browsers. Progressive Networks, which would become RealNetworks, pioneered the effective delivery of audio/video with RealPlayer in 1995. RealPlayer was among the first to use 'streaming'

technology over the Web. Previous forms of audio/video delivery required that users transfer entire files to their computers and then launch a media player to listen to them, a process
that could take minutes or hours. Streaming media technology, just like radio and television,
permits the listener to hear audio and see video within seconds of requesting it.

RealNetworks aggressively marketed RealAudio and RealVideo throughout the late
1990s and now claims 'to deliver content on more than 85 per cent of all streaming media-
enabled Web pages'.[12] However, Apple and Microsoft have not conceded the delivery of
audio and video to RealNetworks. Apple's QuickTime software has been around for as long
as the RealPlayer and was the delivery system of choice for early attempts at multimedia
Webcasting such as the Cable News Network's *CNN Interactive*, which formed in January
1995 and hosted about four QuickTime 'movies' (as Apple calls them) per day.[13] Microsoft
has been catching up to RealNetworks and Apple with its Windows Media Player, which
it has made integral to Windows in much the same way as it integrated its Web browser.

Despite RealNetworks', Apple's and Microsoft's efforts, most users still have trouble
watching video over the Web. The image and sound quality is poor or choppy, and the
video window is often very small. These technical difficulties have contributed to the failure
of older media's attempts to colonise the Web. Television networks and film studios have
effectively used the Web to promote programmes and films (for example, *The Blair Witch
Project* (1999)); however, they have yet to succeed with the distribution of original content
over the Web. This has largely been left to sites that feature independently produced short
films, music videos, games and animation. Indeed, for independent producers the Web
holds out the promise of the worldwide distribution of video produced on a shoestring
budget. Ever since the invention of 8mm film, it has been possible for independent, avant-
garde, student and amateur film-makers to make works for very little money, but until now
there has been no method for them to distribute those works internationally. *Ifilm.com*,
MediaTrip.com, *Shockwave.com* and other Web sites encourage independent video producers by distributing their work globally. Web evangelists are already predicting a video
revolution with new, previously disenfranchised voices being heard, but it seems more likely
that marketing will become the main factor determining which voices are heard above the
ever-increasing din of media texts competing for users' attention.

The limitations to Web-based video delivery will not last forever, as audio and video formats improve and users obtain faster connections to the Internet. We have already seen in
the early 2000s that audio (without video) can be 'transmitted' very effectively across the
Internet. Thousands of conventional radio stations began sending their air signals over
the Net once a critical mass of Web users had the capability to receive Internet audio transmissions and computers equipped to play audio. Full-screen, full-motion video cannot be
far off. It seems likely that in the near future, television stations and film studios will have the
same delivery capability as radio stations.

Merely having the appropriate video technology does not guarantee that traditional television or film corporations will succeed on the Web. They also must revise the mode of
presentation of their products. Television and film are fundamentally 'push' media. The

entertainment/information is pushed at viewers from traditional television or cinema screens without viewers being able to pick ('pull') some bits while rejecting others, or change what is happening on-screen. The television remote control has made television into a more inter-active medium providing viewers with some 'pull' to their viewing experiences. But the television remote control is still nowhere near as interactive as the computer mouse. Moreover, the Web is a fundamentally pull medium. *Nothing* appears in one's Web browser until the user requests it by clicking on the screen or typing in a Web address.[14] In terms of the client-server model, while standard broadcasting stations (servers) are always sending their signal, pushing/beaming it towards television sets (clients), Web servers only transmit data when the client specifically pulls/requests it. Moreover, Web clients can also transmit data back to servers through forms and interactive games, which is impossible in traditional television systems.

There have been attempts to transform the Web into a broadcasting-style, push experi-ence, but they have so far met with failure. The most notable among these was PointCast, an application that sent news, weather, stock prices and so on to users' desktops, without them being specifically requested. PointCast was released in 1997 amid a flurry of media attention that presented it as the vanguard of a new Web. The cover of *Wired* magazine declared, 'The Web browser itself is about to croak. And good riddance. In its place . . . PUSH!'[15] But three years later, PointCast and the other 'push' applications met their demise. The PointCast failure does not necessarily mean that old broadcasting models will never work on the Internet. Indeed, they may find a new home in the transmission of data to personal digital assistants (PDAs) and cellular phones, as is suggested by the remnants of PointCast found in Infogate, an '*alerting service* offering the prioritized delivery of per-sonalized news, financial information, sports, weather and messages via the Internet to your computer or wireless device'.[16] But PointCast's failure does fuel the debate raging over whether old-guard television/film producers will be able to market interactive television or interactive film successfully, or whether they would even want to do so. As the debate con-tinues, the casualties of television networks' and film studios' Internet attempts mount. For instance, NBC formed *NBC Interactive* (*NBCi*) in 1999 with more than $100 million in cash. It boasted, '*NBCi* is driving the evolution of the Internet with interactive online and on-air content, rich media, search and directory, community features and e-commerce'.[17] Two years later, *NBCi* suffered huge financial losses. In the spring of 2001, NBC's parent company, General Electric, put NBCi out of its misery by folding its remaining services into its television-network business.[18] A similar fate was met in 2001 by *Entertaindom*, an attempt by AOL Time Warner to create a media hub.[19]

NBC and AOL Time Warner may have been thwarted in their Internet forays, but the pur-veyors of sexually explicit video have not. Much as pornographers led the way in the exploitation of the photograph and the videocassette, they have also been at the vanguard of Web-based commerce and putting real-time, interactive video online. Among the most successful of these is Danni Ashe, who created *Danni's Hard Drive* just two years after the initial release of Mosaic and used it to market nude images of herself and others.[20] Ashe, whom the Guinness World Records once named the 'Most Downloaded Woman', and others in the sex industry were quick to pick up on technology linking video cameras, still or motion, to the Internet, but they were not the first with this technology. The first 'Webcam', or, more accurately, 'netcam', went online in 1991, as the Web was being developed at CERN. The Trojan Room Coffee Pot netcam was set up on a computer lab in Cambridge, England, by Quentin Stafford-Fraser, who explained its function:

> Some members of the 'coffee club' lived in other parts of the building and had to navigate several flights of stairs to get to the coffee pot; a trip which often proved fruitless if the all-night hackers of the Trojan Room had got there first. This disruption to the progress of Computer Science research obviously caused us some distress, and so XCoffee [the netcam device] was born.[21]

Although the still image refreshed only three times per minute and was initially limited to this lab's computer network and not the Internet as a whole, the Trojan Room Coffee Pot established that an individual could cheaply transmit video images across a network.

In April 1996, Jennifer Ringley, a student at Dickinson College in Pennsylvania, started a computer-connected camera in her dormitory room that periodically sent images of herself to her personal Web site. Much like a surveillance camera, JenniCam captured her quotidian life, mostly her staring at a computer screen, but also occasional glimpses of her masturbating or, after she graduated and moved to Washington DC, being intimate with her boyfriend. Soon other amateur exhibitionists and the sex industry were also using Webcams. Now there are Webcams showing everything from traffic and weather at key transportation junctures to the view from a Berlin taxi cab to the Dallas site of President John F. Kennedy's assassination (the Dealey Plaza Cam presents 'the ONLY LIVE view available in the world from the Sniper's Perch').[22]

The Webcam, whether created for personal reasons or as an element of a commercial enterprise, typifies the Internet's client-server model that so baffles traditional broadcasters. Users must seek out JenniCam and request its images before they appear on their computer monitors. Just before the decade ended, a variation on this client-server model would further baffle and infuriate the producers of copyrighted audio and video. Shawn Fanning, an individual who is 'driving the evolution of the Internet' much more than NBCi, released the file-sharing software Napster and thereby sparked a storm of controversy and litigation. In defiance of copyright laws, Napster users shared music files in MP3 format. Founded in May 1999, the Napster corporation was sued six months later by the Recording Industry Association of America (RIAA) for 'contributory and vicarious copyright infringement'.[23] Napster lost that case and was driven into bankruptcy in 2002, but Napster users and the RIAA alike realised that the peer-to-peer (P2P) genie had been released from the bottle as other Napster-like services – for example, Gnutella and FreeNet – already arisen.[24]

P2P's basic principle threatens the foundations of the recording, broadcasting, film and publishing industries because it radically restructures and decentralises distribution. In P2P transactions, there is no central server. Even the Web, with its widely distributed information-sharing, still requires an HTTP server to provide data to HTTP clients. This is not the case with P2P transactions. In P2P, individual clients (peers) connect with one another and share data on an equal basis, client-to-client, and not server-to-client. Each P2P client is also able to act as a server. In this regard, Napster was not a pure P2P service. Napster clients or peers connected with their first servers, find out where other clients or peers located, then made a peer-to-peer connection. Because Napster clients connected through its server, the Napster corporation was vulnerable to charges that it was abetting music thieves. However, other P2P software does not use a central server and thus will be more difficult to litigate against. Moreover, the files they share are not limited to music. They can easily contain films or software or anything else that may be contained in a digital format. The essentially decentralised nature of P2P software is obviously anathema to major media corporations and their investment in the copyright system. P2P proponents make no secret of this. As Ian Clarke of FreeNet contends, 'You cannot guarantee freedom of speech *and* enforce copyright law. It is for this reason that FreeNet, a system designed to protect Freedom of Speech, *must* prevent enforcement of copyright'.[25]

ONLINE GAMES AND VIRTUAL REALITY: INTERACTIVITY AND IMMERSION

In the previous segment, we have seen how the Internet is changing the delivery of sounds and images to our homes. We have discussed this transformation in terms that are basically familiar to established media forms such as recorded music and video. The viewing and listening experience of a Napster-obtained MP3 file or a Webcam image is not so different from listening to a CD or watching a videocassette, even if the way users acquired them has changed. Users still do not alter such music or video as they passively hear and view them. What of those media experiences, however, where users *do* affect texts *as they experience them*? What of the new level of interactivity found in online games? What of the immersive experiences that have come to be called 'virtual reality' (VR)? How has the Internet changed the acts of viewing and listening?

One component of any computer game is a strong sense of interactivity between the user and the screen. The actions the user takes, such as mouse clicks, key presses, joystick twists, and so on, have an immediate impact upon what occurs on-screen. The 1970s' video game's interactive interface illustrated a significant shift from television's passive experience, especially at a time when remote control devices were relatively rare. Moreover, video games approached virtual reality when they began to bring the viewer into a navigable space that was viewed from a first person perspective. The arcade game *Battlezone* (1980) and the Apple II game *Flight Simulator I* (1980) both placed users inside virtual machines, providing a sense of space and the ability for users to move forwards into that space, to move along the z-axis, and to *choose* which ways they move.[26] This is a crucial aspect of virtual reality, as it enables virtual reality to simulate how humans move through the real world.

The on-screen worlds of *Battlezone* and *Flight Simulator I* provided a virtual space through which players 'moved', but their imagery was far from photorealistic. In 1992 and 1993, id Software's releases of *Wolfenstein 3-D* and *Doom*, respectively, heralded a substantial increase in the level of graphic detail in personal computer games, as well as establishing a new degree of on-screen carnage.[27] *Wolfenstein 3-D* inaugurated the 'first-person shooter' genre, which has since evolved into games such as *Quake* (1996) and *Half-Life* (1998). In first-person shooter games, players typically adopt the first-person perspective of combatants moving through a virtual arena, as in a cinematic subjective shot. Unlike antecedents such as tank games or flight simulators where one is confined to the space of a cockpit, in a first-person shooter game one inhabits the virtual body of an individual moving through space. First-person shooters, tank games and flight simulators all use first-person perspective, but the first-person shooter games heighten the degree of movement and immersion because it is a virtual human body in motion, independent from a machine.

An essential component of most virtual realities is a sense of a shared space, the illusion that one is inhabiting the same space as objects and, crucially, as other beings whether human or not. *Doom* was a pioneer in this regard because several players could enter a combat arena from different computers on a network. Although *Doom* was designed to be played on small networks or between computers connected by a phone line, it was not natively an Internet game.[28] *Quake*, in contrast, was designed to be played over the Internet, although the set-up for doing so was a bit cumbersome. Late-1990s multiplayer games became increasingly Internet-capable, culminating in 'massively multiplayer online role-playing games' (MMORPGs) such as *EverQuest* (1999).[29] MMORPGs manifest visually what has been done using text in 'multi-user dungeons/dimensions' (MUDs) since 1979.[30] An MUD is a virtual world built by its participants, usually to host *Dungeons and Dragons*-style role-playing, but sometimes with other goals of community construction (for example, *Postmodern Culture*'s PMC-MOO). Hundreds or even thousands of users may simultaneously participate. The virtual world of the MUD is described through words, but the MMORPG presents graphically rich virtual worlds through which the player moves. And, in the case of *EverQuest*, some 80,000 players may be concurrently online 'together'.

In multiplayer games on the Internet, whether 'massively' multiplayer or not, we can clearly see an online virtual reality where a virtual space is shared among participants who experience a simulation of movement through a visual realm and there interact with objects, humans and monsters. There have been numerous virtual reality projects in experimental computer labs and military flight simulators, with elaborate paraphernalia such as wired gloves (for example, the Dataglove, which transmits users' hand movements to the computer), head-mounted displays (small computer displays in helmets) and various boxes into which participants are sealed; however, the most widely distributed form of virtual reality is the online multiplayer game.[31]

AN INCONCLUSIVE CONCLUSION

The Internet and the World Wide Web continue to evolve in ways that repeatedly surprise the technological and financial experts, shift users' methods of receiving and transmitting data, and confound traditional media corporations. Reviewing the short history of net-worked computing (since the first ARPANET (Advanced Research Projects Agency Network) nodes in 1969) and the Web (created in 1991), we can see how the efforts of engineers, government bureaucrats, venture capitalists, digital artists, digital activists and maverick hackers and crackers have constellated around a dispersed, decentralised exchange of data (including text, sound, image) and a human–machine interface that permits, and occasionally demands, new, interactive modes. We have concluded with a consideration of the online multiplayer game and virtual reality not because these phenom-ena are the ultimate, teleological endpoint of the Internet, but because they illustrate the current apotheosis of online characteristics. These include hyperactive interactivity; decen-tralised exchange of data; communication among dispersed participants (that is, combat; although players may chat while 'fragging' each other); a shared virtual space; disrupted, nonlinear narrative trails; and a graphically sophisticated user interface. The future Internet will probably bring new implementations of these characteristics.

Notes

1. William Gibson, *Neuromancer* (New York: Ace, 1984).

2. For histories of inter-networking, see Katie Hafner and Matthew Lyon, *Where Wizards Stay Up Late: The Origins of the Internet* (New York: Simon and Schuster, 1996); John Naughton, *A Brief History of the Future: From Radio Days to Internet Years in a Lifetime* (Woodstock, NY: Overlook Press, 2000); Stephen Segaller, *Nerds 2.0.1: A Brief History of the Internet* (New York: TV Books, 1998).

3. Quoted in Stephen Segaller, *Nerds 2.0.1*, p. 131.

4. There is some debate about exactly when these terms were first used. The official *Xanadu* Website contends that they were chosen in 1963 and first appeared in print in 1965. 'Project Xanadu History', <www.xanadu.net/HISTORY>.

5. 'THE NEW XANADU MODEL FOR THE WEB', <www.xanadu.net/xuWeb.html>.

6. See, for example, Apple's HyperCard and Brown University's HES, FRESS and IRIS projects. See 'HyperCard Past & Future', Apple Computer, <www.apple.com/hypercard/information/pastandfuture.html>; George P. Landow, 'Hypertext at Brown', Brown University, <landow.stg.brown.edu/HTatBrown/BrownHT.html>; James M. Nyce and Paul Kahn (eds), *From Memex to Hypertext: Vannevar Bush and the Mind's Machine* (Boston, MA: Academic Press, 1991).

7. CERN stands for Conseil Européen pour la Recherche Nucléaire (European Council for Nuclear Research), even though its official name is the European Organisation for Nuclear Research. For an explanation of its confusing name, see 'About CERN's Name . . . (And Its Spelling)', <cern.web.cern.ch/CERN/CERNName.html>.

8. According to a chronology pieced together by John Naughton in *A Brief History of the Future*, pp. 235 and 239.

9. According to Robert 'Hobbes' Zakon on *Hobbes' Internet Timeline*, 15 April 2001, <www.zakon.org/robert/internet/timeline>.

10. For the version history of Windows Mosaic see <ftp.ncsa.uiuc.edu/Mosaic/Windows/Archive/

index.html>. For Mac Mosaic, see <archive.ncsa.uiuc.edu/SDG/Software/MacMosaic/Release-info/announce.html>.

11. The remnants of Mosaic remain, however, in Netscape's products. The original code name for Navigator was 'Mozilla', a splicing together of 'mosaic' and 'Godzilla'.

12. 'About RealNetworks', <www.realnetworks.com/company>.

13. Jim B. Grant, 'Start Streaming', *VideoSystems*, January 2001, p. 46.

14. Of course, Web browsers automate this request by setting a default for the user's home page.

15. Quoted in Craig Bicknell, 'PointCast Coffin About to Shut', *Wired News*, 29 March 2000, <www.wired.com/news/exec/0,1370,35208,00.html>.

16. My emphasis. 'Download Infogate Now!', <www.infogate.com/cgi-bin/index.cgi?id=&page=download:index2>.

17. See <www.nbci.com/LMOID/resource/0,566,-5623,00.html>

18. 'GE's NBC Agrees to Buy Rest of NBCi for $85 Million', *Bloomberg News*, 9 April 2001, <investor.cnet.com/investor/news/newsitem/0-9900-1028-5550686-0.html>.

19. Steve Kovsky and Evan Hansen, 'AOL Time Warner Plans to Close *Entertaindom*', *CNET News*, 17 January 2001, <news.cnet.com/news/0–1005–200–4515788.html>.

20. *Danni's Hard Drive*, <www.danni.com>.

21. Quentin Stafford-Fraser, 'The Trojan Room Coffee Pot Biography', <www.cl.cam.ac.uk/coffee/qsf/coffee.html>.

22. For example: weather/traffic on the Tappan Zee Bridge (NY), <www.thruway.state.ny.us/webcams>; a Berlin taxi, <www.berlin.de/livetaxi>; Dealey Plaza Cam, <www.earthcam.com/jfk>. For a list of Webcams, see *Webcam World*, <www.webcamworld.com>.

23. 'Napster's Musical History', *The Industry Standard*, 12 February 2001, <www.thestandard.com/article/0,1902,22139,00.html>. For the specifics of the RIAA suit, see <www.riaa.com/PDF/Napster_Complaint.pdf>.

24. Napster is not the first file-sharing, P2P software. It is just the most notorious. Gnutella, for instance, was around well before Napster. For more information on P2P projects, see David Sims, 'O'Reilly P2P Directory', *OpenP2P.com*, 20 October 2000, <www.openp2p.com/pub/a/p2p/2000/10/20/directory.html>.

25. Ian Clarke, 'The Philosophy behind Freenet', *Freenet*, <freenet.sourceforge.net/index.php?page=philosophy>.

26. An online emulation of *Battlezone* that is remarkably true to the look of the original arcade game may be played at <www.games.com>. *MiGMan's Flight Sim Museum* features screen shots from early games, <www.migman.com/ref/simhis>.

27. As Lev Manovich contends, *Myst* (1993) was also significant in its enhanced graphic detail. Lev Manovich, *The Language of New Media* (Cambridge, MA: MIT Press, 2001), pp. 244–5.

28. Ways around this limitation have been devised: Scott Coleman and Jay Cotton, 'The TCP/IP Internet DOOM FAQ', <www.faqs.org/faqs/games/doom/howto-tcp>.

29. *EverQuest* was not the first MMORPG, but it is currently the biggest. The first such game was *Ultima Online*, released September 1997.

30. MUDs originated in the UK in 1979 when Roy Trubshaw launched MUD1 at Essex University.

31. For further elaboration on the history and theory of virtual reality, see Lev Manovich, *The Language of New Media*; Margaret Morse, *Virtualities: Television, Media Art, and Cyberculture* (Bloomington: Indiana University Press, 1998); and Janet H. Murray, *Hamlet on the Holodeck: The Future of Narrative in Cyberspace* (Cambridge, MA: MIT Press, 1997).

2.0

PRODUCTION

The investigation and analysis of film and media production have typically focused on a number overlapping areas, including industry practice, the legal and regulatory environment, the shifting business models of media financing, and the otherwise more creative aspects of producing films and television programmes. The emergence of digital media technologies has had a profound effect across these areas, influencing how media producers finance, create, market and control their media products – both old and new.

The digitisation of media has been a double-edged sword for producers. While the flexibility of movement across, as well as the ease of editing of, digital properties has generated numerous opportunities for the creation of cross-platform and integrated products, it has also provided the consumer with an increased ability to mould and shape the media experience. This has prompted consideration of new, and reconsideration of old, fundamental questions within the media industry – such as who owns, and thus has the power to modify, copy and/or distribute, a media property and how can media producers protect their financial investment in, as well as the artistic integrity of, their media products against such manipulation and untoward dissemination?

The clash between old media's protectiveness of brands and properties, and the 'sharing ethos' of digital producers and consumers has reinvigorated the legal and ethical consideration of how media content is produced, distributed and consumed. This dialectic is further complicated by the mix-and-match strategy often employed by a single producer, which may release, freely or with very little restriction, certain elements of its digital entertainment package into the public domain (such as free samples of digital recordings over the Web), while restricting the release of other exclusive entertainment and services (such as charging more for access to premium content).

The chapters in the following section approach the production of new media from a variety of angles: Hollywood's shifting production and marketing logics in light of the flexible economies of new media; the intertextual matrix of cross-production and marketing of media properties; the conflicting ethics and goals between media conglomerates and what has been deemed as the 'Napster ethos'; and, finally, the emerging global economy of media production, distribution and exhibition. Together, these chapters provide a snapshot of how media production is interacting with and being transformed by the emerging digital format.

2.1

The Business of New Media

John Caldwell

TECHNOLOGICAL 'REVOLUTION'/INSTITUTIONAL 'EVOLUTION'

> The dotcom category has been through a war. There's blood all over the dance floor, and out of the carnage, a few companies will emerge. Venture capital will flow into the sector by year's-end, once the flush-out is over.
>
> Kevin Wendle, CEO, iFilm, mixing survivalist metaphors in his post-high-tech crash business plan[1]

> Ouch. As it turns out, the magic number was 5,048, which the Nasdaq hit on March 10, 2000. What's happened since seems more like black magic. . . . Our goal was to . . . monitor the rise of technology-enabled borderless economy . . . companies (with) a mastery of . . . innovation, intelligent use of new tools, strategic vision, global reach, and, above all, networked communication. Amid the recent turbulence, the Wired Index got walloped right along with everyone else. It fell nearly 41 per cent.[2]

From the perspective of technology in the new millennium, the 1990s appeared less as a familiar guide ushering in the present than as a dramatic worldwide object lesson framed by the drama of ostensibly unbridled technological growth and precipitous economic collapse. Of course any hubris or tragedy in all of this is in the eye of the beholder. For while high-tech start-ups, the stock markets and venture capitalists cheered on the high-tech run-up, the old medias, old industries, old economies all cast an anxious eye at the upstarts even as they covered their own positions by cautious modifications of industrial practice, initiated in response to the newly wired world that promised to render them obsolete.

In the early and mid-1990s, traditional media companies, television networks and studios, even as they toyed with experimental interactive CDs, gaming and marketing, confidently issued press releases assuring everyone that traditional 'content is king'. Aggressive new apologists for the future, however, such as *Wired* in its inaugural issue, resurrected and championed, with a straight face, the technological determinism and visionary Utopianism of McLuhan. By the end of the decade, both of these public poses had shifted. *Wired* now betrayed its own anxious, hand-wringing with earnest cover stories intended to encourage its apparently vast and despondent high-tech readership. 'Optimism Pays', the June 2001 issue pleaded: 'Tough Times? Hell Yes. . . . Some Advice?: Believe in the Internet More than Ever'. Columns in the 'old' media trades since spring 2001, on the other hand, had taken a very different emotional tack, seldom concealing their glee at new media hard times and celebrating the dotcom comeuppance as long overdue and very much deserved. Now, the newly digitalised television industries at a succession of major conventions (NATPE 2000, NAB 2000) are boasting their shared mantra 'content is king'.

Of course, corporate public relations always deliver a cleaner spin than industrial realities might merit. The ratings of broadcast and cable networks, after all, are still in continuous decline. While Time Warner, Disney/ABC and Vivendi/Universal/Canal+ are very much on their feet with high-profile interactive initiatives in play, they are having a very difficult time in these areas making earnings and profits predictable and credible. Underneath the alternating corporate expressions of tactical glee and strategic despondency, something much more provisional and methodical is under way. Both industrial cultures, old media and new media, now take the need to forge substantive, integrated partnerships with the other side as a house rule and objective. Later, I will describe more specifically how new media and old media have come to augment and interact with each other. Here I simply want to suggest how the discursive turmoil over what are frequently deemed 'marriages' and 'irreconcilable differences' masks deep-seated efforts to maintain a position, with old media learning how to commercialise promising but unproven prototypes from new media; and new media bringing on board, for their very survival, the traditional aesthetic and managerial competencies of old media entertainment companies.

For many who create and theorise new media, my summary of the soap opera of explosive dotcom emergence, NASDAQ collapse and old media resurrection in the digital age may seem to have little to do with the kinds of concerns that have preoccupied new media artists, critics and writers over the past century. However, this historic expansion and collapse makes it difficult to continue to theorise about new media in the same way that it has typically been done in the arts and humanities in the past; the aforementioned, globalised high-tech shift makes it almost impossible to talk usefully about new media in terms that are primarily or solely formal, artistic, phenomenological or psychological. Taken alone, all four of these categories now seem intricately interdependent on much broader forms of institutional and industrial practice. To pretend otherwise is to fall prey to the same lazy conceptual schemes – for example, intentionalism, expressionism – and formalism that propped up the avant-garde during its extended period of high modernism. Belief in the agency of the artist or new media creator, or in the need to make 'counter' or 'resistant' media, may be essential to effective new media creation. However, doing so without acknowledging how new media creation is interdependent and with industrial and institutional forces is myopic at the least.

Although doom and gloom at the prospects of globalisation and conglomeration is not the most useful response, new media artists and critics would do well to at least consider how both artists and academics are only in place because of institutional privilege. My colleagues in digital production suites occasionally surmise, 'Hey, we're all going to work for Bill Gates or Rupert Murdoch eventually.' What such a statement might mean in the future, or even now, is worth considering as part of the very ground upon which new media creation and theorisation occur.

ECONOMIES OF SCALE VERSUS NICHE ECONOMIES OF SCOPE

> Thespians log on to ABC dot-com pilot, [and] star as co-owners of a struggling dot-com who face either shutting down their business or bringing in outside 'suits' to save the company.
>
> One of two television shows for autumn 2001 that parody the collapse
> of dotcoms and their rescue by old-media-like 'suits'[3]

> Indigenous programming continues to gain popularity in key international markets.
>
> 'Mass market potential of niche localism at Mipcom Market'.[4]

New media production and distribution typically demands of its makers a high degree of capital; certainly higher than that needed for many low-technology art forms, but comparable to film and television in ways that are frequently unanticipated. This may seem somewhat ironic, as many digital devices hype and promise to *lower* costs dramatically per unit. But while this may be true for individual content production (for example, utilising a DV camcorder to make digital cinema, or a mini-disc recorder and a CD burner to create new music), actually delivering such content on a widespread, accessible, cost-effective and income-generating basis is still extremely difficult, risky and costly. Utilising Powerbooks for nonlinear editing and DVD burners for interactive authoring clearly makes media producing more democratic, but grassroots digital producers still face the same kind of formidable challenges faced for decades by independent film- and video-makers before them: gatekeeping, distribution, advertising, marketing and technical capabilities for widescale streaming and interactivity are still more effectively controlled by others. Increasingly, these others have emerged as the very same corporate brands that controlled the old studio and television network systems, but usually in a merged and morphed form, for example, Time Warner/AOL, NBC/snap.com, Disney/ABC/Go.com, or by far smaller, aspiring new media brands, such as iFilm.

Individuals can make no-budget independent features, or interactive DVDs, but unless such a producer contracts or affiliates with one of the recognisably branded sites or players, the film will probably stream with little or no visibility. With hundreds of millions of users, the Internet now stands like a global Grand Canyon, ready to accept and immediately efface any digital expression tossed into its void. So if real and 'discrete' eyeballs and/or use and distribution revenues are on an independent, new media entity's charter, then a far more challenging and costly form of 'production' is required: one involving corporate networking, server-leasing, affiliation, contracts and exclusivity. Such things have revived the very forms of old media commercialism that the Internet, in its early stages, promised to transcend. Cable television and Madison Avenue had, in the 1980s, proved the commercial effectiveness of producing for narrow but high-spending niches, which were termed 'quality demographics'. No-budget digital cinema and digital music clearly evoke niches themselves, everything from X-gen to hip-hop to survivalist to Sundance sensibility. Like the garage band phenomenon, however, such handmade, niche new media come without high-spending consumerism attached to their digital content.

In a few short years, the Internet has been effectively commercialised. Lacking the regulatory protections and sanctions necessary to establish widespread distribution networks during the start-up phase of any new media (as with television during the network era), the landscape of digital media in 2002 is a harsh and unforgiving place. With hundreds of players vying for fewer eyeballs per site, only the players with very deep financial pockets tend to last the distance. To establish brand identity, to elicit and reward users through compelling forms of interactivity, to develop tangible 'revenue streams' from advertising, subscriptions, licensing, merchandising or e-business, tends to require the standby industrial competencies that old media possessed: economies of scale and reach.

As if the vast scale of the Internet were not formidable enough, many now recognise that 'portals' have become the key battleground in Internet traffic. The Internet may originally have been bi- or multi-directional, a pull-medium rather than a push-medium, and rhizomatic in structure rather than linear or hierarchical, but many new media corporations are in business precisely to find ways to make the Internet highly regulated and exclusive. Some do this by 'tiering' users; others do it with graduated payment-for-access schemes; yet others do this via subscription policies that allow new media companies to push or distribute their content to a select group of subscribers or members. Elaborate encryption schemes are set up to prevent unauthorised Web site or server trespassing. The pervasive form of exclusivity is so ubiquitous and 'helpful' that few criticise its effect. All portals – the first or main Web site that your Internet provider brings you to when you go online or the search engine you choose – are not created equal, and all portal roads and searches do not lead to the same destinations. Critics of AOL, Lycos, Earthlink, Go.com and other portals protest at the bias that leads 'open' searches only to those sites that have contractual alliances with the portals. Vested economic interests regularly drive the ostensibly open searches, in the same way that block-booking in film distribution and network licensing in television greatly delimited the free market choice film and television audiences faced in old media. In an Internet landscape made open-by-design, the only real way to generate revenue is by establishing and legitimising some form of exclusivity.

There is, however, one complication in this regard. Yes, gate-keepers and durable distribution deals rule both the old and now the new media worlds. However, the scarcity of the means of production shows old and new to be very different in other ways. Regularly invoking 'broadcast standards' and 'wide-screen production values', respectively, network television and Hollywood effectively excluded alternative media production by establishing and marketing their own heavily capitalised means of production as somehow proprietary and exclusive. As a result, the network and studio era inculcated and rewarded viewers who acknowledged that the gulf that divided 'producers' from 'audiences' was reasonable and legitimate. Now that digital manufacturers vigorously sell users the idea that everyone can be a digital producer, the lustre of Hollywood exclusivity has faded somewhat. Since digital photographic e-mailing, chatrooms, videoconferencing, digital home movie distribution, group Internet gaming and interactive DVD authoring on PCs have become commonplace, the 'magic' of Hollywood has far less to do with an exclusive means of production than with the continuing draw of celebrity personalities on the other side of the studio wall. In this context, with the means of production now increasingly ubiquitous, moving image and sound productions have become far more vernacular (like speech) than spectacular (like cinema). While this may be more democratic and empowering on one level, the trend reduces most individual digital expressions to the 'background'; to the level of nondescript conversation; to a kind of digital graffiti that hardly anyone sees and that few can or want to understand. So the niche economy of focus personalises expression with digital tools for many. However, a very different economy of scale is also necessary, both for the manufacturing operations at Sony and for the streaming or server sites which were established to give widespread visibility to independent digital work. The old media 'society of the spectacle', an optical ideology, gives way here to the new media 'society of digital conversation', a wired paradigm.

DIGITAL PRACTICES: INSTITUTIONAL NEGOTIATION AND MARKET LOGIC

> FirstLook offers turnkey entertainment content sourcing and development solutions to Web
> site partners worldwide. FirstLook syndicates promotions and rich media preview experiences
> to build consumer demand for their products.[5]

Digital media have altered a number of fundamental categories and distinctions in 'Hollywood' (a cultural site I take here to refer to the constellation of creative industries behind network television and films in the Los Angeles region that produce and distribute globally). As the epigraph above indicates, FirstLook is one of many new companies in the region that are working the potentially lucrative ground that now exists between two formerly estranged competitors: Hollywood and new media. In the old days, a fairly clear understanding existed of the differences between film and programme production on the one hand, and marketing and distribution on the other. Crossing over these distinctions brought with it regulatory risk and business uncertainty. In the digital age, however, companies benefit precisely by complicating and confusing the distinctions between production, marketing and distribution. By creatively describing its product as 'turnkey entertainment content sourcing', FirstLook transforms entertainment content in two ways. It is now both a 'technology' (it is 'turnkey', or ready to operate or go upon delivery) and a verb

(a manner of 'sourcing', rather than *a* programme or *a* film). These kinetic and technological paradigms for content fit the unstable parameters of new media, whether on the Web
or elsewhere. Web and wireless delivery are still mired in a quagmire of technical incom-
patibilities in streaming protocols, bandwidth, formats and standards. Numerous dotcoms
have collapsed precisely because they were unable to materialise their strategic business
objectives in functional and deliverable ways. By 'syndicating promotions', alongside short
films, music, television programmes and video games, FirstLook also unabashedly makes
selling commercials the very content of its 'network'. Marketing emerges here as foregrounded content, the old familiar genre distinctions collapse, and corporate specialists
enter the picture to 'syndicate' promotions instead of authored content. In the current old
media/new media world, new technology companies have thus hijacked the roles once
reserved for production companies, broadcast programmers *and* advertising agencies. By
featuring demo reels, short films and television in this way, FirstLook also intends to function as a 'packager' or agent. The implications of these 'border crossings', and there are
many other variants of it, are now only beginning to be understood.

In many ways it is simplistic to talk of 'digital media' or 'new media' as if they were one
thing. Even a cursory look at the changing industry in Hollywood shows very different digital practices and digital economies at work. It is useful to demarcate a number of discrete
'digitals' within the current constellation of 'new media'. This includes at least four different
creative communities: first, digital effects (CGI/animation); second, high-resolution film and
television (HDTV/DTV/24p); third, video gaming; and, finally, media/dotcom configurations.
The first two groups, digital effects and high-definition (or 'hi-def') film/television, are built
around broad economic conditions tried and proved over many decades in Hollywood. I
term both of these high-end practices 'macro-digital', for despite that fact that audiences
may associate special effects or hi-def with a specific film, television title or company
(*Terminator 2*, LucasFilm), the practices depend upon production methods that have been
built around predictable revenues from advertising-supported commercial television on the
one hand and theatrical motion picture distribution on the other. The second set of digital
practices, video gaming and media/dotcom configurations, does not have the relative
luxury of prime time or blockbuster box-office revenue streams. Video gaming emerged
with a fairly narrow demographic or user base (pre-adolescent and adolescent males), even
though this niche is dependent upon mass market digital products, for example, consoles
by Sega, Nintendo, and Sony. Media/dotcom entities ('micro-digital' practices) have an
even more difficult time amassing an audience of users, lost as they are in the infinitely multi-
niche world of the Web. Few 'Webcasters' successfully emulate 'broadcasting' by aggre-
gating splintered taste cultures and user groups as deliverable economic commodities.

MACRO-DIGITAL

Two macro-digital industrial subcultures are extensions of traditional practices in Hollywood.
Special effects for film and television grew out of traditional optical–mechanical effects in the
1980s, when a range of new, independent digital studios such as Boss, PDI, Digital

Domain, and Industrial Light and Magic emerged. With individual specialisations far more focused and demanding than most comprehensive film or television studios could justify, these effects houses became known as 'boutiques'. As independent contractors, the digital boutiques provided effects on a project-by-project basis. Costs-per-minute for high-resolution effects escalated due to the higher end computerisation requirements. These technology specialisations became prohibitively costly to large studios and networks obliged to fund and maintain a competitive edge across a range of different technical crafts and production areas. By contrast, the new and smaller digital boutiques had the advantage of capitalising in one area and providing this specialisation to many different clients. With no back lots and sound stages to maintain, the boutiques began to break down traditional institutional barriers in the industry.[6] Digital shops such as PDI provided work for an impressive array of genres and production companies. Although feature film effects helped to fuel the audience desire for effects in general, PDI and Boss assumed prominence because of the work they provided for commercials, advertising agencies and music videos. In some ways, starting in the 1980s, the music video and commercial industries became R&D laboratories for effects houses. These short-form clients provided endless opportunities for experimentation on television, cable and video, without the box-office (and corporation-killing) risk that inevitably came with big-budget feature film work at the majors. Such experimentation, furthermore, made high-resolution effects and animation work ubiquitous across the general mediascape.

However, digital effects work did not just splinter business relations and the production methods among the majors. It also fundamentally altered labour relations in Hollywood. Unions became increasingly irrelevant for digital effects artists and animators outside the studios. As 'contract labour', the boutiques were not obligated to the labour constraints of the majors who were signatories to the unions and guilds. In the mid-1990s, the trades marvelled at the high incomes earned by the new digital work force, but seldom remarked on a corresponding dark side that was emerging. The digital boutique became for some a digital 'sweatshop', with seven-day working weeks and 18-hour work days not uncommon. A shortage of skilled effects artists and animators sent companies scrambling to recruit and develop new talent, in some cases at the high-school level. By 1997, digital effects and animation houses frequently had workforces who averaged 22 to 23 years of age. These cash-intensive non-union shops proved immensely profitable for some, but brought with them a drawback. Twenty-five year-olds might earn six-figure incomes, but 80-hour weeks promised to 'burn out' many of the digital artisans who seemed to be going through mid-life crises by their late twenties.

Visionary owners from profitable boutiques such as Rhythm and Hues flaunted the fact that they were successfully confronting the sweatshop aspect of effects work, by offering their young workaholics 'sabbaticals' to recuperate and grow as individuals, before heading back to the digital production frenzy. Workers at less profitable outlets were not so lucky. By 2000, the industrial need for a phalanx of new digital artists had faded, salaries had dropped, and even major animation houses such as Disney were laying off animators.

Some surmised that the glory days of high-priced animation had passed. What had really happened was that the cost of high-end effects work plummeted as digital technologies developed. Lower-end and less expensive Intel- and Mac-based workstations, running Adobe After Effects and Maya software, began taking on the work that had once been restricted to expensive, high-end Silicon Graphics, Quantel and Flame workstations. The industry expressed concern about the demise of high-end effects houses such as Boss studios in 1998, but failed to note how digital work had actually proliferated, albeit now in the hands of even more and smaller boutique operations.

In other parts of Hollywood, 'digital' tends to refer to the shift of what was, until recently, termed HDTV (high-definition television), but is now broadly deemed DTV (digital television). Unwilling to dictate a single 'consensus' technical standard for HDTV, the FCC allowed the 'market to decide', then sanctioned 14 different, allowable digital standards (from 480p to 1080i). The result was four years of technical volatility and confusion, despite FCC dictates that broadcasters must shift to digital delivery by 2003. Even as television recognises the utility of high-definition imagery for certain prime-time genres, they still balk at this perceived top-down model of technological change. With ambivalent broadcasters mired in conflict with consumer electronic manufacturers, television's stunted transition to digital has proved problematic. In the midst of this broadcast HDTV logjam, Hollywood film studios and pro-gramme production companies have gradually settled on their own high-definition format ('24progressive HD') in the arena once called 'film origination'.[7] The 24pHD standard perfectly matches the frame rate of celluloid, suggesting to the industry that theatrical pro-duction with electronic hi-def, and not television's HDTV, will be the trigger application for a successful shift to digitalisation. High production values have always legitimised Hollywood's mode of production as distinctive and marketable globally. The 24pHD stan-dard has been embraced by the majors as a logical next step.

However, because Hollywood involves so many other players and companies at every level of budget and genre, the prohibitive cost of high definition has led other executives and producers to justify very different and more cost-effective 'digital' formats. CNN, for example, recently shocked high-definition manufacturer Sony by discontinuing purchases of Digital Betacam SX equipment (whose cameras sell for $32,000) in favour of Sony's DSR-DVCAM line of industrial digital equipment (whose cameras sell for $4400). CNN argued that the extreme portability would bring 'exceptionalism' and more personality to 'multi-talented' journalists.[8] Skeptical analysts, however, noted a bottom-line logic behind the downgrade: CNN had just laid off 400 of its employees, and cost-cutting came in the 'aftermath of parent Time Warner's merger with AOL'.[9] The break evident here – when prime time and features go 'up' to 24pHD, and prime-time news moves 'down' to industrial digital standards – shows just how variegated 'the' industry continues to be. Even as the shift in features to 24pHD brings with it a range of new technical staff on the production set, DVCAM breaks the obligation to field three- or four-person crews in ENG work by replacing them with one- or two-person units.

Outside Atlanta, National Association of Broadcast Employees and Technicians (NABET) cynically questioned the motives of a major network such as CNN shifting to small format DV by challenging it to cover Timothy McVeigh's execution with a single, amateurish and unproven DVCAM camera. CNN, long known for its non-union workplace, now justifies DV journalism for its 'professional' reporters, while the IATSE-governed shoots in Hollywood, on the other hand, sanction the shift to 24pHD as a natural extension of elite 35mm film usage, the latter a process that Bordwell, Thompson and Staiger have referred to as 'trended change'.[10]

MICRO-DIGITAL

The third and fourth digital-industrial communities examined here, media/dotcoms and video gaming, emerged essentially outside the matrix of Hollywood and faced even tougher market conditions than the high-definition groups due to the unpredictable forms of exchange, revenue and value that arguably accompany the introduction of any new media technology. Despite the early, public cynicism of their trade publications on the subject, traditional entertainment companies never really wrote off the upstarts from Silicon Valley. After the ad agency and dotcom crash of 2000, entreaties came from the high-techs as well, lured by Hollywood's boasted expertise in 'windowing' and 'syndication'.[11]

To understand the institutional practices and economies of digital media, one has to understand syndication, or what has come to be known as 'repurposing and migrating content'. Consider the repurposing possibilities that emerged when the formerly traditional NBC took on the market share challenge of cable and the Internet. Of all of its divisions, network news served to drive the proliferation of NBC texts, by repurposing news stories and talk shows for CNBC, MSNBC and the MSNetwork. Corporate heavyweights Microsoft and NBC invented these kinds of synergies in a cross-media, cross-delivery onslaught, and by 2000 NBC threw down the gauntlet to even bigger globalising Net success stories AOL and Yahoo when it rebranded its own online Internet activities (then named *snap.com*) as a comprehensive, one-stop entertainment and shopping Web 'portal' called 'NBCi'. All of the erstwhile hype about how 'new media' will replace 'old-media' dinosaurs such as network television carried little credibility at GE/NBC. NBC would assume its place at the new media table even as CNN and ABC/ESPN/Disney had done. Bits and pieces of hybridised news anchor Brian Williams now show up in the form of migratory texts customised and endlessly individuated as e-content for NBC, MSNBC, CNBC, MSNetwork and NBCi.

At industry summits, conventions and trade shows, a newer generation of market-conscious 'developers' at NBC, ABC, CBS, Time Warner and Paramount spread the gospel of 'repurposing content' and 'migrating content' to this or that 'platform'. The old media corporations, defined historically by the entertainment experience of the screen, the narrative, the star and the genre, now live to calculate, amass, repackage and transport entertainment product across the borders of both new media technologies and forms. WB Online criticises studio-Internet projects in the 1990s which 'gave away content for free' (as value-added promotions) and instead lauds the success of majors who now 'recapture their brands, their business from the new media companies that at first moved faster and smarter'.[12]

Other trends that have fuelled the volatility and economic possibilities of old media form in the digital era are 'convergence' and 'conglomeration', practices apparent in numerous television/dotcom sites. Almost every old media industry forum now hails the imminent arrival of 'convergence', but many still disagree about what the phenomenon will mean in practical terms. 'Broadband' (a big enough digital 'pipeline') is currently the key word and the trigger delivery system that will allow for the transmission, multiplexing and interaction of multiple streams of digital content. While the computer industry presupposes broadband as the holy grail of real-time interactivity, networking, data management, communications and gaming, the film industry has added broadband to its equation and plans for the domestic delivery of 'electronic cinema'. The television industry, on the other hand, brings to the groundswell of anticipation for broadband and the Internet its founding obsession with advertising, sponsorship and programming practices. Looking beyond the costly high-resolution goals of HDTV, television saw in the extreme bandwidth of broadband a more profitable alternative, the possibility of 'multiplexing' – the ability to offer ancillary digital streams of data, image, sound and interactivity simultaneously. Multiplexed content now includes everything from background information, stock market quotations, commentary, ancillary image and sound streaming, and the numerous forms of merchandising that are added onto the ostensible focus of television's broadband transmission: the programme or content. Television has always been defined by and demeaned because of its 'clutter'. By placing its bets on multiplexed windowing, television continues this dubious distinction. However, few critics of the banner advertisements and graphic morass that make the Net cluttered acknowledge that television has also always known how to make money from merchandising clutter. Faced with the lure of high-resolution alternatives (which would enable video-on-demand delivered digitally in the form of pay-per-view or subscription), most television–Net initiatives are targeting far more complex and lucrative forms of multiplexed broadband streaming. Many current television/dotcom sites provide a full array of e-commerce options: from solicitations and online chats, to narrative and plot interactions, to back-story and character biographies, to merchandising and 'virtual product placement'.[13]

As total worldwide revenue for video games, a fourth discrete digital industrial culture, begins to approach those of the cinema film, many traditional entertainment companies now talk about their 'convergence' with gaming. Implementing such a convergence, however, has proved largely frustrating. Blockbuster game hits such as *Mortal Kombat* and *Final Fantasy* proved lacklustre when adapted for the big-screen feature film box-office. Yet the economies of video gaming have had a much longer period to mature and to standardise in ways that the Net-based dotcoms never could. In this way, the prosperity of the video game industry represents one route out of the debilitating micro-economics and the narrowly specialised digital user-bases of the Net. After almost three decades of development, and the Darwinian corporate shakedown of Atari and Sega, only two significant players remain: Nintendo and Sony. While Microsoft has entered the fray, Nintendo and Sony prospered by integrating software and hardware into singular mass-marketed, consumer, electronic goods: their respective consoles. Moving these products off shelves also means moving very similar or common digital experiences along with it, thereby at last creating the economies of scale possible in a mass market. With millions of units sold, the cost per unit of a game console is far less than a comparable PC equipped with games and far more likely to remain usable because of its locked-down software/hardware integration.

This hardening of software and hardware into a single commodity technology makes the marketing of video games far more predictable and rational than the marketing of amorphous dotcom start-ups such as the failed *Pop.com*, even with their fee-based, value-added sponsorship and/or licensing schemes. Actual audience use is far more predictable with franchised games than with Internet services, and companies such as Microsoft, Sony and TiVo, with various prototypes for digital set-top boxes, know that selling either software or navigational experiences on the Web is far less profitable than achieving market share advantage with patented user-friendly devices that integrate software and hardware. Matsushita's successful VHS standardisation in the video format wars of the 1980s provided a model for Nintendo in its mass-market video game-world survival of the fittest in the 1990s.

PROSPECTS AND CULTURAL IMPACT

Regardless of the confident, new media makeovers unfolding in many old media companies after the dotcom crash, uncertainties about digital media still lurk as threats to the established media companies and studios. I would like to conclude by summarising three areas in which digital technologies are forcing substantive changes in industrial practice. These include issues of: proprietary content and intellectual property; syndication and repurposing; and production culture labour relations within the digital context. All of these factors have an impact on the institutional authoring of new media and thus the cultural impact of those forms as well.

First, digital media technologies threaten the centrality of proprietary content. The much reported legal soap opera surrounding MP3 and Napster downloading was just the tip of a very large and only partially submerged iceberg involving unauthorised duplication and piracy. 'Meta-browsers' such as Octopus.com, for example, allow users the ability not just to 'copy' someone else's proprietary Web content, but also to strip such content of its original contractually based context (away from the advertisements of sponsors and licensors) and to automate this process on a weekly basis, in order to reconfigure it as one's own personal Web publication. DVD distribution similarly raises the stakes considerably by circulating infinitely reproducible, high-quality 'masters'. While the studios labour endlessly to improve encryption schemes that technically block copiers, hackers are always just a few steps behind, and many boast that the coding protocols on DVDs can always be broken by anyone with even a rudimentary understanding of programming. The international situation creates even more anxieties. In countries such as China, the technical possibilities of unauthorised duplication join with a broad range of cultural forces that sanction piracy. These sanctioning forces include the traditional Confucian notion of sharing knowledge as a moral posture and the Marxist Chinese notion that the people own all state properties. In such a climate, guarding new media content to send revenues elsewhere makes little sense. As Michael Keane has shown, Chinese television now institutionalises what the West sees as piracy by addressing it as 'reformatting', essentially discounting ownership by explaining the shared nature of all genres.[14] So the threat of digital culture is not one thing in all places. The CD-ripping assemblage of Napster and meta-browsing in the US is very different from the nationalised effort in China to find justifiable ways to extend media and develop creative industries nationwide.

Second, digital media has fundamentally altered the conditions under which the economies of film and television have traditionally been rationalised. Both box-office (in film) and ratings (in television) are based on the consensus view that the economic value of any media property is determined by a snapshot picture of its 'market share'. By this, I mean that Nielsen ratings and weekend box-office numbers create a static picture of how each competitor performed at a single point in time. This single-point analysis inherent in market-share models provides predictable rules that give the market stability. I would argue that digital media, by accelerating the shift to a multi-channel, rather than regulated or controlled, media marketplace has actually broken the market-share benchmark by establishing performance over time as a far more important index of economic value. In the digital age, the economic value of any media content is determined by its temporal performance in syndication and by its ability to be repurposed or resurrected endlessly for subsequent releases, distribution windows and ancillary markets, both those already known as well as those not yet anticipated. The current widespread success of syndicated 'repurposing' has in fact made 'multi-purposing' across media platforms a starting point for many new media projects. Albie Hecht, president of Film and TV Entertainment at Nickelodeon/Nick at Nite/TNN explains the multimedia logic behind *Jimmy Neutron: Boy Genius*:

> Rather than merely repurposing from one medium to another, Jimmy was created to exist in
> comic books, television, movies, video games, on the Internet and other places right from the
> start. Jimmy is virtual. He's everywhere. When kids are listening to music, playing games,
> watching TV, Jimmy will be there.[15]

Digital media projects such as Nick's *Jimmy Neutron* ensure that front-end syndication deals and content development based on a project's potential for reiteration across platforms, are as crucial today as initial air dates were in electronic media's analogue era (see plate 03). The kind of calculus needed for projecting and determining economic value in the new media era is, therefore, far less rational and predictable than old media corporations would like. This creates additional volatility and makes publicity, marketing and spin even more crucial in fortifying media properties for the ancillary lives they aspire to in the long haul.

Third and finally, digital media unsettles the social relations and communities at both the production and consumption ends of the media exchange. The WGA strike negotiations in spring 2001 were widely feared as a momentous first step that might start to dismantle the

tried and proven continuities that had somehow kept all of the craft unions and guilds profitably employed over time. Reactions critical of the writers came from all corners, including
IATSE and the other unions, and not just from Wall Street or management's executive
suites. While this hand-wringing was couched as a concern for the economic health of the
region, much less concern was focused on the actual cause of the strike threats. Digital
media technologies had out-paced the industry's ability to keep track of, to account for and
to reimburse on a uniform contractual basis revenues from the new ancillary markets. When
the writers gave in, and management acquiesced, many observers realised that the agreement was only a very provisional and partial holding action. Development of digital
technologies continues to threaten sweetheart deals, union privilege and network affiliation,
even as it unsettled the willed affinity and public confidence of an extensive labour–
corporate coalition that teetered when faced with it. This pushing-and-pulling, merging and
jockeying for position in the face of digital technology has had a dramatic effect on the communities working within the industry. The studios, network control rooms and guild halls in
Los Angeles and New York all began to evidence great anxiety and volatility during this
period. Members of the television and production communities arguably faced a far more
uncertain future than those above them in the boardrooms. For while Hollywood and television have jumped into digital technology with great public confidence, the communities
that make up such public bodies have had to navigate and negotiate change in ways that
have substantially transformed what television and film look like and sound like in the digital
age.

In the early 1990s, 'interactivity' was touted by academic theorists as the key to
liberating the top-down, push-media industries from their dominance over viewer/user/
subordinates. Such theorists, betraying little apparent awareness for almost a century of
electronic media history, ignored the fact that broadcasting and television have always
necessarily been interactive in fundamental ways. For while television never had pull-down
menus, it did have free telephone numbers, sweepstakes, viewers' editorial comments,
telethons, public affairs and public service departments, FCC licensing reports on stations'
responsiveness to local communities, marketing research, and constantly articulated product consumption numbers (the advertising industry's Holy Grail). All of these provided
important forms of audience data needed to keep the industrial engines of electronic media
churning away. In the commercial sphere today, at least outside academic research labs
and new media galleries, the very same concern with quantifying and leveraging audience
behaviour informs almost any new media development. Multi-platforming, repurposing,
syndication, meta-browsing, bots and multitasking all mean new media has to develop
more sophisticated ways to rationalise its economies. Fortunately for developers, the very
network connections, portals, fibre-optic cables and broadband lines employed by digital
users also enable new media producers to 'lock-on' to viewer/user behaviours and tastes
with great confidence. The flexibility of digital economies requires that responsiveness, not
hegemony, must be a corporate house rule for digital developers as well. No longer clearly
agents of hegemony, new media artists and developers at industry gatherings now obsess

on questions about what users want or need. Their corporate livelihoods depend upon mastering this posture of flexible responsiveness.

Notes

1. Quoted in Paul Bond, 'Ifilm Gets an Additional $10 Mil', *Hollywood Reporter*, 5 February 2001, p. 3.
2. 'The Wired Index', *Wired* 9.06, June 2001, p. 93.
3. Michael Schneider, 'Thesps Log-on to ABC Dot-com Pilot', *Daily Variety*, 3 April 2001, p. 1.
4. Jacqueline Lee Lewes, 'Local Heroes', *Hollywood Reporter*, 27 March–2 April 2001, p. S19.
5. Ad for 'FirstLook: Your Entertainment Connections', *Daily Variety*, 20 March 2001, p. 14.
6. Sheigh Crabtree, 'Digital Domain Lays-off 17', *Hollywood Reporter*, 3–9 April 2001, p. 2.
7. Billy Hulkower, 'Shooting Tape for the Reel World', *Hollywood Reporter*, 30 March–1 April 2001, p. S1.
8. Michael Grotticelli, 'CNN Moves to Small-Format ENG', *Broadcasting and Cable*, 14 May 2001, p. 47.
9. Ibid.
10. David Bordwell, Kristin Thompson and Janet Staiger, *The Classical Hollywood Cinema* (New York: Columbia University Press, 1985).
11. Ken Kerschbaumer, 'Internet Reality Check', *Broadcasting and Cable*, 30 April 2001, p. 61.
12. Michael A. Hiltzik, 'Net Effect: Old Media, New Tech', *Los Angeles Times*, 12 April 1999, p. 14.
13. Alex Frangos, 'Between Shows: For Fans of *Dawson's Creek*, the Angst Never Stops', *The Wall Street Journal*, 26 March 2001, p. R9.
14. Michael Keane, 'Cultural Technology Transfer: Redefining Content in the Chinese Television Industry', *Emergences: Journal for the Study of Media and Composite Cultures*, vol. 11 no. 1, 2001.
15. Chris Marlowe, '"Jimmy" is Nick's Boy Wonder: Character's Multimedia Formula Includes TF, Web, Games', *Hollywood Reporter*, 5 February 2001, p. 14.

2.2

The New Intertextual Commodity

P. David Marshall

When an industrially major film appears on the horizon of public consciousness via its promotional trailers and publicity that refer to the processes of production, the audience is imbricated in an elaborate intertextual matrix. This matrix, designed to encircle, entice and deepen the significance of the film for the audience, is not a newly constituted phenomenon. The industrial strategy of massaging the filmic text into something larger has been inherited from entertainment's Hucksterism, developed by P. T. Barnum to constitute and produce the new 'mass' audiences of the nineteenth century and passed on to film most visibly through the development of the star system.

What has altered is the intensification and elaboration of the intertextual matrix. Film, music, video and computer games, Websites, television documentaries, books and product licensing are elaborately cross-referenced in the contemporary entertainment industry through the usual suspects of magazines, newspapers, entertainment news programmes, industry-related consumer and trade magazines and electronic journals. The audience 'learns' about a product through its associations in other cultural forms. This chapter investigates the operation of this new intertextual commodity that has permeable boundaries among cultural forms. It argues that the intricate cross-linkages of cultural forms, which produce this new intertextual commodity, are the industrial response to the heightened value of both interactivity and play for audiences. Interactivity is simultaneously an industrial strategy of patterning and guiding the audience and its opposite, the risk of entropy where the cultural commodity becomes lost in less patterned interconnections produced not by the industry, but by the audience. Similarly, despite its inherent indeterminacy, play has been increasingly colonised by the culture industries well beyond childhood in recognition of its heightened importance in the formation of the audience's pleasures at the beginning of the new millennium. To comprehend this interconnected matrix, this chapter traces some of the origins of the new intertextual commodity, from the growth of promotion and the historical antecedents of the interactive in play's commodification to the wider integration of game aesthetics. From that vantage point, the chapter establishes four emergent patterns of cultural production that emphasise how new media forms are part of an industry's attempt to capture the interactive audience.

DEFINING THE NEW DIMENSIONS OF INTERTEXTUALITY

The most useful way of understanding this changed industry is through the term 'intertextual'. Intertextuality has been used by various writers to describe how any particular text implies or calls forth other texts.[1] A film, as it narrates its own particular story, pushes the audience to connect its content to films it resembles. Thus genres of films are relatively stable intersections of the audience's understandings and expectations, and an industry attempting to match those expectations. Moreover, genres of television programmes such as situation comedies or medical dramas are stable structures that allow for a patterning of production. Genre as a form of intertextuality implicates the commodity structure of a cultural form through its provision of a blueprint for future production. Although intertextuality is dependent on an audience's reading of a particular film or television programme, ultimately it is connected back to the industrial process. Intertextuality identifies the exchange process of cultural knowledge that flows back and forth between the audience and the individual text as the audience member injects other sources into the text. The industry's role is to provide the related material for that injection.

The clear industrial precursor of the new intertextual commodity, where the industry actively works on the interrelationship of cultural forms, was developed in the music industry. Goodwin's analysis of music video underlines popular music's 'multidiscursive' quality where music was a combination of distribution formats from disks and cassettes, to film and television soundtracks, concerts, to promotional paraphernalia from T-shirts, cards and bags to figurines. The most intriguing innovation in this mix of musical commodities was the emergence of the videoclip in the 1980s. The videoclip was a blending of content and promotion; its promotional dimension was able to spawn a transformation of the television and cable industry through the emergence of MTV, which literally captured the elusive marketing niche of a youth demographic audience.[2]

COMMODIFICATION WORK

The development of music video serves as a window into the way in which cultural commodities are now further linked in an intertextual tapestry. Closely connected to these intertextual links is the concentration of media ownership which has continued throughout the 1990s, reaching a pinnacle with the media giant Time Warner subsuming its operations into the Internet giant AOL since 2000. As these industrial processes have developed, there have been concerted efforts to connect the various cultural industries whether in ownership structures or singular relationships around a particularly prominent cultural commodity. Instead of an end product, there is a serial form of production where each product in the series is linked through a network of cross-promotion.

There are unique features of the cultural commodity that make its analysis somewhat different from readings of other types of commodities. The Marxist approach that identifies the gap between use value and exchange value in the capitalist economy has served as a useful point of departure for scholarship into the cultural commodity. Dallas Smythe's work on the idea that what is produced by the culture industries is the 'audience-commodity', which is sold to advertisers, has provided a starting point for several other approaches to contemporary cultural forms.[3] Thus the purchase of a cultural commodity is rarely pure: when we buy a newspaper, watch a television programme, go on a Web site or pick up a magazine, advertisers have projected themselves into the content. In a very real sense, there is a cluster of demographically linked meanings when we attempt to consume a cultural form.

On a parallel plane of analysis, two other writers have investigated whether a cultural commodity's value predates its consumption. Haug explains that the use-value of any cultural commodity must precede its actual purchase; in other words, in some way, the film, the recording, or, as Haug describes it, the 'aesthetic', must float as a semblance of its future use and use-value in order for it be consumed.[4] Wernick underlines the theatre of desire that surrounds cultural consumption: 'A promotional message is a complex of significations which at once represents (moves in place of), advocates (moves on behalf of), and anticipates (moves ahead of) the circulating entities to which it refers.'[5] Without being the actual cultural form, the promotional form simulates the cultural product's presence.

There are thus two key shifts in contemporary culture. First, on an empirical level, there is a great deal more promotional material produced about any given cultural product than previously.[6] There are just quantitatively more television programmes, more newspaper space and more magazine material devoted to promotional coverage. News and journalism are often subsumed into the promotional juggernaut of cultural events and production. Second, the promotional material is often commodified itself. Thus the plethora of 'Making of' films from *Titanic* (1997) to *The Planet of the Apes* (2001) become programmes that attract advertising revenue for television networks. The line between forms of promotion and the cultural product is blended and hybridised in contemporary production. The culture industries have attenuated the audience's attention to ponder their future affective investments and have increasingly provided varied paths for engaging with the cultural form. With the expansion of this promotional discourse, which provides both a thick packaging of our cultural forms and wider range of material for interaction, contemporary culture has naturalised the representation of anticipation and normalised the space of desire's perpetual deferral. Like narrative delay, the pleasure of promotion is at least partially in its extension of the possibilities and potential for satisfaction that the cultural form promises.

THE PAEDOCRATIC REGIME: KID CULTURE ORIGINS

Building from this promotional network, the emerging new intertextual commodity has relied on a longer history of marketing to children that has expanded and proliferated throughout most of the past century. Marketers progressively have tried to colonise the world of play. As Stephen Kline has explained 'most Victorian children had few or no toys'.[7] Many of the toys that we associate with that era or earlier centuries, for example, toy soldiers and dolls, were in fact bought and played with by adults. Children's 'toys' were often found, discarded objects that were given significance by the child through play and imagination. If a toy was actually made for a child, it was much more likely to be unique and handcrafted. By the early twentieth century, however, toy making had been industrialised with mass-produced objects. The mass production of toys, which could be produced much more cheaply than handcrafted versions, was closely aligned to the origins of sophisticated marketing and promotional strategies to give meaning to these new toys. For instance, the teddy bear, which emerged in 1906 from a licensing agreement between Ideal Toy Company and then US President Theodore (Teddy) Roosevelt, was emblematic of how these new products achieved massive national sales through intertextual flows between the publicity of politics and the world of children.[8]

Other marketing patterns emerged to deepen the meaning of any particular toy. The *Rudolph the Red-nosed Reindeer* storybook was developed and then given to Christmas shoppers at one of the major department stores in the 1930s and thereby created a seasonal icon. The image of Santa Claus became closely aligned with Coca-Cola® from the late nineteenth century onwards. Macy's Department Store sponsored the New York Thanksgiving Day parade and by 1927 had the cartoon character Felix the Cat showcased as a giant balloon.

In a broader sense, toys were being connected to other products and other cultural commodities to provide a wider range of interactions and forms of play. Breakfast cereal and other pre-packaged foods designed for children were sold with toys and surprises inside from the 1930s and 1940s. In the same era, comic book heroes became the source for film serialisation in the tradition of Tarzan and Flash Gordon. This clustering of products and activities was integrated into the way television developed for children. *The Mickey Mouse Club*, produced by Disney for ABC Television, became an afternoon staple for 1950s' American children. What was unique about the programme was its ability to connect films, cartoons, young hosts, advertised products and the accoutrements of club membership, specifically the mouse ears, into an alluring mix that produced a massive age-group loyalty.[9]

Other toy companies worked to provide similar packaged patterns for their toys that emulated the overall linked packaging of Disney's *Mickey Mouse Club*. In the guise of educative value, Lego's interlocking plastic block toy began providing guides and specialised pieces for the construction of particular models. Mattel's Barbie was not sold as a simple doll, but was provided with narrative scenarios as starting points for children's play: Fashion Barbie, Malibu Barbie, Teenaged Barbie, Beauty Queen Barbie and so on were all partial narratives that worked to provide more elaborate starting points for girls and clear directions for buying new versions of the doll.[10]

This patterning of play became the way in which toy companies could further commodify the experience of childhood. When, under the Reagan administration, the FCC deregulated children's television, the work toward cross-promotional linkages and providing narratives for toys was further completed.[11] The best-selling toys of the 1980s were generally linked to television programmes with the same characters as cartoon entities. Care Bears, Strawberry Shortcake, My Little Pony and He-Man were both toys and popular cartoons. The narrative had been expanded from television commercials into half-hour programmes.

In all, the development of kid's culture as a promotional form demonstrates an elaborate model of intertextuality that is designed to pattern the consumption of children. Child's play becomes an interesting combination of the commodified pattern and the open-endedness of what children do with the toys. John Hartley described television itself as a paedocratic regime because it is constantly telling the viewer how to watch and how to enjoy television.[12] What now needs to be identified is how the paedocratic regime extends beyond television and beyond children's culture. The culture industries are providing elaborate patterns of play across media forms.

THE NEW MEDIA: THE RESURGENCE OF THE PLAY AESTHETIC

In the last decade of the twentieth century, the key insight to permeate the various cultural industries, but particularly film and television, is that play is not limited to childhood or to sports. Where the novel, film and television drama seem to have discrete narratives and storylines, play within games has patterns and permutations that give the player a sense of engagement, agency and transformation. The success of video and computer games in the past two decades is that they have been able to translate that pleasure of play, where there are both ritual, patterns and rules, as well as possibilities, potentials and performance, into adult entertainment culture.[13] Computer-developed games are highly structured entities; however, within those structures, the best games encode 'tricks' or 'cheats' which allow a myriad of transformations possible for any player. Electronic games have developed exactly in that area: with greater complexity of possibility and with more sophisticated graphics and narratives, games have challenged the hegemony of narrative forms such as television and film as the dominant entertainment modes for adults in contemporary culture. Games are a combination of structure and open-endedness that resemble the best of the promotional patterning of engagement developed by the toy companies for children.

From the development of millions of game players – one American statistic claims that 60 per cent of Americans or 145 million people over the age of six play electronic games – a different kind of subjectivity is developing around entertainment culture.[14] Games are certainly highly structured and yet they engender a sense of agency. Whether playing in an online community of gamers, playing a friend through PlayStation or playing against the machine of the game itself, the player is moved by electronic games beyond filmic narrative identification into a hybrid state of 'game play' subjectivity.[15] The player is an agent or actor in the drama unfolding and usually possesses a chosen identity.

Game coding to produce the effect of game play for this 15 billion dollar industry is essentially about producing cybernetic feedback loops.[16] The player plays within the cybernetic system and the goals of that system as long as they are engaged in the game. The cybernetic quality of the game, where the parameters of activity are demarcated by the producers of the game, is the general goal of the contemporary cultural industries as they have learned to incorporate the play aesthetic into their industrial strategies. If the industries can keep the audience, viewer or player within the system of entertainment choices, they are effectively maintaining their market. Metaphorically, all of the cultural industries are engaged in a form of game coding of their products by providing the various relationships and links among the various forms for their audience.

THE DIALECTIC OF INTERACTIVITY: CONTROL AND CHAOS

Increasingly, it is difficult to define the parameters of any cultural commodity because of the effort by the industry to provide interlinkages in order to capture this new active, gameplayer agency of the cultural consumer. Although technological convergence of media has occupied the centre stage of popular and critical commentary, a more elaborate form of convergence is developing across media forms. What is being played is an elaborate dance between the techniques of containing and servicing the desires of the 'audience', and the audience itself venturing into unserviced and uncommercial areas of cultural activity. This dance of control and chaos is most clearly seen in the development of the cultural industries' and the audience's presence on the Internet's World Wide Web, as well as the interlinked products they have created.

To understand this dance, it is worthwhile beginning with the techniques of the new intertext as established by the industry and how it attempts to control the potential for entropy in its cultural production. Recent films provide some typical examples of cross-connections that have become industry standards; however, it is important to bear in mind that the films are often not the starting point for the proliferation of cultural production and structured forms of interactivity. Films now operate as one of the major methods of heralding the confluence of cultural forms or regenerating a flagging intertextual brand. To organise this analysis of something that is rarely a single cultural form, I have grouped these styles of the intertext into four recognisable patterns: the 'game–film–game', the multimedia event, 'kid cultural interconnections' and the interactive game of the cult film.

GAME–FILM–GAME

In the Summer of 2001, two films, *Lara Croft: Tomb Raider* and *Final Fantasy*, were derived from existing video and computer games. Both are rich intertextual examples, but I will focus specifically on *Lara Croft: Tomb Raider*.

The animated pneumatic character of *Tomb Raider*, Lara Croft, had already become an established cultural icon of the late 1990s and represented the movement of game culture into the mainstream. Her appearance on the cover of *The Face* in June 1997 helped establish her wider cultural credibility and celebrity status. Not only was Lara Croft subject to debate as a physiologically impossible female archetype (in the same way Mattel's Barbie and supermodels had been for more than a decade), but also her cartoon character became the object of speculation as to who could possibly play the lead role of Lara in a film version. The game thus was discussed in several different sections of the newspaper, entertainment programmes and innumerable newsgroups on the Internet. The game had ceased being just a game and mutated into a source for massive discursive proliferation over a three-year period prior to the release date of the film.

Tomb Raider originated in 1996 as a PlayStation adventure/role-playing game designed by UK-based Core Design and published by Eidos. It was quickly released in PC game format as well. Four sequels appeared before the movie was released. What extended its reach as an intertextual cultural commodity was the celebrity status of Lara. Requests for product endorsements circulated. For instance, Timberland, a footwear company, wanted to make an arrangement so that Lara wore their brand of boots. A diveware company, Sola, successfully negotiated a deal with the game company. Further cross-media connections have developed with Lara appearing in the comic book *Witchblade*, then with Cow Productions and their game company in a comic book series of her own since 1999. Official models were chosen to represent *Tomb Raider* specifically for the E3 game trade conventions and became sources for further discussion and fan Web sites.

Further associations with other products emerged with the film and the types of equipment that Lara Croft used on her quests. Ericsson, the Swedish telecommunications equipment company, was associated with the mobile telephony prevalent in the film and developed a parallel Web site to underline that the technology employed in the film was not science fiction, but could be purchased. From the bluetooth headset to the Communicator, Ericsson intones that Lara is 'powered by Ericsson' to save the world from evil.[17] Cross-marketing in a similarly open and normalised fashion were the rest of the 'team' behind *Tomb Raider*: the Land Rover was the vehicle of choice and featured prominently in the film; Taco Bell was the fast food franchise for associated toy licensing; Pepsi was the soft drink team member. What is clear about these cross-associations is that they create an elaborate and cross-linked promotional culture where the film's images provide both the newness and the attractiveness on any product's site. Land Rover and Ericsson have a cultural channel through which to explain their wares that has a connection to a wider cultural imaginary of both the film and the game. They have a legitimate and paid-for connection to Angelina Jolie's image as Lara Croft, who thus served as their summer spokesperson online. The products become part of the expanding rings of a cultural form that is continually reinventing itself in these new related contexts.

The extensions of *Tomb Raider* expand further outwards via the film and its official Web site into other realms of popular culture. The official Paramount Web site launches with the U2 song 'Elevation' which initiates a whole other series of intertextual connections to both the film, game and a summer concert tour. Thirty-second clips of the soundtrack, including 'Illuminati' by Fatboy Slim, Missy Elliott and Nine Inch Nails, are linked through an Elektra Records Web site. The soundtrack crosses back over to the demographic that is most closely connected to the original game. Because of the character of Lara and her reincarnation in film as Angelina Jolie, both presented as sexual objects (albeit active ones), the core market for the *Tomb Raider* ensemble of products is teenagers and 20-something males. Although this is not the exclusive market for *Tomb Raider*, much of the intertextual fibres and links move concentrically to interpellate such an audience or user.

The mantle of the brand of *Tomb Raider* is temporarily passed to the film and film Web site for a 90- to 120-day run from pre-release to theatrical launch (15 June 2001) to launch of the DVD. The film operates as the promotional engine for the array of products now associated with *Tomb Raider* and the Web site serves as the anticipatory mainframe for this intertextual matrix. Links back to the original Eidos game are evident as the intertextual super-commodity tries to provide all of the possible connections available for the interested audience. Webrings, a term meaning that certain sites agree to cross-link formally and thereby try to construct a patterning of Web surfing for the audience or user, are part of the *Tomb Raider* site to provide the sanctioned territory of fan sites. The Eidos game site's Webring is an elaborate 105 sites that dwarfs the film Web site's circumscribed ring of six. The game Webring includes all forums and newsgroups, Web site shrines to Lara and to the game itself, and many other sites that are closely or loosely related to each part of the *Tomb Raider* game series. The Web points out the location for further investment into the intertextual commodity. Through Webrings that are centrally connected to the product itself, the companies that have developed the intertextual commodity can monitor its application by its fans. It can gauge the level of investment of users, whether they leave evidence of their presence on the official Web sites via 'cookies' or whether they reconstruct their con-nection to the game–film–game via downloaded pictures or a complete Web site with related images and text. The intertextual commodity has to possess the elasticity to incor-porate the imaginary reconfigurations of its images, stories and products by users. Although corporations protect their trademarks and images, they have also developed sophisticated structures and architectures that allow certain images of their film or game to float freely across the Internet as promotional sirens of their cultural commodity.

THE MULTIMEDIA EVENT

Within the film industry, the greatest development of the intertextual commodity has emerged from the blockbuster. Others have written extensively about this pattern of ensur-ing the dominance of a particular film in the marketplace and there is no need to replicate that work here.[18] Nonetheless, Hollywood continues to produce films that manifest an 'event-effect'; in other words, through massive promotion, large media advertising buyouts, the publicity junkets for entertainment journalists and vast spending on the film itself, the release of the film becomes newsworthy. The blockbuster has at least a 25-year lineage in its contemporary form and has antecedents back to Cecile B. DeMille's Biblical epics of both the 1950s and the 1920s. From *Jaws* (1975) and *Star Wars* (1977) to the more recent *Waterworld* (1995) and *Titanic*, the industry has used the blockbuster to concentrate its resources, promotion and advertising, and thereby actually make fewer films. Recent examples of these efforts include *Star Wars* (the digitally developed re-release in 1999), *Star Wars Episode 1: The Phantom Menace* (1999), *Pearl Harbor* (2001) and *Harry Potter and the Philosopher's Stone* (2001). Because of the long history of the blockbuster, this can be seen as one of the traditional methods of creating an intertextual commodity. Several elements have changed in this era of interactivity, including the development of Web sites, games, toys and collectibles, as well as the proliferation of information about the 'making of' the cultural commodity.

One change has been the development of Web sites well in advance of the release of the film. The use of promotional material prior to the release of the film has been increased, particularly with the re-release of *The Phantom Menace*. Although countdown clocks were in place up to three years before the film appeared, the most startling development was how the release of the promotional trailer led to an Internet downloading frenzy. Moreover, as Axel Bruns has uncovered, the Web resources for *Star Wars* were (and are) astronomical just in the sheer number of fan sites devoted to some aspect of George Lucas's epic film series.[19] In a similar fashion, *Pearl Harbor* depended on its Web site to prepare its viewers for the way trailers position the pleasure of the film prior to its release.

Additionally, there has been the co-development of games associated with the cultural commodity franchise. Although notoriously bad, *Star Wars* developed a game that was timed for the release of the film. The James Bond film *GoldenEye* (1995) not only established Pierce Brosnan in the title character role, but equally has to be seen as a breakthrough video, computer and arcade game of enormous popularity as well. Moreover, in a strange twist, Spielberg's *AI* (2001) was pre-launched with a Web site game three months before the film was released. It generated a group of users who were drawn to the elaborate and intricate Web murder mystery game. For online game players, the game was much more compelling than the film and relatively unconnected in content. Indeed, the game's interactive investment outlasted the film's limited box-office success.[20]

A third change has been the proliferation of toys and collectors' items advertised directly on the Web site. This development acknowledges that alighting on a film Web site constitutes a higher level of effective investment in the cultural commodity. Connections to other products associated with the film are a natural extension of recognising that the techniques of interactivity are concerned with the development of information about the audience or consumer, which will be fed back into a cybernetic system. There is no question that licensing agreements for models, toys and other transformations and mutations of the cultural commodity have been commonplace for blockbuster films. The subtle difference is that the Web provides the glue to hold the wider rings of cultural commodities together.

Finally, there has been a proliferation of information about the making of the film or cultural commodity. A multimedia event is incomplete without the programme on the making of the epic film sponsored by network television. The text is deepened in some way through this process. For example, the *Titanic* documentary had two objectives. It was intended to build an aura of authenticity about the film's re-creations and it was designed to underline special effects, from hydraulics and lighting to CGI reconstructions, to emphasise their integral value to the film. There has been a dramatic promotional push to expand the repertoire of information about films. Film's relationship to information is part of the array of Web sites now devoted to background about cast and crew involved in the film. From the *Internet Movie Database* to *Hollywood.com* and *Entertainment Weekly*, the semi-official information sources provide the detailed texture about how the fiction of film is constructed. Added on to this development is the emergence of the DVD, where the movie is transformed into an information package of alternative endings, background cast and director narrations and explanatory visual notes on how the illusion was fabricated for the camera.

The multimedia event can originate from venues other than film. Reality television, from *Survivor* to *Big Brother*, has developed into parallel events with co-ordinated Web sites complementing the more controlled screen narrative. Film, however, still occupies a privileged position in developing a multimedia form of saturation. With the possibilities of enormous financial returns, the multimedia event with its labyrinth of related cultural commodities continues to stitch the Hollywood industry together.

KID CULTURAL INTERCONNECTIONS

Because play is central to how interactivity is now conceptualised by the cultural industries, there is a frenzy of interconnected cultural commodities that are closely aligned with children's culture. In the colonisation of play, the development of new children's toys are elaborated from television programme to video games to material toys and books. The trendsetter in developing the new intertextual commodity is Pokémon. Emerging simultaneously in 1996 in Japan as a television programme and a Nintendo game made for the Gameboy hand-held console, Pokémon was designed for heightened levels of interactivity for children.[21] Children attempt to capture fabricated creatures in all versions of the game/programme/toy/game cards. Whether it is the ten-year-old Ash in the television and three-film series or whether it is a five-year-old playing with their Pokémon and ball, the high-concept cultural form provides hundreds of characters and clear objectives of collecting or 'catch[ing]-'em all'.

On a similar plane, the television channel Nickelodeon constructs an environment of interactivity that draws children into a loyalty to the service, rather like a club membership. The shows are pieced together with a unity that is simply not achievable by the old networks given their mass audience, but can be achieved through targeting different age groups at different times. In a co-ordinated manner unparalleled in the culture industries, Nickelodeon's Web site, which combines games and educatively designed information with the animated television characters and is geared to different age groups, manages to build a coherence for its cultural products and a strong connection to its target audiences.[22] Characters remain consistent from their animated origins to the simple game structures on the Web site. Certain characters such as those in *Rugrats* mutate further into other cultural forms such as animated films. *Sponge Bob Squarepants* is following a similar trajectory from cartoon to game Web site to licensed toys.

From film itself, there is emerging a new kid cultural aesthetic in the deployment of new visual production technologies such as CGI. The experimentation of realism has been developed in the narrative parameters of films such as *Toy Story* (1995) and *Toy Story 2* (1999), *A Bug's Life* (1998), *Antz* (1998), *Shrek* (2001) and *Final Fantasy: The Spirits within* (2001). Matching this development are the video and computer game promotional trailers for games such *Tekken* and *Doom*, where the generation of a new hyperrealism is emerging. Producing children's cultural commodities has developed into the natural source for the new intertextual commodity.

PLAYING THE GAME OF INTERACTIVITY: THE CULT MOVIE

With the focus of industrial energy towards the convergence of the interactive and the promotional, different cultural commodities were destined to emerge from the cauldron. *The Blair Witch Project* (1999) appears to represent a watershed for the new pattern of both constructing an engaged audience and channelling that audience into a particular commodity. As Telotte has detailed, the film's promotional development was an integral part of the experience of the film and the phenomenon of the film's success. Telotte explains that the aesthetic of the film and film's Web site was modelled around narrative pleasures associated with electronic game forms. He relies on Janet Murray's terminology for this form of narrative pleasure: 'immersion, agency, and transformation'.[23] While the Web site produces the sense of interactive agency, the film co-ordinates that sensation by providing the feeling of immersion and transformation. The ultimate effect is that the audience is drawn into the Blair Witch experience because of the additional level of involvement. As Telotte also emphasises, the development of the film's success depended on a 20 million dollar marketing strategy that worked to transform the 1.1 million dollar film without losing the interactive feel of investment that the film's narrative and Web site fostered. Ultimately, the film connected strongly to a young adult demographic and produced a cult film relationship with its audience. New media forms such as the Internet have been instrumental in nurturing a fundamentally different level of engagement with cultural forms. *The Blair Witch Project* was able to capitalise on these new synergistic connections and forms of play and pleasure.

BMWfilms.com represents another parallel pattern of building an audience, but hiding none of the promotional environment.[24] BMW commissioned five famous directors (John Frankenheimer, Ang Lee, Wong KarWei, Guy Ritchie and Alejandro Innaritu) to make short films with the only condition that a BMW car was somehow integrated into the plot. The films are rich in texture and colour, and are equal in look and style to any feature film. The distinctiveness of the BMW campaign is that they have positioned their site on the cutting edge of Web site video technology and have provided an exclusive push to the convergence of media forms. The computer becomes the channel for the short digital film to be exhibited. Through that process, they have linked BMW to quality via the film-maker's cultural capital and to technical excellence through the film reader technology that is downloaded. In this new style of promotion, BMW is part of the content, not appended to the content via a commercial. The promotional aesthetic initiated through television and perfected through music videos reaches its naturalised apotheosis in *BMW.films.com*. Like the audience for *The Blair Witch Project*, the audience of *BMWfilms.com* has to invest in the process of experiencing the films. The downloading of the exclusive player and the download time for each film demand a viewer who is intrigued enough by the film-making process that they will wait more than an hour to see one of the five films for the first time. Although not exactly cult films, the films do cultivate a very specific audience at the convergence of film and Internet culture that is perceived to be wealthy enough to be interested in their various car models.

CONCLUSION: THE CENTRALITY OF PLAY
WITHIN A CULTURE OF PROMOTION

The nature of the new intertextual commodity is that it expands outwards through a series of linked cultural forms. The analysis of patterns could continue here to include how television programmes spawn fan Web sites in the tradition of *Buffy the Vampire Slayer* or *The X-Files* and are often reconstructed as films, games, books, fanzines or e-zines. Moreover, the relationship of popular music to video and computer games, where certain electronic representations of extreme sports or games have co-ordinated their content with a particular musical style, is a burgeoning growth area of the new intertextual commodity. What unifies this analysis that defies containment is that this industrially driven intertextuality is a response to a shifting formation of pleasure in the audience. The audience is not defined by narrative relationships of pleasure and mastery of the text, but a form of interactivity with cultural forms. Narrative is part of this new mix, but not as central as it has been in the golden eras of television and film. In ascendancy is a new subjectivity that is derived from the transformative agency of games and the playful development of the Web 'user'. To comprehend this change, play and kid's culture have moved to centre stage for the various industries, not so much to produce for children, but to glean insights that can be used to market to this mutated adult audience. In effect, the various entertainment industries are setting the stage for adult play by providing patterns across media forms and by converging those patterns through technology. The culture industries are providing a circumscribed agency for the new audience by providing complex patterns of engagement and exploratory architectures. Wedded to this development of the complex and new intertextual commodity is the expansion of the pleasure of anticipation through more elaborate strategies of product promotion. Various forms of promotion are aligned with providing background information on cultural forms that are designed to deepen the investment of the audience in the cultural commodity.

The investment in play is a new dialectic for the industry. Play as defined by an industry is patterned for the proliferation of cultural commodities through their interlinkages. Play as defined by the audience or actor is precisely the moment when patterns are altered and shifted. The new intertextual commodity identifies the attempt by an industry to provide the rules of the game, while recognising that the pleasure of the game is that rules are made and remade, transformed and shifted by the players.

Notes

1. John Fiske, *Television Culture* (London: Methuen, 1987), pp. 109–27.
2. Andrew Goodwin, *Dancing in the Distraction Factory: Music Television and Popular Culture* (Minneapolis: University of Minnesota Press, 1992), p. 25.
3. See Dallas Smythe, 'Communications: Blindspot of Western Marxism', *Canadian Journal of Political and Social Theory*, vol. 1 no. 3, Autumn 1977, pp. 1–28; Sut Jhally, *Codes of Advertising* (New York: St Martin's Press, 1987).
4. Wolfgang Haug, *Critique of Commodity Aesthetics* (Cambridge: Polity Press, 1987).

5. Andrew Wernick, *Promotional Culture: Advertising, Ideology and Symbolic Expression* (London: Sage, 1991), p. 182.

6. Graeme Turner, Frances Bonner and P. David Marshall, *Fame Games: The Production of Celebrity in Australia* (Cambridge: Cambridge University Press, 2000), pp. 29–43.

7. Stephen Kline, *Out of the Garden: Toys, TV and Children's Culture in the Age of Marketing* (New York: Verso, 1993), p. 144.

8. Ibid., pp. 148–50.

9. Ibid., pp. 165–6.

10. Ibid., p. 170.

11. See Tom Englehardt, 'The Shortcake Strategy', in Todd Gitlin (ed.), *Watching Television* (New York: Pantheon, 1986).

12. John Hartley, *The Uses of Television* (London: Routledge, 1999), pp. 218–19.

13. See Rebecca Farley, 'How Do You Play?' *M/C – A Journal of Media and Culture*, vol. 1 no. 5, 1998, <www.media-culture.org.au/9812/how.html>; Rebecca Farley, 'Game', *M/C – Journal of Media and Culture*, vol. 3 no. 5, 2000, <www.media-culture.org.au/0010/game.html>.

14. Interactive Digital Software Association, 'Interactive Digital Software Association Reports Popularity of Computer and Video Games with Adults', Press Release, 12 September 2000, <www.idsa.com/releases/9 13 2000.html>.

15. See John Banks, 'Controlling Gameplay', *M/C – Journal of Media and Culture* (Issue on 'Play'), vol. 1 no. 5, 1998, <www.media-culture.org.au/9812/game.html>.

16. See P. David Marshall, 'The Video and Computer Game Industry', in Stuart Cunningham and Graeme Turner (eds), *Media and Communications in Australia* (Sydney: Allen and Unwin, 2001); Kevin Durkin and Kate Aisbett, *Computer Games and Australians Today* (Sydney: Office of Film and Literature Classification, 1999), p. 30.

17. See Ericsson's *Tomb Raider* Campaign, <www.ericsson.com/tombraider/US/Tombraider_frameset.htm>.

18. See Thomas Schatz, 'The New Hollywood', in Jim Collins, Hilary Radner and Ava Preacher Collins (eds), *Film Theory Goes to the Movies: Cultural Analysis of Contemporary Culture* (New York: Routledge, 1993); Justin Wyatt, *High Concept: Movies and Marketing in Hollywood* (Austin: University of Texas Press, 1994); Kevin Sandler and Gaylyn Studlar (eds), *Titanic: Anatomy of a Blockbuster* (New Brunswick, NJ: Rutgers University Press, 1999).

19. Axel Bruns, 'Browse the Force: Star Wars on the Web', *M/C Reviews*, July 1999, <www.media-culture.org.au/reviews/features/starwars/starwars.html>.

20. David F. Gallagher, 'Online Tie-In Outshines Film It Was Pushing, Some Fans Say', *New York Times*, 9 July 2001, p. C1.

21. Character Products Inc., 'Pokémon History', <www.characterproducts.com/info/character histories/pokemon doorway.htm>.

22. Nickelodeon.com, <www.nick.com>.

23. J. P. Telotte, '*The Blair Witch Project*: Film and the Internet', *Film Quarterly*, vol. 54 no. 3, p. 30.

24. *BMWfilms.com*, <bmwfilms.com>.

2.3

Innovation, Piracy and the Ethos of New Media

Douglas Thomas

With the development of broadband Internet connections and increasingly sophisticated means of compression, new media is radically reshaping our communication environment. The emerging environment, however, is the product of two distinct sets of technology. On the one hand, 'old' media, from the age of print through broadcast and film, have a long-standing corporate tradition and are clearly regulated both in terms of issues of content and distribution. Issues of ownership, marketing and distribution are well understood and have decades of legal precedent demarcating boundaries. On the other hand, 'new' media, which focuses primarily on transformation from analogue to digital, are too recent to have a well-established tradition of regulation and are too different from their predecessors to be easily regulated by older laws.[1]

Regulation, old media proponents argue, is necessary to protect copyright, ownership and intellectual property rights. New media proponents see regulation as a barrier to innovation, dismissing more traditional notions of intellectual property as an outdated way of thinking about information. The tension between old media claims of piracy and new media claims of innovation reveal two different perspectives on the same phenomenon, primarily sparked by the Internet and World Wide Web's ability to distribute information instantaneously on a global, public scale.[2] What new media champions see as innovation in communication, old media proponents are likely to see as a threat to the stable system of information management and distribution which has long regulated music, film and broadcast economies. The problems multiply as more forms of old media are transformed into digital content and made available on the Net.

This chapter is an attempt to understand both piracy and innovation by addressing the historical trajectory that new media have taken, particularly the development of computer software, in order to define an *ethos* of new media. In short, the history of new media production, from the earliest forms of software for the personal computer to video games, sound and full-motion video files, can be understood more fully by examining the context of development and innovation in which these forms of communication emerged. That history helps explain not only how new media function, but also how mainstream culture has come to think about new media and how we have come to resolve the long-standing tensions between piracy and innovation.

WHO OWNS INFORMATION?

Of all the questions that new media have raised, perhaps the most hotly debated is the question of intellectual property, 'Who owns information?' Nowhere has that debate been more fiercely fought than around notions of 'piracy' on the Internet. The question of Web piracy is often reduced to a matter of financial loss. Microsoft, in fact, goes so far as to argue that the impact of piracy, in addition to causing 'higher prices', 'reduced levels of support' and 'delays in the funding and development of new products', harms 'all software publishers' as well as 'the local and national economies', resulting in 'lost tax revenue and decreased employment'.[3]

Those who write, market or sell software, music or film, for example, see piracy as cutting into their bottom line. At the most basic level the argument is irrefutable. Those who pirate software or entertainment media are not paying for it. As a result, it is tempting to think of piracy as theft and that provides an adequate explanation both for the casual 'pirate' who would prefer to not pay if he or she does not have to and large-scale piracy operations where thousands of videocassettes of the latest film or CD-ROMs for the latest software titles are made and sold on Manhattan street corners.

There are important elements of the new media landscape that complicate such a simple formulation. New media have shifted the idea of intellectual property onto new ground. Instead of considering information from the vantage point of content creation (the essence of old media), new media invite us to think in terms of two different concepts: reproducibility and distribution. In terms of old media, our laws of copyright are straightforward in assigning ownership of property, even intellectual property, to those who create or produce information. In terms of new media, however, the landscape appears to be shifting. Because of the digital nature of new media and the availability of extensive networks, those who purchase or otherwise obtain new media, almost from the moment of purchase, are poised to become distributors as well as consumers.[4] That transformation has altered not only the way in which we purchase media content, but also the way in which we think of it as reproducible.

Whereas old media were reproducible in terms of content, the act of reproducing it often resulted in loss of quality (for example, taping an album or duplicating a videotape). By way of contrast, because information in new media is reduced to 'code', it is capable of nearly instantaneous, unlimited duplication with no loss in quality or content. Old and new media, then, follow two different logics of reproduction and, as a result, two different ethics for distribution.

LOGICS OF REPRODUCTION: FROM ART TO CODE[5]

Understanding what is at stake in a discussion of the impact of technology on intellectual property, ownership and piracy necessitates rethinking our basic notions of what it means to reproduce digital media. The traditional notions of reproduction, based on the idea of a copy of an original, begin to break down in the face of digital transformation. This transition is marked by the logics of two different systems of reproduction. The first, I refer to as an 'artistic' logic of reproduction. The second, marked by the introduction of digital technology, I refer to as a logic of 'code'.

The idea of artistic reproduction is drawn from the notion of representation, literally the re-presentation of an image, object or idea, and is animated by the concept of difference. It is a logic sustained through the idea of the copy. The notion of a copy in Western thought, since the time of Plato, has been based on a differential relationship between an original and a reproduction of that original.[6] That sense of duplication is in fact defined by the degree of difference interjected into the reproduction and the degree to which the copy fails to corre- spond to the likeness of the original (or, alternatively, the degree of resemblance to the original and minimisation of difference). Those notions of similarity and difference become the basis for rendering judgment about all forms of reproduction. These degrees of similar- ity, and particularly difference, are responsible as well for what Gilles Deleuze has called the 'process of individuation', the means by which reproduction already presupposes a form of difference which makes repetition (the production of an identical copy) impossible.[7]

It is in this sense that Walter Benjamin discusses the reproduction of the work of art in what he has deemed the 'age of mechanical reproduction'.[8] The notion of difference, for Benjamin, stems from the possibility of spatial and temporal dislocation. 'Even the most perfect reproduction of a work of art,' Benjamin argues, 'is lacking in one element: its pres- ence in time and space, its unique existence at the place where it happens to be.'[9] It is that grounding, both in a physical place and a fabric of tradition, which gives art its value. Accordingly, the value of art for Benjamin rests with what is unreproducible (what he defines as an 'aura'), qualities which are unique and inseparable from the object in its status as an original. Mechanical reproduction, Benjamin contends, destroys that aura: 'By making many reproductions, it substitutes a plurality of copies for a unique existence.'[10]

A second logic, that of code, emerges as a function of digitisation. The digital is literally a coding of information into 1s and 0s with the goal of making perfect reproduction poss- ible without difference or loss. As a moment of perfect reproduction, it removes the relevance of difference in the determination of judgment. In short, it is no longer possible to judge the distinction between the copy and the original and, as a moment of perfect repro- duction, the copy and the original become indistinguishable. Unlike artistic representation, the logic of code does not exalt the original over the copy. Instead, the original is seen as already multiple, designed for reproduction and distribution. Once complete, there is no material way to distinguish the copy from the original.

This second logic of reproduction, then, confounds what we know about systems of reproduction. Once copies become indistinguishable from originals, reproduction loses a sense of authenticity. In order to maintain a standard for judgment, something else must substitute for the ability to distinguish between copies and originals, should that distinction be seen as an important one to maintain.

Digital reproduction is not animated by a distinction between a copy and its original, but, instead, by a sense of authority. The notion of the copy has been transformed from an object to an activity. In fact, the very definition of the copy in the digital age makes no mention of the relationship of the copy to an original. According to Microsoft's 'End User Licence Agreement' (EULA):

> You make a 'copy' of a software program whenever you: (1) load the software into your computer's temporary memory by running the program from a floppy disk, hard disk, CD-ROM, or other storage media; (2) copy the software onto other media such as a floppy disk or your computer's hard disk; or (3) run the program on your computer from a network server on which the software is resident or stored.[11]

In the digital age, the copy is defined by the act of loading, copying or running a program. Nowhere does it specify the relationship of a copy to an original. Instead, the distinction, and therefore the basis for judgment, is grounded in *authority*, literally the conditions under which reproduction is allowed. The definition of the copy is still differential, but now the relationship is expressed as a ratio of who may and who may not engage in the act of copying. The copy, for Microsoft, is therefore defined as matter of the *right* to reproduce software, rather than in terms of the reproduction itself. Accordingly, Microsoft's definition of piracy is grounded in activity, rather than product.

Software piracy is the unauthorised copying, reproduction, use or manufacture of software products. On average, for every authorised copy of 'computer software in use, at least one unauthorized or "pirated" copy is made. In some countries, up to 99 unauthorized copies are made for every authorized copy in use'.[12] The difference between piracy and software production and distribution does not rest with the activity of copying. The actions of the pirate and Microsoft itself are identical. Both transfer bits to storage media in precisely the same way and each produces a product identical to the other. The distinction is no longer a matter of quality of reproduction.

In essence, the world of the image and text, the world of representation, has been transformed in the digital age into a world of code, of 1s and 0s, easily repeated and distributed through ever-increasing communication networks. Because the relationship between the copy and original no longer serves as the basis for judgment, content no longer serves as a valuable basis for judgment or evaluation. There simply is no distinction between the copy and the original and no way to distinguish between them in a system of digital repetition.

Judgment is, therefore, displaced from the object reproduced to the activity of reproduction. That activity is defined as the movement of information (bits) from one place to another, whether it is from a disk to the computer's memory or from one computer to another. In short, reproduction, as a function of movement, has become synonymous with distribution. As a result, piracy and ownership in the digital age, from software to emerging forms of new media, are more about the right to distribute than the right to reproduce information. In what follows, I trace out a series of cultural moments which have helped to shape and define the ways in which digital information has come to be regarded differently from its more traditional analogue counterparts and how what is seen as innovation from one perspective is seen as piracy from another.

A BRIEF HISTORY OF DIGITAL DISTRIBUTION

I want to emphasise two distinct moments in the history of digital distribution that have shaped an *ethos* of the digital community: the development of peer-to-peer file sharing and the growth of underground pirate communities (warez boards) which emerged in the late 1980s. Each moment delineates not only a set of circumstances under which a new form of digital distribution became possible, but also an *ethic* that accompanied that form of distribution. That ethic emerges from the idea that technology subcultures, while often operating outside the law or in direct confrontation with it, are generally heavily self-policed. Because the law tends to do a poor job of regulating new media effectively (or wisely), those who work in the environment tend to engage heavily in self-regulation. Accordingly, the history of new media is also the history of an ethic, which has developed in response to new forms of communication media. Understanding that history is crucial to understanding how it is that old media face new problems in the new media landscape. Each of these moments documents a critical point at which the question of distribution has conflicted with a set of broader corporate interests and in doing so has called into question the basic logics of capital, which underwrite notions of control and, ultimately, ownership of information. As more classically corporate forms of media (music and film in particular) enter the digital landscape, which is to say as they are transformed from 'art' to 'code', they enter a new domain where issues of content distribution have a radically different history.

Perhaps the most significant 'ethos' to develop in relation to systems of digital distribution grew out of peer-to-peer file sharing systems which emerged in the late 1990s. Software such as Napster (and its increasingly decentralised cousins Kazaa, Morpheus, Bearshare and Gnutella) extended the idea of information exchange to a new level. With programs such as Napster, commercial music (and now film and video) were able to be freely exchanged online. Virtually any song, album or performance desired could be found in digital form and downloaded to a user's machine free of charge (see plate 4). The significance of Napster rests less with the technological advances of peer-to-peer file sharing than it does with the ethos that it spawned among computer users.

As the world of free music opened up, users began to co-opt the earlier hacker ethic, which had given rise to most of the technology that was now being used to allow free file exchanges. This ethos grew out of one of the earliest mantras of the computer community, the idea that 'All information should be free'.[13] However, when this generation of computer programmers and enthusiasts spoke of freedom in the 1960s and 1970s, they were not thinking of it strictly in a financial sense. They were speaking more about the *free flow of information*. Anything which made access to information more difficult or which blocked the transmission of information was considered undesirable. What was at stake for these programmers was not software that was 'free' financially (though most of it was free from cost), but the *freedom* to explore, alter and improve on the software.

The Napster *ethos* translated that ethic in the most basic and, perhaps, most convenient terms. However, it is important to note that what music company executives and some artists saw as stealing, many users considered to be free. As a result, the Napster ethos has three interrelated elements: corporate resistance, freedom to redistribute and entitlement to digital content.

First, on what is perceived as an increasingly corporate Internet, users see trading of MP3s and digital music as an act of resistance against precisely those corporate agents who seek to control and regulate the Internet. In that sense, at the most basic level, file trading is seen as an act that embodies the spirit of the Internet, keeping information free and open in the face of corporate control. Second, a large percentage of users who trade on Napster-like sites feel that they have the right to redistribute music they have purchased, provided they do not profit financially from the act. The analogy is often made to taping albums for friends, trading tapes or recording songs from the radio. The only difference, they argue, is the technology being used. Third, and perhaps most important, many users feel an entitlement to digital content based both on a presumption that anything appearing in digital form in public is (and should be) free, as well as the sense that the intermediate technology has already been purchased. In short, after paying $2000 for a computer and between $20.00 and $40.00 per month for Internet access, many users see the content as already paid for in their monthly network access fees. Moreover, after paying an additional $13.99 for a CD, they feel they have the right to duplicate and share it as they see fit.

These three elements, corporate resistance, freedom to redistribute and entitlement to digital content, have created a sense of how digital information should flow and have marked the site of redistribution as the place in which users can battle corporate control of the Internet. As the means of distribution becomes increasingly decentralised, the corporate focus will also need to shift towards a system of distribution that makes digital reproduction increasingly difficult as well.

The first shots in that battle have already been fired with the passage of the Digital Millennium Copyright Act (1998), which states that 'No person shall circumvent a technological measure that effectively controls access to a work protected under this title.' In effect, the DMCA makes it illegal to provide tools, information or technological devices which allow any form of copy protection to be broken or any form of unauthorised reproduction. One of the first tests of the DMCA has come as a result of a link posted to the *2600* Web site (the Web site for the hacker magazine of the same name). In 1998, *2600* posted a link to *DeCCS*, a software algorithm that was capable of decoding DVD recordings, allowing them to be reproduced and distributed.

The battle is one that pits the traditional hacker ethic of exploration and free sharing of knowledge and ideas against corporate interests to protect their products. The response from industry (and government) illustrates their misunderstanding of the problem of distribution. They believe that if they can make their music or film secure by prohibiting the dissemination of information which would make it insecure, then they will not have to address concerns about redistribution, duplication and piracy. What the industry is failing to account for is the fundamental transformation that has occurred in the medium of dissemination. That is to say that, while hackers have adopted the logic of code, industry is still fighting the battle from the perspective of art.

The problem that industry faces stems from its reliance on traditional models of distribution, where one needed to purchase an album, CD, VHS cassette or DVD in order to consume their product. Today's model of digital distribution challenges the primacy of the physical medium and in doing so sets a new dynamic in motion. The difference between these two models of distribution makes note of the distinction that Nicholas Negroponte uses to introduce his work *Being Digital*, the distinction between 'bits' and 'atoms'.[14] Bits parallel the Napster, peer-to-peer, Open Source model, the digital encoding of information into 1s and 0s which flow effortlessly on the information superhighway (and for the most part Open Source software is available online, rather than in a physical medium). Atoms, the material stuff of the world, follow a different set of rules. Unlike bits, which are nothing more than information, atoms have physical presence and it is that idea of physical presence that facilitates notions of ownership as the concrete possession of an item or, by extension, an idea. Entertainment content and software, which had traditionally been sold as atoms (media such as floppy disks, CD-ROMs or DVDs), is now becoming more widely available as bits (through direct download on the Internet), particularly as bandwidth increases.

This moment, then, is defined by conflicting modes of distribution, one that facilitates freedom and openness (and embodies the Napster *ethos*), the other which attempts to maintain rights based on exclusive possession and ownership (the corporate model). As the computer began to take on a heightened role as a communication medium in the 1990s those notions of distribution would, once again, clash. As a result, out of the computer underground would emerge a new group of hackers with an entirely new ethic.

In the mid-1990s, after the formation of the Internet, but prior to its widespread public use, small groups of self-described pirates began utilising a network of small, private BBSs (bulletin board systems) to trade and distribute software. These software traders, who were usually teenage boys, prided themselves on cracking the copy protection on software the day it was released, or even sooner if they were able to get access to pre-release copies, and would distribute that software via an underground community on self-described warez boards. These warez traders were, and continue to be, relatively few in number and tended to provide access to software to other teenagers, allowing access to games or to applications that they would not be likely to afford or purchase independently.

The focus of these groups, with names such as RiSC (RiSE iN SUPERiOR COURiERiNG) and PWA (Pirates with Attitudes), was not on their skill as programmers or even copy protection crackers, but in their ability to distribute the software within hours of its release. Advertised as 'zero day' or even '0–12 Hour Warez', the programs would be transmitted via modem to BBSs all over the country, which allowed other users who had gained membership the ability to access programs. BBSs were chosen by the groups and given varying degrees of affiliation, ranging from 'World and US Headquarters' to 'Member Sites'. In most cases, the BBS systems employed a quota system, measuring the user's contributions as well as their downloads. Those not contributing their fair share were branded as 'leeches' and were either banned from the board or would have their account name published on the board in an effort to shame them publicly.

The BBS as a distribution medium prefigured much of what would follow with the Internet, initially with FTP sites and later with trading on Internet relay chat (IRC) and, eventually, the World Wide Web. In 1992, Bruce Sterling described the BBS as 'a new medium . . . even a *large number* of new media' with unique characteristics:

> Boards are cheap, yet they can have a national, even global reach. Boards can be connected from anywhere in the global telephone network, at *no cost* to the person running the board. . . . Boards do not involve an editorial elite addressing a mass audience. . . . And because boards are cheap and ubiquitous, regulations and licensing requirements likely would be practically unenforceable.[15]

Within this context, it is easy to see how unauthorised software could be distributed quickly, at little or no cost, with a great incentive to reach a national or even international audience as a matter of reputation. Moving from BBSs to the World Wide Web was only a shift in the degree rather than the type of distribution.

The emphasis with pirate BBSs or pirate groups was on the speed with which they were able to make software available, not on the cost-free nature of the software itself. In fact, many of the pirate groups would specifically disavow any financial motivation. Both RiSC and PWA would add information files marked with an .nfo extension to the software they distributed, often providing information about the software and its installation, but more usually as a form of advertising for the group. The .nfo files would tell the end user who was responsible for the cracking and the distribution of the software.

Perhaps the most interesting and notable element of the warez ethic has to do with the constant and specific disavowal of financial motivation. Cracking copy protection for profit is anathema for warez traders. In 1996, PWA's .nfo file would include the following disclaimer: 'Please note that PWA is NOT accepting pay sites of any nature. We're in this for fun and entertainment, not to try to make ourselves rich.'[16] RiSC would add a similar statement in their .nfo file:

> RiSC is the longest lasting courier grp by far, and continues to bring honor and respect to the courier scene as only RiSC can. RiSC does not take donations of any sort for our services. We work on merit alone, the way the scene should be run.[17]

The soldiers of any pirate group were not the programmers, but usually held the title 'courier', and it became their responsibility to spread the cracked software as quickly and as widely as possible. The ethic that emerged in the warez underground is similar to the ethic that has always driven computer enthusiasts: to make quality software immediately and completely accessible.

That ethic has extended to other forms of new media as well, with pirate and warez groups setting up anonymous Web and FTP sites (often using free server space) to distribute digital music and video. Because these accounts are routinely deleted by service providers, the knowledge of distribution networks becomes essential for warez traders. Pirate copies of software, music or video are short-lived (often lasting less than 24 hours on a server), so warez trading continues to remain a question of access, providing those who are 'in the know' with virtually unlimited access to digital music, film and software.

EVERYTHING OLD IS NEW AGAIN

The most recent moment in the history of digital distribution has been shaped by the fusion of old and new media, particularly in the forms of digital music and video onto the Internet. Peer-to-peer networking (such as Napster and a host of Napster-like clones) has provided a revolutionary method of file sharing, taking full advantage of the decentralised nature of the Internet's packet-switching nature. The transformation of analogue content such as film, images and music into a digital medium is more than just a translation of wave forms into 1s and 0s – it represents a transformation in how information is communicated and distributed as much as how content is managed. It also means that a history of strict regulation and control of old media is continually being challenged by the ethical framework of new media technology.[18]

It is not surprising, given the history of digital distribution, to discover then that a large segment of the public perceives content on the Internet as free, even while they acknowledge that it may be copyrighted and regulated in its distribution in other media. The *ethos* of new media has fostered a belief that, while content can be owned, controlled and regulated, *distribution* cannot and should not be. As a result, the value of the Internet is not found in the information it provides, but in the *way* in which it provides that information. File sharing, with products such as Napster, differs little in form from the traditional ways in which music and even film have been traded among friends (for example, tape recording a CD or album for a friend). The difference rests with the degree to which the network of distribution has become public and global.

The problem that old media face is that the ethic which has always driven new media is one which celebrates the idea of sharing information. If something *can* be shared, this ethic dictates, then it *should* be shared. Hardware, the physical computer itself (the set of atoms), must be purchased. Information, however, as merely the arrangement of 1s and 0s, flows too freely and too easily to be regulated. Whether that information is an e-mail sent to a friend or full-motion video of the latest blockbuster release, it is all reducible to the arrangement of 1s and 0s to be interpreted by a machine.

As entertainment media such as music, videos, films and books, which have undergone the transformation from analogue to digital, begin to outstrip the physical media which were once necessary for their distribution, old media content providers are going to find it increasingly difficult to stake claims of ownership of networked bits. Notwithstanding recent legal rulings, which have in all cases upheld the rights of content owners, it is going to become increasingly difficult to enforce intellectual property rights as the more fully decentralised nature of the Internet plays a more prominent part in media distribution and as long as the tradition of the hacker ethic, demanding the free flow of digital information, subsists within the network and the networked community.

Notes

1. One example worth noting is the Communication Decency Act (CDA) of 1996, which attempted to control indecent content on the Internet by subjecting it to the same standards used to control broadcast. The CDA was, in fact, an amendment to the 1934 Telecommunications Act that established, among other things, the FCC. The CDA was ruled unconstitutional based primarily on its uniqueness as a communication medium and was found to merit, because of its nature, the highest standards of protection.

2. Much of the tension stems from a number of high-profile contestations of the legitimacy of intellectual property law in cyberspace. Most notably, John Perry Barlow's essay 'Selling Wine without Bottles: The Economy of Mind on the Global Net', published in *Wired* under the title 'The Economy of Ideas: A Framework for Rethinking Patents and Copyrights in the Digital Age (Everything You Know about Intellectual Property Is Wrong)', vol. 2 no. 3, March 1994, pp. 84–90.

3. Microsoft, 'What is software piracy?' *Windows ME*, 2000.

4. This issue is taken up by Mark Poster in his book *The Second Media Age* (London: Blackwell, 1995), particularly focusing on notions about the ways in which consumption and production are blurred by new media.

5. I used these terms not to suggest a binary distinction, but rather as a means to discuss the only the means of reproducibility. I do not want to suggest that computers are incapable of producing art or being used in an artistic fashion any more than I want to suggest that art functions without codes or rules. Instead, I use the terms 'art' and 'code' to discuss the primary means by which these different media are rendered reproducible.

6. Plato, *Sophist*, 236b.

7. Gilles Deleuze, *Difference & Repetition*, trans. Paul Patton (New York: Columbia University Press, 1995), pp. 38–9.

8. Walter Benjamin, 'The Work of Art in the Age of Mechanical Reproduction', in Hannah Arendt (ed.), *Illuminations*, trans. Harry Zohn (New York: Schocken Books, 1969), pp. 217–52.

9. Ibid., p. 220.

10. Ibid., p. 221.

11. Microsoft, 'End User Licence Agreement', *Windows ME*, 2000.

12. Microsoft, 'What Is Software Piracy?', <www.microsoft.com/uk/licenses/faqconcerns.htm>.

13. Steven Levy, *Hackers: Heros of the Computer Revolution* (New York: Bantam, 1984), p. 40.

14. Nicholas Negroponte, *Being Digital* (New York: Viking, 1995), pp. 11–17.

15. Bruce Sterling, *The Hacker Crackdown: Law and Disorder on the Electronic Frontier* (New York: Bantam, 1993), p. 66.

16. PWA, .nfo file, 21 November 1996.

17. RiSC, .nfo file, 21 November 1996.

18. For a very sophisticated discussion about the relationship between the Internet and regulation, see Lawrence Lessig's *Code and Other Laws of Cyberspace* (New York: Basic Books, 1999). Lessig argues that code, as the self-inscribed architecture of the Internet, creates an internal system of regulation that will ultimately be the means by which intellectual property rights on the Internet are negotiated.

2.4

Emerging Global Ecologies of Production

Tom O'Regan and Ben Goldsmith

Report after report, commentary after commentary envisaging futures for multimedia, digital film and television, and convergent media alike speak of the increasing impact of the global market on production. International considerations are thought to impinge at earlier stages in the production process and increasingly shape and re-order the entire field of production. 'Content creators' are being encouraged to think not only of multiple windows or platforms for their product, but also of different versions as their 'product' becomes an idea with multiple manifestations – a feature film, a large-format film (IMAX), a theme park ride or attraction, a video game, a Web site and online fan presence. They are also being encouraged to think beyond this or that local or national market, or the horizon line of their own particular region, nation or language group, and conceive of global opportunities and markets for the circulation and development of their content. Such considerations suggest the existence of a new production ecology. This chapter is about this emerging ecology and its close but insufficient entailment, globalisation.

When we talk about an emerging production ecology, we are not only talking about identifiably new forms of expression on new platforms such as computer games, online interactive drama, varieties of 'electronic art', but also the transformation of existing cultural forms and the platforms that 'carry' them. Considering new media production, therefore, requires us to hold together the old and the new; to recognise the presence of the new in the old; the consequences of the old for the new; and the mixing of old and new. The production ecology forming at this intersection is complex and multifaceted. The development of digital technology does not only involve the development of new formats and platforms for content delivery and new ways of producing content and thinking about working with audiences. It also involves renovating the production and distribution of existing formats and platforms, from feature films and television programmes to the cinema and prime-time television. Interactive television is not only emerging in new formats and distribution platforms such as the Internet, but is also an added element thoroughly at home with existing old analogue media such as prime-time television and film festivals.

There are then two stories we can tell about the new production ecology: one stresses innovation at every level of the production, distribution, exhibition and consumption cycle and so emphasises revolutionary change and new structural models and modes of expression. We can see this writ large in the games industry. The computer games industry has grown over the past decade at a phenomenal rate. It now has a higher turnover than the cinema as its core audience has aged to become 18- to 30-year-old gamers with time and disposable income. As a new form, gaming is constantly mutating in its business, distribution and playing forms so that there are now several differentiated gaming models across a number of different platforms. As gaming increasingly incorporates online elements, expectations of interactivity, gamer input and user-pays are creating games some distance from either the 'publishing model' of the stand-alone game available through retail outlets and the more televisual-based e-commerce models for online services with their banner advertising.[1]

By early 2000, games were starting to routinely provide several online gaming opportunities within the same game alongside stand-alone gaming possibilities, and purpose-built online games were becoming more commonplace as multiplayer strategy and role-playing games assembled opposing 'clans' and teams online. At the same time, game designers are increasingly incorporating fan communities in the very creation and development of games. Fans are being enlisted to contribute add-ons, plug-ins, lay-outs and characters, or to model machinery to be utilised within the game. The designer of *The Sims*, Will Wright, for example, sees games' production processes as heading in the direction of 'where it's truly a collaborative effort between us, the developers, and the people that buy our products'.[2] Gamer communities are not only involved in the marketing of the product, but also in co-creating product. In response, games companies are developing 'community relations' positions to handle their online community relations. In this model the gamers who contribute to the development of the game can be located in other countries, other continents or other hemispheres.

If this is a story of one kind of globalisation of audiences, product development and global distribution, it is also a story where for Pierre Levy 'the production of added value is shifted to the consumer' such that the 'very notion of consumption should be replaced by that of the co-production of merchandise or interactive services'.[3] And this is a 'a qualitatively different transaction space in which the roles of consumer and producer are undergoing profound change'.[4] New media mean here new market paradigms, new production processes, new mindsets and new expressive forms.

The second story we can tell about the new production ecology can be glimpsed in the first. It stresses the incremental transformation of 'old media' as new media are incorporated into old media production processes, formats and platforms. This is a story of continuity of production, format and platform in which 'new media' support, revive and amplify the possibilities of old media. This story documents how new media platforms have become new distribution outlets for old media forms: the standard television and cinema formats. This is fundamentally a story of continuity. It is about an enlargement of horizon that is producing difference. In this story, globalisation is present but alongside continuing local, regional, national and international scales. It is a story of incremental change that is cumulatively reshaping the ways in which these geographical scales interact.

An example of this is the international syndicated television format *Big Brother*. This reality television series is not only a high-rating television programme worldwide, but also a highly orchestrated, multi-platform media event delivered across television, the Internet, radio, telephony, newspaper publishing and outdoor advertising.[5] In its Australian manifestation, it incorporated a 24-hour video stream available live on the show's Web site, archived audio and video coverage of the house, chatrooms, forums and news updates which attracted on average over 350,000 viewers per day from a total population of 18 million. With this programme, Roscoe claims that the prime-time television programme is the site for sophisticated and intense levels of cross-media interaction between the Web and television. Here that old staple of the television trade, 'programme formats' or 'copycat TV' in Albert Moran's happy phrase, is becoming the basis for multi-platform media events centred on network television.[6]

A similar story of enhancement which is incorporating new media is the increasing number of film festivals that are no longer just the physical realities delimited to a particular place, set of cinemas and time, but are also 'virtual festivals' featuring streamed short content and other materials enabling virtual audience participation at a distance.[7] In these circumstances, the 'old platform' is a vehicle for the 'new'. Perhaps in time the new could grow to replace the old, but it is more likely that the new will continue to become a way of enhancing, amplifying and enlarging the brand of the festival, including the places and spaces where the films are being screened.

The new production ecology is certainly shaped by new platforms and forms of expression, but it is just as importantly shaped by the incremental transformation wrought on existing media platforms and forms of expression by new processes, technologies and distribution platforms. What we have is flux: not only at the level of the venue, the format and our interaction with it, but also in the very boundaries of the work itself as content streaming encourages creators to think about the repurposing of the 'idea' in multiple formats. In 'old media' such as cinema and television there has not been a time since the early days when so many different aspects in production, distribution, exhibition, formats and marketing have been in such flux.

The very circumstances of this new ecology give rise to both optimistic and pessimistic scenarios for independent production in a globalising environment and to different estimations of the consequences of digitisation for the organisation of production. Below we will develop both optimistic and pessimistic scenarios with reference to the place of the 'studio' system in each.

DIGITAL DIVERSITY AND A 'STUDIO WITHOUT WALLS'

On the face of it, independent producers have increased options available to them in a globalising environment as media systems fragment and new platforms develop from large format cinema (IMAX), to computer games, to interactive television. With more outlets, greater varieties and styles of product (formats), and greater differentiation within these styles, there are many more production opportunities, many more opportunities for specialisation, many more niche products for different tastes, and much more chance of reaching the demographically, politically and socially like-minded.

Producers can source payments for product from a variety of distribution platforms. Freelance film workers can transfer their skills and work across several formats including Web sites, museums, galleries and games enabling them to have a richer and varied experience of scriptwriting, directing, film shooting and producing. Independent film producers are increasingly transferring their skills to other compatible 'digital environments' from computer games to interactive museum exhibits to the 'new corporate video/film' in CD-ROM and DVD multimedia presentations, which are helping to sustain local screen production capacities.

Operating without the distribution bottleneck of the older broadcast television and cinema system which conferred such power on the networks and cinema chains, the new production ecology is built on the availability of alternative platforms for product.[8] The cinema chains and networks dominated the system through their monopolisation of cinema and television outlets and were supported by national systems of television regulation and territorial copyright systems in the cinema. With additional distribution systems these 'conduit' systems become so many transmission paths for content providers – distributors and producers – as the balance between 'content, conduit, and creation' changes to favour content providers.[9] This gives rise to expectations that, in this new environment, content would be 'king' and producers, in reality intellectual property owners, would be the new gate-keepers.

With digital television likely to lead to multi-channelling by existing stations, maturing pay-TV systems, new developments such as interactive television and alternative online-based platforms for the distribution of content including pay-per-view, the independent producer's long-term interests appeared served by this mix. With such open television and new media environments, content creators and content providers have more scope, opportunities with increased numbers of outlets and so should benefit from this additional leverage. These environments are characterised by multi-channel markets, minimal technological barriers for the entry of new players, the existence of various delivery platforms and a pervasive move towards digitisation and the inexorable expansion of online services.

The range of possibilities available to the producer is enhanced by the increased production capacity among populations as film-making competencies and technology capable of delivering sophisticated images become more affordable. With the falling cost of access to previously expensive audiovisual technologies and distribution systems, many more players can now afford to produce ultra-low-budget films for specific local communities and communities of interest nationally and internationally, and expect to have these 'presented' in a range of media systems from online to pay-TV systems predicated on small niche audiences.

Here digital technology seems to make possible a 'studio without walls' built on this fundamental and exponential increase of both access to screen production technology and to distribution networks. In October 1999, Rob Kenner argued in *Wired* magazine that breakthrough technological developments heralded a new era for do-it-yourself and low-budget film-making:

> Until recently, filmmakers hoping to find a large audience were caught in a vicious circle: you can't make a movie without shelling out serious money for crew, gear, and film. Raising the cash requires signing away rights, schmoozing investors, or plunging into debt, all of which encourages artistic compromise or, at best, diverts attention from the creative task at hand. Now, suddenly the cinematic landscape is changing.[10]

Movie production was becoming 'more accessible, personal, and spontaneous than ever before'[11] as the costs of shooting and editing became more 'affordable':

> In particular, prices of digital video cameras and desktop editing suites have plummeted in the last couple of years, demystifying and democratizing the world of moviemaking. What has been a costly and elaborate collaborative process is quickly becoming a one-person show.[12]

The result is a kind of garage film-making which blends screen formats and technologies: shot on Super 8, analogue video or 16mm, edited on digital video; shot on digital video, similarly edited and burned onto film or DVD, 'then hire or buy a projector and player and hey presto you are a portable cinema (without comfy chairs)'.[13] Unprecedented standards of imaging and special effects can now be achieved on desktop computers using software programs that were formerly beyond the price range of independent or low-budget film-makers. Talented individuals are pushing the boundaries and developing a new digital film-making vocabulary that extends the limits of the technology and the software. Much of this work can be distributed online via one of a number of sites, or screened at film festivals or through alternative microcinema circuits.

The underground microcinema culture is political and cultural in intent. The aim of many 'guerilla film-makers' is to use varieties of technology old and new, often against the grain and for one's own specific, political, cultural (non-digital) ends. Microcinema film-makers pose their film-making not as Hollywood 'wannabes', but as alternative practitioners opposed to 'slick, Hollywood FX films'. For this reason they are just as likely to be using 16mm, Super 8 and regular video which are 'considered more cool for being retro, for being not digital'.

For independent film-makers and critics such as David Cox, the microcinema economy of film 'can only really exist outside the mainstream, independent of the formats shown'.[14] Cox's work on other people's pictures in the US and Australia is governed by systems of exchange which have 'little to do with commercial models' and more to do with 'community-based systems of barter'. David, like many others in the burgeoning alternative media spaces, sees himself as part of an international underground film movement dedicated to realising the anarchic, expressive and anti-authoritarian potential of the Web. Alternative media oppose the 'aims and objectives of the commercial sector and its claims to the imagination of the global population'. In the case of alternative media and the protests it covered and developed in Seattle and afterwards, the digital revolution does reach downwards. It is no longer the preserve of a film-making elite or powerful corporations, but of ordinary interactions among activists wishing to define themselves against large corporations, globalisation and the international trading regime.

The story of microcinema is a story about the broader social distribution of the capacity to produce audiovisual images that new media technologies are enabling. It is located in the blurred edges of the film industry (where exactly does it begin and end, and where does it become multimedia?). It is a story about the democratisation of film-making, enabling people who would not previously have been able to tell stories on film to do so. The creative horizon has been extended as format and concept become open to new forms of experimentation and speculation.

Technological developments have enabled 'studios without walls'. In their new-found ability to manipulate images digitally, ordinary film-makers can access technology and special effects previously only available to the studios because of their prohibitive costs.[15] This begs the question whether such digital innovations render redundant the heavy contemporary investment in studio infrastructures? One powerful proof that it does is *The Blair Witch Project* (1999); another is the international reality of credit card film-making and the development of an additional tier of ultra-low-budget film-making. From this perspective, the studios do look like dinosaurs and the future seems to be in the hands of the Net Generation.[16]

Such developments provide grounds for the much touted optimism about convergent media systems and digital networks: that they will allow new players to emerge, will encourage greater diversity of expression and involvement, will permit more responsive media content adjusted to local, ethnic and regional circumstance, and will allow greater participation in new media content development. If we just stick with this story then we would in all likelihood agree with Nicholas Negroponte's oft-cited remark that the digital revolution means that 'the monolithic empires of mass media are dissolving into an array of cottage industries . . . the media barons of today will be grasping to hold on to their centralized empires.'[17]

CONSOLIDATION, ANIMATED PAINTING AND 'STUDIOS WITH WALLS'

However, the same conditions give rise to serious concerns for the capacity of independent production to respond to opportunity; amid such unbridled optimism is profound pessimism. The media barons look like they have indeed found a way of holding onto their centralised empires and growing even larger. The anxiety facing domestic production industries around the world was well encapsulated by the European Union's High Level Group on Audiovisual Policy in 1998:

> At the heart of the matter is the question of whether the predicted explosion in demand for audiovisual material will be met by European productions or by imports. The European

audiovisual market is already fragmented, due to linguistic and cultural diversity. The danger is
that the channel proliferation brought about by digital technology will lead to further market
fragmentation, making it even more difficult for European producers to compete with
American imports.[18]

Here market fragmentation is the enemy not the ally of the producer. This is the spectre
of more platforms benefiting a narrow range of producers and a limited variety of product.
Here market fragmentation seems to assist the larger players, the apex of the audiovisual
system, while precipitating the marginalisation of existing production capacity, production
and financing models. These larger players are themselves increasingly international in
outlook and orientation, as testified by the worry on the part of US-based film-makers
about the loss of production to Canada, the UK, Australia, Mexico and Eastern Europe.

Television producers and domestic film and television policy-makers worry away at the
consequences of steep competition for audience share from competing media outlets as
new television systems, games and the Internet erode the market dominance of broadcast
television. Local producers increasingly need to source a growing proportion of their production costs from other parts of the television system beside their traditional national
broadcasters and international broadcasters. However, these parts of the distribution chain
are often either not sufficiently developed or are unwilling to take up the slack. Where once
international sales were expected later in the life of a drama programme, often after a library
of episodes had been created, now a high-rating series or serial needs international sales
through a variety of windows as a condition for proceeding with the show.

The problem producers face here is the difficulties and costs they incur in negotiating a
pathway through the array of 'platforms' for the delivery of basically the 'same' product. It
used to be easier when the content and underlying delivery mechanism were co-terminus,
when, for example, free-to-air television meant terrestrial 'broadcast' television signals for a
local geographical area and when getting a video meant accessing a local video library.
Producers had a one- or two-stop shop, in reality the broadcasters and cinema distributors
who were dealing through national intermediaries and then international intermediaries.
However, increasingly there is a structural separation between the content and the underlying delivery mechanism. This has the consequence, for example, that free-to-air television
is as likely to be delivered by cable and satellite as being broadcast terrestrially in markets
such as Germany; of video transactions through video libraries beginning to occur through
online servers as well as physical visits to video libraries; and of the previously distinct
boundaries among television, video, cinema and pay-TV blurring as media systems
become more differentiated and fragmented.

In this process, previously separated and settled geographical scales of the local, the
regional, the national, the international and the global are becoming increasingly complex
and intermixed. Where once a limited set of television stations had a monopoly over 'broadcasting' in a particular geographically defined area, the same geographical community is
becoming increasingly serviced by television organised on the basis of a variety of

geographical scales ranging along the continuum from the local to the regional, the national, the international and the global. Here services originated on the basis of several geographical scales are operating at once. In these circumstances, it is very difficult for domestic producers to influence more distant distribution or conduit systems such as CNN and internationally delivered news channels. Such national and international media systems have local and sometimes national geographical scales (for smaller countries) as an inevitably minor component of their business model.

Similarly problems emerge for content creators when they seek to repurpose their content. They require increased 'negotiation' skills to navigate a pathway for content through different formats and delivery systems; and they need to make significant readjustments to production processes as greater co-ordination, levels of collaboration, additional skills and a change of horizon are needed on their part. In such circumstances, producers need both to spend more time negotiating an increasingly complex distribution pathway for their productions and to spend more time in product development for repurposing to be effective. This raises both transaction and production costs. Because organising distribution pathways is integrally linked to organising production funding, these higher costs mean that content creators often need more rather than less money and time with which to organise the flow of their product through a variety of windows.

Market fragmentation may have increased the scope for product development and circulation, but it has required a significant increase in the resources and leverage required by producers to take advantage of it. So while product development opportunities have certainly been enhanced, permitting new participants in the audiovisual industries, there are significant costs and changes of outlook required to take advantage of them. The structural separation of content from platform has inevitably privileged those with the leverage and resources to organise the trajectory of product through a variety of platforms and handle the repurposing of content.

In these circumstances, 'studios' which represent the coming together of a variety of financing, production and post-production resources become more not less significant. Here digitisation supports the renovation of the centralised production system studios represent. Alongside the 'studio without walls' there is another story to be told which focuses on the sustained programme of studio construction and redevelopment happening around the world. It sees this as, in Thomas Schatz's words, a 'regeneration of the studio system'.[19] The 'studio idea' is widely seen as a means to secure the future of production industries, to generate additional domestic capacity and to ensure that local film-making milieux remain technologically competitive. There simply has not been this global enthusiasm for the studio idea since the coming of sound in the 1930s. Governments around the world are busily developing direct or indirect assistance packages to offer to production companies in a bid to construct competitive studios and maximise opportunities for 'footloose', migratory or 'runaway' production. Such studios are built on new alliances between private and public sectors – media production companies, studio infrastructure providers and governments. These alliances are characteristic of broader trends in cultural policy-making which stress cross-sectoral partnerships between government and private enterprise.

The response to market fragmentation has not only been the emergence of a plethora of new players, but also the consolidation, merger and takeover of previously independent and nationally owned companies by larger international production companies. The Hollywood majors, the larger domestic media proprietors and the increasingly international production houses are better placed to co-ordinate, cohere and advance a fragmented and fragmenting media system. They are better placed to handle the economies of scope implied by the development of product for multiple platforms as they are better able to cohere disparate media activity.[20] These circumstances encourage ownership concentration and this concentration has been a feature of the late 1990s and early 2000s. Major broadcasters and telecommunications companies now have significant interests in content production, and multinational media conglomerates typically have production arms in a number of different territories. The production sector has been an integral part of some of the global trend towards consolidation and vertical integration as 'global conglomerates own significant interests in the broadcasting and production sectors, and are pursuing risk-reduction strategies based on vertically integrated self-dealing'.[21] These multinationals appear to be simultaneously pursuing a policy of localisation, regionalisation and globalisation. One instance of this is the Sony Columbia TriStar International production of *Crouching Tiger, Hidden Dragon* (2000).[22]

While digitisation – digital television, Web-TV, datacasting or online content streaming – will facilitate more outlets, more channels, it will also in Allan Brown's words 'generate economic forces conducive to concentration of *ownership* of those channels'. While it is now easy and cheap to produce extremely good audiovisual images with digital technology, the standards of imaging, and the expectations audiences have for film, television and new media imaging, have increased with the rise of standards. Television series and video games alike have to meet increasingly high standards of imaging to remain competitive.

In this scenario the larger players such as the incumbent Hollywood majors and major games producers have particular advantages over unaffiliated independent producers because they already have available to them a greater number of people (audience members, users, gamers) in different countries to pay for their high-budget programming. These companies can invest more in production. Hollywood can use its high-budget blockbusters – the major research and development arm of the Hollywood system – to continually ratchet up audience expectations and standards as competition for audiences is 'waged mainly in terms of the attractiveness of media products'.[23]

In a recent report on the effects of migratory or runaway production on below-the-line film workers, the US Department of Commerce notes that digital technologies have meant that post-production facilities no longer need to be located close to sound stages. Director Robert Zemeckis made a similar observation in 1996: 'It's not like there's one great fx house where you have to go to get beautiful images. All you need is the talent of the film-maker and the graphic artists, and the machinery can be put anywhere.'[24] In the new or refurbished studio developments in Australia, Mexico, Germany and the Czech Republic, digital effects and other companies are important parts of the studio precinct. Many of these studios are partly or fully owned by one of the major studios or an associated company. They are a response to a number of factors. They service the growing demand for 'international' content occasioned by the new multi-channel and multimedia audiovisual landscape. Most are directly related to the development of an extensive market for migratory or 'runaway' productions as the production infrastructure, including large-scale studio facilities, digital effects and editing expertise capabilities, has become more extensive and innovative in other principally English-speaking countries.[25] Perhaps most critically of all they are a response to digitisation and media convergence. The very same digital technology that is raising questions about its long-term viability with the development of studios without walls is also fuelling this development of studios.

Films such as *The Matrix* (1999) are unthinkable without their combination of digital technology and studio production environments. These are films that are premised on the creation of special effects and images never seen before. However, their creation requires powerful computer hardware, substantial digital manipulation and elaborate studio set-ups. Take, for example, a key sequence in *The Matrix*:

> The impressive 'bullet time' or 'frozen moment' shots in *The Matrix* required a ring of 120 still cameras each taking a single frame of film simultaneously from a different angle. These were subsequently assembled into a single progressive shot using digital imaging techniques – freezing a Kung-Fu action as 'the camera' appeared to circle around the actor. To avoid other cameras appearing in each frame, the actor was shot against a green screen, and the background to each shot was filmed separately and combined with the foreground later. The entire set-up was modelled using video and 3D computer-generated graphics (CGI) to ensure an accurate and lifelike movement.[26]

Compositing, modelling, rendering and 3D animation tools can be identified as genuinely 'new' innovations wrought by the possibilities of digital manipulation of sound and image. Early attempts to incorporate CGI and live-action footage in the films *Tron* (1982) and *The Last Starfighter* (1984) were hampered by expense and the need for high-powered supercomputers to achieve the necessary result at film resolution. The boom in computing in the 1980s, and the exponential growth in computing memory and speed, reduced the expense and increased the sophistication of digital effects. Morphing was first used in a Hollywood film in *Willow* (1988), but the film which is widely regarded to have raised the profile of digital effects to new heights was James Cameron's *Terminator 2: Judgment Day* (1991) with its liquid metal robot. The spectacular financial success of *Jurassic Park* (1993) has been argued to have 'fully legitimated the use of CGI in film' and 'marked an historic threshold in the relation between cinema and the computer'.[27] The recent animated feature *Final Fantasy* may mark another.

If microcinema is often built on the 'raw and edgy', these studio films conform to a different aesthetic of spectacle and display predicated on possible worlds, storybook worlds and virtual worlds. If the cinema has been, in Jean-Jacques Annaud's words, 'built around an animated picture' in a slew of films from *Terminator 2* to *The Matrix*, cinema 'has the option of becoming an animated painting'.[28] As Scott McQuire continues 'the dominant frame for computer artists working in cinema is not simply to create high resolution images, but to make these images look *as if they might have been filmed*'.[29] The setting for the storyspace of these films does not take place somewhere, but takes place in a place which could not only be somewhere, but might also be everywhere. For Scott Renshaw, the setting in *Babe: Pig in the City* is 'no longer Anywhere, but Everywhere; the story isn't just a fantasy where anything could happen, but one where the film-makers try to make everything happen'.[30] The results can be formidable.

> *Babe: Pig in the City* is littered with landmarks such as the Sydney Opera House and harbour, the Eiffel Tower, the Statue of Liberty, the Golden Gate Bridge, the World Trade Centre, the Seattle Space Needle and the 'Hollywood' sign, amongst others, amalgamated into the City's fantastic skyline. . . . With its surrounding canals and small bridges, the hotel at the heart of the story seems to be located at the intersection of Hong Kong and Venice.[31]

The result is a quite wonderful absurdity. Here the fatal coincidence of digital production processes and studio production appears liberating, allowing film-makers to play with the very plasticity of the medium. Such opportunities will have an impact on content, narrative and style as scriptwriters, designers, directors and producers explore the different possibilities of studio and location production. In addition, this more centralised form of production, coupled with state-of-the-art technology and expertise, presages increasing standards of imaging and production. Digital media enable the creation of 'whole imaginative environments' of media spaces that engage the viewer. In both studio stories the focus is on creating possible worlds rather than actual worlds, and there is an enthusiasm for exploring the 'virtual' worlds familiar in computer gaming. There is a rising generation of film-goers who are not only familiar and comfortable with these environments, but have come to expect them.

CONCLUSION

With Thomas Elsaesser, we want to propose that we are encountering a 'cultural shift, the consequences of which seem to be to leave everything the same while simultaneously altering everything'.[32] By this he means 'the digital is not only a new technique of post-production work and a new delivery system or storage medium, it is the new horizon for thinking about cinema'.[33] In these circumstances it is best to think of the cinema, television and new media as an assemblage of quite different things which have been assembled in particular ways, but may end up being reassembled in other ways.

The digital revolution seems to make possible a truly double vision. It enables a lot more activity, a wider distribution of film-making capacity and a veritable explosion of credit card film-making, and it supports a vibrant alternative film culture; however, it also enables the larger global media companies to take advantage of both the economies of scale and the scope represented by digital production, distribution and exhibition technologies. There is no doubt that studio production has fuelled the internationalisation of the audiovisual sector and this internationalisation is taking place alongside a recent burst of alliances and mergers which have created large, vertically integrated media conglomerates which are themselves involved in online services.

Supporting both developments and scenarios are the same recent advances in data compression and digitisation which have opened up the possibilities for making audiovisual content at both ends of the production spectrum. High-budget, high-revenue content has benefited from the new manipulability and interoperability of high-definition digital video as it has from the craft and sophistication of a phalanx of animators and digital sound and visual effects technicians. The fact that digitised sound and images do not degrade or suffer generation loss when copied has benefited production processes such as the laying of soundtracks or compositing images, and contributed to their increasing specialisation.

But at the same time as it has enhanced professional specialisation, digitisation has more banal resonances. At the domestic and low-budget end of the scale, the increasing affordability of digital video cameras and the widespread availability on desktop computers of major motion-graphic tools have inspired innovations in form and content, some of which have fed back in to the international circuits of money, imagination and risk which characterise commercial screen media production.

New modes and practices in the production of audiovisual media content for commercial distribution are both dictated by and able to form the screen experience of 'viewsers' (viewers/users) familiar with the aesthetics and conventions of film and television, and the interactivity enabled by networked computers. Interactivity, at some levels, transforms the relation between consumer and producer as the 'viewser' is intimately involved in mixing or producing their screen media experience. These transformations create opportunities particularly at the lower end of production, but pose considerable challenges for producers operating in the medium-budget ends of production. To a great extent change in the scale, scope, technological sophistication and location of screen media production is due to new production and distribution technologies enabled by digitisation and the much-documented but rarely satisfactorily defined 'convergence' of telecommunications, information technology and audiovisual media.

Notes

1. See John Banks, 'Gamers as Co-Creators: Enlisting the Virtual Audience', in Mark Balnaves, Tom O'Regan and Jason Sternberg (eds), *Mobilising the Audience* (St Lucia: University of Queensland Press, 2002).

2. Will Wright in Amy Jo Kim, 'Interview with Will Wright', *Great Places: The Newsletter for Savvy Community Builders*, 1.2, 5 September 2000, <www.naima.com/community/greatplaces/v1n2-2.html>. For an insider's discussion of these trends, see John Banks, 'Gamers as Co-Creators'.

3. Pierre Levy, *Becoming Virtual: Reality in the Digital Age*, trans. Robert Bononno (New York: Plenum Trade, 1998), pp. 80–1. For a discussion of the working out of these dynamics in the context of games development, see John Banks, 'Gamers as Co-Creators'.

4. Ibid., p. 78.

5. Jane Roscoe, '*Big Brother* Performing the Real 24 Hours a Day', *International Journal of Cultural Studies*, vol. 4 no. 4, 2001.

6. Albert Moran, *Copycat Television: Globalisation, Program Formats and Cultural Identity* (Luton: University of Luton Press, 1999).

7. See Tom O'Regan, 'The End of Cinema? The Return of Cinema?', *Metro*, nos 124–5, 2000, pp. 64–74.

8. For two useful discussions of this bottleneck and its dissolution, see Eli Noam, *Television in Europe* (New York: Oxford University Press, 1991), pp. 336–8; Department of Communications, Information Technology and the Arts (DoCITA), *Convergence Review* (Canberra: DoCITA, 2000).

9. Eli Noam, *Television in Europe*, p. 338.

10. Rob Kenner, 'My Hollywood!: So You Wanna Be in Pictures? Pick up Your Tools and Shoot', *Wired*, October 1999, pp. 214–21.

11. Ibid., p. 217.

12. Ibid.

13. 'Budgie Budgets', *Filmnet Daily: The Free Online Daily Australian Film Industry Newsletter*, 2.132, 7 October 1999. <filmnet.org.au/issues/2132.html>

14. Cox, correspondence with author, 11 January 2000.

15. This phrase is borrowed from Scott McQuire. See his essay 'Digital Dialectics: The Paradox of Cinema in a Studio without Walls', *Historical Journal of Film, Radio and Television*, vol. 19 no. 3, 1999, pp. 379–97.

16. See Don Tapscott, *Growing up Digital: The Rise of The Net Generation* (New York: McGraw-Hill, 1999).

17. Nicholas Negroponte, *Being Digital* (New York, Knopf, 1995), pp. 57–8.

18. High Level Group on Audiovisual Policy, *The Digital Age: European Audiovisual Policy* (Brussels: European Commission, 1998), p. 6.

19. Thomas Schatz, 'The Return of the Hollywood Studio System', in Patricia Aufderheide, Erik Barnouw and Richard M. Cohen (eds), *Conglomerates and the Media* (New York: The New Press, 1997), p. 86.

20. Andrew Graham and Gavyn Davies, *Broadcasting, Society and Policy in the Multimedia Age* (London: John Libbey Media, 1997), pp. 12–13.

21. CFTPA in association with PricewaterhouseCoopers, *Profile 2001: Canadian Independent Production: Growth Opportunities in a Period of Consolidation* (Ottawa: CFTPA, 2001), p. 7.

22. Philip Kemp, 'Stealth and Duty', *Sight and Sound*, vol. 10 no. 12, December 2000, pp. 12–15.

23. Allan Brown, 'Media Ownership in a Digital Age: An Economic Perspective', *Media International Australia Incorporating Culture and Policy*, no. 95, May 2000, pp. 49–61. See also Peter Goodwin, 'Concentration: Does the Digital Revolution Change the Basic Rules of Media Economics?', in Robert Picard (ed.), *Evolving Media Markets: Effects of Economic and Policy Changes* (Turku: The Economic Research Foundation for Mass Communication, 1998), pp. 173–89.

24. Shilo T. McClean, *So What's This All About Then? A Non-User's Guide to Digital Effects in Filmmaking* (Sydney: AFTRS, 1998), p. 61.

25. A number of recent reports chart these production trends. See Department of Commerce, *The Migration of US Film and Television Production: Impact of 'Runaways' on Workers and Small Business in the US Film Industry* (Washington DC: Department of Commerce, 2001); Monitor Company, *The Economic Impact of US Film and Television Runaway Film Production*, Report for the Directors' Guild of America and the Screen Actors' Guild (Monitor Company, 1999); Malcolm Long and Associates, *A Bigger Slice of the Pie: Policy Options for a More Competitive International Film and Television Production Industry in Australia*, Report for AusFILM International, 2000.

26. Prime Minister's Science, Engineering and Innovation Council, *Innovation in the Australian Film Industry*, Occasional Paper no. 4 (Canberra: Department of Industry, Science and Resources, 2000), p. 40.

27. Scott McQuire, *Crossing the Digital Threshold* (Brisbane: Australian Key Centre for Cultural and Media Policy, 1997), p. 27.

28. Jean-Jacques Annaud, 'Digital Future', *Sight and Sound*, vol. 6 no. 5, 1996, p. 15; cited in Scott McQuire, 'Digital Dialectics', pp. 379–97.

29. Scott McQuire, 'Digital Dialectics', p. 386.

30. Scott Renshaw, '*Babe: Pig in the City*', *Scott Renshaw's Screening Room*. <www.interconnect.com/~renshaw/babeinthecity.html>

31. Tom O'Regan and Rama Venkatasawmy, 'A Tale of Two Cities: *Dark City* and *Babe: Pig in the City*', in Deb Verhoeven (ed.), *Twin Peeks: Australian and New Zealand Feature Films* (Melbourne: Damned Publishing, 1999), pp. 187–203.

32. Thomas Elsaesser, 'Digital Cinema: Delivery, Event, Time', in T. Elsaesser and K. Hoffmann (eds), *Cinema Futures: Cain, Abel or Cable?* (Amsterdam: University of Amsterdam Press, 1998), p. 222.

33. Ibid., pp. 204–5.

3.0

TEXTS

What is meant by the term 'the moving image'? Is it the literal moving of photographic pictures along a celluloid strip? Is it the constantly moving lines of the analogue television signal? Or does the term encompass a much broader scope of sounds and images (media texts) that move, if not on a variety of screens, then in our minds? This section provides a number of explorations into what is meant by the term 'moving image' – for example, television programmes, films (in the cinema, on the Web, on DVD), electronic games, comics (paper-based and online) and Web sites – and investigates how the digital has recast a number of important issues relating to textuality, including intertextual referencing, notions of narrative interactivity and the constitution of aesthetic boundaries.

New media's impact on film and television aesthetics has been in play for some time with computer-generated titles, graphics and special effects adding a dazzling array of flash to traditional media products. Additionally, the cinematic and the televisual have had an effect on how digital media texts are produced and consumed – and it is this intersection between these aesthetic traditions that arguably makes contemporary media so engaging and exciting. Such mutual influencing tendencies between old and new media in terms of aesthetics, narrative and structure also assist in finding new ways to 'tell a story' or create a media experience.

All of the chapters in this section touch upon the intertextual circuit of meaning production and consumption in the contemporary media environment. New media texts quite often rely on this intertextual circuit in order to tap into established traditions of narrative exposition while simultaneously offering new ways to move through the narrative. Due to these increasing levels of intertextuality, one is even tempted to move away from using the more singular term, media 'text', and instead towards terms that highlight this increased intertextuality such as media 'experiences' and 'projects'.

The chapters in this section explore the potentialities and realities of such highly touted concepts as 'interactivity', 'convergence' and 'virtuality' from a variety of perspectives, including narratology, phenomenology and quantitative textual analysis. It is, in fact, quite refreshing to see some good old-fashioned 'textual analysis' in many of these chapters – a form of analysis so often displaced in writings about new media under the repeated mantra of 'the medium is the message'.

3.1

The Impact of Digital Technologies on Film Aesthetics

Michael Allen

Computer-based digital imaging technologies and techniques have had a substantial impact on contemporary film-making over the past ten to fifteen years. From hesitant beginnings, these technologies and techniques, and the particular kind of images they have helped create, have become increasingly central to many films of the period. This chapter will look at the effect of the digital on previous media technologies – namely, celluloid film – and examine the ways in which digitally produced images have changed the formal parameters of the modern film text. It will also look closely at specific instances of this development across the past decade or more, in order to determine in which ways these effects and changes are historically specific. As I hope to demonstrate, the reality is a combination of change and continuity over time.

Although computer-generated imaging (CGI) technologies have been around for some time, even before what is commonly seen as their landmark arrival in the film *Tron* (1982), it is really only since 1989, in James Cameron's *The Abyss*, that CGI has become a significant element in modern film-making. Since that time, its role in the creation of spectacular images in big-budget films has grown considerably. While certainly this has often been the result of hype and expectation as much as actual reality, CGI has now become the focal point around which the promotion of a major new release might be organised. Indeed, it could be said that the dominant identity of mainstream big-budget film-making of the past decade is one framed by such images and such image-making technologies.

This growing dominance is testimony to a certain sense of historical development both of the hardware and software programs and of the techniques they facilitate and make possible. The failure of *Tron* was at least partly perceived to have been the result of the much-heralded CGI effects falling some way short of expectations, of a palpable sense of disappointment about the capability of such effects to produce convincing images. The success of *Jurassic Park* (1993) a decade later, conversely, was due to an acknowledgment of the quantum leap such effects work had taken in the intervening years. I mention these two seminal moments in order to stress, at the outset, the need to keep in mind the several specific, historical moments when the films under discussion were created. This is important because it is only by doing so that the true effect of CGI on the formal level of these films can be adequately and accurately analysed.

Within this general historical framework, the assumed trajectory of CGI, for many observers, has always been towards the perfecting of a photo-realistic quality for the images, an endeavour encapsulated in the following comment by Phil Tippett, the stop-motion supervisor on *Jurassic Park*:

> Artistic realism was the goal on all of the animation. We worked to get rid of all anthropo-
> morphic actions. We wanted the dinosaurs to be as naturalistic as possible. It was the
> subtlety and all the refinements to the animation that allowed us to make those creatures look
> like real animals and not like movie monsters.[1]

In this sense, digital imaging technologies and techniques are striving to replicate what already exists: the photographic representation of reality. The success or failure of any digital image lies in the degree to which it persuades its spectator that it is not digital, but *is* photographic. The difference between the two, as has been widely analysed, is that whereas the photographic record automatically assumes a referent, an original object whose image has been captured by light passing through a camera lens and altering the chemical make-up of a strip of celluloid, a digital image need have no such referent. This difference, seemingly impossible to reconcile, lies at the heart of the matter in hand: how to combine photographic and digital imaging to create a coherent and seamless filmic world. This chapter aims to examine how this process has been formally achieved in some of the most significant films that have employed computer-generated imagery in recent history.

SHOT LENGTH

One of my working hypotheses going into the researching and writing of this chapter was that the advent and development of computer-generated images has led to changes in editing patterns and scene construction in some films of the past decade or so. My basic supposition was that the visual 'fragility' of the computer-generated image made it difficult for it to be scrutinised for very long before its essential artificiality became obvious to the observer. Consequently, it might be assumed such images had to be given short, fleeting appearances on screen, so that the spectator's eye could not settle upon them, could not 'see through' them.

There would be little new in this. Effects sequences created before the digital revolution, such as the mining car ride at the end of *Indiana Jones and the Temple of Doom* (1984), rapidly edited together live action with more traditional models and animation. While this was partly because of the narrative demands of speed and action, it was also designed to mask the potentially disruptive shots of model-work, the artificiality of which, if allowed to remain on screen long enough, would have become obvious to the audience.

A close examination of several seminal CGI films from the past decade or so shows an historical specificity to the use of such effects works in constructing sequences and scenes in the films. This historical perspective also complicates the simple hypothesis suggested above concerning the brevity of CGI images. In *The Abyss*, for example, the only sequence to use CGI comes halfway through the film and consists of 53 shots, from the first point of view of the creature as it approaches the submarine bay of the underwater rig, through to its final retreat back into the water as it flees from attack by the film's chief villain. The sequence runs five minutes in total. Of the 53 shots, some 20 contain CGI work and 33 are traditionally photographed shots of the actors only. The CGI shots make up a total of 67 seconds of the 300 seconds that the sequence lasts; that is to say, while the ratio of CGI to traditional shots is roughly 1:1.5, the ratio of total lengths of the two types of shot is 1:5. The CGI shots are on screen far shorter amounts of time than the photographed shots: an average of three seconds per shot, as opposed to around seven for the photographed shots. The screen time for each CGI shot is enough to register each effect, but not usually long enough to scrutinise it fully. The creature's first emergence out of the water is in a shot lasting around four seconds, but it only begins to form its shape in the latter half of the shot. The next few appearances each last around two to three seconds and establish the crea-ture's presence within the space of the scene. Longer duration shots are then used to allow the creature to form the facial features of the two main characters, Bud and Ace.

Contrast this with the first explicit appearance of CGI effects in *Jurassic Park*: the scene in which Alan Grant (Sam Neill) and Ellie Sattler (Laura Dern) are shown the brachiosaurs. From the jeeps coming to a halt through to the end of the scene, where Richard Attenborough offers to show them how he made the creatures, there are 25 shots, six of them CGI, ten non-CGI. The scene lasts three minutes. The six CGI shots run a total of one minute, the non-CGI shots the remaining two; an average shot length of ten and 6.3 seconds, respectively. Now the CGI shots run longer, on average twice as long, as the non-CGI shots.

Why the difference? It is partly to do with the narrative purpose of the two scenes. While in some ways similar – the first contact of the main characters with, respectively, alien and extinct creatures – in other ways the two scenes differ significantly. In *The Abyss*, the scene depicts a tentative and nervous meeting in which the two parties are cautious about full contact. The tension then increases with the appearance, and aggressive behaviour, of the film's villain, who scares the water creature away. In *Jurassic Park*, the purpose of the scene is to stun the two main characters, to impress them overwhelmingly by allowing them to gaze long and closely at the dinosaurs. Hence they, and we as fellow gazers, are given lengthy views of the creatures.)

Partly, it also has to do with sophistication of the CGI software itself. In *The Abyss*, the uncertainty surrounding the programs, and the images produced by them, meant that the film-makers felt comfortable in using them only in short bursts. In *Jurassic Park*, the cre-ators had far more faith in the software and were far more confident in allowing the images to remain on screen for far longer. They *wanted* the audience to stare at them and still be amazed. Talking about this scene, the film's effects supervisor, Dennis Muren, commented that: 'In the sequence, the graceful animals are revealed in long, lingering shots that are in marked contrast to the quick, flaw-concealing cuts typical of "creature" films.'[2] The scene is really an announcement of the arrival of a state-of-the-art image-creating process, especially explicit coming so near to the beginning of the film. If this is the first display of their image-making capabilities, what more is to come?

Finally, in *Godzilla* (1998), the length of shot is carefully controlled for dramatic rather than for technical reasons, in spite of the fact that the makers admit that the imaging software programs they used improved as production went on. The computer-generated images are overwhelmingly brief in the first scene in which Godzilla appears to the people of New York. But this fleetingness is not the result of the fragility of the technology so much as a means of teasingly suggesting the huge size of the creature and the panic induced by it in the people on the streets. But when much longer shots of the creature are needed, such as the one that comically ends the sequence, in which the news anchorman with his back to the window does not see Godzilla passing by, the shot is held for a noticeable length of time (around ten seconds).

Therefore, far from limiting their screen time, the gradual lengthening of shots featuring ever more photo-realistic computer-generated images, made possible by advances in the imaging software programs, can be said to present the images overtly for the gaze of the spectator. They become moments of sheer spectacle, their length intended to announce their importance as new kinds of image.

FRAMING

The scene in *Godzilla* mentioned above indicates another element of film form that has come under scrutiny in terms of CGI. In a production in which all objects and figures are physically real and inhabit the same real space, the combining of some or all of them within one shot, one framing, is not particularly problematic. The determinant is one of artistic choice, rather than technical constraint. In early CGI work, conversely, the latter rationale applied. Michele Pierson has observed the tendency of computer-generated objects in these early films to be separated from the flesh-and-blood figures in a scene: 'Beginning with *The Abyss*, the arts-and-effects direction for films produced in the first half of this decade [1990s] emphasised the alterity of the computer-generated special effect by formally bracketing the presentation of it off from the action.'[3] The problem of combining CGI with real objects within the same shot was sufficiently difficult, technically, to result in a separation of the two, resulting in an alternation between CGI image and non-CGI image. As Pierson notes, this can be seen in the CGI scene in *The Abyss*, where, although a few of the framings show the CGI creature and the human actors in the same shot, most show the CGI creature alone.

By 1991, with *Terminator 2: Judgment Day*, this tendency was still in place. Most of the CGI effects in the film take place either in a separate shot or in the empty half of a shot containing humans or other real objects. For example, take the scene in which the T-800 has just rescued John Connor from the T-1000 who has been chasing him through the storm drains in a truck. After the truck has crashed and burst into flames, the T-800 and the boy stare back at the flaming wreck to check that the terminator has been destroyed. When they feel assured that he has, they ride away from the scene. A cut to a shot framing the wreckage is held for several seconds before the T-1000 appears, morphing back to the cop as he walks through the flames. This shot, explicitly separated from the preceding sequence of shots, presents a spectacular moment of CGI; a moment in which, while there is narrative content (the T-1000 is alive and still in pursuit), the foregrounded element is of the image being computer-generated; of having a particular visual quality which is unreal, but also situated in ostensibly 'real' space.

Again, this particular formal parameter altered over time as the software programs became more sophisticated and allowed computer-generated images to be seamlessly combined with real objects and people. *Jurassic Park* does this throughout its first scene involving the digital dinosaurs, as does *Godzilla*, in which the fragmented body of the huge creature is continually obscured by objects in front of it in the frame. Shot length and framing combine together to present the CGI object in a particular way that also has developed across time. In 1989, in *The Abyss*, the creature is generally framed in short, separate shots. By 1993, the dinosaurs are composited with the humans and the shots showing the two together are held for far longer. By 1998, CGI creature and real objects and humans are composited together in short shots, for dramatic rather than technical reasons.

CAMERA MOVEMENT

Until the appearance of motion-control camerawork in *Star Wars* (1977), there was a tendency in model-based effects work for the camera to have to remain stationary. The blocking out of specific areas of the image into which the animated models would later be optically inserted worked against the possibility of moving the camera and tended to implement instead a regime in which scenes were constructed of separate static shots. Motion-control, as the name suggests, freed the camera again and allowed it to follow models as they moved through space, in a kind of continuous frame-by-frame animation process whereby camera and model moved incrementally as single frames were photographed, sometimes in operations lasting several hours.

Early digital effects tended to immobilise the camera once again. In the scene in *The Abyss*, almost all of the CGI shots have a static framing and stand in stark contrast to both the fluid tracking shots from the creature's optical point of view as it enters the crew's quarters and the hand-held camerawork as the team chase after the creature later in the scene. There are two exceptions to this: first, when the creature moves towards Bud and Ace in the second shot of their encounter, there is a very slight track in towards the actors as the creature itself moves forward; second, in the very last shot, when the creature, having been scared off by the film's villain, whips back into the water, an upward tilt and then a rapid pan down right follows the creature as it disappears. However the latter's position at the very end of the scene, together with its speed and brevity, however, make it a coda more than an integral stylistic feature of the scene. The governing formal parameter of the scene is to have static framing for the CGI shots to simplify the image-creating process.

Once again, contrast this with the scene of the first dinosaur sighting in *Jurassic Park*, in which the camera movements are explicit and made obvious to us, and work to confirm the authenticity of what we are witnessing, essentially by suggesting that only real objects can be tracked by the camera in such a complex way. The registers of the real world (perspective, depth cues, light and shade) work with the camera movement to overwhelm our means of analysing the effect.

However, the camera movements in this scene from *Jurassic Park* are kept frontal to the action; both dinosaurs and humans are kept to one side of the laterally moving camera. Even the extravagant low-angle shot which tracks as it tilts up steeply to frame Alan and Ellie in the foreground and the brachiosaur rising up behind them maintains this frontality. Later scenes, however, such as the herd of gallimuses which run past the characters, present a more complex spatial situation, the camera tracking backwards as the creatures run past on either side. A reverse angle then shows them running away from camera as it tracks forwards. But the presentation of space is somehow discontinuous; separate spaces each allowing the CGI creatures to be re-positioned anew.

It is only in the past couple of years that the presentation of continuous 3D space containing CGI objects and spaces has been achieved. In the scene in *Godzilla* in which the creature first appears in New York, there is a sweeping shot in which the camera tracks backwards as a cabdriver begins to run from Godzilla, whose giant feet and lower legs are just visible in the background. As Godzilla approaches the foreground, the camera swings around 180 degrees, temporarily losing sight of the creature before it reappears in frame, its foot smashing down onto the street. The presentation of continuous space achieved by the 180-degree camera movement serves to reinforce our belief in the reality of the scene we are witnessing. The same effect is achieved in *Gladiator* (2000), when, as the gladiators enter the arena of the Coliseum, the camera swirls around them, showing computer-generated walls and tiers of spectators present continuously behind them. CGI space appears to be really there, behind and around the live actors.

An important point must be made here. These camera movements try to mimic as precisely as possible identical camera movements which might be used in a wholly live-action film. In one sense, they try to become invisible, to hide the role they play in persuading the spectator that the image they present is a computer-generated illusion. In another, however, their very extravagance, their overt sweep and style, are intended to be noticed by the spectator. They are in some sense pulled out of the constant and invisible flow of images that go to make up the scene and allowed to stand apart as moments for awed appreciation. Therefore, they both confirm the spatial reality of the scenes in which they appear and simultaneously announce their amazing presence as illusion. This tension between the real and the illusory lies at the heart of the impact computer-generated images often have for their spectators.

LIVE AND VIRTUAL

More generally speaking, a specific formal structure has developed which establishes the rules by which CGI and live action are combined. While CGI shots, in themselves, might be lengthy, allowing the spectator to gaze at and to scrutinise them, it is rare that several CGI shots are run together in a sequence at any one time. More normally, a CGI shot will be bracketed by live-action shots before and/or after it. The moment of 'artificiality', therefore, is both set up as coming out of, perhaps extending, the real and is also retrospectively reconfirmed by the real. This interaction can occur with non-CGI effects work using models and/or animatronics instead, as evidenced by the comment made by Mark Goldblatt, the picture editor on *Terminator 2*, on the commentary track of the DVD edition of the film: 'You have to use the stuff [model effects and animatronics] judiciously and keep referencing it with the real actors so that you never get the impression that you're looking at a puppet.' But it could be argued that the necessity for such strategies of confirmation is heightened with CGI, in that the models at least have a physical reality, whereas the CGI is pure imma-terial illusion. The need to refer back to real objects, in order to continually convince the viewer that the computer-generated object really exists, is thereby greater and becomes a determining formal strategy in the construction of sequences containing CGI work.

To take an example: in *Deep Impact* (1998), the complex, digitally composited shot of the large number of helicopters taking off across Washington is framed before and after by shots of, one assumes (perhaps dangerously), hundreds of real cars jamming a highway upon which another of the main characters is trying to find his new wife. The large number of cars and trucks in the framing shots echoes, and somehow confirms by association, the unfeasibly large number of helicopters all flying in the same air space during the middle CGI shot. Furthermore, the reality of 'helicopters' is verified by having one land on the rooftop helipad at the beginning of the CGI sequence while another flies past in the background (an entirely feasible production logistic). Finally, at the end of the sequence, Tea Leoni's char-acter is shown clutching two photographs of her father, to whom she will now return so they can face death together, as confirmation of the notion of the existence of originating referents. The potentially 'fragile' CGI moment, lasting at most four or five seconds in an otherwise live and photographed event, but still capable of being 'seen through' by the vigilant spectator, therefore has considerable, one might say overwhelming, real-world, live confirmation. This relationship between real and photographed and simulated and com-puter-generated images, in which the latter is carefully framed by the former in order to boost its chances of establishing and maintaining a weight of authenticity, will inevitably change as CGI systems and techniques become ever more sophisticated.

This interaction between real and simulated images can be placed within the framework of Stephen Prince's theory of correspondence.[4] Prince argues that with objects and beings that are outside our actual real-life experience, such as the dinosaurs in *Jurassic Park*, we bring to our assessment of the believability of such beings a set of prior knowledges. So, generally, we refer to the scientific laws of gravity, weight, mass and so on. Specifically, we draw upon our knowledge of the texture of the thick skin of a large mammal, such as an elephant or rhino, light as it falls on such a skin, and so forth.

This theory of referencing allows us to understand the dynamic interaction between CGI effects and shots of live action, in which the live-action shots explicitly give us the infor-mation to which we will refer as the simulated equivalent in the following CGI shot appears on screen. While it might be thought that this could work to undermine the integrity of the diegetic world, especially if the CGI version fares poorly when directly juxtaposed with the 'real thing', generally the shift into the 'virtual world' and back out to the real repairs any momentary viewer scepticism about the believability of the former.

It is perhaps significant in this respect that many of the substantial CGI sequences are prefaced, and thereby mediated, by already known audiovisual systems within the diegetic world of the films themselves. In *Godzilla*, the creature is initially represented as a physical reality by a radar display on the Japanese fish-processing ship. In *The Abyss*, characters communicate via videophone monitor, fixing in place a known set of images that lay the groundwork for the later, further step to take place in representing the water creature. In *Jurassic Park*, we are given an audiovisual presentation that sets out the scientific and technical premise of the film. Though this context is constructed retrospectively; we have already seen the CGI dinosaurs for the first time. The ultimate effect, however, is the same: the known and believable audiovisual form provides a link and bridge from the real world to the virtual CGI one.

THE PLACING AND TIMING OF CGI SEQUENCES

I would now like to move on to consider whether there is anything significant about how CGI sequences are positioned in terms of their film's shape and flow as a whole. Essentially, it is a question of the timing of the initial presentation of computer-generated imagery in any of the films in question. What is revealed is a range of strategies, rather than a standard template. Once again, this range is partly, but by no means wholly, historically conditioned. In *The Abyss*, the CGI images are withheld for over an hour (exactly halfway through the film) before the water creature is revealed to us. In *Jurassic Park*, as just indicated, the first sustained sight of the CGI dinosaurs comes after only 19 minutes and is not preceded by any suggestion or foretaste to whet the audience's expectations. In *Godzilla*, several brief but violent events introduce us to the presence and potential of the eponymous creature; scenes largely created using models as well as the mystery of the unseen. All fleeting sightings of the lizard are fragmentary and intentionally confusing.

The contrast between these films is the result both of narrative and historical pressures. In *The Abyss* and *Godzilla*, the rationale is certainly one of building narrative suspense, of positing the presence of a massive and/or fantastic creature, then delaying the moment when that creature is finally revealed to the viewer. However, it is also a question of the sophistication of the technology and software programs available at the time when each film was produced. In *The Abyss*, the imaging software was so new and untested that director James Cameron both protected his production by arranging traditional processes for producing the same images and allowed the film to spend an hour establishing the physical reality of its world. Indeed, the extreme and real physicality of the film's production was hyped in all promotion and word on the film.

In *Godzilla*, the software capability has less of an uncertainty. Indeed, proof of concept could be said to have passed the test several years earlier in *Jurassic Park*. The moment of revealing the full image of the creature has therefore become far more one of dramatic necessity than technical protectionism.

The case of *Jurassic Park* represents a perfect balance between these two points. Coming 20 minutes into the film, the first viewing has narrative logic; it is imperative that the two main characters see the dinosaurs as soon as possible so that they sign up to support the park. It also has industrial logic, spectacularly and almost arrogantly announcing the arrival of a significant advance in the field of CGI effects. The two logics, effectively, map onto one another; a mapping illustrated by the stunned, open-jawed reaction of the two characters. This is also a representation of the reaction the film-makers hope the audience would be having as they first see the CGI creatures.

The presence and incorporation of computer-generated images within feature films involving traditionally photographed actors, objects and spaces, therefore, has resulted in a number of changes to the parameters of conventional film form, as well as a number of continuities. Except, perhaps, in the very early attempts, there have been no radical changes in shot length, or in framing or camera movement either. Each of these elements has continued to be varied and determined according to the dramatic requirements of the scenes in which they are used. Shots get shorter as action sequences build. Framings change with the dramatic content of a scene. Camera movement is still used to follow moving objects or to reveal new spaces in which new actions take place. In these senses, at least, CGI has fitted into existing formal properties of feature films. The conventional two-shot, for example, is now used to provide a space within the framed image where a computer-generated object can later be added. The framing, unbalanced in the original filming, becomes balanced and conforms to conventional aesthetic rules, due to the later computer-generated additions.

If there have been few major changes to film form, there have been modifications to some of the existing parameters. A series of computer-generated shots will often begin with shorter length shots intercut with live-action equivalents, before a later, longer shot spectacularly presents the climactic computer generated image. This flow of images is slightly different from ordinary scene construction and shows one way in which CGI, in demanding a privileged space for a final display of itself as spectacular image, is subtly modifying the rules of film grammar. Similarly, the sweeping 180-degree or circular, space-to-reverse-space camera movements operate not so much to follow live, on-screen action as to convince their spectators that the non-real action being seen on screen is actually happening.

Repeatedly, therefore, we see CGI sequences taking the accepted rules of film form and scene construction and either using them, unaltered, to confirm the reality of the digital images by editing them together with images of real objects to persuade us they exist in the same world or to present them as images which are spectacularly apart. In this latter case, it is the minor abuse of conventional film form that opens up a space for this display: the slightly 'too-long' contrasting with the series of 'just-long-enough' shots, or the too perfectly executed camera movement. In using and manipulating the formal parameters of mainstream film-making in this way, CGI sequences construct themselves as simultaneously ordinary *and* extraordinary, as photo-realistic elements of transparent film-making and as non-real, spectacular images designed to be noticed, to be separated from the flow of the rest of the film's images, and appreciated for their non-photographic visual qualities. The tension between these two states, between these two kinds of film form, has come to typify the experience of watching any film with a significant degree of CGI in it. Whether this relationship will change again, as CGI processes continue to develop, remains to be seen.

Notes

1. Mark Cotta Vaz and Patricia Rose Duignan, *Industrial Light and Magic: Into the Digital Realm* (London: Virgin, 1996), p. 218.

2. Jody Duncan, 'Jurassic Park: The Beauty in the Beasts', *Cinefex*, no. 55, August 1993, p. 64.

3. Michele Pierson, 'CGI Effects in Hollywood Science-Fiction Cinema 1989–95: The Wonder Years', *Screen*, vol. 40 no. 2, Summer 1999, p. 172.

4. Stephen Prince, 'True Lies: Perceptual Realism, Digital Images and Film Theory', *Film Quarterly*, vol. 49 no. 3, Spring 1996.

3.2

Narrative Equivocations between Movies and Games

Marsha Kinder

FOREPLAY

When the film version of the popular role-playing game *Dungeons & Dragons* (2000) was advertised on television, despite the commercial's emphasis on fast-cut visual spectacle moving at the speed of gameplay, it ended with the punchline, 'It's not a game!' This equivocating insistence on both the similarities and differences between games and movies is growing shriller, in both the popular press and cultural theory, as the convergence between these two forms increasingly appears inevitable.

In exploring this equivocation, I will focus on the comparison not only between electronic games and movies, but also more broadly between games and narrative. I come to this subject as a cultural theorist who has been writing about narrative since the 1960s, first in literature, then film and television, and now 'new media'. Since 1997, I have been directing a research initiative on interactive narrative, the Labyrinth Project, where we daily confront these equivocal relations while producing electronic fictions in collaboration with film-makers and writers known for nonlinear experimentation in earlier non-digital forms.

I will argue that narrative experimentation in cinema from earlier decades provides a valuable legacy for those interested in designing productive combinations of games and movies, especially as transmedia adaptations have thus far been so disappointing. Film adaptations of popular games, such as *Lara Croft: Tomb Raider* (2001), *Mortal Kombat* (1995) and *Super Mario Bros*. (1993), usually restrict themselves to the original sketchy characters and narrative shell, fleshing them out with generic clichés while highlighting the action, which, no matter how spectacular, still loses kinetic force. Game adaptations of films have fared somewhat better because they usually have richer characters and more elaborate narratives to draw on, especially in works such as *Blade Runner* and *Star Wars* that inaugurated paradigmatic shifts in visual culture, which can be enhanced by kinetic action and new modes of identification. Even if on-screen representations of characters prove disappointing, particularly when computer-generated or second-rate stand-ins for the original stars, players can bring memories of the original actors and back-stories to the game and put them into play, as kids do with action figures.

The hybrids I find most productive move beyond transmedia adaptations by combining the distinctive conventions and pleasures of games and movies in original ways. Perhaps because cinema is the medium threatened with extinction, these expressive possibilities have been explored in a wide range of movies: in vintage game films such as *Tron* (1982) and *The Last Starfighter* (1984); in recent complex action films such as *Run Lola Run* (1998), *Crouching Tiger, Hidden Dragon* (2000) and *The Matrix* (1999); in comedies and thrillers with experimental narratives such as *Groundhog Day* (1993), *Being John Malkovich* (1999), *Sliding Doors* (1998), *XistenZ* (1999) and *Memento* (2000); and in demanding experimental films such as *The Pillow Book* (1996), *Until the End of the World* (1991) and *Timecode* (2000).

This kind of experimentation is harder to find in games, even in today's most exciting genre – those online massively multiple player games, such as *Anarchy*, *Ultima*, *EverQuest*, *Asheron's Call* and *The Sims*. Although these profitable role-playing games provide rich narrative fields where thousands of players personalise their own avatars and objects with customised behaviours as they collaboratively spin open-ended stories, their narratives are simplistic and their pleasures interrupted by frustrating time-lags. These games could learn valuable strategies from earlier cinematic experimentation with open narratives, yet, when I made this suggestion at a recent game conference, several game designers indignantly rejected the notion.

One finds traces of this resistance even in those new media theorists who freely acknowledge continuities between electronic games and earlier narrative forms and deliberately avoid a McLuhanesque technological determinism, the dangers of which Raymond Williams exposed back in the early days of television.[1] In seeking to define 'new media' specificity, many adopt a formalist methodology I call 'cyber-structuralism', which disavows crucial discursive debates of post-structuralism and cultural studies. The most fascinating example is Lev Manovich's *The Language of New Media*, the most ambitious and rigorous book on this topic yet published.[2] For, despite the comprehensive range of his concerns and his broad historical contextualisation, Manovich establishes a formal rhetoric of new media without addressing cultural differences among players and practices. He ignores the crucial shift from structuralist to post-structuralist approaches to narrative, so succinctly described by Teresa de Lauretis:

> Today narrative theory is no longer or not primarily intent on establishing a logic, a grammar, or a formal rhetoric of narrative; what it seeks to understand is the nature of the structuring and destructuring, even destructive, processes at work in textual and semiotic production . . . a production of meaning which involves a subject in a social field.[3]

To demonstrate the usefulness of narrative experimentation in cinema to contemporary gameplay while simultaneously addressing the theoretical limits of cyberstructuralism, I have chosen as my case study five experimental films produced in the highly politicised context of Paris in the 1960s and 1970s, the historical period when the shift to post-structuralism took place. By rereading these 'game films' in the light of new media, I hope to illuminate what was at stake in these comparisons between games and movies for that period and how these texts can still be useful to our own context of convergence.

DEFINITIONS AND DISTINCTIONS

The perception of differences between games and films hinges on how one defines narrative and the primary functions it performs. Manovich rejects the broad definitions of narrative from film theorist Edward Branigan, who said, 'Narrative is increasingly viewed as a distinctive strategy for organizing data about the world,' and historian Hayden White who claims:

> Far from being one code among many that a culture may utilize for endowing experience
> with meaning, narrative is a metacode, a human universal on the basis of which transcultural
> messages about the nature of a shared reality can be transmitted.[4]

Within the context of new media, Manovich rejects using 'narrative' as 'an all-inclusive term', claiming it is used 'to cover up the fact that we have not yet developed a language to describe these new strange objects'.[5] Like David Bordwell, he chooses a narrower neo-formalist approach that deliberately avoids ideological considerations; defining narrative through a list of essential components and questioning whether a text 'qualifies', rather than what functions it performs. Manovich adopts the specific list of criteria prescribed by literary theorist Mieke Bal:

> It should contain both an actor and a narrator; it also should contain three distinct levels
> consisting of the text, the story, and the fabula; and its 'contents' should be 'a series of
> connected events caused or experienced by actors'.[6]

Like Branigan and White, I see narrative more broadly as a discursive mode of patterning and interpreting the meaning of perceptions, an operation crucial to culture. Thus, its distinctive components – characters and events interacting within a space-time setting with change and causality – always carry specific historical, cultural and generic inflections, which enable us to contextualise its primary functions in three ways: aesthetically, ideologically and cognitively.

Aesthetically, the function of narrative is to arouse emotion or give pleasure; to create a simulacrum of the world or preserve one's experience in the face of death. The key question is which stories arouse the greatest range and depth of response. Ideologically, the function of narrative is to transmit or challenge the dominant values of a culture, as in myths, religion and history. The key questions are: how do narratives interpellate us as subjects who accept the prevailing order or, more interactively, how can we re-inscribe them for our own ends? Cognitively, the function of narrative is to contextualise the meanings of perceptions, a process involving montage and other modes of selection and combination, as well as the hermeneutic pleasures of problem-solving. The key question is: how do stories shape the way we process new data or enable us to design new narratives and algorithms? Whereas most electronic games address the aesthetic function by constantly improving graphics and the cognitive function by requiring mastery of increasingly difficult skills, their ideological dimension is usually limited to a simplistic struggle between good and evil, leaving other social assumptions unexplored.

The ideological and cognitive functions of narrative are inextricably fused: the cognitive is the operational form of the ideological, and the ideological represents the political consequences of the cognitive. The more aesthetically powerful a story, the more effectively it performs its ideological and cognitive ends. With these interwoven functions, narrative maps the world and its inhabitants and locates us within that changing textual landscape, constantly broadening our mental cartography.

This broader definition of narrative enables one to see games as a special kind of narrative, rather than a rival form. Ordinarily defined as a playful leisure activity, games usually involve a contest between participants competing for amusement, money, fame or some other stake. Thus, most games are built on dramatic conflict like other narrative forms, and the stakes are ideologically charged for they become a means of defining power, for example, who is stronger, luckier or more worthy of becoming a cultural hero. While the term 'game' is used literally in sports and in the leisure worlds of playgrounds, casinos and arcades, it is applied figuratively in contexts where the border between leisure and other activities is ambiguous. One thinks of the mind games people play in psychological interactions; the zero-sum, mini-max games of economics, which have worldwide social and political consequences; the informal usage in business professions, such as the law game and teaching game, where people's livelihoods depend on adherence to codes of behaviour; or hunting and war games where the stakes can be amusement or survival.

In the contemporary discourse comparing games and narratives, three main distinctions are usually emphasised:

1. Whereas games require active participation by players, most narratives encourage passive readings.
2. Whereas the game world is purposely cut off from reality, most narratives are designed to represent and influence real life.
3. Whereas rules, goals and results are clear cut in games, they are usually ambiguous in narratives.

Instead of functioning as binaries, these distinctions can be treated more productively as a continuum.

ACTIVE PLAYERS VERSUS PASSIVE READERS

Unlike earlier 'new media' theorists such as Andy Lippman and Sandy Stone who fetishised interactivity as the ultimate value,[7] Janet Murray, in her influential and useful book *Hamlet on the Holodeck*, avoids the term altogether, switching the focus to 'agency',[8] while Manovich calls it a misleading myth.[9] However, both realise the emphasis on interactivity in new media enables us to rethink its analogues in earlier forms.[10] The crucial task is distinguishing between these forms of agency.

According to Murray, whereas stories do not require us to do anything except pay attention, 'games always involve some kind of activity and are often focused on the mastery of skills'.[11] To make this distinction more precise, Manovich introduces the concept of algorithm, yet soon blurs the boundary by applying the term figuratively to novels and their readers:

> In contrast to most games, most narratives do not require algorithm-like behavior from their
> readers. However, narratives and games are similar in that the user must uncover their
> underlying logic while proceeding through them – their algorithm. Just like the game player,
> the reader of a novel gradually reconstructs the algorithm (here I use the term metaphorically)
> that the writer used to create the settings, the characters, and the events.[12]

Both accounts present a limited view of narrative reception, one that assumes readers merely decipher the author's intention or underlying design, without inflecting the text with their own personal associations or appropriating it for their own pleasures. They ignore conceptions of active readership that have been promoted by cultural studies over the past 30 years, whether through the 'negotiated' readings posited by Stuart Hall and the Birmingham School, or 'reading against the grain' (the phrase used by feminist film theorists in the 1970s), or 'textual poaching' (Michel Certeau's term popularised by Henry Jenkins), or 'queering' a text (the reading strategy operative in gay studies). At this point in history, any simplistic distinction between active game players and passive movie spectators would be naive.

One could also argue that all narrative forms accommodate more passive modes of response, even games. Individuals alternate between functioning as players or observers, not only in spectator sports such as basketball and chess, but also in electronic games, when friends play at home, at work or in the arcade. The consumption and awareness of games played and stories told by others help shape one's own active performance. There is a more complex mix of active and passive modes than is usually acknowledged.

REPRESENTATION VERSUS RETREAT

Intrigued with a different kind of mix, Manovich begins with the assumption that 'computer programming encapsulates the world according to its own logic'[13] and claims the cognitive oscillation between interactivity and illusion found in computers and their electronic narratives generates a 'new kind of realism'. Although he starts to address its ideological implications, his attention quickly shifts to aesthetics:

> The old realism corresponded to the functioning of ideology during modernity – totalization of
> a semiotic field, 'false consciousness', complete illusion. But today ideology functions
> differently: it continuously and skillfully deconstructs itself, presenting the subject with
> countless 'scandals' and 'investigations'. . . . The oscillation analyzed here is not an artifact of
> computer technology but a structural feature of modern society, present not just in interactive

media but in numerous other social realms and on many different levels. This may explain the popularity of this particular temporal dynamic in interactive media, but it does not address another question: does it work aesthetically? Can Brecht and Hollywood be married?[14]

Although hundreds of films have specifically addressed that question, Manovich chooses a provocative electronic example the ideological implications of which for 'real world' applications are obviously problematic:

> In my view, the most successful example of such an aesthetics already in existence is a military simulator, the only mature form of interactive narrative. It perfectly blends perception and action, cinematic realism and computer menus. . . . In this art form, the roles of viewer and actant are blended perfectly – but there is a price to pay. The narrative is organized around a single and clearly defined goal – staying alive.[15]

Manovich maps this combat model of survival games over the mediascape, where he finds one-on-one serial screen wars, this time between cinema and computers, with the latter clearly in command. Claiming that 'new media embeds cinema-style illusions within the larger framework of an interactive control surface', he paints a pathetic picture of an ageing cinema's humiliating decline:

> From commanding a dark movie theater, the cinema image, this twentieth-century illusion and therapy machine par excellence, becomes just a small window on a computer screen, one stream among many others coming to us through the network, one file among numerous others on our hard drives.[16]

But it is possible to argue, as Murray does, that the combination of interactive control and narrative illusion provides new pleasures:

> Games are recreational because they offer no immediate benefit to our survival. Yet game-playing skills have always been adaptive behaviors. Games traditionally offer safe practice in areas that do have practical value; they are rehearsals for life.[17]

Or rehearsals for death, in those military war games that prefigured Desert Storm and in those 'mature' military simulations Manovich admires. On the one hand, the separateness of the game with its hard and fast rules provides refuge from the chaotic nature of the real world. Despite the pressures to win, playing offers a certain kind of serenity, for you know exactly what you are dealing with and can choose to withdraw at any time from the game. There is also a contrary desire to transfer these feelings of control over to the real world, a dynamic operative in games from 'fort/da' to *Doom*. Yet this contradiction also occurs in films and novels. The ratio between desires may differ, but it oscillates within all narrative forms.

GAME RULES VERSUS OPEN NARRATIVE

Despite their subjection to the laws of causality, most narratives create the illusion that any-thing can happen, whereas most games present a closed world with a clearly defined set of rules. According to Murray, 'games are goal directed and structured around turn taking and keeping score. All of this would seem to have nothing to do with stories'.[18] Manovich argues exactly the opposite, claiming that not only are computer games 'experienced by their players as narratives', but also that it is precisely the 'well-defined task' assigned to the player ('winning the match, . . . or attaining the highest score') . . . 'that makes the player experience the game as a narrative'.[19] Manovich continues:

> Often the narrative shell of a game ('You are the specially trained commando who has just landed on a lunar base; your task is to make your way to the headquarters') masks a simple algorithm well-familiar to the player – kill all the enemies on the current level, while collecting all the treasures it contains.[20]

From this perspective, the narrative premise is always the illusion, whereas the underlying algorithm, whether literal as in games or figurative in films and novels, is the deep structure that controls the user's reception. This cyber-structuralist assumption fails to acknowledge the great array of differences in class, gender, sexuality, ethnicity and generation among players or in the specific historical and cultural contexts in which these games are being played.

As a special form of narrative with explicit goals and a clear-cut set of rules, games pro-vide an excellent opportunity to negotiate the relationship between social conventions and the degree of leeway allowed for variations in performance. This negotiation is precisely what is at stake in three recent popular game movies when a young gifted player performs innovative moves that alter the algorithms of the game and thereby challenges the oppress-ive social structure it upholds: whether it is finding a new rhythm to save a loved one in *Run Lola Run*; or taking a suicidal leap of faith in *Crouching Tiger, Hidden Dragon*; or combining these tactical moves with an Althusserian deconstruction of realism to become the assertive messiah who brings down *The Matrix*.

Although such abilities could be seen as fantasies restricted to films, even in those sports whose narrative dimension is minimal, we frequently find similar stories refocused around players – their hardships, team play and rivalries are a dimension now central in the tele-vision coverage of the Olympic games. We have seen the rules of the game change in response to shifting cultural and historical circumstances, such as the entry of African American and female players such as Jackie Robinson, Muhammad Ali, Tiger Woods and the Williams' sisters into the sports of baseball, boxing, golf and tennis; the use of new materials to make golf clubs, baseball bats and footballs; and the ingestion of new drugs and hormones to enhance performance and erase boundaries between genders. There is always an interaction between individual performances and their material contexts, relations that leave us wondering who are the best players of all time. In the world of electronic games, this ongoing enhancement is mobilised to sell new playback systems, processors and patches that keep accelerating performance goals for both games and players.

In films and novels where goals and outcomes are ambiguous, we still find rules of causality and generic conventions, which guide authors in writing stories, readers in interpreting their meanings and distributors in marketing them to consumers. While some narratives follow these conventions very closely, others blatantly violate the codes, encouraging readers to take a more active role in reading or, in Barthes's terms, to perform a 'writerly' reading of the text. Openness lies at the centre of the narrative illusion; it can be read aesthetically as merely another stylistic choice or ideologically as a means of empowering readers to make meaningful interventions in the fiction and the outside world it represents. That presupposes readers acquire some kind of knowledge from the text, even if they interpret or apply it in different ways.

In online role-playing games, procedural narratives seem designed to expand the range of possible customisations of such textual knowledge. According to Murray, they offer 'the highest form of narrative agency the medium allows'.[21] Dismissing this ideological potential as an illusion, Manovich sees this genre as simply more evidence for his general principle of transcoding ('the projection of the ontology of a computer onto culture itself') and for his cyber-structuralist assumption that 'an algorithm is the key to the game experience'.[22] After quoting Will Wright, the 'legendary author' of *The Sims* games, Manovich concludes:

> The world is reduced to two kinds of software objects that are complementary to each other – data structures and algorithms. Any process or task is reduced to an algorithm, a final sequence of simple operations that a computer can execute to accomplish a given task. And any object in the world – be it the population of a city, or the weather over the course of a century, or a chair, or a human brain – is modeled as a data structure, that is, data organized in a particular way for efficient search and retrieval.[23]

Reminding us that a database 'is anything but a simple collection of items',[24] Manovich sets narrative and data structures in dialectic opposition: as 'two competing imaginations, two basic creative impulses, two essential responses to the world' with modern media as 'the new battlefield for the competition between database and narrative.'[25] Whereas he was willing to use the term 'algorithm' metaphorically when referring to the reader's search for the writer's logic, he refuses to deviate from a strict operational definition of database. In pursuing media specificity, he resists the notion of database narrative.

Conversely, I see database and narrative as two compatible structures that always function together. All narratives are constructed by selecting items from databases and combining them to create a particular story, while each retrieval of information from a database has a narrative dimension, but only in the broad cognitive definition of narrative rather than the narrower neo-formalist definition that Manovich appropriates from Bal and Bordwell. This compatibility enables one to perceive closer similarities between narratives and games, which both have underlying database structures that frequently remain hidden.

I use the term 'database narrative' to refer to those narratives, whether in novels, films or games, whose structure exposes the dual processes of selection and combination that lie at the heart of all stories and that are crucial to language: the selection of particular characters, images, sounds, events from a series of paradigms, which are then combined to generate specific tales. Raising meta-narrative issues, such structures reveal the arbitrariness of the particular choices made and the possibility of making other combinations, which would create alternative stories.

Although Manovich grants that a 'poetics' of database structure will someday be realised in cyberspace, he finds its cinematic precursors to be rare. Only two auteurs qualify, Dziga Vertov and Peter Greenaway, who conveniently represent modernism and postmodernism, respectively.[26] In contrast, I find database narrative throughout the entire history of cinema, from the early cinema of attractions, through modernist film-makers such as Buñuel, Leger, Eisenstein and Vertov, to narrative experimentation in the post-structuralist period of the 1960s and 1970s, to recent hybridisations of movies and games, yet inflected differently in each period.

My definition of 'database narrative' is consistent with Buñuel's own 'synoptic table of the American cinema', a bizarre document he allegedly constructed when he was in Hollywood trying to 'learn some good American technical skills.'

> There were several movable columns set up on a large piece of pasteboard: the first for 'ambience' (Parisian, western, gangster, etc.), the second for 'epochs', the third for 'main characters', and so on. Altogether there were four or five categories, each with a tab for easy maneuverability. What I wanted to do was show that the American cinema was composed along such precise and standardized lines that, thanks to my system, anyone could predict the basic plot of a film simply by lining up a given setting with a particular era, ambience, and character.[27]

Buñuel's exposure of the database structure within Hollywood narratives was performed as a subversive act. However, for Manovich, the database remains tied to the computer, whose encapsulation of the world justifies a return to structuralism, a discursive move that makes it more difficult to read the ideological implications of narrative in general and games in particular.

CINEMATIC CASE STUDY

Finally we turn to the context of Paris in the 1960s and 1970s, when the experimental fusion of games and films was in direct dialogue not only with radical changes in narrative theory through the movement from structuralism to post-structuralism, but also with the political events of May 1968, which helped to politicise film and narrative studies worldwide. The interest in games was partially motivated by the emergence of narratology and its attempts to define the deep structure of narrative as a closed system, whose complete formal possibilities could be charted, and by the subsequent mobilisation of this theory in the political sphere where it helped to challenge dominant master narratives and their ideological assumptions and where in the process it, like the *nouvelle vague* itself, was transformed. Although these theoretical and political currents were also in dialogue with narrative experimentation in the novel, cinema was considered a privileged arena for this struggle, partly because the firing of Henri Langlois as director of the Cinémathèque Française helped to spark the uprisings against de Gaulle's government and also because the mass medium of cinema in general and the transparent realism of the prevailing Hollywood aesthetic were perceived as powerful transmitters of a political hegemony that was culturally colonising the world. Thus, an effective alternative cinema had to de-naturalise realistic illusions and expose the ideological functions of their pleasures. While these historical dynamics are well known, what has been overlooked is the role that games played in the mix.

I have selected five films made in this context which show how the line of narrative experimentation with games became increasingly politicised. Yet all of these works contain strategies that could be useful for the hybridisation of games and films, for all of them have a game embedded in the centre, which functions as one of three narrative modes through which a story is being told.

1. *The documentation of an open yet specific narrative field*, where characters and spectators wait for the 'real story' to emerge. Relying on the recording function of cinema, this mode privileges the iterative, the representation of what usually happens repeatedly in this space and its connection with the outside social 'reality'.[28]

2. *A game*, which functions as a microcosm for narrative contrivance and its algorithms. The choice of game helps define what is at stake and thereby offers a reading of the overall narrative system.

3. *The singulative fictional narrative*, which tracks a spatial journey within a limited stretch of time, focusing on individuated characters, their chance meetings and changing relationships.

By combining the three modes, the film prevents us from seeing any of them as the truth. What emerges instead is a formidable narrative machine whose ideological operations are exposed.

The simplest example is Agnes Varda's *Cleo from 5 to 7* (1961), which uses tarot cards, a serious game of prophecy, to set up the contrived plot of a seemingly frivolous pop star faced with the melodramatic prospect of cancer. The algorithm is extended into the narrative by means of the temporal limits imposed on her playtime by the film's title ('from 5 to 7') and by the segmentation of the narrative into titled episodes that name each person she encounters and record the elapsing of time. Although Cleo at first seems as stereotypical as the avatars in the tarot deck, once she moves into the open narrative field of the city, filmed with the kind of 'city symphony' documentary style with which Varda began her career, the avatar becomes humanised and the temporal countdown a reminder that we are documenting her movements in 'real time'. In this space she meets a young soldier on leave from Algeria who is also facing death, a chance encounter that locates her in history and redirects the 'woman's film' towards an open ending that the driving endgames of tarot, cancer and melodrama did not lead us to predict.

The game is more pivotal to the experimental structure of *Last Year at Marienbad* (1961), which was called 'a documentary about statues' by its collaborators, film-maker Alain Resnais and novelist Alain Robbe-Grillet. It opens with the protagonist wandering through the winding corridors of a baroque hotel describing its lavish decor in repetitive detail, as if archiving these items for a database. The hotel serves as a labyrinthine narrative field in which both characters and spectators become lost in a mélange of interpretations and reflective echoes of their own situation. Despite the rigid formalism of the setting, the repetition compulsions of the protagonist and the clichés of the romantic triangle (including a princess who must be rescued), the narrative resists closure. Everything in the film – even time, space and causality – remains totally open to interpretation, waiting to be replayed.

Yet the game at its centre provides a contrary reading that exposes the driving power of the narrative engine. Early in the film, the antagonist introduces the game of Nin, carefully arranging playing cards and other objects in parallel rows and explaining the rules to his opponent and on-screen spectators: whenever it is a player's turn, he can remove as many objects from a single row that he pleases, but the player left with the last piece is the loser. Despite this explanation, the algorithms for Nin and the narrative remain mysterious because no matter how many times the game is played, the antagonist (who claims he can lose) in fact always wins. Is he cheating or merely lucky? Is there some underlying principle that only he has mastered? Or is this winning streak a contrivance of the narrative in which the game is embedded? We never find out. Not only is this game an analogue for the two men's competition for the woman, but also its patterned rows are repeatedly reflected in the *mise en scène*: in the artworks displayed in the hotel's corridors, in the checkered rows of dark and illuminated windows, and in the multiple photographs and mirror reflections of the woman displayed in her bedroom. The database structure of the game controls our reading of the outcome: despite the openness of the labyrinthine narrative and the erotic obsessions of the protagonist, we conclude he is the loser, for he is the one left with the woman.

The political implications of the game are more apparent in Chris Marker's celebrated short film *La Jetée* (1962), which made it more powerful than its high-tech 1990s remake, *Twelve Monkeys*. The film demonstrates how a narrativising voice-over can transform what looks like a simple database of documentary stills into a compelling sci-fi story, a popular genre that ordinarily relies on expensive special effects to dramatise humanity's powers of survival. However, in Marker's low-tech, low-budget approach to the genre, it is conceptual power (the use of narrative to recontextualise the meaning of visual and audio perceptions) that can reanimate the dead and save the world. The narrative is driven by two opposing forces: the nonlinear narrative field of one man's memories (an open database of documentary images) versus the militaristic mind games of experimental scientists who impose procedural algorithms on this subject in order to mobilise his mental wanderings as a linear mode of time travel, first backwards to find resources from the past, then forwards to build a brave new world. The key to winning this game is finding the crucial image, which can simultaneously be read both as a flashback and flash forward and thereby function as a warp zone to provide entry into another historical era or level of experience. Once they find it in the protagonist's vision of death, they transform his primal scene into a search engine that can access whatever they need. Although these ingenious mind games are supposedly designed to save mankind, in the larger narrative scheme they function as a ruthless form of murderous oppression. By keeping our attention focused on the individual subject and his love for a particular woman whom he encounters in the narrative field, Marker enables us to distinguish the scientists' relentless narrative drive from the over-arching omniscient voice-over, which deconstructs the ideological dangers of the game. Still, the rivalry between these two modes of contextualisation exposes the vulnerability of all discrete images and signs, which, like the haunting vision of death that frames the film, can always be redefined by any narrative machine.

The transformative power of games is explored much more fully within the endless narrative shuffle of Jacques Rivette's films, whose long running times (usually over three hours) and repetitive structures enable him and his collaborators to suggest the full range of possibilities for any given character or narrative premise and thereby demonstrate the endless playability of cinema. With their long, slow stretches and serial improvisations, his films may have the most to offer online role-playing games. His most brilliant use of games occurs in *Celine and Julie Go Boating* (1974), where tarot readings and magical incantations launch the collaborative interplay of two women, a magician and librarian. Like two little girls playing house, together they create a house of fiction where they collaborate on saving a princess, with whom they both identify. This young girl in peril is being held captive in an alternative melodramatic narrative, based on a story by Henry James, which, first through spectatorship, then interactive interventions, these two women customise with their own childhood memories, inventive fantasies and improvisations. Within this fiction, they take turns playing one of the minor characters (Miss Terry Angel) and participate in familiar games (frozen statues and which hand has the bonbon?). The Games seem to delight, but actually are designed to eliminate the young girl so that the stereotypical female avatars can get down to their one-to-one mortal combat over her father and his fortune, a game at the heart of many women's melodramas.

Despite the satisfactions of the happy ending, *Celine and Julie* ends with the same image with which it began: a woman sitting alone on a park bench in an open narrative field reading a book of magic. At first nothing happens; the camera merely documents the casual games within its field of vision – children playing ball, a cat stalking a bird. Eventually, after a ritual incantation performed by the reader, a young woman passes by and drops an object, a combination that creates the illusion of causality and sets their collaborative narrative in motion. At the end of the film, the same scene is repeated, but with the women's positions reversed, as we are told, 'This time it began like this.' This line extends the film's playability by demonstrating how repetition can open any closed narrative.

Buñuel's films made in Paris during this period are equally provocative in their metanarrative use of games, a subject I have elaborated on elsewhere.[29] In his penultimate film,

The Phantom of Liberty (1974), a country inn (the traditional stopping place in picaresque fiction) provides two analogues that expose the database structure of all narratives, including this radical film. A central hallway connects several rooms, which contain mini-stories and characters competing for this central narrative space. In one room, a game of poker is being played by a woman and four Dominicans, who repeatedly shuffle the cards into new syntagmatic combinations while betting medals, Virgins and Sacred Hearts, which, like their own religious order, become paradigmatic suits. Despite the film's rigorous linear structure, no singular story emerges and events prove as unpredictable as the random shuffling of cards.

With the exception of Buñuel (who died in 1983) and Rivette (whose exploration of games never ceased), these new wave film-makers recently returned to their experiments with database game films, now filtered through the tropes of new media. Chris Marker's *Immemory* (1999), a CD-ROM comprised of stills organised into interwoven databases, and his feature film *Level 5* (1999), the protagonist of which is designing an electronic game about the Battle of Okinawa, exploring the complicity of representational practices in many kinds of warfare, both return to concerns he addressed in pre-digital database films such as *La Jetée* and *Sans soleil*. Resnais's pair of multi-branching films *Smoking/No Smoking* (1993), based on the eight plays in Alan Ayckborn's *Intimate Exchanges* (1982), play out the full range of narrative possibilities in the relationships among a limited number of characters (played by only two actors). Though at first they seem narrow, they keep growing in unpredictable ways despite their restrictive settings, a premise similar to the one he explored in *Marienbad*. Agnes Varda's *Gleaners and I* (2000), a documentary with a database structure, uses a digital video camera to 'glean' a fascinating collection of rural and urban scavengers living off the surplus waste of a consumerist culture; in the process she proves the most accomplished gleaner of all, especially as she turns the camera on her own ageing hands advancing towards death and recycles techniques and issues that have preoccupied her from *La Pointe courte* (1954) to *Vagabond* (1985). Varda demonstrates all filming is a form of collecting and all gleaning (whether historic or contemporary, material or conceptual, economic or artistic, autobiographical or communal) is an essential part of constructing the database narratives crucial to historical memory.

All of these films, those vintage works from the 1960s and 1970s as well as the recent ones they have helped spawn, infuse the interplay between games and movies, database structures and stories, with a conceptual power that fully engages the aesthetic, cognitive and ideological functions of narrative in the broadest sense of the term. That is why they offer such a valuable legacy for those interested in conceptualising the future equivocal relations between films and games.

Notes

1. Raymond Williams, *Television: Technology and Cultural Form* (New York: Schocken Books, 1975).
2. Lev Manovich, *The Language of New Media* (Cambridge, MA: MIT Press, 2001).
3. Teresa de Lauretis, 'Desire in Narrative', *Alice Doesn't: Feminism, Semiotics, Cinema* (Bloomington: Indiana University Press, 1984), p. 105.

4. Edward Branigan, *Narrative Comprehension and Film* (London: Routledge, 1992), p. 36; Hayden White, 'The Value of Narrativity in the Representation of Reality', *The Content of the Form: Narrative Discourse and Historical Representation* (Baltimore, MD: The Johns Hopkins University Press, 1987).

5. Lev Manovich, *The Language of New Media*, p. 228.

6. Ibid. See also Mieke Bal, *Narratology: Introduction to the Theory of Narrative* (Toronto: University of Toronto Press, 1985), p. 8.

7. Allucquère Rosanne Stone, *The War of Desire and Technology at the Close of the Mechanical Age* (Cambridge, MA: MIT Press, 1995). See pp. 10–11 for her discussion of Andy Lippman's definition of interactivity.

8. Janet H. Murray, *Hamlet on the Holodeck: The Future of Narrative in Cyberspace* (New York: The Free Press, 1997), p. 128.

9. Lev Manovich, *The Language of New Media*, pp. 55–61.

10. See Erkki Huhtamo, 'From Cybernation to Interaction: A Contribution to an Archaeology of Interactivity', in Peter Lunenfeld (ed.), *The Digital Dialectic* (Cambridge, MA: MIT Press, 1999), pp. 96–110.

11. Janet H. Murray, *Hamlet on the Holodeck*, p. 140.

12. Lev Manovich, *The Language of New Media*, p. 225.

13. Ibid., p. 223.

14. Ibid., pp. 208–9.

15. Ibid., p. 210.

16. Ibid., pp. 210–11.

17. Janet H. Murray, *Hamlet on the Holodeck*, p. 144.

18. Ibid., p. 140.

19. Lev Manovich, *The Language of New Media*, p. 221.

20. Ibid., pp. 221–2.

21. Janet H. Murray, *Hamlet on the Holodeck*, p. 148.

22. Lev Manovich, *The Language of New Media*, p. 222–3.

23. Ibid., p. 223.

24. Ibid., p. 219.

25. Ibid., p. 233.

26. Ibid., p. 239.

27. Luis Buñuel, *My Last Sigh*, trans. Abigail Israel (New York: Vintage Books, 1984), p. 132.

28. For a discussion of the iterative in cinema, see Marsha Kinder, 'The Subversive Potential of the Pseudo Iterative', *Film Quarterly*, vol. 43 no. 2, Winter 1989/90, pp. 2–16.

29. Marsha Kinder, 'Hot Spots, Avatars and Narrative Fields Forever: Buñuel's Legacy for New Digital Media & Interactive Database Narrative', *Film Quarterly* (forthcoming).

3.3

Online Comics and the Reframing of the Moving Image

Scott Bukatman

Throughout cinema's history, the expectation that things will move, or at least could move, has been balanced by the surprise generated by the kinds of movement displayed. The issue is not only that things move, but also how that movement continues to generate wonder or engagement. The kinesthetic impact of moving objects, supplemented by camera trajectory and the manipulations of special effects, still attracts the spectator and continues to serve as a nearly irresistible form of address. The cinematic moving image interpellates and embodies the viewer, providing a space to occupy and the means to occupy it. In this key moment of transition from mechanico-chemical to digital modes of moving image production, the conditions and functions of the moving image remain a powerful force. The nascent medium of online comics has already generated significant debate around its appropriation of movement, sound and other elements of electronic culture's multimedia synthesis, and this debate, historically situated, can help us understand the place of the moving image within the expanded arena of new media.

Comics have long possessed a sophisticated vocabulary for expressing movement and the passage of time in ways that converge with, and diverge from, the time-based forms of cinema and new media. As with film and television, and other conduits of vulgar modernism in their turn, comics have been slow to gain recognition as a legitimate object of study. David Kunzle, for example, begins his elegant, two-volume history of the medium with an elaborate apologia fortunately counterbalanced by a gentle indictment of academic short-sightedness. But academic interest is indeed on the rise and with good reason. Cheap to produce and distribute, energetic and easy to understand, illegitimacy clinging to them like a cheap suit, comics pervade the history of the twentieth century. For me, there are few media that present, so sustainedly and forcefully, the dialectic between movement and stasis. This chapter will concentrate on some of these temporal properties of comics, highlighting two specific moments in which the comic's image was invested with motion: one within the history of early cinema, the other in what we may presume to be early in the history of digital culture.

The comic strip (or pictorial narrative, *bande dessinée*, or other preferred term) has existed as a printed form throughout Europe and Asia since the fifteenth century. It developed into a medium for the representation of continuous movement in the nineteenth century with the introduction of the looser, more exaggerated line associated with carica- ture. David Kunzle notes that the Hogarthian model of large, complete, 'richly accoutred' compositions yielded to a new model. A flowing, more improvisational line, the sense of an illustration as incomplete unless viewed as part of a sequence, an increasing emphasis on what Scott McCloud categorises as moment-to-moment rather than scene-to-scene or action-to-action transitions between illustrations – all contributed to the increasing associ- ation of comics and movement (the work of Rodolphe Töpffer is seminal in this regard).[1]

What Kunzle describes is actually the advent of 'rhythm' in the presentation of a picto- rial narrative, and this tendency towards greater fragmentation and interruption of actions is indeed recapitulated in the history of filmic cutting.[2] Of course, later comics would marshal overlapping action, oscillating or blurred outlines, motion lines, and other effects to convey a sense of movement within a single panel and would also expand the repertoire of panel- to-panel transitions to convey more complex temporalities.

What comics uniquely present is a combination of static images, often infiltrated by visual cues of captured or continuing movement, arranged in temporal sequence. McCloud has emphasised the importance of the 'gutter', the space between the panels, as a defining condition of the medium. McCloud adds that, 'Comic panels fracture both time and space, offering a jagged, staccato rhythm of unconnected moments.' The gutter demands that the reader must simultaneously grasp the continuities and discontinuities that connect panel A and panel B, just as cinematic viewers do when confronted by a cut between two shots. We mentally construct 'a continuous, unified reality'. In comics, though, A and B both remain visible: the reader can move back and forth. 'In contrast to film, a comic page poses the dimension of time on a visible linear continuum. Even after the reader has proceeded from picture to picture, the panels continue to relate to one another on the page.'[3] Time is represented as territory in space, and the experience of the flow of time can be very care- fully regulated. This dialectic between the stasis of an individual image and the spatio- temporal movement of the sequence – a dialectic that exists diegetically, but also in the experience of the reader – is what he calls 'the temporal map', and it is a conceptual fun- dament of the medium.[4]

Although it is easy to exaggerate the connections between film and comics, they clearly share some concerns partly determined by the historical ground against which they devel- oped. John Fell has written that 'a number of . . . relationships emerge between film and the comics if we broaden our perspective to view the strip artist and the filmmaker as confronting common problems of space and time within the conventions of narrative expo- sition'.[5] Donald Crafton has debunked the easy assumptions Fell and others have made about the overlapping developments of film and newspaper comics. There is, first of all, an historical fallacy at work. David Kunzle has established the long history of the comic strip, which was a thriving form from the seventeenth century forward. Even the modern comic strip predated the emergence of cinema by about a decade. Furthermore, film did not borrow many devices, other than gag structures, from the comics.[6] In fact, early borrowings from the conventions of comics, such as the use of speech balloons in place of intertitles, led precisely nowhere.

But Crafton's revisionist nuancing of history should not blind us to relevant correlations. Crafton may underestimate the historical connection between two media, both of which inherited something from the magic lantern and the phenakistoscope, and the experiments of Marey.[7] Similarities exist less in shared techniques as in their 'confronting common problems of space and time within the conventions of narrative exposition'. The broad shifts in spatio-temporal experience associated with the culture of modernity were coded in both the fine arts and popular media as an experience of accelerated and permanent movement.

Comics were well suited to respond to the mechanical rhythms of industrialism. In comics of the late nineteenth century, 'The body is experienced as machinoid or a machinable substance, and both fear and fascination reside in the artist's rendering of the body as machined almost beyond recognition.'[8] The body in comics was thus figured in terms of shock:

> In its more industrially conscious phase, the comic strip imagines the human body violently flattened, stretched, twisted, kinked or wrapped around a spinning drum. When whole social substances, or institutional structures, were being deformed and torn apart by capitalism in its most dynamic phase, it was logical to depict the constituent unit of those structures, the individual human body, as literally deformed by (or as if by) the real-life agency of that reshaping: the machine.[9]

If comics represented the body as reconfigured and recognised within the parameters of technological shock, cinema was the apparatus that embodied that shock in the critical imagination. For Maxim Gorky, writing in 1896, the cinematograph presented movement stripped of life, it was a kingdom of shadows. Screenings of the Lumière brothers' earliest films began with the projection of the initial frame as a still image. 'You anticipate nothing new in this all too familiar scene,' Gorky reported, 'for you have seen pictures of Paris streets more than once. But suddenly a strange flicker passes through the screen and the picture stirs to life.'[10] The still frame lulls the viewer, while movement assumes its powerful immediacy against the ground of that stillness. Kinesis, under the right conditions, produces a shock. Dziga Vertov, that magician-*cum*-epistemologist,[11] produced film sequences that resound with the rediscovery of such kinesthetic astonishment.

A great cinematic sleight-of-hand occurs in the 1911 film presentation of Winsor McCay's *Little Nemo*. McCay had unveiled Slumberland and its denizens in the colour comics section of the *New York Herald* some years earlier. McCay's comic strips were meticulously realised, the very completeness of each image rendering them resistant to movement and change even as his elaborate graphic matches and magic lantern-like dissolves imbue his comic strip world with elaborate, endless metamorphosis. He had also become a popular entertainer on the vaudeville stage, producing lightning sketches for the crowd (until Hearst made him stop).

In the film, McCay has bet his colleagues that he can bring his characters to life; he can make them move. The audience, the one in the film and that of the film, gets a glimpse of the laborious process of creating a sequence of animated drawings. With his buddies assembled, the projectionist gets cranking, and the demonstration begins. McCay's hand produces a drawing of Flip labelled 'WATCH ME MOVE' that is inserted into a slotted frame. The camera tracks in on the illustration, which abruptly takes on colour and movement as Flip smoothly turns and blows a voluptuous cloud of smoke in our direction.

While the audience has been painstakingly prepared for this movement by the narrative, the repeated sequences of drawing, and the dramatically mobile camera, the eruption into colourful animation could not be more surprising or satisfying, thanks to what we must understand as a masterful act of misdirection. The drawings displayed in the film had been either full-frontal figures or facial profiles: flat and undynamically conventional. When the animation commences, it immediately evokes the third dimension. The animated world takes on a depth that the single images actively denied.

The comic strip was reinvigorated as a mass medium in the American newspaper culture of the late nineteenth century. Early Sunday comics were elaborate showcases for new, inexpensive printing technologies that allowed for subtle, dynamic coloration. In their deployment of colour and fantasy, they provided a deliberate departure from the rest of the paper (and were thus as driven by technology as any new media). The first masters of the form, luxuriating in the space of a full page, resisted or played with the grid that structured most of the paper. In this sense, McCay's images in the *Little Nemo* film are impoverished, with none of the dazzling architectures of the page or the phenomenal detail of his backgrounds.

The passage into animation recapitulates the shift from still to moving image that marked those screenings by the Lumières, but what surprises the spectator of *Little Nemo* is the *re*-cognition of the moving image at a time when narrative had increasingly incorporated spectacle within its natural structures. Noël Carroll has written of the horizon of epistemic expectation that the spectator brings to bear upon different sorts of images. It would be irrational to expect a photograph suddenly to move, he points out: 'one commits a category error if one expects movement', and, concomitantly, we understand that 'movement is a permanent possibility in the cinema'.[12] But of course the wonderment experienced by early audiences of the cinema is partly the wonder of expectations overturned, Gorky's grey images of Paris yielding to a new kind of real-time experience of movement. At a time when Winsor McCay was best known as the artist behind the detailed, precise, static images of Slumberland or a vaudevillian master of the lightning sketch, the apparently autonomous movement of Flip, Inky, Nemo, the Princess and Doctor Pill results in the delight of a categorical redefinition.

Now consider the World Wide Web. When I visit a Web site, it is not clear exactly what kind of text/image/motion nexus I will be encountering. There might be plain text, text augmented with simple graphics, an elaborate graphic design or, assuming I have the right plug-ins, some kind of image manipulation up to and including full motion. The user must hold expectations in abeyance until the page has fully loaded. Of course, users are demonstrably drawn to sites with advanced graphics and movement, and, increasingly, these might be the only kinds of sites encountered, or at least browsed. But there is no question that we occupy a transitional moment where variant experiences become possible because a single system, the Web, channels information using an array of different media forms. Is movement a 'permanent possibility' on the Internet? Do categorical boundaries remain? Who has not spent time fruitlessly pointing-and-clicking their way across an image, searching for the links, the 'hot spots' that will activate movement or change?

All of this raises questions pertinent to Carroll's discussion of 'epistemic states' and audience expectation. The moving, apparently photographically based image, once the province of the cinema and later shared with television, is now encountered on a more continual basis in everyday life. There also exists an increasing uncertainty regarding the status of any given image: does it move and how does it move? This is true not only for images on the Internet, but also for digital manipulations in cinematic images, through which new species of movement flourish. In *Terminal Identity*, I argued that, by undermining the fixed ontology of the photographic image, science-fiction film staged and narrated an ontological crisis for the human subject.[13] In the succeeding decade, however, digital manipulation has become ever more mundane, and what I am arguing here is somewhat more modest: the uncertainty of the status of the image in the cinema and on the Internet produces something more like an epistemological hesitation.

McCay's forays into animation represent an early example of the melding of comics and cinematic motion. The developing technologies of digital media have created another site of intersection, the nascent medium of online comics. McCloud's *Reinventing Comics*, the follow-up to his brilliant *Understanding Comics*, drew sustained fire from the comics community, not only for its vision of economic egalitarianism in cyberspace, but also for its proclamations regarding the creative possibilities offered by the online environment. The attacks centred less on McCloud's specific propositions as on the medium in general, with some of the greatest skepticism and opprobrium reserved for the incorporation of moving images into comics-style narrations. This debate regarding the proper 'place' of movement was waged largely in the pages of *The Comics Journal* and its online bulletin board, but the dispute received broader coverage when *salon.com* picked up the story.[14]

Gary Groth, publisher of Fantagraphics Books, and Art Spiegelman, creator of *Maus*, defended comics as a print-based medium whose impact would be diluted by any tendency towards animation. For students of media history, the terms of debate are achingly overfamiliar. Groth laments the 'inconsequential distraction' of Net culture: 'the Net is all about short attention spans'. As creators and publishers, Groth and Spiegelman both have a vested interest in the future of long-form comics, and, indeed, the turn of the millennium was a remarkable time for the genre, with lavish, hardcover publications by Chris Ware, Daniel Clowes, Joe Sacco, Art Spiegelman, François Mouly and others. Ironically, however, given the still-prevalent perception of comics as an immature medium for immature minds, figures such as Groth remain determined to defend the terrain of serious comics against the medium's more distracting and kinetic incarnations as either superhero narratives or online comics. Movement is, once again, the barbarian at the gate, seducing through the distractions of 'multimedia' while destroying the possibility of sustained attention and engagement represented by 'pure' comics.[15]

Reinventing Comics was hardly unforgiving in its review of online comics' tentative investigations into the possibilities of digital media. Gag-a-day strips or continuing adventure series use a screen-sized page-by-page or panel-by-panel layout, cleaving to pre-existing models of print (the page) or film and television (full-frame images in successive temporal sequence).[16] Other online comics are hypertexts, using links to generate separate and intertwining narrative branches.

Online comics produced by larger multimedia companies such as Dark Horse, Marvel or the short-lived Stan Lee Media tried to generate plenty of 'synergy' and 'buzz' by incorporating 'the interactive bag of tricks associated with multimedia gaming and "infotainment"', moving steadily towards the state of full animation. The result was a slow-loading 'new media' form that, with its static, laterally sliding figures and static backgrounds, resembled film less than it did a particularly crude magic lantern show. 'Whatever their relative quality,' McCloud writes, such 'additive approaches sidestepped the question of comics' own evolution by letting comics become an undigested lump in multimedia's stomach [,] without ever expanding on the ideas at comics' core'.[17] The bells and whistles of Flash animations, for instance, fail to contend with the specific implications of sequential, pictorial forms that define comics *conceptual* terrain.

The animated image in online comics does not feel like its cinematic counterpart. In the animated *Little Nemo*, it is movement that gives the characters 'a life of their own', separate from the hand of the artist McCay. The immediacy of kinesis supersedes the process of its own creation. In the cinema, the moving image is situated as an immersive perception that, phenomenologically, belongs to *me* (or, as Sobchack argues, a perception that belongs simultaneously to me, to the film-maker and to the film itself).[18] The darkened theatre, the screen as focal point, the proprioceptive cues (including cues of movement) – all contribute to the cinematic image's unique power to incorporate me (and vice versa). The spectator is embodied and, further, projected as a site of consciousness in dynamic relation to a mobile world. The effect of animation within online comics is altogether different. The movement is not 'mine'; it belongs not to me, not to the diegesis, but only to the work. Movement is more limited; the aesthetically primitive looping of Flash animations tend towards lateral movements rather than mobility in depth, and so animation here tends to close off the third dimension, in radical distinction to McCay's invocation of volume, presence and character through the movement of Flip. The limitations of quick-loading online animation tools produces a machinic rotation and repetition, but with none of the frenzy or fluidity that defined both comics and film in the early twentieth century.

For McCloud, however, successful online comics can *fulfil*, rather than *redefine*, the potential of comics, but not through recourse to full animation. After all, he acknowledges, 'when it comes to time-based immersion, the art of film already does a better job than any tricked-up comic can'.[19] The trick for online comics is to 'preserve comics' silent, static nature while exploiting other capabilities of digital media'.[20] He finds an alternative aesthetic in certain pictorially based narratives that existed before the advent of print culture. Citing the precedents of walls of hieroglyphs, the Bayeux Tapestry, Trajan's Column and the Codex Nutall, he notes that each produced an 'unbroken reading line' that exists in contradistinction to the later experience of reading that followed from print culture's segmentation of information onto separate pages. This represented a particularly strong example of temporal mapping, as a single line, straight, winding or zigzag, represented a linear passage of time in both the diegesis and the reader's experience.[21]

McCloud argues that the advent of multiple windows and scroll bars again opens the possibility of experiencing a pictorial narrative in an extended, continuous space: the 'infinite canvas of comics'. By reconceiving the screen as a window rather than as a page, larger – literally *longer* – arrangements of continuous images can be viewed. 'There may never be a monitor as wide as Europe, yet a comic as wide as Europe . . . can be displayed on any monitor, simply by moving across its surface, *inch-by-inch, foot-by-foot, mile-by-mile!*' he crows, seemingly possessed by the force of his own hyperbole.[22]

Online comics, then, offer the potential and the opportunity to restore protocols of reading less accessible since the onset of the dominance of the book. McCloud himself opened up some of this potential through the online version of his superhero comic *Zot!*.[23] Each chapter of the futuristic saga appears within a single browser window with individual panels linked by lines ('trails'), both of which flow vertically through the space on-screen, at the user's own pace. This configuration, one of many that he suggests, has the advantage of replicating the most familiar online reading strategies of linking and scrolling. In the clearest example of McCloud's continuous reading space, the third episode illustrates Zot's plummet from sky to earth in a single 'panel' six feet high (see plage 05).

There has been some justifiable criticism of McCloud's attempt to define and delimit the medium, although he avoids the most obvious trappings of medium-essentialism, and his discussion of reading protocols could use some scholarly nuance. Trajan's Column might read as he suggests (in the abstract, as no actual body could read it continuously), but the Bayeux Tapestry, as Suzanne Lewis has demonstrated, depends upon a more elaborate set of reading protocols to produce a more multivalent description of time.[24] The forward movement of the main narrative of the Norman Conquest is interrupted, not least by a series of drawings in the upper and lower borders comprising animal figures in retellings of some of Aesop's fables (not unlike the tiny tier of comics beneath George Herriman's *The Family Upstairs* that introduced Krazy Kat and Ignatz). 'The irregular diagonal lines framing each episode form jagged, disruptive patterns that tend to deflect the viewer's gaze from the continuous progression of the dominant plot line,' Lewis writes, further noting that the small scale of the fable becomes a signifying other to, and commentary upon, the epic scale of the main narrative.[25] (Similarly, Krazy Kat and Ignatz might comment on the action taking place in the strip above them).[26] McCloud's reduction of reading to linear progress stands in sharp contrast to his more nuanced analysis of panel juxtapositions in *Understanding Comics*.

When I Am King by Swiss artist Demian.5 (née Demian Vogler) is a pantomime 'strip' in the tradition of *Henry* (Carl Anderson, 1932) and *The Little King* (Otto Soglow, 1934–75).[27] Savvy in the ways of comics, *When I Am King* also evokes the hieroglyphics that are its narrative source. The saga, which appeared on the Internet in 63 instalments between October 1999 and July 2001, presents a desert king whose quest for a single, simple flower is interrupted when his pants are eaten by some sort of desert animal, who falls in love with him. Subplots involve the quest for new pants, the animal's ardour for the king and a competition between the king's guards around the issue of penis size. Grotesque and innocent, *When I Am King* sustains a happy admixture of elements in its narrative, structure and aesthetics. The strip is framed on screen within a large window, separated into upper and lower frames. The first instalments most often appear as a horizontal strip in the upper frame, referring to the form of the daily comic strip by the way in which the line of reading is broken up by individual panels. Unlike a newspaper strip, however, most episodes do not fit onto the screen, and the reader must scroll laterally to read them in their entirety. Demian.5 sets up a series of reading and aesthetic protocols as well as reader expectations, most of which will be playfully challenged by the saga's end.

At first the panels are uniformly square, although the length of each strip can vary greatly: the first instalment consists of 25 panels, the second of only two, which are symmetrically rectangular rather than square. One week might feature a single panel, referring to another common form of comics, or blossom into a larger dream space reminiscent of the more free-form, sometimes downright hallucinatory Sunday pages by McCay and others in the 1920s and 1930s. Meanwhile, the strip produces a strong continuity across these aesthetic and structural variations through the continuing narrative, the stylised iconography of the drawing, the deliberately limited colour palette. Demian.5 arranges a series of delightfully unexpected effects, readers scrolling to read one week's episode or clicking to begin the next might encounter a sequence of images, a single panel (no. 5), parallel narratives on upper and lower tiers, looping animations (no. 27), CGI modeling (no. 49) or elaborate scrolling designs (no. 45). The strip happily establishes and disrupts visual and narrative rhythms.

When I Am King establishes a ludic zone that restores the pleasure in learning 'what comes next', narratively and aesthetically. The reader might well experience a growing sense of freedom and possibility in (literally) moving through this extended sequence of variations occurring within flexible but never arbitrary strictures. In this it resembles the classic children's book *Harold and the Purple Crayon*.[28] Readers should remember that Crockett Johnson's 1955 work followed Harold through the night as he drew the scenery and spaces that his body would occupy. He draws the moon to see by and the ground beneath his feet, and 'he made a long straight path so he wouldn't get lost'. Much of the act of reading *Harold and the Purple Crayon* involves tracing the line that the crayon makes. Metamorphosis and passage combine. When Harold becomes frightened and his hand shakes, the wavy line his hand produces suddenly become real waves, beneath which Harold quickly sinks (fortunately, the stalwart fellow is a quick thinker and draws himself a boat). The organisation of pictures, one per page, establishes an unvarying movement from left to right, and the right side of the pictures frequently depicts the trailing, unfinished line. The story is nevertheless circular. Harold, searching for his bedroom, draws a window around his room. 'And then Harold made his bed. He got in it and he drew up the covers.' Younger readers may be forgiven for missing the puns as Harold indeed 'makes' his bed and 'draws' the covers.

The movement that the reader makes in following the line within an illustration and from picture to picture is reiterated and extended in *When I Am King*. The horizontal scrolling always moves the reader from left to right, a directional movement reinforced by the actual arrows that indicate a character's trajectory. The king runs from some bees from left to right, with an arrow pointing the way as the reader scrolls. Two panels later, however, the king runs back towards the left; the arrow behind him points left. Through it all, however, the reader continues his or her unidirectional scroll, as trail lines weave and wind down, across and up the screen.

If cinema models and reflects our own activity of perception (the underlying principle of the phenomenon of film), then we might consider that what comics construct is a model of reading. The iconic nature of the pictorial sign, the interplay of pictorial and linguistic signs, the gutter between frames, the organisation of panels in sequence and within the organising unit of the page (what Will Eisner refers to as 'the super-panel') – all point to an elaborate semiotics as well as a phenomenology of reading. Comics often combine simple, iconic characters with more realistic depictions of setting, McCloud observes. 'This combination allows readers to mask themselves in a character and safely enter a sensually stimulating world. One set of lines to *see*. Another set of lines to *be*.'[29] Or, one might also add, one set of lines to *read*, another set *to see oneself reading*. 'There will always be a borderline between comics and animation,' Demian.5 comments, 'There is a difference: in comics, it's the space between images that defines time. And in animation, the time is determined not by the viewer but by the creator.'[30]

Louis Marin reminds us that Michel de Certeau defined all narrative as a space narrative, a travel narrative. Moreover, travel is a dominant mode of the comic strip, according to Kunzle, especially in the late nineteenth century when the subject matter was often 'the process of traveling (or of getting stuck or lost)', for example, *Little Nemo in Slumberland*.[31] Is this merely a sign of the *fin de siècle* times, thick as they were with packaged tours, world expositions and railway journeys, or is there some deeper relation between travel narratives and the metonymic, iconic form of comics? Marin, in considering the nature of *Utopia*, emphasises its condition as narrative. Utopia is defined by its paradoxical state of boundedness and infinitude. While the map may be bounded, static and asynchronous, the narrative of journey or quest, the following of a particular trail, awakens the process of change, temporalises the map, and endows it with the infinite space–time of possibility:

But at the very moment that I look at the map – when I follow with my finger the route of a road, a contour line, when I cross here and not there a frontier, when I jump from one bank of a river to the other – at this moment, a figure is extracted from the map ground, the figure of a projected journey, even if it is an imaginary one, a dreamed one. With that figure a narrative begins, with a before and an after, a point of departure and a point of arrival, a happy coming-back or a final permanent exile. The locus has become space: directions, speeds, travel-timing give motion to the map with the tracings of various routes. With all these temporal processes, these potential action programs, with all these proximities and distances, space 'awakens' to narrative and *loci* are opened up to various practices that change and transform them through variations, transgressions, and so forth.[32]

The lateral, bounded and looping animations that constitute a weakened version of the kind of moving image most familiar to students of film and video study do not *take* us anywhere, but only return us, repeatedly, to an initial state (and stasis). These small, limited movements are a far cry from the real-time immersion of cinema or their close analogue, computer games, and are far less definitive of world or being. Yet the surprising encounters with these movements and variations as we scroll through *When I Am King* give them liveliness, if not life. The movement of the image through scrolling repositions the moving image as a syntagm within a larger signifying structure. Scrolling along one of McCloud's or Demian's 'trails', I am put in motion, I follow the map as it maps me into a particular space and time, and system of signage. 'It is the reader who unfolds the network of possible connections, and it is the reader who then makes a selection from that network,' writes Wolfgang Iser, while McCloud points out: 'Whether by choosing a path, revealing a hidden window, or zooming in on a detail, there are countless ways to interact with sequential art in a digital environment.'[33] Enframed rather than immersive, the moving image becomes a single element within the syntagmatic structure of reading; part of a temporal mapping that reading produces and that comics and online comics model particularly well.

Notes

1. David Kunzle, *The History of the Comic Strip: The Nineteenth Century* (Berkeley: University of California Press, 1990), p. 348; Scott McCloud, *Understanding Comics: The Invisible Art* (Northampton, MA: Tundra Publishing, 1993), p. 74.

2. David Kunzle, *The History of the Comic Strip*, p. 348. Kunzle uses the term 'montage' to describe Töpffer's use of compositional variety in sequence.

3. Scott McCloud, *Understanding Comics*, pp. 67 and 91.

4. Scott McCloud, *Reinventing Comics* (New York: Paradox Press, 2000), pp. 206ff.

5. John L. Fell, *Film and the Narrative Tradition* (Berkeley: University of California Press, 1986), p. 89.

6. Donald Crafton, *Before Mickey: The Animated Film 1898–1928* (Chicago, IL: University of Chicago Press, 1993), p. 225.

7. See David Kunzle, *The History of the Comic Strip*, pp. 349–50.

8. Ibid., p. 357.

9. Ibid., p. 361.

10. Maxim Gorky, 'The Kingdom of Shadows', reprinted in Gilbert Adair (ed.), *Movies* (New York: Penguin Books, 1999), pp. 10–11.

11. I am of course paraphrasing Annette Michelson. See her introduction to *Kino-Eye: The Writings of Dziga Vertov*, Annette Michelson (ed.), trans. Kevin O'Brien (Berkeley: University of California Press, 1984), pp. xv–lxi.

12. Noël Carroll, *Theorising the Moving Image* (Cambridge: Cambridge University Press, 1996), p. 64.

13. Scott Bukatman, *Terminal Identity: The Virtual Subject in Postmodern Science Fiction* (Durham, NC: Duke University Press, 1993).

14. On 9 August 2001 in 'No Laughing Matter', an article by Damien Cave. <www.salon.com/tech/feature/2001/08/09/comics/index.html>.

15. At least Spiegelman, unlike Groth, had the historical awareness to cite McLuhan's dictum that each new medium cannibalises its dominant predecessor.

16. The first run of *Arkon Zark* or *Astounding Space Thrills* is an example of the former approach; *Crazy Boss* is indicative of the latter.

17. Scott McCloud, *Reinventing Comics*, p. 209.

18. See 'Phenomenology and the Film Experience', in Vivian Sobchack, *The Address of the Eye: A Phenomenology of Film Experience* (Princeton, NJ: Princeton University Press, 1992).

19. Scott McCloud, *Reinventing Comics*, p. 210.

20. Ibid., p. 213.

21. Ibid., p. 218.

22. Ibid., p. 222. In a show of responsible journalism and club-footed literal-mindedness, *Comics Journal* publisher Gary Groth has pointed out that 'If you can scroll across a comic at 15 seconds a foot, which is a pretty good clip, it would take 46,200 hours – or 5.27 years [–] to read a comic as wide as Europe.'

23. *Zot! Online* is available online, along with other online comics work, at <scottmccloud.com>.

24. Suzanne Lewis, *The Rhetoric of Power in the Bayeux Tapestry* (Cambridge: Cambridge University Press, 1999).

25. Ibid., p. 60.

26. 'As Herriman had done in other strips in his brief but crowded past, he occasionally filled the bottoms of [*The Dingbat Family*, later *The Family Upstairs*] panels with miniature comic animals. They could play the role of a Greek chorus or engage in their own farcical adventures . . .' Richard Marschall, *America's Great Comic Strip Artists* (New York: Abbeville Press, 1989), p. 103.

27. The strip, which was also featured in *salon.com*'s explication of the McCloud/Groth debate, is available online at <www.demian5.com>.

28. Crockett Johnson, *Harold and the Purple Crayon* (New York: HarperCollins, 1955).

29. Scott McCloud, *Understanding Comics*, pp. 43–4.

30. Damien Cave, 'No Laughing Matter'.

31. David Kunzle, *The History of the Comic Strip*, p. 377.

32. Louis Marin, 'Frontiers of Utopia: Past and Present', in *Critical Inquiry*, 19 (1993), pp. 413–14.

33. Wolfgang Iser, *The Act of Reading: A Theory of Aesthetic Response* (Baltimore, MD: The Johns Hopkins University Press, 1978), p. 126; Scott McCloud, *Reinventing Comics*, p. 229.

3.4

The Myths of Interactive Cinema

Peter Lunenfeld

Charlie Chaplin and Leni Riefenstahl still strike me as odd figures to sell the masses on computers, but then again, I am not, nor have I ever been, an ad man. And so it was in the first half of the 1980s, when computers underwent a makeover, that I watched the Little Tramp morph into a corporate pitchman and the athletic Valkyries from *Olympiad* (1938) recast as digital 'revolutionaries'. At the very moment when technology marketers discarded mainframe mandarins in favour of 'empowered' populations of personal computer users, the two biggest PC manufacturers, IBM (desperate to shed the image of sober white-coated scientists, with which they had built their fortune) and Apple (the very embodiment of the computer 'revolution'), both chose to invoke the cinema directly in their most important advertising campaigns. In 1981, IBM licensed Charlie Chaplin's image as spokesperson for their new line of PCs and used a Chaplin impersonator to sell the concept of an IBM computer for the little man in both print and television ads. That the impersonator was female was weird enough, but not half so odd as the decision to hire the Little Tramp, an icon of the battle between the romantic spirit and the brutalism of the machine age, to sell the portal to the information era. Like the robber barons who built mechanised factories while stocking their Victorian-era houses with all kinds of hand-crafted decorative arts, IBM was counting on the lag between technology and aesthetics to sell their machines.

Three years later, in 1984, Apple's television commercial for the first Macintosh computer took direct aim at IBM's PC, and Apple, too, referred to the cinematic. It was 'helmed', as they say in *Variety*, by Ridley Scott, one of England's most accomplished directors of commercials and the man who had just created *Blade Runner* (1982), inarguably the most influential film of its era. Its premiere was during the Super Bowl for American football, the US's single most important and expensive venue for advertisements, and it made a huge impact. A young woman bursts into a totalitarian screening room, IBM's Big Blue conflated with Orwell's Big Brother. She runs down the aisle hefting a sledgehammer in both hands, lets it fly, shatters the screen and liberates the enslaved audience from the tyranny of command line interfaces and C//: prompts with the power of Mac's GUI (graphical user interface). Gifted bricoleur that he is, Scott also lifted freely from a range of totalitarian cinematic images, from Orson Welles's *Citizen Kane* (1941) to Riefenstahl's other fascist masterpiece, *Triumph of the Will* (1936).

These two advertising campaigns can jumpstart any number of discussions, from a debate about Marshall McLuhan's provocation that the content of any new medium is actually always an old one, to an earnest condemnation of capitalism's willingness to enlist every aesthetic to fulfil the needs of consumerism. However, I use the example of Charlie and Leni as a way to literalise the connection between computers and the cinema, a relationship that when analysed too often fuzzes out into aesthetic banalities, technological generalities and market futurism. Of course, the computational and the cinematic are now such massive and intertwined cultural and economic forces as to make a general dis-cussion of them all but impossible. So, perversely, I choose to discuss not one of the endless successes of this marriage, everything from computer-generated special effects (CGfx) to DVDs to digital film-making, but a failure: 'interactive cinema', a much-hyped hybrid that never did quite make it. Interestingly, however, the failure of this form has never dampened the enthusiasm of its proponents, and its very lack of success has occasionally inspired even greater fervour to 'get it right'.

In this, interactive cinema has ascended into the realm of the mythic. There are seminars on interactive cinema from San Francisco State to the University of Southern California; tool development workshops from the University of Washington to Princeton; scholarly confer-ences from NYU to Brown to MIT; and festivals from Telluride's International Experimental Cinema Exposition to the Rotterdam Film Festival to the so-called first Interactive Film Festival in the Portugal Media 2001 programme. In the Summer of 2001, a random search engine pulls up over 2000 hits for the phrase 'interactive cinema' on the World Wide Web. Journalists continue to a spout a dewy sort of techno-optimism when they cover this, as witnessed by a recent story from Sydney: 'Imagine a cinema screen surrounding you, showing a panoramic scene from which you can pick which action you want to watch, zooming in on certain events and viewing something different from that being viewed by the person next to you.' Indeed, 'imagine' is the operative word. In the pages to follow, I hope to explore the myths of interactive cinema to generate a kind of abject insight into our con-temporary techno-cultural moment.

First, however, a discussion is needed on what interactive cinema actually is. From the medium's short history, I offer three examples. The first is an experiment by Glorianna Davenport, director of MIT's Interactive Cinema Group and without a doubt the foremost proponent of the form in the world. On the screen, a flock of birds appears, pecking at the ground. As the spectator approaches, the birds take flight. Another screen offers an Indian dancer going through her complex choreography. As the spectator turns to leave, the image cuts to a close-up of the dancer, her nostrils flaring with anger at the effrontery of the spectator daring to turn away from her per-formance. Davenport characterises her approach to interactive cinema storytelling as follows:

A novel approach ... celebrates electronic narrative as a process in which the authors, a networked presentation system, and the audience actively collaborate in the co-construction of meaning. ... A spreading-activation network is used to select relevant story elements from a multimedia database and dynamically conjoin them into an appealing, coherent narrative presentation. ... Connected to the narrative engine through rich feedback loops and intuitively understandable interfaces, the audience becomes an active partner in the shaping and presentation of story.[1]

This narrative stresses novelty, the database and the empowerment of the viewer. All these are ideas that cohere perfectly with the Media Lab's commitment to fostering ties between university and industry, and to the goal of convergence, a virtual mantra there under the reign of founding director Nicholas Negroponte.

In the longer, more aesthetically compelling works of the artist Grahame Weinbren, including *The Erl King* (1986) and *Sonata* (1990), existing stories are retold using many classical cinematic tropes, but under the 'cloak' of the interactive cutaway, a signature grammar that allows the user to control the movement from one scene to another. This is most memorable in *Sonata*, Weinbren's retelling of Leo Tolstoy's most nihilistic story, 'The Kreutzer Sonata'. A husband is tormented by thoughts that his violinist wife is having an affair with her accompanist. The climactic scene of both the originating tale and the interactive cinema comes when the husband rushes into the music room and stabs his wife to death. Weinbren offers the prelude to this shocking violence with a view of the wife playing and the husband in distress outside the door. The user can 'slide' either perspective however far 'over' the other he or she chooses. This allows for a kind of simultaneity that the classic montage between the two scenes would not. Weinbren has analysed his own practice:

The basis of the interactive cinema is that the viewer has some control over what is on-screen. He or she knows that what is there will change if she or he acts, that it would have been different if he or she had acted differently earlier. Thus, the viewer is aware of a fundamental indeterminacy ... the viewer must be kept always aware that it is *his, her* action on a particular image that has produced these new sounds or pictures, and techniques to foster this awareness must be developed. In my judgment, the most immediately available techniques can be found in the language of montage. A deliberate use of film editing strategies can keep reconvincing the viewer of the non-arbitrariness of connection between old and new elements, between the elements already there and those produced by viewer action.[2]

This artist's narrative also stresses the viewer's sense of control, but begins to delve into the formal strategies that would make such work compelling. It offers a different strategy for content, less like coherent storytelling and more akin to the condensation of the dream work.

If Davenport's and Weinbren's comments underlie two of the originary myths of interactive cinema, engineering and aesthetic, what of that given by the market? Max Whitby, an interactive media producer, offers the following:

> Something happens to people, especially people who come from a film or television background, when initially exposed to the idea of interactive multimedia. When you first realize that computers are not just tools, but a new medium through which information can be delivered in completely new ways, a light bulb goes on – it certainly went on in my head and I've seen it go on in lots of other people's heads. Instead of the high priests in their ivory towers deciding what a TV programme will be, you can hand over your programme material to your audience and they can construct their own experiences.[3]

Whitby goes on, however, to offer this demurral: 'Now that basic premise is very exciting. The trouble is it doesn't sustain. When you actually get in there and try to make things in an interactive way, the premise falls apart.'[4] This is the restraining power of the market, the digital dialectic in action: the flights of theory balanced against the constraints of practice in the world.

This becomes clear when looking at my third example, *I'm Your Man*, directed by Bob Bejan, which claimed to be the 'The World's First Interactive Movie' when it premiered in a select number of cinemas in 1992. It is a short interactive movie in which viewers, pushing buttons on their armrests, decide at specific points in the narrative to follow a specific character and the trajectory of that character's movements. Each version of the film runs only 15 minutes. *I'm Your Man* is ostensibly the tale of a female whistle-blower, her corrupt boss and an FBI agent who inserts himself between them. Depending on the viewer's choices, however, the story can evolve differently, and various aspects of the character's backgrounds reveal that choosing an alternative path would indeed lead to very different conclusions.

Yet how interactive is such a proposition, such a product, and, more to the point, how radical is its notion of interactivity? As Lev Manovich points out in *The Language of New Media*, 'all classical, and even more so modern art is "interactive" in any number of ways'.[5] However, as computers moved out of the workplace and into the home, their capacity for nonlinear assemblage – linking, if you will – disrupted their users' expectations of linearity and fuelled a hunger for interactivity as an end in itself, rather than simply a means. The privileging of the interaction between user and machine became the Holy Grail of computer-based media, and the quest for this interaction generated a potent combination of technological, cultural, and economic narratives.[6]

What of the cinema's own mythologies? Film is more than a medium; it is a system that is inseparable from the myths that drive it and which the cinema forms in turn. There are the myths that surround the industry – the myths of stardom, the gilded dreams and wretched excess of wealth and the lottery of luck. There are the myths of the technology of cinema itself, from the apocrypha surrounding its origin – the notions that Brazilians shot at screen villains and that Parisians ducked as a locomotive passed over them – all the way through to André Bazin's myth of total cinema.[7] It is worth mulling over Bazin's notion that the cinema has striven since its inception to become the highest art form, replacing opera as the culture's supreme *gesamtkunstwerk*. Yet Bazin wrote this at the tail end of the classical age of the cinema, just before the onslaught of the medium that would supersede the cinema and indeed bring together all manner of consumption, namely television.[8] Less than half a century after television as a medium overtook the cinema, television was in turn challenged by the computer. As noted above, when the computer moved into the home, that previously unchallenged realm of the colour console, new myths of usability, connectivity and personal empowerment emerged.

At this point, I could offer some sort of nostrum about how all that is needed to prove the viability of the myths is for someone, some day, to demonstrate them successfully. I could say this, but I will not, for, as the pioneering Russian net.artist Olia Lialina noted about her own medium, 'saying that net art is just beginning isn't very different from saying it's dead'.[9] However, it is precisely within the realms of myth that beginnings and endings co-exist in an eternal presence. The new myths that emerged revolved around the notion that the narrative impact of film could be grafted onto the networked nonlinearity of the digital to create a liberatory, new interactive cinema.

It is farcical to speak of a single interactive cinema when in fact there were interactive cinemas. Computer science initiated projects that pushed back boundaries in interface, intelligent agency and computing expertise. On the European media festival circuit, one could encounter the more aesthetic explorations, the results of solitary artists toiling away in whatever the digital equivalent of a garret might be, or those who had won a residency at a place such as Canada's Banff Centre for Computing and the Arts. Finally, and for the shortest time, one could even wander into the multiplex cinema (at least in Hollywood) and pay money to see an 'interactive movie' such as *I'm Your Man*, complete with a hackneyed plot and a technological updating of the entertainment industry's obsession with story arcs and plot points.

That few have heard of these actual instantiations of interactive cinema, much less actually experienced them, has not been an impediment to people waxing philosophical, and even Utopian, about them. This is because, like its technological cousin virtual reality, the interactive cinema functions best in the realm of myth. There will be no definitive unmasking, for the myths of interactive cinema fill creative, technological and even financial needs. One example is the elaborate executive fantasies about 'Silliwood', that much-ballyhooed melding of Silicon Valley and Hollywood fostered by computer techies and film business sharpies in the mid-1990s. The triumph of Silliwood would have done much to justify the faith of venture capitalists and other investors in the notion of a technologically deterministic aesthetics, that myth that the machine would somehow give birth sui generis to a new medium that would transform authorship and experience.

What, then, transcends the realm of fantasy and exists in the real world? The answer lies in shifting from the fixation on interactivity within the narrative object to thinking instead about a system-wide application of new technologies of augmentation and communication. This would follow my own interest in the digital media's aesthetics of unfinish and move the discussion from hypertexts to hypercontexts. As more and more contemporary cultural production follows a Duchampian arc, in which the presentation of the object defines that object's function within culture, the shaping and moulding of context come to the fore. This is not news, and, in fact, a quarter of a century's work on defining the differences between the high modern moment and that which followed it hinged precisely on this elevation of context to parity with the text itself. The word 'telematic' has been around for almost as long as this debate, but it has only been within the past decade that the combination of computers and communication networks has shown how it can contribute to the creation of context. This context takes many forms, especially in relation to popular media: there is the pre-planned marketing of tie-ins from music CDs, to television spin-offs, to lunch boxes, and there is the efflorescence of discursive communities generated by fans. In certain cases, all of these combine to create something far more interesting than back-story and more complicated than synergistic marketing. This is what I call 'hypercontext', a rhizomatic and dynamic interlinked communicative community using networks to curate a series of shifting contexts.

If we recast the interactive cinema around the concept of hypercontextualisation, rather than the mythic grail of nonlinear narrative, a phenomenon such as *The Blair Witch Project* (1999) functions as an unusually successful example of the interactive cinema.[10] When the film arrived in cinemas, it was presented as if it were a documentary. It began with a title card informing the audience that what was to follow consisted of footage found in the Maryland woods one year after the disappearance of three young film-makers, who had gone in search of a legendary local supernatural presence. The genre, the specific treatment of the subject, the pseudo-realism of the delivery and some very convincing improvisational acting (the three stars of the film were indeed isolated and terrified by the directors for a week in those real Maryland woods) all combined to create what Brenda Laurel speaks of as the 'affordances' a narrative object offers to the development of fandom.[11]

Shot for very little money, the film was a huge commercial success, and the dominant cinema has been copying its hypercontextual strategies ever since. Central to the impact of this project, which surely was and remains more than a 'film', was the choice to use a new communications medium to play off the tension created in the spectator by the false documentary. The hypercontext was established a full year in advance of the release of the film itself. A poster campaign across college campuses, aimed at the target demographic group, asked for help from anyone who might have information about the 'missing' student film-makers. Meanwhile, the directors and their small studio put up a Web site that contained the kernel of the film's narrative and created a set of interlinked pseudo-documentary elements – video clips, news reports, audio fragments – that engaged that sense that, while information wanted to be free (to use a 1990s cliché), it did not seem to have any corollary imperative to be accurate. Here, the communicative potential of the Net was deftly deployed to create a hypercontext of remarkable depth, something both pre- and post-extant to the film itself. The Web site primed the target audience and survived after the film left cinemas and moved to video and DVD. The DVD's links back to the Web complete the circuit, while simultaneously opening up new layers of hypercontext as *The Blair Witch Project* main site features links to non-commercial fan sites built from the affordances of the narrative object and its explicitly commercial hypercontexts.

Having said that, *The Blair Witch Project*, and whatever its progeny in the dominant cinema, or even the sham that passes for 'independent' cinema today, will hardly be developing every facet of hypercontextualisation. Indeed, the phenomenon is as much a function of entertainment's capacity within networked capitalism to co-opt anything onto its promotional agenda. In any case, the hypercontextual explosion initiated by *The Blair Witch Project* has not really manifested itself in full bloom since 1999. The attributes of the interactive cinema we have been searching for in other modes really find their apotheosis in the 'expanded' DVD, in which the linear narrative object is embedded in a system of ever-expanding self-reflexive media (see plate 06). Such an extra-textual and ever-expanding cocoon is the real future of the hopes invested in the interactive cinema.

The 'expanded' hypercontextual DVD is part of an historical narrative of home-based playback technology. This begins with the commercial release of videotaped films in the 1970s and that market's subsequent explosion in the 1980s. In that same decade, videophiles, as they came to be known, started to become interested in laser-discs because of their superior picture and sound. They also offered, for the first time in commercial formats, randomised, nonlinear access to the material and the ability to have alternate audio tracks and ancillary materials such as stills and even written articles attached to the filmic 'object' at their centre. At that time, a new product emerged on the market – the expanded laser-disc, especially as perfected by the Criterion Collection. This was a joint venture of Janus Films, one of the oldest distributors of what once went by the name 'art films', and the Voyager Company, run by pioneering multimedia publisher Bob Stein. Stein then built upon the success of the Criterion Collection to release early multimedia CD-ROMs. Now there are Criterion Collection DVDs, the fourth technological substrate for this kind of augmented narrativity.

What goes little questioned in all of these 'added features' is their promotion of the intentionalist fallacy. The pleasures of expanded hypercontextual DVD are manifest, but they foster an ever-stronger authorial voice on theorists and audiences alike. One of the most routine features on DVDs is the addition of a soundtrack featuring the director commenting on the action, sometimes with the addition of interviews with stars and other crew. While fascinating in themselves, and marketed as a way for viewers to expand their understanding of and appreciation for the art of cinema, these augmentations can also tend to circumscribe the audience's readings of a film text, using the technological novelty of the hypercontext to calcify the director's version as the definitive way to read a film.

Film-makers will be driven primarily by an impulse towards raw promotion, building in the greatest number and variety of affordances to hook an audience, while the audiences that do latch onto these products and systems are more likely to engage in a relatively unre-flexive fandom than the transgressive bricolage so beloved of cultural studies. One of the myths of the interactive cinema that was particularly intoxicating was that which promised, through the combination of technology and aesthetics, to liberate the cinema from the nar-rative ruts into which it had fallen. This was the idea that new technologies would generate not just new stories, but new ways of telling those new stories. The record on the screen, however, indicates that the real impact of digital technologies was not to strengthen narra-tive, whether linear or not, but to contribute to its decimation.

The contemporary blockbuster has been noted for its departures from the normal narrative model developed during the classical Hollywood period. There has been an evacuation of narrative from contemporary media, but that is as much a reflection of the surfeit of narrative as it is a sign of its demise. Indeed, it would be ludicrous to claim some sort of 'death of narrative' in the midst of its ever-broadening triumph. The more that tele-vision extends its sway around the globe, the more the human race is suffused in story, bathed in narrative. From the 30-second advertising spot to the half-hour sitcom, to the 90-minute film, to the two-hour-plus sporting event, the televisual experience is equally a telenarrative experience. It should strike no one as shocking that the dominant Hollywood cinema, especially in its blockbuster mode, should seem to care less and less about nar-rative convention and coherence. When Bruce Willis, the star of Luc Besson's *The Fifth Element* (1997), was confronted at a press event about the amiably shambling incoherence of that digital effects-driven film, he laughed and let the scribes know that nobody cares about story any more. While we do not generally expect our action heroes to moonlight as narratologists, Willis's observation was at least partially accurate.[12]

We have so much narrative surrounding us that it is often enough merely to refer to it. Like sampling within contemporary music and so much of our endlessly self-reflexive adver-tising culture, the nod to an established and overflowing narrative tradition is sufficient. In other words, the movement towards a referential rather than developmental narrative strategy has grown out of the sheer plentitude of narrative, exemplified by the glowingly accessible archive of everything. Indeed, the Web's 24/7 access promises to make the video store seem as archaic as the repertory cinema. But let us not forget that the art of cinema, and film culture itself, flourished far more healthily in the era of the repertory cinema than it does now. The very proliferation of narrative, even the highest quality narrative, can have the paradoxical effect of making it seem that much less important – Willis's sense that 'nobody cares'. This is the effect of communications technology on freedom of access and even discourse: when the samizdat culture of Eastern Europe and the Soviet Union during the 1970s mutated into the Western-style market of the post-1989 era, something both ineffable and important was lost. The Web offers a marvellous explosion of access, but the law of unintended consequences could usher in a world in which anything can be obtained, but nothing is special.

This would be a dour chapter indeed if we were to stop here: myths of interactivity slain, the death of a certain kind of film culture bemoaned, the forces of hypercontextualisation firmly under the control of Hollywood studio flacks, narrative coherence as anachronistic as Tin Pan Alley's well-crafted popular lyrics. If we want relief from this barrage, I would suggest we move away from the cinema and start to think about art. Alfred Barr, the famous curator from the Museum of Modern Art's glory days in the middle of the twentieth century, used to speak confidently of 'the art of our time' when referring to the painting, sculpture and photography that so defined his institution, from Pablo Picasso to Walker Evans to Jackson Pollock. Barr could count on and indeed was personally responsible for the sense of a coherent narrative of the 'avant-garde arts'. Although we live in what I have characterised as a period of ferocious pluralism, I am intrigued by the concept of proposing the 'media of our times'.

The past ten years have seen the flowering of a rich body of large-scale video art installations, and it is to these I turn as the next step in this mythopoesis. I will discuss the work of artists Sam Taylor-Wood and Jane and Louise Wilson in relation to the myths of interactive cinema, as these artists offer a range of approaches to the 'surfeit' of narrative. I made reference to this plenitude earlier and noted how the Hollywood blockbuster offers one way to confront this deluge of story: simply ignore it and its conventions and learn to create a 90-minute cinema of attractions, this time around with bankable stars. The few attempts at a computer-driven interactive cinema failed to prove themselves capable of offering a viable nonlinear narrative form to compete with the standard models. The video artists I am interested in offer a third strategy: they accept the omnipresence of narrative and up the ante, creating installations that distil narrative while at the very same time confound plentitude.

Sam Taylor-Wood's *Atlantic* (1997) is a three-screen space that condenses the narrative trope of romantic trouble into a short, endless loop of feeling without narrative substrate. It is installed in a large, rectangular gallery, so that the viewer enters to face the largest of the three walls and there confronts an establishing shot of an upmarket restaurant. Redolent with the kind of obsessive details the art world has come to expect from the photographic tableaux of Andreas Gursky, Taylor-Wood's restaurant becomes exactly the kind of theatre that high-ticket restaurateurs invoke in their descriptions of their spaces. There is, however, little in the way of drama taking place on this exquisitely rendered stage, at least if we think of drama as evolving over time and involving at least a modicum of narrative. What Taylor-Wood offers here instead is a nod to drama, a condensation of the cinema's romantic arc, distilling it down into two looped scenarios playing opposite each other on the walls perpendicular to the projection of the restaurant space. One is a close-up of a woman's teary-eyed face, the other an extreme close-up of a man's hands, wringing nervously.

The room is suffused with a soundtrack seemingly more ambient than scripted, with the woman's voice plaintively imploring, 'Why?' as the three loops cycle in an eternal present. From 1977 to 1980, Cindy Sherman made a series of *Untitled Film Stills*, which perfected a certain semiotic reference to the cinematic imaginary – with the artist herself taking on a variety of pitch-perfect incarnations of the Office Girl, the Femme Fatale and the Moll, all deployed in subtly art-directed environments. Taylor-Wood's piece can be seen to have dynamised the Sherman film stills to a certain degree, spatialising and slightly temporalising them without going all the way towards actually making a film. If anything, the Sherman stills are turned into a weird variety of animatic by Wood's installation. Here, the plenitude of narrative is so much taken for granted that the artist can assume we know precisely that thing to which we refer when invoking the Latin phrase *in medias res*.

If Taylor-Wood is following Sherman's reference to the narratives we know so well as to obviate the need for their presence, Jane and Louise Wilson practise a reference to the narrative which we have lived through, but, at least in the West, have not yet internalised enough to understand fully. The Wilsons are twins, fully aware of the inherent freakishness of a collaboration between the mostly identical. In pieces such as *Stasi City* (1997), *Proton, Unity, Energy, Blizzard* (2000) and *Star City* (2000), they use their natural affinity for the intertwined to deal with the intersection of space and politics inherent in the big story of the past 20 years – the dissolution of the Berlin Wall and the end of the Soviet Union. This is a story that, as mentioned earlier, everyone knows but no one really understands, at least not yet. The Wilson sisters have been taking these strategies and applying them to one of the central questions of our time: what becomes of art after the great divide between communism and capitalism was so abruptly sundered in 1989? It is a narrative that cries out to be regarded as central, but that is drowned out by the din of celebrity culture that bubbles along in a rich, peaceful, easily distracted West. The Wilsons create multi-screen environments which destabilise the act of spectatorship, upping the ante on celebrity culture's premium on distraction while at the very same time cataloguing the spaces and objects of the structuring narrative of the second half of the twentieth century – the Cold War. They have been inside Stasi headquarters in the former East Berlin, in the abandoned missile silos of NORAD in Wyoming and in the cavernous environs of Star City, the former Soviet Union's cosmonaut training centre. The spaces they create have both the menace and sterility of security installations, but the technological artifacts they uncover offer a poignant historicism. Here we confront the electronics of the Cold War, not the sleek and streamlined consumerism of the Sharper Image catalogue. They fetishise the clunky apparatus of spies who never came in from the cold. This presents electronics as raw wires and wood-housed transformers, a back-story to our present fascination with the embedded and seamless, for example, the PDAs, Web-enabled cell phones and wireless modems that form our fluid-free notion of sexy. The Wilson sisters aestheticise the return of the politically repressed. After all, it was only a few decades ago that the impulse towards civil defence, a narrative that culminated in thinking the unthinkable, in the complete end, was dominant. The Wilsons make it impossible to lay claim to a single vantage point to take all of this in. The spectator moves from place to place in the installation, and the totality of the visual experience is, just like the totality of the historical narrative, always impossibly and implausibly beyond us. They create a cinema interactive with history, defeat, fear and triumph. Yet these spaces of eviscerated history and depleted power offer such sheer visual seduction and interactive immersion that they become as enthralling as the celebrity-addled pop culture that forms their overall cultural context.

Sam Taylor-Wood and the Wilson sisters do not make interactive cinema, but they do capitalise on the doomed genre's aspirational myths, the best hopes of the digital to reanimate the art forms that preceded it. I have written elsewhere that it was precisely because video as a medium moved through its Utopian phase that the past decade's video installation artists were able to come into their own; they were freed of the psychic burdens imposed by the impossibly lofty expectations of the early years of videos. In the same way, when technologists, artists and Hollywood *luftmenschen* work through the myths of 'interactive cinema', compelling syntheses of film and the digital could come into being.

Notes

1. Glorianna Davenport's comments are from an article co-written with M. Murtagh titled 'Automatist Storyteller Systems and the Shifting Sands of Story', originally published in the *IBM Systems Journal* in 1997. It can be accessed through the Interactive Cinema Group's copiously documented Web site: <ic.www.media.mit.edu/icpublications/biblio.html>.

2. Grahame Weinbren, 'In the Ocean of Streams of Story', *Millennium Film Journal*, no. 28, Spring 1995, <mfj-online.org/journalPages/MFJ28/GWOCEAN.HTML>.

3. Quoted in Andy Cameron, 'Dissimulations: Illusions of Interactivity', *Millennium Film Journal*, no. 28, Spring 1995, <mfj-online.org/journalPages/MFJ28/Dissimulations.html>.

4. Ibid.

5. Lev Manovich, *The Language of New Media* (Cambridge, MA: MIT Press, 2001), p. 56.

6. John Caldwell develops his own analysis of the myths of interactivity in *Televisuality: Style, Crisis, and Authority in American Television* (New Brunswick, NJ: Rutgers University Press, 1995).

7. André Bazin, 'The Myth of Total Cinema', in *What Is Cinema?*, vol. I, essays selected and translated by Hugh Gray (Berkeley: University of California Press, 1967). In this context, it is interesting to note Bazin's offhand comment in that essay that 'the cinema owes virtually nothing to the scientific spirit', p. 17.

8. Simon Frith succinctly describes television's hegemony: 'In the western world, television has been the dominant medium of the second half of the twentieth century . . . The other mass media – radio, the cinema, recorded music, sport, print – feed off television. . . .', in 'The Black Box: The Value of Television and the Future of Television Research', *Screen*, vol. 41 no. 1, Spring 2000, p. 33.

9. Olia Lialina posted her comments to the seminal <nettime> listserve on 18 February 2001, archived at <nettime.org>.

10. J. P. Telotte, '*The Blair Witch Project*: Film and the Internet', *Film Quarterly*, vol. 54 no. 3, Spring 2001, goes into some detail on the BWP's hypercontexts.

11. Don Norman popularised the term 'affordances' within interface design, drawing from the work of the perceptual psychologist, J. J. Gibson, in 'The Theory of Affordances', in R. E. Shaw and J. Bransford (eds), *Perceiving, Acting, and Knowing* (Hillsdale, NJ: Lawrence Erlbaum Associates, 1977). Brenda Laurel discusses affordances in relation to narrative systems and fan culture in *Utopian Entrepreneur* (Cambridge, MA: MIT Press, 2001).

12. The Bruce Willis press conference at Cannes in 1997 is described at <www.citypages.com/databank/18/860/article3513.asp>.

4.0

CONSUMPTION

The vast complexities of media consumption have long interested scholars and critics. What meanings do we derive from such encounters? Who 'controls' such meanings? What does our interaction with media say about ourselves? The emergence of digital production, distribution and exhibition has only added to this complexity, as consumers access entertainment content from an expanded media menu. Now we not only ask the questions posed above, but also query how we watch, interact with and use new media technologies and content. Similarly, we question how these encounters affect how we watch more traditional modes of media entertainment.

The consumption of media can be viewed from a number of vantage points: from the ways in which a spectator interacts with a text, to the ways in which consumers and producers mutually influence each other's activities, to the various ways in which media consumers interact with each other. The chapters in this section tackle all three of these points and explore pertinent issues relating to the audience's increasingly active participation in the consumption process; the ways in which audiences can (and cannot) be interactive; the variety of viewing strategies consumers utilise as they 'multitask' and participate on various levels of engagement; and the emerging role of the consumer-as-producer. In fact, as noted in a number of the chapters in this section, the division between media production and consumption has become increasingly blurred as consumers continue to 'dive into' the production process.

Each of the chapters in this section investigates different modes of consumption from a variety of perspectives: the increasingly active levels of audience participation and the related increase in consumer-led 'DIY' production and recirculation of media material; the creation of hybrid strategies of spectatorship that combine media viewing with computer using; the constitution of 'self' in and by new media; and, finally, the shifting modes of distribution and exhibition in the moving image industries. Together, these chapters provide a compelling assessment of the ways in which we make meaning in the contemporary media environment.

4.1

Interactive Audiences?

Henry Jenkins

'You've got fifteen seconds. Impress me.'

An advertisement for Applebox Productions depicts the new youth consumer: his straggly dishwater blonde hair hangs down into his glaring eyes, his mouth is turned down into a challenging sneer and his finger poised over the remote. One false move and he will zap us. No longer a couch potato, he determines what, when and how he watches media. He is a media consumer, perhaps even a media fan, but he is also a media producer, distributor, publicist and critic. He is the poster child for the new interactive audience.

The advertisement takes for granted what cultural studies researchers struggled to establish throughout the 1980s and 1990s, that audiences are active, critically aware and discriminating. However, this advertisement promises that Applebox productions has developed new ways to overcome his resistance and bring advertising messages to this scowling teen's attention. The interactive audience is not autonomous, still operating alongside powerful media industries.

If the current media environment makes visible the once invisible work of media spectatorship, it is wrong to assume that we are somehow being liberated through improved media technologies. Rather than talking about interactive technologies, we should document the interactions that occur among media consumers, between media consumers and media texts and between media consumers and media producers. The new participatory culture is taking shape at the intersection between three trends:

1. New tools and technologies enable consumers to archive, annotate, appropriate and recirculate media content.
2. A range of subcultures promote do-it-yourself (DIY) media production, a discourse that shapes how consumers have deployed those technologies.
3. Economic trends favouring the horizontally integrated media conglomerates encourage the flow of images, ideas and narratives across multiple media channels and demand more active modes of spectatorship.

It would be naive to assume that powerful conglomerates will not protect their own interests as they enter this new media marketplace, but, at the same time, audiences are gaining greater power and autonomy as they enter into the new knowledge culture. The interactive audience is more than a marketing concept and less than 'semiotic democracy'.

COLLECTIVE INTELLIGENCE

In *Collective Intelligence*, Pierre Levy offers a compelling vision of the new 'knowledge space', or what he calls 'the cosmopedia', which *might* emerge as citizens more fully realise the potentials of the new media environment. Levy explores how the Web's 'deterritoriali-sation' of knowledge might enable broader participation in decision-making, new modes of citizenship and community, and the reciprocal exchange of information. Levy draws a pro-ductive distinction between organic social groups (families, clans, tribes), organised social groups (nations, institutions, religions and corporations) and self-organised groups (such as the virtual communities of the Web). He links the emergence of the new knowledge space to the breakdown of geographic constraints on communication, of the declining loyalty of individuals to organised groups and of the diminished power of nation-states to command the exclusive loyalty of their citizens. The new knowledge communities will be voluntary, temporary and tactical affiliations, defined through common intellectual enterprises and emotional investments. Members may shift from one community to another as their interests and needs change, and they may belong to more than one community at the same time. However, they are held together through the mutual production and reciprocal exchange of knowledge. As Levy explains:

> Not only does the cosmopedia make available to the collective intellect all of the pertinent knowledge available to it at a given moment, but it also serves as a site of collective discussion, negotiation, and development. . . . Unanswered questions will create tension within cosmopedic space, indicating regions where invention and innovation are required.[1]

Online fan communities are the most fully realised versions of Levy's cosmopedia. They are expansive self-organising groups focused around the collective production, debate and circulation of meanings, interpretations and fantasies in response to various artifacts of contemporary popular culture. Fan communities have long defined their memberships through affinities, rather than localities. 'Fandoms' were virtual communities, 'imagined' and 'imagining' communities, long before the introduction of networked computers.[2] The his-tory of science-fiction fandom might illustrate how knowledge communities emerged. Hugo Gernsbeck, the pulp magazine editor who has been credited with helping to define science fiction as a distinctive genre in the 1920s and 1930s, was also a major advocate of radio as a participatory medium. Gernsbeck saw science fiction as a means of fostering popular awareness of contemporary scientific breakthroughs at a moment of accelerating techno-logical development.[3] The letter column of Gernsbeck's *Astounding Stories* became a forum where lay people could debate scientific theories and assess new technologies. Using the published addresses, early science-fiction fans formed an informal, postal network, circulating letters and amateur publications. Later, conventions facilitated the face-to-face contact between fans from across the country and around the world. Many significant science-fiction writers emerged from fandom. Given this history, every reader was understood to be a potential writer and many fans aspired to break into professional publication; fan ideas influenced commercially distributed works at a time when science fiction was still understood predominantly as a micro-genre aimed at a small but passionate niche market.

This reciprocity between readers, writers and editors set expectations as science fiction spread into film and television. *Star Trek* fans were, from the start, an activist audience, lobbying to keep the series on the air and later advocating specific changes in the programme content, the better to reflect its own agendas. *Star Trek* fandom, in turn, was a model for other fan communities to create forums for debating interpretations, networks for circulating creative works and channels for lobbying producers. Fans were early adopters of digital technologies. Within the scientific and military institutions where the Internet was first introduced, science fiction has long been a literature of choice.[4] Consequently, the slang and social practices employed on the early bulletin boards were often directly modelled on science-fiction fandom. Mailing lists focused on fan topics took their place beside discussions of technological or scientific issues. In many ways, cyberspace is fandom writ large. The reconstitution of these fandoms as digital enclaves did not come without strenuous efforts to overcome the often overtly hostile reception female fans received from the early Internet's predominantly male population. Operating outside technical institutions, many women lacked computer access and technical literacy. Heated debates erupted at conventions as fans were angered at being left behind when old fan friends moved online. At the same time, fan communities helped many women make the transition to cyberspace; the group ensured that valued members learned to use the new technologies.[5]

Nancy Baym has discussed the important functions of talk within online soap fandom: 'Fans share knowledge of the show's history, in part, because the genre demands it. Any soap has broadcast more material than any single fan can remember.'[6] Fans inform each other about the programme's history or recent developments that they may have missed. The fan community pools its knowledge because no single fan can know everything necessary to appreciate the series fully. Levy distinguishes between shared knowledge (which would refer to information known by all members of a community) and collective intelligence (which describes knowledge available to all members of a community). Collective intelligence expands a community's productive capacity because it frees individual members from the limitations of their memory and enables the group to act upon a broader range of expertise. As Levy writes, within a knowledge community, 'no one knows everything, everyone knows something, all knowledge resides in humanity'.[7] Baym argues:

> A large group of fans can do what even the most committed single fan cannot: accumulate, retain, and continually recirculate unprecedented amounts of relevant information. . . . [Net list] participants collaboratively provide all with the resources to get more story from the material, enhancing many members' soap readings and pleasures.[8]

Soap talk, Baym notes, allows people to 'show off for one another' their various competencies while making individual expertise more broadly available. Fans are motivated by 'epistemaphilia', not simply a pleasure in knowing, but a pleasure in exchanging knowledge. Baym argues that fans see the exchange of speculations and evaluations of soap operas as a means of 'comparing, refining, and negotiating understandings of their socio-emotional environment.'[9] Fan speculations may, on the surface, seem to be simply a deciphering of the material aired but, increasingly, speculation involves fans in the production of new fantasies, broadening the field of meanings that circulate around the primary text.

For example, in the early 1990s, *alt.rec.arts.twin-peaks*, a group devoted to discussing David Lynch's cult mystery/soap opera series, sought to 'break the code and solve the crime', that is, to predict successfully future revelations about the Laura Palmer murder and thus to arrive at the 'truth' of the series.[10] However, as members mobilised and interpreted the series' 'evidence', they introduced a range of different potential narratives, centring on alternative assumptions about 'who done it' and how Laura's death fitted within larger schemes. Their ability to recognise previously undiscovered narrative possibilities enlarged their pleasure in watching *Twin Peaks*, and the group actively recruited new members to expand the range of interpretations. This collective exchange of knowledge cannot be fully contained by previous sources of power which depended on maintaining tight control over the flow of information, for example, 'bureaucratic hierarchies (based on static forms of writing), media monarchies (surfing the television and media systems), and international economic networks (based on the telephone and real-time technologies'. The dynamic, collective and reciprocal nature of these exchanges undermines traditional forms of expertise and destabilises attempts to establish a scriptural economy in which some meanings are more valuable than others.[11] The old commodity space was defined through various forms of decontextualisation, including the alienation of labour, the uprooting of images from larger cultural traditions, the demographic fragmentation of the audience, the disciplining of knowledge and the disconnection between media producers and consumers. The new information space involves multiple and unstable forms of recontextualisation. The value of any bit of information increases through social interaction. Commodities are a limited entity and their exchange necessarily creates or enacts inequalities. However, meaning is a shared and constantly renewable resource and its circulation can create and revitalise social ties.

HOW COMPUTERS CHANGED FANDOM

For Levy, the introduction of high-speed networked computing constituted an epistemological turning point in the development of collective intelligence. If fandom was already a knowledge culture well before the Internet, then how did transplanting its practices into the digital environment alter the fan community? The new digital environment increases the speed of fan communication, resulting in what Matthew Hills calls 'just in time fandom'.[12] If fans once traded ideas through letters, they now see the postal service as too slow ('snail mail') to satisfy their expectations of immediate response. Hills explains, 'the practices of fandom have become increasingly enmeshed with the rhythms and temporalities of broadcasting, so that fans now go online to discuss new episodes immediately after the episode's transmission time or even during ad-breaks perhaps in order to demonstrate the "timeliness" and responsiveness of their devotion'.[13] Where fans might have raced to the phone to talk to a close friend, they can now access a much broader range of perspectives by going online. Hills worries that the broadcast schedule may be determining what can be discussed and when. This expectation of timeliness complicates the global expansion of the fan community, with time lags in the distribution of cultural goods across national markets hampering full participation from fans who will receive the same programme months or even years later. International fans often complain that they have an additional disadvantage because their first experience of the episodes is 'spoiled' by learning too much from the online discussions.

The digital media also alters the scope of communication. Fandoms centring on Asian popular culture, such as Japanese *anime* or Hong Kong action films, powerfully exploit the Internet's global reach. Japanese fans collaborate with American consumers to ensure the underground circulation of these cultural products and to explain cultural references, genre traditions and production histories.[14] *Anime* fans regularly translate and post the schedule of Japanese television so that international fans can identify and negotiate access to interesting programmes. American fans have learned Japanese, often teaching each other outside a formal educational context, in order to participate in grassroots projects to subtitle *anime* films or to translate *manga*. This is a new cosmopolitanism: knowledge-sharing on a global scale.

As the community enlarges and as reaction time shortens, fandom becomes much more effective as a platform for consumer activism. Fans can quickly mobilise grassroots efforts to save programmes or protest against unpopular developments. New fandoms emerge rapidly on the Web, in some cases before media products actually reach the market. As early participants spread news about emerging fandoms, supporters quickly develop the infrastructure for supporting critical dialogue, producing annotated programme guides, providing regular production updates and creating original fan stories and artwork. The result has been an enormous proliferation of fan Web sites and discussion lists. Kirsten Pullen estimates, for example, that by June 2000 there were more than 33,000 fan Web sites listed in the *Yahoo! Web Directory*, dealing with individual performers, programmes and films.[15] One portal, *Fan Fiction on the Web*, lists more than 300 different media texts that have generated at least some form of fan fiction, representing a much broader array of genres than previously suspected.[16]

As fandom diversifies, it moves from cult status towards the cultural mainstream, with more Internet users engaged in some form of fan activity. This increased visibility and cultural centrality has been a mixed blessing for a community used to speaking from the margins. The speed and frequency of communication may intensify the social bonds within the fan community. In the past, fans inhabited a 'weekend only world', seeing each other in large numbers only a few times a year at conventions.[17] Now, fans may interact daily, if not hourly, online. Geographically isolated fans can feel much more connected to the fan community and home-ridden fans enjoy a new level of acceptance. However, fandom's expanded scope can leave fans feeling alienated from the expanding numbers of strangers entering their community. This rapid expansion outstrips any effort to socialise new members. Online fan discussion lists often bring together groups who functioned more or less autonomously offline and have radically different responses to the aired material. Flame wars erupt as their taken-for-granted interpretive and evaluative norms rub against each other. In some cases, fans can negotiate these conflicts by pulling to a meta-level and exploring the basis for the different interpretations. More often, the groups splinter into narrower interests, pushing some participants from public debates into smaller and more private mailing lists. Levy describes a pedagogical process through which a knowledge community develops a set of ethical standards and articulates mutual goals. Even on a scale much smaller than Levy's global village, fandoms often have difficulty arriving at such a consensus. Andre MacDonald has described fandom in terms of various disputes; between male and female fans, between fans with different assumptions about the desired degree of closeness of the producers and stars, between fans who seek to police the production of certain fantasies and fans who assert their freedom from such constraints, between different generations of fans, and so forth.[18] MacDonald depicts a community whose Utopian aspirations are constantly being tested against unequal experiences, levels of expertise, access to performers and community resources, control over community institutions and degrees of investment in fan traditions and standards. Moreover, as Nancy Baym suggests, the desire to avoid such conflicts can result in an artificial consensus which shuts down the desired play with alternative meanings.[19]

Networked computing has also transformed fan production. Web publication of fan fiction, for example, has almost entirely displaced printed 'zines'. Fanzines arose as the most efficient means of circulating fan writing.[20] Fan editors charged only the costs of reproduction, seeing zines as a vehicle for distributing stories and not as a source of income. In some fandoms, circuits developed for lending individually photocopied stories. In other cases, readers and editors came to see zines as aesthetic artifacts, insisting on high-quality reproduction and glossy colour covers. Fans have increasingly turned to the Web to lower the costs of production and to expand their reading public. Fans are also developing archives of older zine stories, helping to connect newer fans with their history. The higher visibility of fan fiction on the Web has inspired many new writers to try their hand and spread the practice to new fandoms, yet older fans complain of the lack of editing and nurturing of emerging talents. In several cases, fans have organised themselves to map out alternative story arcs and to script their own episodes when series were cancelled or took unwelcome turns.

Digital technologies have also enabled new forms of fan cultural production. Elena Garfinkle and Eric Zimmerman have documented the emergence of *Kisekae* or digital paper-dolls, which can be dressed and undressed by the user and programmed to perform simple actions. The *Kisekae* become vehicles for erotic play and fantasy, primarily among *anime* fans.[21] Similarly, game fans have produced short, animated films using game engines, developed to enable *Quake* enthusiasts to record and replay their gameplay. Fans call these new works '*machinema*' after a Japanese word that refers to puppetry.[22] Game avatars become, in effect, puppets that enable fan artists to tell their own stories. The scrapbook function in *The Sims* has similarly enabled new forms of fan fiction, as fans play the game in order to create the images necessary to illustrate their stories. In some cases, they also develop 'skins' designed to represent favourite television or comic book characters. Fan artists have been part of the much larger history of amateur film and video production. George Lucas and Steven Spielberg were themselves amateur film-makers as teenagers, producing low-budget horror or science-fiction movies. *Star Wars*, in turn, has inspired Super 8 film-makers since its release in the early 1970s. As the video recorder became more widely available, fans re-edited series footage into music videos, using popular music to encapsulate the often-unarticulated emotions of favourite characters.[23] As fan video-makers have become more sophisticated, some fan artists have produced whole new storylines by patching together original dialogue.

The World Wide Web is a powerful distribution channel, giving what were once home movies a surprising degree of public visibility. Publicity materials surface while these amateur films are still in production, most of the films boast lavish posters and many of them include downloadable trailers to attract would-be viewers impatient with download times. *Star Wars* fans were among the first to embrace these new technologies, producing more than 300 web movies at the last count.[24] These fan film-makers have used home computers to duplicate effects LucasFilm had spent a fortune to achieve several decades earlier; many fan films create their own light sabre or space battles. Some of these fan film-makers have had offers for professional projects or had their films screened at international film festivals. When *Amazon.com* offered videos of one favourite amateur *Star Wars* production, *George Lucas in Love*, it outsold *Star Wars Episode 1: The Phantom Menace* (1999) during its first week in circulation. Amateur film culture has already made an impact on the commercial mainstream. Spike Jonze, the director of *Being John Malkovich*, for example, began his career by making amateur films within the skateboard subculture. Similarly, MTV's *Jackass* took its inspiration from the Web-based distribution of amateur stunt films, while *Celebrity Death Match* adopts an aesthetic remarkably similar to action figure cinema. In the future, amateur productions may initiate many innovations in popular culture that gain higher visibility as they are pulled into mainstream media, just as the fans appropriate and recirculate materials from commercial culture.

KNOWLEDGE CULTURE MEETS COMMODITY CULTURE

Levy distinguishes between four potential sources of power: nomadic mobility, control over territory, ownership over commodities and mastery over knowledge. He suggests a complex set of interactions and negotiations between them. The emergent knowledge cultures never fully escape the influence of the commodity culture, any more than commodity culture can totally function outside the constraints of territoriality. However, knowledge cultures will, he predicts, gradually alter the ways that commodity culture operates. Nowhere is that transition clearer than within the culture industries, where the commodities that circulate become resources for the production of meaning: 'The distinctions between authors and readers, producers and spectators, creators and interpretations will blend to form a reading–writing continuum.'[25]

Creative activity, he suggests, will shift from the production of texts or the regulation of meanings towards the development of a dynamic environment, 'a collective event that implies the recipients, transforms interpreters into actors, enables interpretation to enter the loop with collective action'.[26] Room for participation and improvisation is being built into new media franchises. Kurt Lancaster, for example, has examined how commercial works (including computer, role-playing and card games) surrounding the cult science-fiction series *Babylon 5* facilitate a diverse range of fan performances, allowing fans to immerse themselves in the fantasy universe.[27] Cult works were once discovered, now they are being consciously produced, designed to provoke fan interactions. The producers of *Xena: Warrior Princess*, for example, were fully aware that some fans wanted to read Xena and Gabrielle as lesbian lovers and thus began to consciously weave 'subtext' into the episodes. As Levy explains, 'The recipients of the open work are invited to fill in the blanks, choose among possible meanings, confront the divergences among their interpretations.'[28]

The new cultural works will have to provoke and reward the production of collective meaning through elaborate back-stories, unresolved enigmas, excess information and extratextual expansions of the programme's universe in order to be marketable.[29] Over the past decade, there has been a marked increase in the serialisation of American television, the emergence of more complex appeals to programme history and the development of more intricate story arcs and cliff-hangers. To some degree, these aesthetic shifts can be linked to new ways of receiving information arising from the home archiving of videos, Net discussion lists and Web programme guides. These new technologies provide the information infrastructure necessary to sustain a richer form of television content, while the programmes reward the enhanced competencies of fan communities. Television producers are increasingly knowledgeable about their fan communities, often courting their support through networked computing. *Babylon 5* producer J. Michael Straczinski went online daily, responding to questions about his complex and richly developed narrative, sometimes actively engaging in flame wars with individual fans, as well as conducting what he saw as a continuing seminar on the production of genre television.[30] While Straczinski sought to be more accessible to fans, he found it difficult to shed his authority or escape a legal and economic system designed, in part, to protect corporate interests from audience appropriation. His lawyers warned him that he would have to leave the group if there were danger that he would be exposed to fans' speculations that might involve him in potential plagiarism suits. Straczinski is perhaps unique in the degree of exposure he has had to fans; however, other producers have shown a similar awareness of online fan discourse. For example, when the WB Network postponed the season finale of *Buffy the Vampire Slayer* shortly after the Columbine shootings, producer Josh Whedon made a notorious public call for Canadian fans to 'bootleg that puppy' and distribute it over the Web to American viewers. Fans, in turn, rallied to Whedon's defence when the religious right launched a letter-writing campaign against the introduction of a lesbian relationship involving regular characters.[31] By contrast, *Survivor* producer Mark Burnett engaged in an active dis-information campaign to thwart audience efforts to predict the winner of its million-dollar competition, burying false leads in the official Web site to be discovered by fan hackers. When long-time World Wrestling Federation announcer Jerry Lawler was fired, he brought his side of his disputes with Vince McMahon directly to online fans.

For many media producers, who still operate within the old logic of the commodity cul-ture, fandom represents a potential loss of control over their intellectual property. The efforts of the recording industry to dismantle Napster demonstrated that the traditional media companies were prepared to spend massive sums in legal action against new forms of grassroots distribution.[32] Television producers, film studios and book publishers have been equally aggressive in issuing 'cease and desist' letters to fan Web sites that transcribe programme dialogue or reproduce unauthorised images. If new media have made visible various forms of fan participation and production, then these legal battles demonstrate the power still vested in media ownership.

The horizontal integration of the entertainment industry, and the emergent logic of syn-ergy, depends on the circulation of intellectual properties across media outlets.[33] Transmedia promotion presumes a more active spectator who can and will follow these media flows. Such marketing strategies promote a sense of affiliation with and immersion in fictional worlds. The media industry exploits these intense feelings through the marketing of ancillary goods from T-shirts to games with promises of enabling a deeper level of involvement with the programme content. However, attempts to regulate intellectual property undercut the economic logic of media convergence, sending fans contradictory messages about how they are supposed to respond to commercial culture.[34] Rosemary Coombes and Andrew Herman have documented intensifying legal and political skirmishes between corporate lawyers and consumers. Many fan Webmasters post their 'cease and desist' letters in order to shame the media industries: shutting down grassroots promotional efforts results in negative publicity.[35] Often, the conflict boils down to an issue of who is authorised to speak for a series, as when a Fox television executive justified the closing of *The Simpsons* fan sites: 'We have an official Web site with network approved content and these people don't work for us.' Levy sees industry panic over interactive audiences as short-sighted: 'by preventing the knowledge space from becoming autonomous, they deprive the circuits of commodity space . . . of an extraordinary source of energy'. The knowledge culture, he suggests, serves as the 'invisible and intangible engine' for the circulation and exchange of commodities.[36]

The online book dealer *Amazon.com* has linked bookselling to the fostering of online book culture. Readers are encouraged to post critical responses to specific works or to compile lists of their favourite books. Their associates programme creates a powerful niche marketing system: Amazon patrons are offered royalties for every sale made on the basis of links from their sites. Similarly, the sports network ESPN sponsors a fantasy baseball league, a role-playing activity in which sports fans form teams, trade players and score points based on the real world performance of various athletes.[37]

Attempts to link consumers directly into the production and marketing of media content are variously described as 'permission-based marketing', 'relationship marketing' or 'viral-marketing', and are increasingly promoted as the model for how to sell goods, cultural and otherwise, in an interactive environment. As one noted industry guide explains, 'Marketing in an interactive world is a collaborative process with the marketer helping the consumer to buy and the consumer helping the marketer to sell.'[38]

Researchers are finding that fandom and other knowledge communities encourage a sense of passionate affiliation or brand loyalty that ensures the longevity of particular product lines.[39] In viral marketing, such affiliations become self-replicating as marketers create content which consumers actively want to circulate among their friends. Even unauthorised and vaguely subversive appropriations can spread advertising messages, as occurred with Internet spoofs of the Budweiser 'whazzup' commercials.

Building brand loyalty requires more than simply co-opting grassroots activities back into the commodity culture. Successful media producers are becoming more adept at monitoring and serving audience interests. The games industry, which sees itself as marketing interactive experiences rather than commodities, has been eager to broaden consumer participation and strengthen the sense of affiliation players feel towards their games. LucasArts has integrated would-be *Star Wars* gamers into the design team for the development of their massively multi-player online game. A Web page was created early in the design process and ideas under consideration were posted for fan feedback.[40] Maxis, the company that manages *The Sims* franchise, encourages the grassroots production and trading of 'skins' (new character identities), props and architectural structures, even programming code. *The Sims*' creator Will Wright refers to his product as a 'sandbox' or 'doll house', where consumers can play out their own stories. Ultimately, Wright predicts, two-thirds of *The Sims* content will come from consumers.[41]

It remains to be seen, however, whether these new corporate strategies of collaboration and consultation with the emerging knowledge communities will displace the legal structures of the old commodity culture. How far will media companies be willing to go to remain in charge of their content or to surf the information flow? In an age of broadband delivery, will television producers see fans less as copyright infringers and more as active associates and niche marketers? Will global media moguls collaborate with grassroots communities, such as the *anime* fans, to ensure that their products achieve visibility in the lucrative American market?

FROM JAMMERS TO BLOGGERS

In his 1993 essay, 'Culture Jamming: Hacking, Slashing and Sniping in the Empire of Signs', Mark Dery documented emerging tactics of grassroots resistance ('media hacking, informational warfare, terror-art and guerilla semiotics') to 'an ever more intrusive, instrumental technoculture whose operant mode is the manufacture of consent through the manipulation of symbols'.[42] In Citizens' Band Radio slang, the term 'jamming' refers to efforts to 'introduce noises into the signal as it passes from transmitter to receiver'. Dery's essay records an important juncture in the history of DIY media. Over the past several decades, emerging technologies – ranging from the photocopier to the home computer and the videocassette recorder – have granted viewers greater control over media flows, enabled activists to reshape and recirculate media content, lowered the costs of production and paved the way for new grassroots networks.

Many of the groups Dery describes, such as Adbusters, ACT UP, Negativeland, The Barbie Liberation Army, Paper Tiger Television, and the Electronic Disturbance Community, would happily embrace his 'culture jammer' banner. However, Dery went too far in describing all forms of DIY media as 'jamming'. These new technologies would support and sustain a range of different cultural and political projects, some overtly oppositional, others more celebratory, yet all reflecting a public desire to participate within, rather than simply consume, media. Dery, for example, distorts the fan community concept of 'slash' when he uses it to refer to 'any form of jamming in which tales told for mass consumption are perversely reworked.' Culture jammers want to opt out of media consumption and promote a purely negative and reactive conception of popular culture. Fans, on the other hand, see unrealised potentials in popular culture and want to broaden audience participation. Fan culture is dialogic rather than disruptive, affective more than ideological, and collaborative rather than confrontational. Culture jammers want to 'jam' the dominant media, while poachers want to appropriate their content, imagining a more democratic, responsive and diverse style of popular culture. Jammers want to destroy media power, while poachers want a share of it.

Returning to this same terrain at the end of the decade, it is clear that new media technologies have profoundly altered the relations between media producers and consumers. Both culture jammers and fans have gained greater visibility as they have deployed the Web for community building, intellectual exchange, cultural distribution and media activism. Some sectors of the media industries have embraced active audiences as an extension of their marketing power, have sought greater feedback from their fans and have incorporated viewer-generated content into their design processes. Other sectors have sought to contain or silence the emerging knowledge culture. The new technologies broke down old barriers between media consumption and media production.

The old rhetoric of opposition and co-option assumed a world where consumers had little direct power to shape media content and where there were enormous barriers to entry into the market place, whereas the new digital environment expands their power to archive, annotate, appropriate and recirculate media products. Levy describes a world where grassroots communication is not a momentary disruption of the corporate signal, but the routine way that the new media system operates: 'Until now we have only reappropriated speech in the service of revolutionary movements, crises, cures, exceptional acts of creation. What would a normal, calm, established appropriation of speech be like?'[43] Perhaps, rather than talking about culture jammers, we might speak of bloggers. The term 'blog' is short for weblog, a new form of personal and subcultural expression involving summarising and linking to other sites. In some cases, bloggers actively deconstruct pernicious claims or poke fun at other sites; in other cases, they form temporary tactical alliances with other bloggers or with media producers to ensure that important messages get more widely circulated. These bloggers have become important grassroots intermediaries, facilitators, not jammers, of the signal flow. Blogging describes a communication process, not an ideological position. As Levy writes:

> The new proletariat will only free itself by uniting, by decategorizing itself, by forming alliances with those whose work is similar to its own (once again, nearly everyone), by bringing to the foreground the activities they have been practicing in shadow, by assuming responsibility – globally, centrally, explicitly – for the production of collective intelligence.[44]

Bloggers take knowledge in their own hands, enabling the successful navigation within and between these emerging knowledge cultures. One can see such behaviour as co-option into commodity culture insofar as it sometimes collaborates with corporate interests, but one can also see it as increasing the diversity of media culture, providing opportunities for greater inclusion and making commodity culture more responsive to consumers. In an era marked both by the expanded corporate reach of the commodity culture and the emerging importance of grassroots knowledge cultures, consumer power may now be best exercised by blogging rather than jamming media signals.

Notes

1. Pierre Levy, *Collective Intelligence: Mankind's Emerging World in Cyberspace* (Cambridge: Perseus, 1997), p. 217.

2. The phrase 'imagined community' comes from Benedict Anderson, *Imagined Communities: Reflections on the Origin and Spread of Nationalism* (New York: Verso, 1991). Pierre Levy introduces the concept of an 'imagining community' in *Collective Intelligence*, p. 125.

3. A fuller account of Gernsbeck's role in the development of science-fiction fandom can be found in Andrew Ross, *Strange Weather: Culture, Science and Technology in the Age of Limits* (New York: Verso, 1991). For a fuller account of contemporary literary science-fiction fandom, see Camille Bacon-Smith, *Science Fiction Culture* (Philadelphia: University of Pennsylvania Press, 2000).

4. Sherry Turkle, *The Second Self: Computers and the Human Spirit* (New York: Touchstone, 1984) provides some glimpse of the centrality of science fiction in that early hacker culture, as does my study of *Star Trek* fans at MIT in John Tulloch and Henry Jenkins (eds), *Science Fiction Audiences: Watching* Doctor Who *and* Star Trek (London: Routledge, 1995).

5. Susan J. Clerc, 'Estrogen Brigades and "Big Tits" Threads: Media Fandom Online and Off', in Lynn Cherney and Elizabeth Reba Weise (eds), *Wired Women: Gender and New Realities in Cyberspace* (Seattle, WA: Seal, 1996).

6. Nancy Baym, 'Talking about Soaps: Communication Practices in a Computer-mediated Culture', in Cheryl Harris and Alison Alexander (eds) *Theorizing Fandom: Fans, Subculture, and Identity* (New York: Hampton Press, 1998).

7. Pierre Levy, *Collective Intelligence*, p. 20.

8. Nancy Baym, 'Talking about Soaps', pp. 115–16.

9. Ibid., p. 127.

10. Henry Jenkins, '"Do You Enjoy Making the Rest of Us Feel Stupid": alt.tv.twinpeaks, the Trickster Author and Viewer Mastery', in David Lavery (ed.), *Full of Secrets: Critical Approaches to Twin Peaks* (Detroit, MI: Wayne State University Press, 1995).

11. For a useful discussion of the ways that the Net is challenging traditional forms of expertise, see Peter Walsh, 'That Withered Paradigm: The Web, The Expert and the Information Hegemony', <media-in-transition.mit.edu>.

12. Matthew Hills, Fan Cultures (London: Routledge, forthcoming).

13. Ibid.

14. For an overview of *anime* and its fans, see Susan J. Napier, *Anime: From Akira to Princess Mononoke: Experiencing Contemporary Japanese Animation* (New York: Palgrave, 2001).

15. Kirsten Pullen, 'I-Love-Xena.Com: Creating Online Fan Communities', in David Gauntlett (ed.), *Web.Studies: Rewiring Media Studies for the Digital Age* (London: Arnold, 2000). See also Sharon Cumberland, 'Private Uses of Cyberspace: Women, Desire, and Fan Culture', <media-in-transition.mit.edu>.

16. *Fan Fiction on the Net*, <members.aol.com/KSNicholas/fanfic/slash.html>.

17. The phrase 'weekend only world' is discussed in the concluding chapter of Henry Jenkins, *Textual Poachers: Television Fans and Participatory Culture* (New York: Routledge, 1991).

18. Andre MacDonald, 'Uncertain Utopia: Science Fiction Media Fandom and Computer-mediated Communication', in Cheryl Harris and Alison Alexander (eds), *Theorizing Fandom*.

19. Nancy Baym, *Tune In, Log On: Soaps, Fandom and Online Community* (New York: Corwin, 1999).

20. Stephen Duncombe, *Notes from Underground: Zines and the Politics of Alternative Culture* (New York: Verso, 1997).

21. Elena Garfinkle and Eric Zimmerman, 'Technologies of Undressing: The Digital Paperdolls of KISS', in Katie Salens (ed.), *Beyond the Object*, *Zed.5* Center for Design Studies, Virginia Commonwealth University, 1988.

22. Katie Salens, 'Telefragging Monster Movies', in Lucien King (ed.) *Game On: The History and Culture Of Video Games* (London: Lawrence King, 2002), pp. 98–111.

23. For a fuller discussion of fan video practices, see Henry Jenkins, *Textual Poachers*. For a larger context on amateur media production, see Patricia R. Zimmermann, *Reel Families: A Social History of Amateur Film* (Indianapolis: Indiana University Press, 1995).

24. Henry Jenkins, '*Quentin Tarantino's Star Wars*?: Digital Cinema, Media Convergence and Participatory Culture', in David Thorburn and Henry Jenkins (eds) Rethinking Media Change: The Aesthetics of Transition (Cambridge: The MIT Press, 2003).

25. Pierre Levy, *Collective Intelligence*, p. 121.

26. Ibid., p. 123.

27. Kurt Lancaster, *Interacting with Babylon 5: Fan Performances in a Media Universe* (Austin: University of Texas Press, 2001).

28. Pierre Levy, *Collective Intelligence*, p. 125.

29. Amelie Hastie, 'Proliferating Television in the Market and in the Know', Console-ing Passions Conference, Bristol, UK, 6 July 2001.

30. Kurt Lancaster, *Interacting with Babylon 5*, p. 26. See also Alan Wexelblat, 'An Auteur in the Age of the Internet,' in Henry Jenkins, Tara McPherson and Jane Shattuc (eds), *Hop on Pop: The Politics and Pleasures of Popular Culture* (Durham, NC: Duke University Press, 2003).

31. Allison McCracken, 'Bronzers for a Smut-filled Environment: Reading Fans Reading Sexual Identity at Buffy.com', Console-ing Passions Conference, Bristol, UK, 6 July 2001.

32. David Spitz, *Contested Codes: Toward a Social History of Napster*, Masters Thesis, Comparative Media Studies Program, MIT, June 2001.

33. See, for example, Eileen Meehan, '"Holy Commodity Fetish, Batman!": The Political Economy of a Political Intertext,' in Roberta Pearson and William Uricchio (eds), *The Many Lives of the Batman: Critical Approaches to a Superhero and His Media* (New York: Routledge, 1991).

34. This formulation of the issue was inspired by Sara Gwenllian Jones, 'Conflicts of Interest? The Folkloric and Legal Status of Cult TV Characters in Online Fan Culture', Society for Cinema Studies Conference, Washington DC, 26 May 2001.

35. Rosemary Coombes and Andrew Herman, 'Defending Toy Dolls and Maneuvering Toy Soldiers: Trademarks, Consumer Politics and Corporate Accountability on the World Wide Web', presented at MIT Communication Forum, 12 April 2001.

36. Pierre Levy, *Collective Intelligence*, p. 237.

37. For example, see Amy Jo Kim, *Community Building on the Web: Secret Strategies for Successful Online Communities* (Berkeley, CA: Peachpit Press, 2000).

38. Don Peppers, 'Introduction', in Seth Godin, *Permission Marketing: Turning Strangers into Friends, and Friends into Customers* (New York: Simon and Schuster, 1999), p. 12.

39. Robert V. Kozinets, 'Utopian Enterprise: Articulating the Meanings of *Star Trek*'s Culture of Consumption', *Journal of Consumer Research*, June 2001, <www.journals.uchicago.edu/JCR/journal/>.

40. Kurt Squire, 'Star Wars Galaxies: A Case Study in Participatory Design', *Joystick 101*, <www.joystick101.org>, forthcoming.

41. Personal interview, April 2001.

42. Mark Dery, 'Culture Jamming: Hacking, Slashing and Sniping in the Empire of Signs' (Open Magazine Pamphlet Series, 1993), <web.nwe.ufl.edu/~mlaffey/cultjam1.html>.

43. Pierre Levy, *Collective Intelligence*, p. 171.

44. Ibid., pp. 36–7.

4.2

Watching the Internet

Dan Harries

Sitting in front of my computer screen surfing the Web, I recently recognised that my obsessive, nonstop clicking from site to site closely resembled my behaviour in front of the television set: a constant pushing of buttons on the remote control in an endless stream of channel surfing. Had I become bored with the near infinite supply of Internet content, my interest measured in fleeting seconds? Perhaps I had merely settled into a pattern shaped by my habits as a viewer of another little box. Do I 'view' the Web in a way taught to me by television? Am I using the Internet in the same way that I would 'use' any application on my computer? Or am I literally 'watching the Internet' in a way that combines both viewing and using media?

With the growing use of digital video, computer-based editing and special effects, we are witnessing a convergence of media images. As Anne Friedberg notes, 'the movie screen, the home television screen, and the computer screen retain their separate locations, yet the types of images you see on each of them are losing their medium-based specificity'.[1] In fact, we are even seeing these previously discrete screens being merged, particularly in relation to current efforts to fuse both computer and television screens into integrated, interactive entertainment spaces. As Henry Jenkins suggests, 'because digital media potentially incorporate all previous media, it no longer makes sense to think in medium-specific terms'.[2]

In many ways, all screens are becoming, more or less, *new* media screens as we conceptualise their uses in new and different ways. Screens are becoming *loci* of an assortment of media activities and experiences, particularly in the way that the 'screen becomes an "activity center", a cyberchronotope where both space and time are transformed'.[3] These are the screens of an expanding media environment where the modes of viewing and using commingle in ways only previously proposed in the narratives of science fiction.

From its inception, the Internet has long been host to such 'multimedia' screens. Even in the early days of the Internet, using such protocols as Gopher and FTP, users could download and watch small movies (typically short animations demonstrating molecular configurations) while also reading pages and pages of scrollable text linked to other pages of scrollable text. With the rapid expansion of the World Wide Web in 1993, precipitated by the release of the graphic-oriented browser Mosaic, text began to be augmented with images and sounds. Applications such as Shockwave allowed the creation of more inter-active content: an early favourite was the 'Pong'-like game in which one could hit a tennis ball with a 'K-Swiss shoe' racket.

Not surprisingly, the film and television industries were relatively slow in developing con-tent for the Internet (once famously referred to by one advertising executive as 'television without the shows')[4] beyond material that was promotionally tied to marketing other film and television properties, such as film trailers, television schedules and 'interactive' press kits. Yet once the major film studios and television networks realised that the Internet was going to be a major media platform, they dived in with a vengeance, ploughing millions and millions of dollars into the development of entire divisions dedicated to creating online content. These sites have ranged from dedicated online screening rooms to integrated TV-Web shows, although the viewing numbers are still miniscule when compared to tra-ditional media viewership. As one media critic cynically points out, 'more new shows will debut this fall on the Internet than on television, but fewer people will tune in to all of them, taken together, than saw a single episode of CBS's *Survivor*'.[5] Nonetheless, the major film studios and television networks see the Internet as having the potential to reach a vast and global audience and so they continue to develop entertainment products that com-bine the entertainment industries' proven ability to 'entertain' with the Internet's ability to 'connect'.

Increasingly, we are also witnessing a convergence of the ways in which viewers and users interact with media screens and there are a number of ways in which we 'watch the Internet', particularly in relation to the content being created by the entertainment industries. Not surprisingly, one of the central modes encouraged by the Internet is that of 'viewing', literally the online viewing of movies in a manner that loosely emulates the viewing of films in the cinema or on a videocassette recorder. A second mode is that of 'using' new media with users following more 'computer-oriented' activities, such as exploring hyperlinked Web pages or playing online games. Both of these modes are being cultivated by a Hollywood eager to leverage its money-making film and television properties on to the Internet.

Yet what happens when both of these modes are integrated in a manner where the using affects the viewing, and vice versa? What do we call this hybrid mode of both viewing and using? While the term 'viewer' still retains a certain sense of passivity long associated with both film and television viewing,[6] the term 'user' seems equally inappropriate with its con-notations of computational doings and 'too-active-for-narrative-seduction' pursuits. Instead, I call this third emerging mode of spectatorship 'viewsing' – the experiencing of media in a manner that effectively integrates the activities of both viewing and using, such as participating in a real-time online poll that directly affects a live video feed. 'Viewsers' are the new 'connected consumers' who find entertainment pleasure in the multitasking activities being promoted through their computer and television screens. In other words, entertainment value is not only measured by what they see and hear, but also by what they do and the ways in which their activities have a direct impact on a developing narrative.

Together, these three modes of spectatorship engender new strategies of making meaning that, in turn, migrate across media: viewing computer software, using interactive television and viewsing new media. Next, I will examine these three modes of online spectatorship, particularly in relation to how we experience online films, games and integrated media experiences and chart the shifting ways in which we are watching the Internet.

VIEWING THE INTERNET

The activity of 'viewing' has long been of interest to theorists of the moving image, from Jean-Louis Baudry's cinematic 'state of artificial regression' to David Bordwell's cue-following 'rational agent', each of which proposes different levels of 'activity' and 'interactivity' while watching the moving image, including both the visual and soundtracks.[7] The same concepts can be roughly applied to the ways in which we view online moving images, a mode of watching typically anchored in the process of 'narrative immersion' in which texts from other media, such as a movie, a television clip or a radio broadcast, are 'inserted' into the online exhibition venue. There are, of course, many derivations of this, but basically, when a spectator heads for a 'viewing' site, they are seeking access to a small, jerky film trailer or a clip from last night's news.

The amount of interactive functions on such sites is limited, much like a basic video-cassette recorder or DVD player, with the ability to start the film when you choose, to pause, and to skip both forwards and backwards. In fact, the activity involved in watching an online movie is similar to watching a DVD, being far more 'reactive' than 'interactive', a distinction made by Raymond Williams in which reactive media display a range of choices that are pre-set, for example, switching channels on the television set rather than being able to effect a two-way system of communication.[8]

The context of online viewing, then, is marked not by the interactivity usually attributed to accessing the Internet, but rather by a form of 'broadcasting' texts to viewers. As George Landow comments, such time-bounded media primarily 'turns hypermedia into a broadcast, rather than interactive, medium.'[9] In other words, sites that encourage viewing moving images become alternative movie exhibition venues, albeit ones with poor quality and the tiniest of tiny screens.

These new movie exhibition sites rely heavily on strategies of viewership already groomed by watching film and television. Of course, the experience is similar, but not quite the same. As Vivian Sobchack correctly describes downloadable QuickTime movies, they are 'full of gaps, gasps, starts, and repetitions, made "precious" by their small size and "scarce" memory'.[10] Again, it is almost like watching the real thing (films in a cinema, shows on a television), but it is not. And streamed videos are even worse: small, jerky and fuzzy (more like gloppy). As one critic describes her experience of watching an online film, 'Pixelations. Loss of sound. Herky-jerky movement. Sudden shutdowns of service. No response during high traffic. And you can't go in the lobby and yell at an usher.'[11] However, a very important factor to keep in mind is that these films are typically watched for free, hence the attraction for an inferior viewing experience.

Quite often, the movies themselves are either independently produced short films or previously distributed features with little to no legs left in their marketing (although a studio executive did once acknowledge to me that putting old worn-out films on the Net was good business as people usually reacted so adversely to the streamed movies that they ended up going out and buying a good copy of the film on video). In other words, these are films that are rarely seen in other exhibition venues and a good deal of their entertainment value can be placed on the sheer sense of being 'able' even to watch the films, rather than the content of the movies themselves.

One of the earliest attempts to place previously distributed films on the Internet was accomplished by the American Film Institute in 1997 with the launch of the *AFI Online Cinema*. Although QuickTime movies and streaming video had been around for a few years, the Online Cinema was one of the first sites to not only embed the film into a graphic and cinematic interface, but, more importantly, to exhibit films that were known and celebrated as movies released before the arrival of the Internet. People came to the site to watch a Charlie Chaplin or Buster Keaton film, although some of the entertainment pleasure must have been derived from the sheer sense of accomplishment by successfully downloading the plug-in and getting the movie to play somewhat fluidly, and to do this all for free.

What the viewer encountered when they 'entered' the cinema was a three-inch by three-inch screen embedded in a grand, graphic interior of an old movie palace, complete with sheer golden curtains and red velvet seats. When the movie began, the viewer would see a small movie playing on the screen accompanied by an audio track coming through the computer's speakers. The experience seemed almost primitive, like watching a revolving Zoetrope, but, for viewers simultaneously watching the film from across the globe, there must have been some sort of 'collective' excitement attached to the viewing of a real movie being streamed into their own computers from a server based in California.

The formation of online networks and movie portals, much in the same vein as television networks and similar to the *AFI Online Cinema*, has created further opportunities on the Internet for viewers to watch online movies. *BijouFlix.com* (established in 1998 and currently offering streaming feature-length films at 50 cents per screening) and *IFilm.com* (launched in 1999 and funded by Sony and Kodak) are two of the portals that have emerged as leaders in an effort to exhibit independent short films to an ever-increasing online public.[12] In fact, the Web may be *the* ideal medium for distributing and exhibiting short films. As John Geirland writes, 'online distributors see greater financial possibilities for shorts online – where they earn revenues through advertising, sponsorship, licensing fees and e-commerce partnerships – than in admission-paying movie houses.'[13] Although the quality of films that are screened is mixed, as is the quality of films being screened in non-online cinemas, the sheer choice of online films available to watch is impressive, with many of these sites offering hundreds of titles from which to choose.

In many ways, online movie venues have become the world's largest drive-in theatres, complete with plenty of non-film related distractions and equally poor image and audio quality. And with the current limitation of bandwidth and external technological factors, viewing films on the Internet remains a challenging and fairly non-interactive experience. As a mode of media distribution, though, the Internet remains excellent due to its ability to transfer digitised movies around the globe. In the not-too-distant future, the downloading of DVD movies will be the norm and one will then be able to view the films in a more tech-nologically stable and controlled environment such as, ironically, the television set.

USING THE INTERNET

'Using' the Internet, on the other hand, is a spectatorship anchored in the realm of com-puter 'interactivity': the pushing of buttons, the typing of answers, the moving of objects or the solving of riddles. Users have the ability to change many aspects of the entertainment content they are encountering, quite often through multitasking and toggling between mul-tiple windows, as well as navigating through predetermined narrative co-ordinates. This is most commonly seen in the playing of computer and video games where users travel through virtual worlds or decipher encrypted codes. Unlike the 'viewing' experience, controlled interaction within the storyworld is primary, if not necessary, to the 'using' enter-tainment experience. In fact, quite often, such interaction is the *only* narrative occurring in the game. As Lev Manovich succinctly reminds us, 'If the player does nothing, the narrative stops.'[14]

Yet one might also argue that such experiences are still more 'reactive' than 'interactive', as the parameters of the experience are often predetermined, therefore creating more of an activity of enacting and reacting than actually interacting. One of the more overhyped elements of online media is the promise of increased interactivity between user and enter-tainment content. The spectator's pleasure is predicated on the amount of interactivity one can have with both the medium and its content. This is often juxtaposed to the relative pas-sivity associated with both cinematic and television viewing, yet the parallels between Web and channel surfing in terms of interactivity seem to suggest something quite different. In fact, when you consider the amount of interactivity involved in accessing a Web page through a browser (primarily clicking on a hyperlink to retrieve a file), you begin to realise how little interactivity there really is beyond the decision of what pages to 'enact' or what links to 'react' to and click upon.

Some of the earliest attempts by Hollywood to put 'original' entertainment on to the Internet were efforts to create new media properties that had this 'added feature' of limited interactivity. Sites such as *The Spot*, *Eon 4* and *The Pyramid* fostered a spectatorship defined through actions of 'narrative exploration' in which the user explored multilinear options of a story and literally 'read' media content. Usually, however, such narratives evoked broader narrative worlds and contexts, such as film and television, and intertextu-ally relied on these narrative schemata for situating the entertainment experience, rather like reading a novelisation of a hit movie or, even worse, like browsing through a series of film storyboards without getting to see the film. In other words, clicking through Web pages did not provide the immersive experience that one gets with both film and television, and any attempt to replicate such an experience through hyperlinked Web pages was doomed to failure. Not surprisingly, all of these sites quickly became costly failures as users quickly grew tired of the shows' stories and spent more time doing the associated activities, such as sending e-mails to the shows' stars, than getting 'caught up' in the unfolding narratives.

Ironically, in comparison to cinema and television, the computer is, in its own right, already steeped in heavy interactivity. Just think of any word processing program and the instant ability to change fonts, check spelling, or cut and paste a paragraph. The computer is full of interactivity and this is what makes it so powerful for writing, designing and calculating. As Lev Manovich argues, 'to call computer media "interactive" is meaningless – it simply means stating the most basic fact about computers'.[15] Yet how do these computer-based interactive features affect the user's ability to become actually immersed in a narrative experience?

Referring to Benjamin's concept of 'perception in the state of distraction', Manovich argues that new media have become the perfect realisation of this notion as users straddle different modes of interaction. He writes that 'the periodic reappearance of the machinery, the continuous presence of the communication channel in the message, prevent the subject from falling into the dream world of illusion for very long, make [sic] her alternate between concentration and detachment'.[16] The resulting experience of this state of distraction can be unsatisfactory in terms of how we experience traditional entertainment content as the user ends up viewing little and doing even less.

David Rokeby argues that interactivity is, in many ways, a hindrance to narrative immersion, stating that 'it is ironic that wide-open interaction within a system that does not impose significant constraints is usually unsatisfying to the interactor. It is difficult to sense interaction in situations in which one is simultaneously affecting all of the parameters'.[17] In other words, a viewer plunged into a world of total interactivity becomes so involved in conscious decision-making that she or he has less of an ability to 'let go' and enter a realm of narrative seduction.

Recognising this limited spectatorial paradox, major film studios and television networks have realised that, contrary to conventional wisdom centred on the need to *increase* the level of interactivity on the Internet, traditional forms of media entertainment play better when there is a *decrease* in interactivity, making the site even more reactive than interactive. To this end, Web creators have worked to eliminate levels of interactivity, for example, the removal of navigational buttons on customised launched browsers, in order to simulate more traditional notions of immersive entertainment.

Websites based on popular television game shows where the focus centres on inserting the user *into* the text rather than broadcasting the text to the viewer are often characterised by this limited level of interactivity. User interaction within these games is typically based on typing answers into a provided box, submitting the information via a button and having the game 'react' to the answer, sometimes with audio applause, at other times with a graphic proclaiming 'Wrong!'. Another interesting feature of these game sites, and many entertainment-based Web sites, is how the content-centred diegetic world as we traditionally know it in film and television rarely exists with the diegetic and non-diegetic worlds collapsed, creating a space where navigation *is* content, serving as one of the key structural devices for the entertainment experience as well as the sites' more interactive features.[18]

An interesting example of this limitation of interactivity is the 'You Don't Know Jack' online trivia game. Modelled as a generic television game show, 'Jack' is a downloaded program that retrieves new content through an online connection. While its irreverent humour and televisual aesthetics make it a very entertaining game to play, the most compelling aspect of the game is how much it channels user activity by *removing* typical features of computer interactivity. As the game opens up on the computer screen, its interface envelops the entire computer workspace. The screen width is fixed, its fonts cannot be altered and your interactive options have been reduced to the simple pushing of the 'P' or the 'Q' keys on the keyboard. But the game remains fun and entertaining despite such removals because the content is so compelling and the user is led to forget that she or he is playing on a computer connected to a network.

While the 'Jack' online game creates a balance between looking like a television game show and offering a limited palate of interactivity, other sites have had even greater success in combining the identifiable brand of known television game shows with extra features of limited interactivity. For example, ITV's *Who Wants to Be a Millionaire?* game site goes to great lengths to evoke the widely watched television version of the show while still providing a fun game for the user to play. You hear the same theme music as you 'enter' the stage, the lights rapidly dim when you are asked a question and you are even given the chance to go '50/50'. As the television show itself relies heavily on the use of computer graphics to display both the questions and answers during the game, the reappearance of those same graphics on your computer screen is a friendly, intertextual sight as the user begins to feel as if he or she is 'part of the show'. However, there is no Chris Tarrant (the television show's host) prodding you for your 'final answer', no in-studio crowd gasping at your wrong answers and no chance to 'phone a friend'. No matter how hard one tries, the site seems like just another computer game, far removed from the glamour and exposure of national television, with interactive options that narrowly affect only your version of the game.

In contrast to this, Sony's *Station.com* features a number of multiple-player online games based on hit television game shows such as *Jeopardy!*, *Wheel of Fortune* and *The Dating Game*, as well as such classic parlour card games as solitaire and spades, and can easily have well over 100,000 players logged on playing the online games at any moment. The *Wheel of Fortune* site provides a close approximation of how the game is played on television. You spin the wheel, you guess at what the missing letters are and you can even 'buy a vowel'. Yet unlike the *Who Wants to Be a Millionaire?* game site, the entertainment pleasure on this site is derived not only from the pleasures associated with a direct affiliation with a well-known television programme, but also from the interactive 'playing' of the game against other logged-on network users. On the site, your answers are heard, responded to and even applauded as your interaction affects the game for the other players as well. Yet for all of its limited interactivity and canned sound effects, the experience still seems like a popular computer game trying to attain the entertainment value of either film or television, but falling short.

The exploratory activity of the user, therefore, is often couched within a desperate need by the sites to make overt links to the cinematic and the televisual for their larger framing as 'Hollywood entertainment', possibly at the expense of developing innovative means for more direct experiences of interactivity. Of course, if one really does want to experience the 'real' thing, there are ample opportunities on these sites to call the free phone number and sign up to be a contestant on the show, reinforcing a strong link to the television programme and overtly indicating that one's participation here *is* different from the real thing – like playing the related board game in one's own living room.

VIEWSING THE INTERNET

Although sites that encourage either viewing or using entertainment content on the Web have been the prevailing locale for Hollywood's entry into online media, Web sites are now being developed which foster 'viewsing' modes of spectatorship, effectively combining the viewing of moving images with the interactive functions provided by microprocessing and digitisation. One should not, however, confuse this hybrid form of spectatorship with the side-by-side and parallel activity that one can do while sitting at a networked computer; as stated above, it has almost always been possible to play a QuickTime movie in one window while scrolling through text in another. Rather, it is the integration (and mutual influencing) of the two primary spectatorial activities that creates a true 'viewsing' experience on the Internet, much in line with Manovich's concept of 'cognitive multitasking', which is already embedded in modern computer usage and involves a combination of multiple and oscillating activities.[19] Most importantly, in relation to entertainment content on the Web, such 'cognitive multitasking' creates a viewsing experience in which one's interaction with the content has an immediate effect on the outcome of the experience and can be shared between connected viewers.

Whereas the viewing of online movies or the using and playing of online games such as *Wheel of Fortune* have been available for some time now, especially as they have most typically been tied to other film and television properties already in existence, the creation of original, online viewsing experiences by Hollywood is relatively new. As Dan Adler, head of new media for Creative Artists Agency, suggests, 'some of those who have struggled have looked at the Internet as a means of distributing traditional content rather than as an opportunity to create something new'.[20] In many ways, major film studios and television networks have quite literally failed to think outside of the (television) box when developing online sites that might harness the best qualities of both television and the Internet.

This is now changing. Entertainment creators and producers have begun to develop 'programming' that operates effectively across and between different media. Rather than attempting to 'convert' television programmes to an interactive environment (such as *Jeopardy!*), many production companies are developing programmes that are initially conceived as interactive properties in which logged-on viewers directly influence the developing narrative in real time and visibly on the televised and Web-based moving image.[21]

Such viewsing activities have found a particularly fertile home among the assortment of 'reality' TV programmes that have become huge hits on television screens around the world and have generated enormous amounts of 'hits' on Web sites. These shows are built on the premise of spying and constant surveillance, where the audience takes an active role in determining the unfolding narrative events. One of the first attempts to do this was in February 2000, with launch of the companion Web site for the *de Bus* television programme produced by the Dutch television network SBS. Essentially, the show borrows the successful formula of the MTV-produced *Real World* series and loads 11 strangers on to a double-decker bus for a four-month trip around the Dutch countryside. The audience is able to watch the contestants 'live' 24 hours a day via live Webcams.

While the use and prevalence of live Webcams is not terribly new on the Web, what makes this site a bit more interesting in terms of viewing is that the television programme, comprising 45 minutes of 'highlights' six days a week, is parasitic to the 'Webcast'. In other words, you can see the show first on the Internet. Yet even more important to the viewsing experience is how the site's developing narrative is also reliant on the online assembly of viewers who are granted the opportunity to vote for which contestants they like and do not like, and every two weeks the least-liked person is booted off the bus. This mixture of viewing the contestants on the bus and performing associated user activities such as chats and online polling offers a varied spectatorial palette where one votes and keeps a check on the ever-changing tally while watching the bus riders with the lower percentages of audience votes squirm.

Similar to *de Bus* are the Web sites built around the popular television series *Big Brother*, in which ten or 11 people are selected to live in a house together for nine weeks with one person being voted off by the public each week. On the US's CBS *Big Brother* site, there are a number of activities that combine viewing the ongoing lives of the people in front of the cameras with using the site to perform various interrelated tasks, including taking a 3D virtual tour of the house, contributing to the very active chatrooms where fans exchange views on the happenings within the house, taking part in constant opinion polls and being able to watch four live video feeds that are accessible 24 hours a day and only available when one purchases a '*Big Brother* Season Pass' for $19.95 (see plate 07).

The UK's Channel 4 version of *Big Brother* has an even greater integration of viewing and using activities built into the programme as a 'package'. Like its American counterpart, Channel 4 broadcasts the day's highlights each evening on regular broadcast television. Its Web site, however, features chatrooms, online polling, two live camera mixes, a 'fan cam' that follows a particular house member who was voted on by viewers the previous day, and a 'spin camera' that the user can control him or herself. Spectators can also sign up for constant text update messages via their mobile phones for those times when they are not near either a television or a computer. However, probably the most interesting aspect of this show in terms of creating a viewsing experience was Channel 4's decision to broadcast live edited feeds each day and night from 11.00 pm to 5.30 pm on its digital television channel, E4. This created almost 24/7 high-resolution access, in comparison to streaming video, into the house. It provided for some quite unusual viewing, including cameras focused on individual house members sleeping that was often toggled with views provided by the Internet cameras in different parts of the house. This convergence between the television screen, computer screen and the mobile phone screen creates a viewsing opportunity that reaches beyond the expected parameters of traditional entertainment by integrating the entire experience and capitalising on the strengths of each medium.

It is the creation of entertainment 'programmes' that are integrated from their inception that offers the richest experience for future viewers. These are the new generation of integrated entertainment media projects that combine television, live events and the Internet in which all three media are essential components to the experience. A good example of the new integrated viewer experience is LivePlanet and ABC Television's *The Runner*, based on the online game 'Reality Run,' which is in turn based on the film *Running Man* (1987).[22] LivePlanet, a recently launched film/television/Internet venture, whose founders include actors Matt Damon and Ben Affleck, states that it is dedicated to producing 'entertainment experiences that break down the barriers between traditional media, new media, and the physical world'.[23] The way they plan to achieve this is by developing an experience that is integrated from the start. As Chris Moore, CEO of LivePlanet, explains, 'each medium will provide a stand-alone entertainment experience. But when they are combined, people will get a better overall experience because we have built everything to work together from the start.'[24]

The premise of *The Runner* is intriguing and challenging in the way it offers an integrated media experience:

> A 'runner' competes for a $1 million-plus prize by completing a series of 'missions' across the country, while three 'agents' try to 'capture' him. The LivePlanet-designed twist? Not only can potential contestants apply to be runners or agents online, but viewers can win a share of the pot by digging up and sharing clues about the runner's whereabouts on the Web.[25]

What makes *The Runner* so unique and tricky in terms of viewsing, besides the multitude of safety issues involved in generating a nationwide 'manhunt', is the way in which the logged-on and television-watching viewser can help solve the narrative's enigma ('Where is the runner?') while building on the contributions by other viewers. In this manner, the activity of both viewing the television programme and using the online interactive features creates an entertainment experience that harnesses the strengths of both television and the Internet without compromising the unique qualities of each medium. In other words, viewsing becomes the true manifestation of multimedia spectatorship and offers media audiences an interesting and engaging interactive experience.

SWITCHING/LOGGING OFF

Online entertainment spectatorship, at least the spectatorship nurtured by the major film studios and television networks, is obviously one of multiplicity and it is in flux. Media conglomerates are trying hard to work out the best way to leverage their proven ability to create immersive experiences within a context of linked interactivity. This has created an assort-ment of online sites where spectators can learn more about film and television shows, 'view' narratives over the Internet, 'use' interactive games and eventually take part in integrated media experiences as 'viewers'. By integrating the illusory 'realness' of cinema, the 'live-ness' of television and the 'connectedness' of the Internet, true viewsing experiences can now be created and accessed by a global audience.

Notes

1. Anne Friedberg, 'The End of Cinema: Multimedia and Technological Change', in Christine Gledhill and Linda Williams (eds), *Reinventing Film Studies* (London: Arnold, 2000), p. 439.

2. Henry Jenkins, 'The Work of Theory in the Age of Digital Transformation', in Toby Miller and Robert Stam (eds), *A Companion to Film Theory* (London: Blackwell, 1999), p. 250.

3. Robert Stam and Ella Habiba Shohat, 'Film Theory and Spectatorship in the Age of "Posts"', in Gledhill and Williams (eds), *Reinventing Film Studies*, p. 395.

4. Russell Collins, co-founder of the California advertising agency Fattal & Collins, quoted in 'Hitting the Spot/Soap Operas in Cyberspace', *The Economist*, vol. 332, 26 August 1995, p. 44.

5. Marc Gunther, 'Full Stream Ahead', *Fortune*, 9 October 2000, <www.business2.com/articles/mag/ 0,1640,8423,00.html>.

6. As Anne Friedberg rightly points out, 'computer "users" are not spectators, not viewers'. In 'The End of Cinema: Multimedia and Technological Change', p. 448.

7. See Jean-Louis Baudry, 'The Apparatus: Metapsychological Approaches to the Impression of Reality in the Cinema', *camera obscura*, no. 1, Autumn 1976, pp. 104–28; David Bordwell, *Narration in the Fiction Film* (Madison: University of Wisconsin Press, 1985).

8. Raymond Williams, *Television: Technology and Cultural Form* (New York: Schocken Books, 1975), p. 139.

9. George Landow, *Hypertext 2.0: The Convergence of Contemporary Critical Theory and Technology* (Baltimore, MD: Johns Hopkins University Press, 1997), p. 159.

10. Vivian Sobchack, 'Nostalgia for a Digital Object: Regrets on the Quickening of QuickTime', *Millennium Film Journal* no. 34, Autumn 1999, p. 5.

11. Susan Wloszczyna, 'One Critic's Trip to Movies on the Net', *USAToday.com*, 7 June 2000, <www.usatoday.com/life/cyber/tech/cth497.htm>.

12. Although the dramatic and costly failure of DreamWorks to launch *pop.com*, a site devoted to delivering original programming for the Internet, suggests that such large-scale endeavours to make the Web a sustainable entertainment medium might be economically premature.

13. John Geirland, 'Short Attention Span Theater', *salon.com*, 21 July, 1999, <www.salon.com/tech/ feature/1999/07/21/short_films/index.html>.

14. Lev Manovich, *The Language of New Media* (Cambridge, MA: MIT Press, 2001), p. 247.

15. Ibid., p. 55.

16. Ibid., p. 207.

17. David Rokeby, 'Transforming Mirrors: Subjectivity and Control in Interactive Media', in Simon Penny (ed.), *Critical Issues in Electronic Media* (Albany: State University of New York Press, 1995), p. 140.

18. See Sean Cubitt, *Digital Aesthetics* (London: Sage, 1998), p. 79.

19. Lev Manovich, *The Language of New Media*, p. 210.

20. As quoted in Marc Gunther, 'Full Stream Ahead'.

21. Like many aspects of the Internet, this form of viewsing was previously developed by the online porn industry as logged-on users could type instructions to the on-screen 'actors'.

22. As of November 2001, ABC had placed this project on hold following the events of 11 September.

23. LivePlanet Press Release, 'LivePlanet Unveils Integrated Media Concept-Entertainment Experiences that Span Traditional Media, New Media and the Physical World', 14 December 2000, <www.liveplanet.com/inconcept.html>.

24. Ibid.

25. Josh Young, 'Good Will Games', *Entertainment Weekly's EW.COM*, 31 July 2001, <www.ew.com/ew/report/0,6115,169443~6~0~storybehindmattand,00.html>.

4.3

Self, Other and Electronic Media

Tara McPherson

I am supposed to be writing this chapter about identity and electronic forms for the Consumption section of this collection of essays on new media. At least, that is what I was asked to do, but I quickly realised that I could not fulfil this request, as straightforward as it seemed. Try as I might, I could not fix identity at the level of consumption and found myself instead wanting to think through other questions about the networked construction of selves, questions that extend beyond the contours of the consuming subject. The notion of consumption is perhaps not flexible enough for the demands of digital times, implying as it does a neat division from production, making it difficult to see that identity does not align neatly with either term, but, rather, fluctuates between the material forms of the digital and the self engaging those forms, as well as in both the self's and the machine's appropriations of or approaches to the other. The conditions of digitality process identity, reconfiguring notions of the self while also blurring the boundaries between production and consumption. Much of digital theory strives to address the complex ways in which cultural technologies (if not our theories of technology) shape the grounds for identity and consciousness. So, rather than writing about identity in cyberspace, I have come to write about the constitution of the self in and by electronic media.

Specifically, I question two basic assumptions embedded within much of digital theory, now functioning as near truisms. First, I am interested in claims that cyberspace and networked subjectivity have the effect of multiplying the self. This observation is sometimes extended towards an attendant claim that this multiplicity of selves, frequently described as proliferating points of view, sets the stage for seeing as others do, supporting what Janet Murray has called an 'imaginative identification with a surrogate'.[1] While some theorists imply that the ability to inhabit multiple points of view also facilitates increased empathy or understanding, we should think carefully about such claims. How do we gauge the output of cycling through multiple selves? What precisely does it mean to inhabit the other under conditions of virtuality? Second, I suggest that we rethink the blanket call for more bodies in cyberspace. As Sandy Stone, Simon Penny, Katherine Hayles and others have pointed out, it is certainly true that fantasies of digital living sometimes replay familiar Cartesian paradigms, aiming to divorce mind from body and upload consciousness into the network, leaving behind a carcass of devalued skin and bone. Sandy Stone reminds us that 'forgetting about the body is an old Cartesian trick, one that exacts a price from those bodies rendered invisible in the act of forgetting'.[2] However, simply remembering or representing the body is not enough; it matters 'how' we remember the body, calling it up from within the realms of code. We need to exercise care in our moves to flesh out the machine, thinking through which bodies are called into service in today's new media ecologies. Conversely, we might consider that, for some bodies, possibilities reside in moments of dissolution.

I raise these concerns as part of a larger investigation, one designed to introduce new modes of relationality into our considerations of self and machine in the era of digital reproduction. Important work has compellingly argued for probing the intricate connections between body and networks, self and computer, highlighting the degree to which relationality should be central to our understanding of increasingly networked modes of subjectivity. For instance, Katherine Hayles writes that 'refusing to grant embodiment a status prior to relation opens the possibility that changes in the environment . . . are deeply interrelated with changes in embodiment. Living in a technologically engineered and information-rich environment brings with it associated shifts in habits, postures, enactments, [and] perceptions.'[3] In examining the feedback loops between 'mindbody' and technology, Hayles highlights the importance of focusing not on entity, but on relation.[4] This insistence on the relational is crucial, a paradigm which can be usefully extended. However, an understanding of relationality is not inherent in our encounters with digital forms. In fact, the fragmentary nature of the digital, in concert with other fragmentary logics of our times, can impede our experiences of relationality, fixing us in precise and often familiar modes of being. In what follows, I suggest that in our careful parsing of the intricate dance of distributed cognition and embodiment, we need to expand our critical models beyond a dyadic focus on self/machine (in the world) towards a triadic consideration of self/other/machine (also in the world), a positioning that deploys relationality to disrupt the old self/other binary. Here, strategic approaches to the machine can help us to rethink the relationship of self to other, destabilising the default status of whiteness in cyberspace while allowing us to discern how fragmentation can impact everyday life.

Otherwise, we risk reinstalling a new millennial version of the 'universal subject' of 1970s film theory. This new subject is a fragmented and networked subject, but one still strangely universal, meant to speak for us all, somehow not quite mindful of the powerful dialectic of self and other which has profoundly shaped Western subjectivity over the years. Immersed in the critical stylings of thinkers ranging from Homi Bhabha to Toni Morrison to Paul Gilroy to Emmanuel Levinas, we know that the self is constituted in relation to the other.[5] This other need not be a racial other, although that axis of difference is the vector this chapter will pursue. We might also pursue gender, sexuality, class or any other of the multiple markers of identity which engage contemporary theorists of self and other. I turn particularly to race, specifically to blackness, for I believe that race functions as a structuring absence in many of our theories of the digital, displaced onto a fascination with the (more universal, although sometimes gendered) networked self. We would do well to remember that identity has long been distributed for the Western self, bound up with blackness and other markers of difference in intricate and myriad ways. Might our encounters with the digital help us break free from these tired, familiar loops?

LENTICULAR LOGICS AND FRAGMENTED KNOWLEDGES

The Winter of 1991 found me roaming around the Mississippi Delta, beginning my doctoral research on race and Southern femininity. During a midday stop at one of the combination gas station/country store/lunch counter places that dot the region, I came across a dusty postcard tacked up near the cash register. It was one of those plastic, ridged postcards composed of two interlaced images I have always mistakenly called '3D'. This particular card usually depicted – that is, its primary image was – a young hoopskirted belle standing before an antebellum mansion on the scale of Tara, much like the opening moments of the film *Gone with the Wind*. However, if you stood in just the right spot as you paid your bill, this vision of Southern architecture and femininity was supplanted by the familiar iconic image of a grinning, portly mammy. Over the years this card has come to symbolise for me a very particular mode of racial visibility, a prominent way of seeing in black and white in the latter half of the twentieth century that I call a 'lenticular logic'.

A lenticular image is composed when two or more separate images are interlaced or combined via a specialised process. This combined image is then viewed via a unique type of lens, called a lenticular lens, which allows one to see only one of the two views at a time. By slightly rotating the picture, the second image comes into focus, displacing the first. The most familiar use of lenticular images is in '3D' postcards, a form increasingly popular after World War II. That ridged, plastic coating on each card is actually a lenticular lens, a device which makes joining the two images within one view difficult if not impossible, impeding relationality. The postcard described above is capable of representing both black and white, but one approaches the limits of the card's lenticular logic when one attempts to under-stand how the images are joined or related. Such a positioning fixes images and their possible meanings, erasing context and connections. In a book exploring modes of racial visibility in the twentieth-century US South, I argue that this lenticular logic is a covert racial logic, a logic for the post-Civil Rights' era. In distinction to the overt racial logics of the early twentieth century, economies of visibility that powerfully insisted on the interrelation of black and white, limning one against the other, these later logics separate black from white, fixing them in different registers. For example, if *Gone with the Wind* stands as a model of an overt racial (and racist) logic, the sequel *Scarlett* represents the covert strategy. The earlier novel presents the whiteness of its heroine largely in relation to mammy, while the sequel quickly moves to displace blackness altogether, dispatching Scarlett to Ireland, isolating her from blackness. This is the freeze-frame and separatist operation of a lenticular logic, fixating on one image, suppressing the other. A lenticular logic might also be additive, alternating between images of black and white, but still suppressing relation. (Here, recall Ken Burns's documentary, *The Civil War*, which dutifully examined the lives of both whites and blacks while largely failing to frame the war within a relational understanding of race.)

Now what, you might ask, does any of this have to do with the networked selves of the digital era? A lenticular logic is a logic of the fragment or the chunk, a way of seeing the world as discrete elements, a mode which can also suppress relation. The popularity of lenticular lenses, particularly in the form of postcards, coincides historically not just with the rise of an articulated movement for civil rights in the US but also with the growth of electronic culture and the birth of cybernetics (with both, cybernetics and the Civil Rights movement, stemming from World War II). I am not arguing that one mode is causally related to the other, but, rather, that they both represent a move towards fragmentary knowledges, knowledges increasingly prevalent in the later half of the twentieth century that have much to say about the relationship of self, other and machine. They are congruent modes of knowledge production.

While Hayles convincingly illustrates the power of particular digital art works to assert relationality, thus 'teaching us to be posthuman in the best sense', some modes of digital processing can suppress relation.[6] For instance, C++, the programming language that underlies many of our encounters with the digital, at some levels functions as a form of fragmentary knowledge production, making cause and effect and interrelation hard to conceptualise. In large C++ applications, such as the ones fuelling computer games or Windows programs, one programmer may create one group of classes; other programmers create other groups of classes. They work in different conceptual areas of an application, different components of a work space. Programmer B may develop an object based upon a class created by programmer A, but often programmer B knows nothing about the code inside this object. Effectively, programmer A has created a black box of code, limiting programmer B's ability to control certain functions of the object. Programmer B has access to select functions of the object, but not to the code which underwrites the objects and their functions. He only knows the interface to the object, a shallow knowledge at best, useful but fragmented. While relation is important to the application as a whole, and across the parts within it, the workers creating the code (and we can also say being created by these coding processes) often have a limited experience of relationality in a deep sense, working as they usually do on a particular fragmentary group within the code. C++ is an object-oriented programming language, and, as such, it deploys interfaces alternately to hide and access data, manipulating the objects' data beneath the interface. The programmer working with a colleague's 'black box' of code remains at the level of the interface, allowing only partial views, much as the lenticular lens processes its interlaced images into separate entities. The relation between objects is suppressed in favour of ease of use, as is the relationship between programmers. The computer as processing machine, like the lens, here impedes relationality. This calls to mind the factory labour of a century ago, but with a key difference: here the final product is fundamentally malleable until the final moment of production, a malleability that resides within the fragmentation.[7]

This fragmentation also haunts other digital experiences. In interacting with many mainstream computer applications, the user is also distanced from the relationality of the code, moving across the surface of the screen. We often experience our movement through electronic spaces as a rather simplistic A to B: this becomes that, in an instant, in the click, in the reload. Difference and the risks and limits of becoming something else are smoothed over at the surface of the screen. Both the computer and the lenticular lens mediate images and objects, changing their relationship, but frequently suppressing that process of relation. Of course, fragmentation is also the logic of global capitalism in which, as John Hess and Patricia Zimmerman note, 'transnational capital ... reform[s] labor relations through fragmentation and isolation'.[8] Fragmentation need not inherently suppress relationality in electronic texts, but, when it does, it supports modes of distributed identity which are limited and limiting, particularly when networked subjectivity is also hardwired into other lenticular networks of difference and meaning. The fragmentary knowledges encouraged by some experiences of the digital neatly parallel the lenticular logics which underwrite the covert racism endemic to our times, operating in potential feedback loops, supporting each other. As the lenticular lens destroys the relationship between self and other, fixing them into distinct and separate realms, so, too, do many modes of digital production and consumption deploy the machine in order to fracture productive relations between self and other. In order to model different, 'relational' modes of subjectivity in electronic spaces, we need to wed our relations of self and machine to what Paul Gilroy has called a principled exposure to the claims of otherness.

MULTIPLYING THE SELF

In 1995, Sherry Turkle observed that living under conditions of networked virtuality offers people the chance 'to play with their identity and to try out new ones'. This play 'makes possible the creation of an identity so fluid and multiple that it strains the limits of the notion. ... [O]ne can be many.'[9] Such ideas now have an almost viral familiarity in digital theory, and, to anyone who has spent some time lost in the rich textuality of MOOs or chat, it is hard not to agree with Sandy Stone when she asserts that such practices are rewriting the standard of the bounded, embodied individual.[10] Still, these claims often slide seamlessly into other contentions, including the oft-voiced assumption that 'a more fluid sense of self allows a greater capacity for acknowledging diversity'.[11] Here, the multiplying self becomes the ground for greater empathy, a perspective espoused by Jay Bolter and Richard Grusin when they note that 'the path to empathy is the occupation of another's point of view'.[12] In their remediations of old and new, the ability of the virtual self to inhabit multiple points of view becomes 'a new positive good'.[13] Thus, this work moves all too neatly from an acknowledgment of the porous boundaries of the networked self towards the assertion that such extended subjectivity also instantiates relationality, that is, that a connection of self to the machine easily connects self and machine to the other as well. It is reasonable to think of cyberspace as encouraging an exploration of identities, a trying on of various ways of being (or not) in the world. But this is not an entirely innocent pastime. While it might, as Turkle and others maintain, signal a desire for connection and relationality, such identity play might also signal less benign desires. Importantly, there is a difference between 'engaging' the other and 'becoming' the other. Thus, when Bolter and Grusin write that 'the freedom to be oneself is the freedom to become someone or something else', we must ask precisely what they mean.[14] What does it mean to occupy another? The very terms we use to describe our experiences of cyberspace, such as fluidity, merging, disso-lution, networks, morphing, also imply fantasies of escaping into or subsuming the other (as machine, but also as other), movements into a new frontier of 'personal freedom' which are also the fantasies of colonialism. History should give us pause, warning us to be wary of assigning too much progressive potential to easy dreams of inhabiting an other.

Many forms of digitality seem to enact an endless rehearsal of becoming other, from the relentless techno-Orientalism of computer games and game-based cinema to the endemic gender or species swapping of the slippery worlds of chatrooms and MUDs.[15] Here, the self is reconfigured via playful difference, a becoming without inherent accountability. Such identity switching can replay a lenticular logic, porting into the digital realm the additive modes of racial representation which I earlier noted characterised *The Civil War*. Players or viewers are invited to try on other points of view in rapid succession, an exploration of char-acters or perspectives. Click a menu; be a Ninja. Click once more; you're white again. Flick the card; there's Mammy. Flick again; there's Scarlett. We shift frames towards a hollow pluralism, suppressing relation or responsibility. As Jennifer Gonzalez has observed, the realm of the virtual can become 'a matrix of desire that seeks to absorb or orchestrate cul-tural differences'.[16] The lenticular (and technologically enabled) logics of the digital era recall the minstrel shows of the industrial era, appropriations of the other characterised by love and theft, but with a key difference.[17] Now there is a tendency towards seamlessness, a flip-ping of whiteness into otherness without the seams of artifice that the burnt-corked faces of minstrelsy always revealed, a move towards transparency which disavows connection. Thus, the very forms of electronic media can facilitate identity play in ways which restage the dynamics of disgust and desire, demonstrating what Evelynn Hammonds has characterised as a feigned horizontality expressed via 'the facile device of shape-shifting, interchangeability, [and] equivalency'.[18]

If many forms of digital self-creation seem to support an additive lenticular logic, framing the difference of race via the easy sameness of equivalency, others are more prone to the sep-aratist mentality of the sequel *Scarlett*, where the safety of sameness fixes difference as either removed or absolute. For instance, groups such as the Neo-Confederates have an active presence online, busily constructing a new Dixie in cyberspace, actively urging secession and revamping the ideology of the Lost Cause for a new millennium. This virtual South is a mark-edly white world, for, via an appropriation of the rhetoric of the Civil Rights movement, these cyber-rebels call for a defence of whiteness that they insist simply has nothing to do with blackness.[19] Their resort to a separatist lenticular logic provides a hedge against the anxieties wrought from living an increasingly networked existence. Difference vanishes in a white, white world, and identity fixates as rigid sameness. This naturalised whiteness informs other cyber-spheres, from the eerie sameness of commercial sites such as *iVillage* to the vast majority of 'cybertheory' listservers. These sites and forums are not equivalent in their covertness (or in its effects), but all at least partially repress racial difference and impede relationality.[20]

A meaningful electronic relationality must short-circuit the lenticular logics which charac-terise much of contemporary life, bringing together self, other and machine. Such modes of connection are possible, but they are not an inherent extension of the 'freedoms' and multiplicities of digital forms. We need to distinguish between modes of exploring selves online and encourage productive encounters between sameness and difference. Multiple points of view may be deployed in these encounters, even while the outcome of such strat-egies is never given. One promising experiment is found online at *360degrees.org*, a Web site with the subtitle, 'Perspectives on the American Criminal Justice System'. The site sit-uates the prison-industrial complex within the realms of virtuality, remediating documentary, reality TV, video games and radio into a multi-perspectival examination of incarceration, race, class, victimisation and crime. The 'Stories' section examines the complex nexus of events and voices surrounding a particular crime, allowing the site visitor to listen to the audio transcripts of the incarcerated, their victims, various family members, lawyers, judges and prison and social workers. Listening to the diverse voices structures the space for a complex understanding of crime and punishment, while other sections of the site, including quizzes, timelines and chatspaces, position these stories within a broader understanding of the history and importance of incarceration in America. The site offers a broad and relational experience without giving in to the temptation of becoming other, a strategy reinforced through carefully chosen design elements, including the simple circles which float around the splash page, functioning as a menu. These circles swoop and glide across the screen, moving in, through and out of each other, always remaining distinct even in their collisions. A QuickTime VR plug-in allows us to explore, in 360 degrees, the spaces inhabited by the people telling us their stories. These spaces are empty, but our voyeuristic drive to peep into the world of others is redirected by the voices we hear as we explore; the audio excerpts re-mark the spaces, re-inscribing the perspective of the other, and guiding our movements and understanding. The site provides the point of view of others, but in good faith, imagining the possibility of a relationality that cuts across the borders of sameness and difference that a lenticular logic defends. Connection is imagined as a mode of commonal-ity which mediates between a politics of identity and a politics of difference, thinking through consequence and enacting a translation at once routine and also ripe with ethical potential.[21]

BODIES AND SELVES

In her essay 'Virtual Systems', Sandy Stone calls into question the representation of the body in cyberpunk fiction as 'a purely phantasmic body, freed from the constraints that flesh imposes'. She continues, urging us to 'remember that bodies, selves, technologies and culture constitute each other,' so that we might 'prevent virtual systems from becoming unwitting accomplices in new exercises of social control'.[22] While her appeal to culture as a powerful element in the networks of exchange between bodies and technologies gestures towards the triadic structures of relationality I am encouraging, her article focuses primarily on the shakeup of the boundaries of the individual body, the decoupling of many selves from one body in a digital 'spatiality of a different order'.[23] Of course, technologies and bodies do constitute one another, but bodies marked by race (that is, bodies of colour which cannot lay claim to the unmarked privileges of whiteness) disproportionately bear the weight of the geometries of power laced through the technological constitutions of embodiment. The body has long been the ground from which racial 'truths' are deduced, a fertile playing field for practices such as eugenics and fascism. Thus, remembering the raced body in electronic media will require complex strategies that recognise that more is needed than bodily visibility. Indeed, blackness in today's electronic mediascape might best be described as already hypervisible, an economy of visibility that, in the words of Stephen Michael Best, allows white audiences a 'surreptitious, vicarious occupation' of black bodies.[24] Here, blackness is on parade, largely via the electronic networks of sports and entertainment, but in a highly circumscribed fashion fuelled by the visual logics of capitalism. Blackness is singled out, endlessly recirculated for white consumption, a stream of representation which works to counter claims of systemic racism while locating blackness in contained realms largely separate from whiteness, replaying the fixity of the postcard's logic. 'Playing' Michael Jordan's body in a video game is not enough to forestall new exercises of social control.

Confronted with the hypervisibility of the performing black male body, artist Paul Pfeiffer takes a completely different path to remembering the raced body in electronic realms: he erases it. In a triptych of electronically processed videos called 'The Long Count', the artist condenses the final rounds of Muhammad Ali's most famous fights, meticulously eliminating the figures of the fighters from each frame. He enacts an evacuation of bodies: erasing the body of the other as the ground for the fixing/fixated gaze of the majority subject. In installations, the videos are shown on small LCD screens mounted on gallery walls via long, slender poles. The miniature screens comment on our fetish for portability and smallness in our technological toys, while also demanding a more concentrated attention from the spectator, forcing the viewer to move in close, to get intimate with the screen. Defiantly responding to our desires to gaze upon and own the body of the other, Pfeiffer speaks back to his viewer: you will not become me. You will not even see me: I evade you. Your gaze, your joystick, your remote control, all your technological apparatus will not produce my motion. Paradoxically, the dissolution of (the image of) the other's body gives it a new force, perhaps even a new materiality, making the spectator work hard to develop a relation to it. As viewers, we are powerfully reminded of both the technological apparatus's ability to frame bodies and Pfeiffer's ability to direct our eyes and ears, calling us to ponder his desires and motivations. Here the self experiences subjectivity as mediated not only by the technological networks, but also by networks of power, of control, of racial logics. Pfeiffer confronts the hypervisibility of blackness by linking black bodies to both the history of mediation and the cult of celebrity. Indeed, he helps us to realise the degree to which the contemporary hypervisibility of black bodies simply is another manifestation of a lenticular logic, a refusal to see connection or relation while fixating on particular modes of racial imagery. In reducing blackness to the contour of a shadow, the artist also reminds us of the crucial work blackness performs in American identity, particularly as a structuring absence, while also challenging the absence of considerations of race in our theories of the digital.

Other artists working at the interface of self, other and machine script different interventions into the raced body of electronic spaces. The collective, Mongrel, inserts the racialised self back into mediated networks through a range of projects, including strategic hacks of mainstream software. Their work presents this self not as a body to play with, but as a resistant identity speaking back, sometimes from a position of invisibility, sometimes in uniquely embodied forms. For instance, one portion of the expansive project 'Natural Selection' hacks a popular search engine, mimicking its forms. If a visitor types in 'postcard', the site will return much the same list as any search engine. When the user types in racially loaded words such as 'Paki' or 'white power', the site kicks back a vast network of pre-constructed pages that reveal the illogicality of a racist, separatist mentality. As such the project destabilises assumptions of the Internet as a neutral space of data, foregrounding the racial work already undertaken by networks of power and information. Here, the machine, the self and embodiment all have consequences, ones which Mongrel urges us to take seriously. A print component called 'Colour Separation' undermines the evasive logic of the morph by resisting the lure of electronic networks in favour of print. A full-colour poster features a series of faces literally stitched from masks of the other, the seams painfully apparent. This grid of hybrid faces refuses the easy movement of becoming other, insisting on a relationality which also respects difference, moving us towards a language that might adequately conceptualise mixture. Throughout its work, Mongrel sustains a dual movement between the weight of history, on bodies and on identities, and future imaginaries, sketching the digital as a space for possibility and speculation, but also of danger.[25]

TOWARDS RELATIONALITY

This is all an attempt to say that there is no fixed value or meaning inherent in the fragmented forms of the electronic age. Certainly, our digital encounters with a world of mutable, malleable, impermanent digital forms suggests the difficulty of fixity. Neither is this a call to wholeness, a nostalgic return to the unfractured subjectivities of liberal humanism. Instead, my argument builds to a warning, a cautionary tale about the multiple modes of meaning a coded fragmentation can create. While it is perhaps impossible to fix a causal relation between electronically mediated knowing (of self, of other, of world) and the persistent racial logics of the latter half of the twentieth century, the parallels should give us pause and urge us towards new models of relationality.

Relationality is hopeful, a mode Paul Gilroy deems a 'more worthwhile resting place',[26] but it is certainly not guaranteed by electronic media. To realise this hopefulness will require a principled exposure to the claims of otherness and alterity residing not only in the code beneath our screens, but also in the world around us, a world which continually re-inscribes lenticular modes of knowing that, in the best of worlds, our machinic relations might help to trouble. To do so, we will need to be vigilant in our theorising, working towards broader models of relationality. Indeed, our very theories of the digital too often enact a narrow focus on the self and the machine. In this dyadic structure, we risk missing a complex under-standing of how this particular network of relational meanings engages with, shapes and responds to other networks of cultural meaning, networks which have historically func-tioned to produce the meanings of the body in very precise ways.

Many of our theories of new media continue to replay a familiar fascination with form, new variations on formalism that sever representation from materiality, underlining the unbearable whiteness of much of digital theory. Volume after volume has appeared over the past several years tracking digital dialectics, pursuing the specificity of new technologies, mapping their forms. Such work pays scant attention to the dialectics of race, unwittingly producing a body of theory that cannot understand the generative role forms play in the reproduction of racialised (if not racist) epistemologies and aesthetics. In a drive to define the electronic or the digital as inherently new, as fundamentally different from earlier forms, we introduce a backdoor formalism, a technological determinism, that cannot discern the connections between the racialised modalities of lenticular logics and the theories stream-ing forth from The MIT Press.

This technological determinism can take many forms. From aesthetics, to phenomenol-ogy, to psycho-physiological and cognitive theory, to work on video and new media, we re-inscribe colour blindness, a colour blindness at least partially produced by the theories we embrace and circulate. If we are to avoid the naturalised whiteness and universal sub-ject of the early years of film theory, an understanding of the technological production of race must be ground zero for our theories of digital media. Race (or class or gender) cannot simply be 'added on' later, once we have theorised the forms and specified the media. Forms produce race in the crucible of culture. In our moves towards relationality, we must never forget that.

Notes

This essay was written while I was a participant in the 2001 NEH Summer Seminar, 'Literature in Transition', an experience which left indelible marks on my thinking about life in the digital era. My thanks to the seminar's organiser, Kate Hayles, as well as to my fellow seminarians. My thanks, too, to Marsha Kinder for her feedback on this essay and for her work in the digital realm. My deepest debt of gratitude is to Rob Knaack, whose insights into programming and to ethical living continue to inspire me.

1. Janet Murray, *Hamlet on the Holodeck: The Future of Narrative in Cyberspace* (New York: The Free Press, 1997), p. 125.

2. Rosanne Allucquère Stone, 'Virtual Systems', in Jonathon Crary and Sanford Kwinter (eds), *Incorporations* (New York: Zone Books, 1992), p. 620.

3. N. Katherine Hayles, 'Flesh and Metal: Reconfiguring the Mindbody in Virtual Environments'. Unpublished manuscript, p. 3.

4. Ibid., p. 11.

5. It is not enough, at least in today's world, to read the machine as other, as standing in for or subsuming difference among human selves. This replays an old disappearing trick. The machine, in

its many historical and contemporary forms, mediates the relation between self and other, processing difference, cycling through other networks of cultural meaning. Thus, it cannot just stand in for difference.

6.   N. Katherine Hayles, 'Flesh and Metal', p. 10.

7.   My focus here on the human production of code also signals another flaw in many of the formalist readings of the new digitality; that is, such work often proceeds as if the computer generated code solely of its own accord, discounting the importance of both human programmers and the working conditions under which they labour. Important work remains to be done theorising these new modes of production.

8.   John Hess and Patricia Zimmerman, 'Transnational/National Digital Imaginaries', *Mesh*, 1999, <www.experimenta.org/mesh/mesh_1999/articles/jh_rz.html>.

9.   Sherry Turkle, *Life on the Screen: Identity in the Age of the Internet* (New York: Simon and Schuster, 1995), p. 12. Turkle is here speaking specifically of identity play in MUDs, but she later generalises these notions across cyberspace. She writes, '[A]s I discuss MUDs, it is important to keep in mind that they more generally characterise identity play in cyberspace' (p. 186). I am not entirely convinced that MUDs should form the baseline for our theories about digital life, an argument I develop in 'I'll Take My Stand in Dixie-Net: White Guys, the South, and Cyberspace', in Beth Kolko, Lisa Nakamura and Gilbert B. Rodman (eds), *Race in Cyberspace* (New York: Routledge, 2000).

10. Allucquère Rosanne Stone, 1995, p. 43.

11. Sherry Turkle, *Life on the Screen*, p. 261.

12. Jay David Bolter and Richard Grusin, *Remediation: Understanding New Media* (Cambridge, MA: MIT Press, 1999), p. 245.

13. Ibid.

14. Ibid., p. 247

15. For an early take on techno-Orientalism, see David Morely and Kevin Robbins, *Spaces of Identity* (London: Routledge, 1995). Beth Kolko, Lisa Nakamura and Gilbert Rodman (eds), *Race in Cyberspace* (New York: Routledge, 2000), and Alondra Nelson and Thuy Linh N. Tu, *Technicolor: Race, Technology and Everyday Life* (New York: New York University Press, 2001), also take up questions of digital culture and the appropriation of race and ethnicity. In the former, Lisa Nakamura writes that the depictions of the virtual realm often evoke 'a sort of technologically enabled transnationality . . . that directly addresses the first-world viewer' (p. 17).

16. Jennifer Gonzalez, 'The Appended Subject: Race and Identity as Digital Assemblage', in Kolko, Nakamura and Rodman (eds), *Race in Cyberspace*, p. 46.

17. See Eric Lott, *Love and Theft: Blackface Minstrelsy and the American Working Class* (Oxford: Oxford University Press, 1993), for a complex and illuminating discussion of the historical, cultural and psychological dimensions of the minstrel show.

18. Evelynn M. Hammonds, 'New Technologies of Race', in Jennifer Terry and Melodie Calvert (eds), *Processed Lives: Gender and Technology in Everyday Life* (New York: Routledge, 1997), p. 109. Hammonds is here speaking of morphing, a form of digital production which seems to push beyond the limits of the lenticular, blending two images into one. However, we might see the morph as simply the interlaced image which forms the substrate of the lenticular postcard, rather than as a process

which reveals relationality and breaks us free from lenticular logics. The morph can propel a kind of amnesia of the original, erasing relation and context, and underwriting a simplistic pluralism. Paul Gilroy reminds us that 'We do not have to be content with the halfway house provided by the idea of plural cultures. A theory of relational cultures and of cultures of relation represents a more worthwhile resting place. That possibility is currently blocked by banal invocations of hybridity in which everything becomes equally and continuously intermixed, blended into an impossibly even consistency.' Paul Gilroy, *Against Race: Imagining Political Culture beyond the Color Line* (Cambridge, MA: Harvard University Press, 2000), p. 275.

19. For an extended discussion of the Neo-Confederates online, see my 'I'll Take My Stand in DixieNet'.

20. It is also important to recognise that not all racial representations in the digital realm deploy the covert logics of the lenticular. Overt logics of race and racism have not entirely disappeared, vanquished by the covert; they are simply less prevalent in 'polite' society, finding instead a haven in cyberspace. To cite an obvious example, one need only note the widespread prevalence of hate groups online, organisations intent on using the Web not as a playground for the exploration of the boundaries of the networked self, but, rather, as a base camp for the re-entrenchment of the inviolate contours of a pure and total whiteness.

21. For a discussion of the ethics of translation, see Paul Gilroy, *Against Race*, p. 77.

22. Rosanne Allucquère Stone, 'Virtual Systems', p. 620.

23. Ibid., p. 614.

24. Stephen Michael Best, 'Game Theory: Racial Embodiment and Media Crisis', in Sasha Torres (ed.), *Living Color: Race and Television in the United States* (Durham, NC: Duke University Press, 1998), p. 234. When I call upon us to remember the raced body in electronic media, I mean this to include the white body, a body often called to stand in as 'universal' but which is nonetheless raced.

25. Across their various projects, Pfeiffer and Mongrel also move beyond the black/white binary which structures much of this essay. Born in the Philippines, Pfeiffer's work explores race along many registers. Mongrel includes members of various ethnicities and, as its name suggests, is interested in thinking through issues of sameness, difference and hybridity in complex modes.

26. Paul Gilroy, *Against Race*, p. 275.

4.4

The Future of Film Distribution and Exhibition

Janet Wasko

The Internet is revolutionizing TV and motion pictures.

Mayra Langdon Riesman, Film Scouts[1]

You have to open your eyes, and your vision has to encompass the whole picture. You really have to feel it . . . movies, television, DVD, Internet. It's all the same thing, just different configurations . . . It's an incredible landscape.

Quincy Jones, musician and film producer[2]

E-cinema is possibly the greatest revolution since Al Jolson opened his mouth on screen.

Patrick von Sychowski, *Screen Digest*[3]

Even though there is much ado over the Internet and digital media, models of distribution and exhibition for new media forms are still somewhat unclear. Although the future is 'blurred and murky', and the risks of speculating are well known, that does not stop many media observers from engaging in rampant crystal-ball gazing and exuberant predictions.

Rather than being swept into what Vincent Mosco has called 'the near religious transcendence' of cyberspace,[4] it is important to look at what is actually changing, what may change in the future and what may also remain the same because of the political economic context in which these changes are taking place. While predicting new models of distribution for the wide range of new media is a formidable and somewhat perilous task, this chapter will be limited to speculation about future distribution and exhibition models for films. More specifically, it will focus on the commercial film industry in the US, otherwise known as Hollywood. In addition, the focus is mostly on the US market, even though Hollywood companies are all part of transnational conglomerates for which the global entertainment market is increasingly important.

While it is tricky to sort out the various technologies that may be involved and how they may evolve, the following sections will explore unfolding developments in film distribution via video-on-demand (VOD), utilising the Internet, cable, and telephone lines or digital subscriber line (DSL), followed by an overview of digital cinemas or e-cinema. As the evolution of these developments is guided not only by the technology itself, but also by more general economic and political tendencies, some of this discussion may well provide clues as to how the distribution of other forms of new media may evolve.

It also should be noted that some of the projects or systems discussed might be gone by the time this chapter appears in print. Some of the claims should also be considered 'forward-looking statements', a term that US regulatory agencies require corporations to use when speculating about expected future business.[5]

VIDEO-ON-DEMAND: INTERNET

Some of the excitement over the Internet has been prompted by the possibilities for distributing new and interesting entertainment forms. Currently, short films and some independent feature films are distributed via the Internet at sites such as *Atomfilms*, *iFilm.com*, *CinemaNow*, *CinemaPop* and *Hypnotic*. Of course, Hollywood has always looked to such independent and experimental alternatives for innovative ideas, and, these days, everyone seems to be looking for the next *Blair Witch Project* (1999). Nevertheless, the major Hollywood companies mostly have been unsuccessful in developing Internet sites with new content.[6]

Another possibility is the direct release of feature films via the Internet. On 5 May 2000, *SightSound.com* released *The Quantum Project*, billed as the 'first direct-to-Internet movie', with a $3 million budget which allowed for known actors and relatively high production values. Still, major Hollywood films continue to be released first in cinemas, with little discussion of changing this release pattern.

Hollywood seems mostly concerned with the Internet as an additional outlet for the distribution of films some time after they have appeared in cinemas. In March 2001, Motion Picture Association of America (MPAA) head Jack Valenti announced that, within a year, Hollywood features would be available to download from the Internet. 'The studios have a history of watching, waiting and studying. They would have preferred to be able to do that, but the experience with Napster has told them that option is not available,' says Skip Paul, a former Universal executive who is now chairman of *iFilm.com*.[7]

Even though the studios are reported to be formulating serious Internet strategies as of Summer 2003, it is still unclear how the online distribution of Hollywood films will unfold. Several scenarios were possible: independent sites or middlemen; each major with its own site; one site for all majors; or several jointly owned sites.

The only option that does not seem likely is one jointly owned channel, because of obvious antitrust violations.[8] While many may consider the distributors' ownership of any exhibition outlets to be problematic, it seems likely that the majors will gather more additional revenues from distribution to a number of different sites after issues of control are settled, as will be discussed below. A few examples of existing services or plans for future sites will be discussed briefly in the next sections.

EXAMPLE: INDEPENDENT SITE

SightSound Technologies is a six-year-old company that claims to have rented the first full-length film downloaded over the Internet in 1999. In January 2001, the service also offered Miramax's 1999 feature film *Guinevere* to be downloaded (not streamed) for a 24-hour viewing licence at $3.49. The claim is that it was the first Hollywood film offered online in a legal, non-pirated way.[9] The Disney-owned Miramax also made a deal to offer 12 full-length features on *SightSound.com*, which offers other films (mostly pornography and cheap independent films) for downloading.

During the summer of 2001, the company appeared to be struggling to stay afloat, cutting its workforce and complaining that: 'For the last ten years, the major motion picture studios and the major record labels have maintained an unnatural prohibition with their content on the Internet. And it is their unwillingness to utilise this new and useful way to distribute movies and music that has forced SightSound Technologies to where it is today.'[10]

EXAMPLE: MAJOR STUDIO-OWNED SITE

In August 2001, five of the major studios announced plans for a joint on-demand service that would offer old and new releases for broadband Internet users in the US. The participants included MGM, Paramount, Universal, Warner Bros. and Sony. The site was likely to be a version of Sony's MovieFly (but using another name), and planned to allow viewers to browse a 'virtual' video store, look at the front and back of the 'box', and view film stills. Anti-piracy software, or Digital Rights Management (DRM), was to employ codes to prevent unauthorised copying.[11] Significantly, Disney and Fox were not part of the alliance, but were said to be considering a joint project offering their films to Internet customers.

Beyond the antitrust implications of such arrangements, other complications involve the major studios' corporate connections with cable and video companies. For example, Paramount's online activities could run into conflict with sister company, Blockbuster, as would Warner Bros. with Time Warner's cable operations and AOL's online and television ventures.

EXAMPLE: MINOR STUDIO-OWNED SITE

CinemaNow started streaming independent films both for free and for a fee in November 1999. The site is partly owned by Lions Gate Entertainment, but also has received funding from Microsoft and Blockbuster. *CinemaNow* offers fee-based films in their traditional pay-per-view window and a subscription service. In June 2001, *hollywood.com* joined *CinemaNow*, which offers pay-per-view films for $2.99 each, available for streaming at any time during a 48-hour window from the time of purchase. *CinemaNow*'s library includes more than 1000 films, mostly from independent companies (see plate 09).

INTERNET ISSUES

While the Internet continues to attract a good deal of attention, technological and economic questions remain. The technology has developed rapidly, with broadband

Internet connections and compression technology making it possible to transmit large amounts of data relatively quickly. According to the US General Accounting Office, more than 100 million Americans are online in some way; however, only about 12 per cent have high-speed or broadband access. Thus, for most people, receiving feature films via computers still is a relatively slow and cumbersome option and will remain so for the near future. For example, several reporters reported numerous obstacles before managing to download *Guinevere* when it became available in early 2001. One writer reported that, even at optimum speed, it took approximately 24 hours for the actual download to take place. Another noted that, 'Watching a film . . . while leaning forward staring at a computer isn't exactly a bring-out-the-popcorn kind of experience. Fifteen minutes into the film I gave up and took my dog for a walk.'[12]

Besides the gnawing question of whether there are enough people who will pay to watch movies on computers, the other pressing issue, of course, is piracy. In a world where digital copies of films do not deteriorate with each copy, Hollywood is obviously concerned that digital pirates can easily produce huge quantities of copies, quickly, inexpensively and from anywhere. With the industry already claiming a $2 billion loss from the piracy of audiovisual products, digitised versions of Hollywood films present serious problems.

One estimate is that Hollywood films are traded online nearly 500,000 times each day from hundreds of sites. MediaForce, an online company that tracks pirated digital content, claimed that a million pirated downloads occurred during the month of June 2001, including box-office hits such as *Lara Croft: Tomb Raider*, *Shrek* and *Pearl Harbor*.

The industry's anti-piracy efforts are led by the MPAA, which is working on political solutions, trying to convince governments to enact strong legal protections, such as the Digital Millennium Copyright Act of 1998. Like the music labels, the studios have chosen to challenge piracy first in court. The industry took on iCraveTV, an online re-broadcaster based in Canada, and RecordTV, an online video recorder made available to the public by a company based in Agoura Hills, California. It then crippled Scour Exchange, which went bankrupt within months of a suit being served.

In January 2000, the major Hollywood studios won an important battle when a US District Court found in their favour in a case that challenged the public posting of programming code that makes it easy to copy DVD movies. Most Hollywood movies on DVD include CSS (Content Scramble System), which has been used since 1996. With the code breaking system, called DeCSS (Decrypt the Content Scramble System), DVDs can be played on any system. The code was published in *2600: The Hacker Quarterly*, considered the bible of hacker publications, and posted on its Web site (www. 2600.com). One report summed up the court's decision on the case, noting that, 'The trial was a rout. The US District Court judge ruled in favor of the eight studios on every point.'[13]

While technological issues ultimately may be sorted out, with some obvious help from the government, there are still economic questions to be answered. A major concern is how to profit from this new form of distribution. While other distribution outlets have provided additional profits with little added costs (for example, television, cable, videocassettes,

DVD, and so on), Internet distribution may be different. Content providers, such as the major film studios, may have to pay per-stream licensing costs to software companies such as RealNetworks or QuickTime so that customers can view videos, as well as per-stream charges to Internet service providers such as AT&T. As one analyst recently explained, 'The early model for broadband has been TV. But broadband is exactly the opposite of the broadcast world. Your costs go up as your audience grows.'[14]

This also explains why advertising may not be included. The size of audience needed to support advertising may not be possible without prohibitive costs.[15] However, other analysts assume that the major film studios will solve these issues by distributing their films from their own servers, with relatively low distribution costs.[16]

If revenues are forthcoming from some kind of Internet distribution, other questions remain about the timing, or 'window', of a film's Internet release, and whether ultimately it will replace video and/or pay-TV. Rights to Internet distribution will have to be negotiated, especially for past films where such rights have not been imagined, much less specified. These include issues relating to territory, as well as payments to talent and licensors.[17] Certainly, Internet distribution rights will have to become an essential part of Hollywood deals, if they are not already.

OTHER INTERNET USES

While the Hollywood majors are fighting digital pirates and sorting out ways to officially distribute their wares via the Internet, they also are using the technology in other ways. In addition to sites that offer industry news and information, all of the majors have Web sites that promote their various businesses, as well as sites for individual films. Currently, the Internet could be thought of as 'just another medium to market in, like print, radio, theater and television'.[18]

After all, the technology offers new possibilities for 'one-to-one marketing', using databases of moviegoers with preferences and profiles, and targeted e-mail promotions. The sites also can be used to 'build communities'. An example: Sony TriStar's *Starship Troopers* site featured 'Mobile Infantry' that users could employ to join the battle against the giant alien bugs, while Trooper ID screens provided links to other users' sites. The *Starship* site had attracted over 30,000 users by Summer 2000, thus providing free promotion for the film. By 1997, 40 per cent of the movie sites online had interactive attributes, such as games or quizzes, and 30 per cent had community features.[19]

VIDEO-ON-DEMAND (VOD): CABLE

Some commentators believe that the majors would prefer an Internet/television combination, moving from a personal computer platform to a television-like platform. In other words, they would prefer getting the potatoes back to the couch for 'lean back' rather than 'lean forward' technologies. A television setting, with more sophisticated remote control devices and interactive electronic television programme guides, will allow not only films to be delivered on demand, but pizza and other merchandise as well.

VOD revenue is predicted to be $192 million for 2001 and to increase to $4.75 billion by 2005. Enthusiasts predict that VOD households will reach 27.8 million by 2005. However, these estimates are made with the assumption that these services will be able to offer Hollywood films.[20] If 44 million homes are using VOD by 2010, the market may be worth anywhere from $2 billion to $6 billion a year. One report estimates that at least $1 billion in additional revenues may be forthcoming for the studios, which generally get about 50 per cent of pay-per-view revenues from cable and satellite companies.[21]

But VOD delivered by cable is also dependent on the huge multiple-system operators (MSOs), such as Time Warner Cable, Insight Communications, Cox and Comcast. Also involved are the companies producing the technology that will aggregate and store the content, companies such as Concurrent, Demand Video, DIVA, nCUBE and SeaChange. When VOD on cable finally takes off, sales for such equipment is expected to reach $1–2 billion per year within the next five years.

One of the services that could become a major player is iN Demand, the industry pay-per-view consortium owned by AT&T, Time Warner and Comcast, the three largest cable operators in the US. However, cable systems are also developing their own VOD services.

Another version of film distribution via cable is subscription VOD (or SVOD). For a single monthly fee, usually between $6 and $10 above basic subscription fees, subscribers have access to a list of titles that change every month. The movies are available during the usual pay-TV window. Early efforts to implement a version of SVOD included HBO and Time Warner's Full Service Network (FSN) trial in Orlando, Florida, in the early 1990s, and Viacom's Showtime Anytime, tested in Castro Valley, California, in 1993. The services experienced technical and economic challenges, but have contributed important consumer research and business modelling for these companies' current plans.

HBO is testing an SVOD service called HBO On Demand, in Columbia, South Carolina, which allows subscribers to watch original HBO programming, including *The Sopranos* and *Sex and the City*, as well as films from Warner Bros., DreamWorks and Fox. The service is set up like pay-per-view, although subscribers can watch films whenever they want. Showtime planned to begin trials sometime in 2001 with a service that would offer films from Paramount and MGM, plus original programming.

A similar service is already offered by Starz Encore, a subsidiary of Liberty Media, which claims that it is the largest provider of cable and satellite-delivered premium movie channels in the US. Starz Encore owns 15 domestic channels and offers various themed film packages, including films from Disney, Sony and Universal.

VIDEO-ON-DEMAND: DSL

Another VOD option is delivery by way of high-speed telephone lines. An example is Intertainer, a service that sends its signals over private computer networks, connecting to homes either by DSL or digital cable. Consumers buy a device that switches the signal from their computer to their television set. Most customers receive the service via DSL, which involves going to the Intertainer icon on the DSL provider's home Web page that gets them into the computer network. After typing in a password, customers choose a film and are billed either through their credit card or their DSL provider. Intertainer may eventually be available as an added feature of digital cable, available through a set-top box with remote control.

Originally formed in 1996, the project includes a range of investors, including Comcast, Intel, Microsoft, NBC, Sony and Qwest. The service offers recent motion pictures from a number of major studios (Universal, Warner Bros., DreamWorks, Fox, New Line Cinema, Columbia/TriStar) and pricing options that include pay-per-view and package options. While Intertainer currently offers films after their home video release like other VOD services, it is unclear how much of its programme fees go to content providers. Also, Comcast is the only cable operator that is testing the service, so it will probably have to continue to rely mostly on telephone companies' DSL services.

It is unclear how successful Intertainer will become, as much depends on relationships with both the Hollywood content providers and, eventually, cable operators. A similar service was planned between Blockbuster, the video store giant, and Enron, a telecommunications company. EBEntertainment was to be a 'high-speed, closed phone line VOD service'. However, only MGM agreed to offer its film archives, and, without much support from the major Hollywood studios, the project folded in mid-2001. While Hollywood's lack of co-operation may have represented a wait-and-see attitude, it also seems likely that the studios intended to prevent Blockbuster from gaining an advantage in yet another lucrative outlet for their products.

VOD ISSUES

Even though many feel that VOD, in one form or another, is inevitable, there are still some unresolved issues. It seems clear that cable companies want VOD to better compete with satellite services, and they feel that they need Hollywood films. However, one of their big problems is the reluctance of Hollywood companies to supply content. As the head of Viacom explained recently at a cable industry convention: 'Paramount wants to make money with its films, and video-on-demand could end up displacing existing revenue from video rentals and sales'.[22] Of course, home video is the single largest revenue source for Hollywood films, attracting over $15 billion in 2000. Thus, any form of VOD will need to supplement, but not detract from, home video revenues, or else completely replace those revenues.

The timing of VOD releases and the licensing arrangements between the studios and VOD companies are key issues. According to some sources, the studios are demanding around 70 per cent of the revenue from VOD, although Universal's deal with iN Demand is said to be a 60 per cent deal.[23] Until some of these technical and economic wrinkles are ironed out, video-on-demand may continue to be, as many observers have already noted, 'video on delay'.

ELECTRONIC OR DIGITAL CINEMAS

People won't stay away from the theater. They like to be in a crowd, get out of the house, go on dates – they like the whole movie-going experience. I do see online and theaters as different release patterns. The online films will not be considered as good as what's in the theaters. Today, if a movie is released directly to video, or on cable, it is seen to be subtly inferior. That's not always the case, but that's the way people see it. If you made a really good movie, you wouldn't release it online. Theatrical releases will still be the way filmmakers want to get their films out.

Roger Ebert[24]

After years of speculation, the technology and support for electronic or digital distribution of films to cinemas is developing rapidly. E-cinema or digital cinema involves film prints converted to electronic form, digitised and encrypted, then transmitted from a central server to cinemas via DVD, satellite or fibre-optic link, and projected on electronic projectors.

Over the past few years, various demonstrations have shown that the quality is improving and may finally be acceptable to the film industry. Digital versions of major films have been demonstrated at trade shows, including a screening of *Star Wars Episode 1: The Phantom Menace* at Showest '99. (Around that time, George Lucas vowed to release the next *Star Wars* instalment only in a digital format.) In addition, a few digital cinemas have screened digital versions of Disney's *Mission to Mars*, *Dinosaur* and *Toy Story II*, as well as *Final Fantasy*, during the summer of 2001.

The industry is making progress in establishing technical standards through organisations such as the Society of Motion Picture and Television Engineers (SMPTE) and the Motion Picture Experts Group (MPEG), as well as the National Association of Theater Owners (NATO) and the MPAA.[25] Several e-cinema systems seem to be emerging. The one most often mentioned is Texas Instruments' Digital Light Processing (DLP) system, which uses a digital micro-mirror device. The company has three major licensees, Barco, Christie Digital and Digital Projection, and is seen by some as the industry leader. Meanwhile, Hughes-JVC, a company owned by the Victor Company of Japan, is developing a system based on Direct Drive Image Light Amplifier (D-ILA), using liquid crystals on a microchip. Another contender is Technicolor's Digital Cinema, developed in conjunction with Qualcomm. By mid-2001, 31 sites were participating in a demonstration programme that included Technicolor, Texas Instruments and Disney.

As noted above, distribution of digital films is possible by DVD, satellite or fibre-optic link. Ultimately, satellite distribution may be the most efficient method and has been demonstrated with technology developed by the Boeing Company. The system is supported by the company's military satellite experience, presenting interesting potential alliances. Again, Miramax has participated in early tests, offering its feature film *Bounce* for a trial run of the system in March 2000 and *Spy Kids* for another demonstration in March 2001.

Both Disney and Sony, as well as other industry sources, have shown enthusiasm for e-cinema. According to a *Screen Digest* report, there are likely to be an estimated 10,000 digital screens worldwide by 2005 and a complete transition within 20 years. The enthusiastic report also predicts that almost 100 per cent of the major Hollywood studios' films will be available both in digital and conventional 35mm format by the end of 2004.[26]

Many of the advantages cited by e-cinema's supporters are apparent. The most obvious is the elimination of film prints, which cost on average $3 million for a major film, or around $1500 per print. Often 3000 to 4000 prints are produced for each film, with the total global cost of prints estimated at $5 billion each year.[27] Digital versions of films also eliminate the wear and tear that is common with film prints, with fewer scratches and less dust. In addition, multi-language audio tracks become possible, as well as simultaneous worldwide release dates. Distributors would be able to move poorly performing films more easily or possibly alter or re-edit films during their theatrical runs.

E-cinemas are envisioned as multi-format outlets featuring films, live concerts and other special events, corporate meetings, and so on, which could help some cinemas earn desperately needed extra revenues. This type of activity is already happening in Canada at Viacom's Famous Players cinemas, which feature live pay-per-view wrestling from the World Wrestling Federation, employing Bell ExpressVu satellite operations. Another additional source of income might be advertising from local sources, which may be enthusiastically welcomed by some, while dreaded by others. With digital projection, individual cinemas might also be able to schedule screenings more easily to accommodate public demand, as well as saving on less labour-intensive projection. Although cinema projection is already often automated, further reductions in labour costs may be possible.

While there are clear advantages and most believe that digital cinema is an inevitability, there are some formidable questions that will need to be answered before widespread digital exhibition is a reality. Again, security and control are key issues. Even with encryption systems, the potential for pirating cinema-quality versions of new films is far more ominous than with current pirated prints, which often are copies of tapes shot from projected films in cinemas.

With a number of companies developing digital cinema technology, there are likely to be compatibility issues. It is still unclear whether there will be one standard or 'open architecture' allowing more than one system to be used. In addition, questions prevail regarding the compatibility of encryption and compression equipment.

Another issue that e-cinema enthusiasts seem to overlook has to do with the advantages of film projectors that are not only less expensive, but more rugged and universally adaptable as well. Even if the costs come down for electronic systems, the e-cinema equipment may rapidly become obsolete, with constant new developments in digital technology.

Moreover, there is the critical issue of cost. Although prices for digital projectors are dropping (from $220,000–$240,000 to $160,000 in just one year), they still are major investments compared to a 35mm projection system that is currently priced at around $30,000–40,000. Most analysts agree that digital systems must be around $100,000 to be viable. With the total cost of converting 100,000 screens around the world at an estimated $25 billion,[28] the big question is: who will pay?

In a recent trade paper article, one exhibitor expressed the sentiments of many other cinema owners, explaining: 'We know exactly what we are prepared to pay to move to digital: nothing.'[29] Many of the major US cinema chains will be hard-pressed to make such substantial investments, as recent cinema upgrading has left a number of them in or near bankruptcy. One proposal has suggested that a consortium of the major studios fund the new projection systems, but it is unlikely that the majors will agree. More than one studio executive has explained that it is up to the exhibitors to fund the new technology as one of the costs of doing business. Another option is from Technicolor Digital: the company will install systems at no cost to exhibitors or distributors, but charge exhibitors 12.5 cents per customer and charge fees to studios to distribute films electronically. Clearly, this is a crucial issue that will need to be resolved before e-cinemas become the norm.

Furthermore, even though the distributors seem to be the most obvious benefactors of the new systems, it is unclear whether they will be willing to give cinema owners any advantages in new exhibition licensing arrangements, where many would argue that the distributors now have the upper hand.

Nonetheless, the enthusiasm over e-cinema is growing, with glowing reports and claims by industry spokespeople, who anticipate major changes and increased opportunities. Patrick von Sychowski, author of the previously mentioned *Screen Digest* report, comments: 'Electronic cinema is an entirely new medium and as yet the industry hasn't had the opportunity to grasp its full impact.'[30] E-cinemas may be commonplace sometime in the future; however, it is unlikely that these thorny issues will be sorted out in time for an all-digital first run of *Star Wars Episode III* when it is scheduled to open in 2005.

THE UNCERTAIN BUT PREDICTABLE FUTURE

From this brief and speculative overview, it seems certain that there will be changes in film distribution and exhibition in the future. In addition, these developments will continue to be accompanied by a series of familiar promises and hopes. As with the introduction of cable and video technologies, new forms of digital distribution and exhibition have been associated with the prospect of more consumer choice and content diversity, as well as more independent production and expanded competition. Some have again predicted a 'shift of power' from the studios to independent film-makers. Others have suggested that, when all is said and done, major films will still appear in cinemas with electronic equipment, and Web-enabled television will feature different tiers of content: mass market fare, 'edgy' pay-cable channels, and independent and experimental fare for niche audiences.[31]

However, as this discussion suggests, it may be safe to predict that the major Hollywood studios, as part of well-heeled transnational conglomerate organisations, will continue to be the dominant forces in guiding whatever models prevail, at least in the US market. They have the desired content, they already dominate other distribution outlets and they will continue to receive whatever help is necessary from a political system that mostly supports their success. In other words, it is clear to at least some observers that video-on-demand and e-cinema promise to maintain and extend the studios control over distribution

Thus, despite the uncertainty about the future, it is safe to predict that some things will remain the same. Again, there is continuity as well as change in store for the entertainment industry. Moreover, it is certain that profit will continue to be the major motivation for change. Despite the rhetoric of providing choices and access for consumers, the self-stated aim of the studios is to make money. More money. Lots of money. Decisions will be made with that goal in mind.

MPAA head Jack Valenti, has observed that the future is 'blurred and murky', and the only thing that is certain is that the studios will not distribute films in the same way any more. What also seems certain is that the entertainment and media transnational corporations will continue to dominate whatever new distribution and exhibition models evolve, operating under the same overall strategies as in the past.

Notes

1. Quoted in 'HP Promotes Convergence of Entertainment and Technology', *IT News*, 5 February 1999, <www.dit.net/ITNews/newsfeb99/newsfeb48.html>.

2. Quoted in Marc Levey, 'Hollywood Meets Silicon Valley: A New Era of Media Convergence', *The Motion Picture & Television Industry Magazine*, 1 July 2000, <www.empire-pov.com/media.html>.

3. 'Electronic Cinema: The Big Screen Goes Digital', *Screen Digest*, September 2000, <www.screendigest.com/press_ecine.htm>.

4. Vincent Mosco, 'Myth-ing Links: Power and Community on the Information Highway', *The Information Society*, vol. 14 no. 1 (Jan.–March, 1998), pp. 57–62.

5. Unless otherwise noted, the information that this brief overview is based on is drawn primarily from the Web sites of the various companies and organisations referred to in the discussion.

6. Examples include Digital Entertainment Network, Warner's Entertaindom and pop.com.

7. Quoted in L. Rich, 'Hollywood Braces for "Napsterization"', *CNN.com*, 20 January 2001, <www.cnn.com/2001/TECH/computing/01/10/hollywood.napsterization.idg/>.

8. The majors tried a jointly owned channel (called Premiere) to distribute its films on pay cable, but could not get away with the blatant flouting of antitrust law. See J. Wasko, *Hollywood in the Information Age* (Cambridge: Polity Press, 1994), pp. 78–9.

9. C. Tristram, 'Broadband's Coming Attractions', *Technology Review*, June 2001.

10. P. Sweeting, 'SightSound Shrinks Workforce', *VideoBusiness Online*, 9 July 2001, <www.videobusiness.com/news/070901_sightsound_layoffs.asp>.

11. J. Shprintz, 'Hack to the Future', *Premiere*, March 2001, <www.premiere.com/Premiere/Features/301/hackers.html>.

12. C. Tristram, 'Broadband's Coming Attractions', p. 72.

13. J. Shprintz, 'Hack to the Future'.

14. C. Tristram, 'Broadband's Coming Attractions'.

15. J. Healey, 'Streaming Video Slows to a Trickle Amid Preoccupation with Profit', 28 June 2001, <www.latimes.com/business/cutting/20010628/t000053624.html>.

16. S. M. Moore, *The Biz: The Basic Business, Legal and Financial Aspects of the Film Industry* (Los Angeles: Silman–James Press, 2000), pp. 199–200.

17. Ibid., pp. 199–208.

18. I. Rubenstein, Director of Marketing of Columbia/TriStar Interactive, 17 November 1997, from an interview by Jennifer Lee cited in 'How Will the Internet Affect the Marketing and Distribution of Movies?', *Active Minds*, May 1998, <www.activeminds.com/ideas_jlee_comps.html>.

19. S. Chowdhury, W. M. Bluestein and K. S. Davis, 'Promoting Films Online', *The Forrester Report: Entertainment and Technology*, vol. 1 no. 5, August 1997.

20. P. Sweeting, 'Vod Is MIA at NCTA', *Video Business Online*, 13 June 2001, <www.videobusiness.cothem/news/061301_ncta_VOD_no-show.asp>.

21. J. Black, 'Video-on-Demand: Hollywood Is Missing the Big Picture', *Business Week*, 26 March 2001.

22. P. Sweeting, 'Vod Is MIA at NCTA'.

23. P. Sweeting, 'Universal Opens Window on In Demand Cable VOD Deal', *Video Business Online*, 20 July 2001, <www.videobusiness.com/news/072001_universal_vod_indemand.asp>.

24. Quoted in David Ferris, 'Roger Ebert on Digital Movies', *CNN.com*, 2 August 2000, <www.cnn.com/2000/TECH/computing/08/02/ebert.interview.idg/>.

25. M. Quan, 'Standards Body Pushes Digital Movie Making', *Electronic Engineering Times*, 11 August 2001, pp. 4–5.

26. 'Electronic Cinema: The Big Screen Goes Digital'.

27. Ibid.

28. Ibid.

29. Matthew Doman, 'Exhibitors, Studios Show Caution over Digital Offer', *Hollywood Reporter*, 8 March 2001, p. 1.

30. 'Electronic Cinema: The Big Screen Goes Digital'.

31. For instance, see J. Perry, 'Online with the Show', *US News & World Report*, 4 December 2000, pp. 52–5.

5.0

CONTEXTS

The final section of this book investigates the broad contexts of both new and old media. While each of the chapters in the previous sections account for contexts in one way or another, this section acknowledges media contexts on a more macro level. The following chapters address how media contexts can be highly determining factors in how new media technologies are developed, used, consumed and either embraced or suppressed – especially in light of the relatively long historical traditions of what we quite loosely call 'old' media: namely cinema and television.

It would be difficult to deny that there have been significant shifts in the cinema and television industries towards increased digitisation at the levels of production, post-production, distribution and exhibition. Few films or television programmes encounter no level of digital transformation. Such shifts pose many new and old questions regarding the status of media identity. Can new media find its own voice, its own vision – detached from the traditions of the cinematic and the televisual? Can we draw a meaningful differentiation between new technologies and their older media siblings? And what can we learn about film and television through the exploration of digital media?

Of course, we also return here to the question of what makes new media 'new'? Possibly one of the more visible 'new' items to land on the media agenda is the increasing level of uncertainty (technological, economic, aesthetic and spectatorial) experienced by an entertainment industry that traditionally banks on its ability to forecast certainty. This has led to an exciting yet hard to monitor cultural situation that transforms as quickly as it stabilises.

All four of the chapters in this section explore the discursive, aesthetic and economic implications of new media, particularly the mutual-influencing activities of the media industries – both old and new. By considering a broader historical and cultural context of media production, distribution and consumption, we can better appreciate the delicate and complex ways in which all media affect the way in which we live in contemporary society.

5.1

Old Media as New Media: Cinema

Lev Manovich

If Mike Figgis's remarkable *Timecode* (2000) exemplifies the difficult search of digital cinema for its own unique aesthetics, it equally demonstrates how these emerging aesthetics borrow from cinema's rich past, from other media and from the conventions of computer software. The film splits the screen into the four quarters to show us four different actions taking place at once. This is, of course, something that has been common in computer games for a while; we may also recall the computer user's ability to open a new window into a document, which is a standard feature of all popular software programs. By tracking the characters in real time, *Timecode* follows the principle of unity of space and time that goes back to seventeenth-century classicism. At the same time, as we are presented with video images which appear in separate frames within the screen and which provide differ-ent points of view of the same building, the film also makes a strong reference to the aesthetics of video surveillance. At the end, we may ask if we are dealing with a film that is borrowing strategies from other media; or with a 'reality TV' programme that adopts the strategies of surveillance; or with a computer game that heavily relies on cinema. In short, is *Timecode* still *cinema* or is it already *new media*?

The role played by cinematic heritage in shaping new media is the main focus of my recent book, *The Language of New Media*.[1] Ideally I would like this chapter to present an overview of the different ways in which cinema and new media interact, but this would mean repeating the arguments of the book and trying to compress 250 pages into ten. This chap-ter, therefore, will present a new thesis, but first I will summarise the arguments set out in *The Language of New Media*, so that I can give you an idea of what some of these inter-actions are.

In the book, the theory and history of cinema serve as the conceptual 'lens' through which I look at new media. The topics explored include the parallels between cinema his-tory and the history of new media; the identity of digital cinema; the relations between the language of multimedia and nineteenth-century pre-cinematic cultural forms; the functions of screen, mobile camera and montage in new media as compared to cinema; and the his-torical ties between new media and avant-garde film. Another way in which cinema enters into the book is through its structure. Although a textbook on film may begin with film technology and end up with film genres, this book progresses from the material foundations of new media to its forms. The last chapter is called 'What is Cinema?' and it mirrors the book's beginning. I begin by pointing out that many of the allegedly unique principles of new media, such as random access, can be already found in cinema. The subsequent chapters continue this perspective of using film history and theory to analyse new media. Having discussed different levels of new media, such as the interface, the operations, the illusion and the forms, in the last chapter, I turn my conceptual 'lens' around to look at how computerisation changes cinema itself. I analyse the identity of digital cinema by placing it within a history of the moving image and also discuss how computerisation offers new opportunities for the development of film language.

My chapter for this book addresses one of the key themes which accompanies both the evolution of new media technologies during their four-decade-long history and the current ongoing shift of cinema towards being computer-based in all aspects of its production, post-production and distribution. This theme is 'realism'. The introduction of every new modern media technology, from photography in the 1840s to virtual reality in the 1980s, has always been accompanied by the claims that the new technology allows to represent reality in a new way. Typically it is argued that the new representations are radically different from the ones made possible by older technologies; that they are superior to the old ones; and that they allow a more direct access to reality. Given this history, it is not surprising that the shift of all moving image industries (cinema, video, television) in the 1980s and 1990s towards computer-based technologies, and the introduction of new computer and network-based moving image technologies during the same decade (for example, Webcams, digital compositing, motion rides) has been accompanied by similar claims. In this chapter I will examine some of these claims by placing them within a historical perspective. How new is the 'realism' made possible by digital video cameras, digital special effects and computer-driven Webcams?

Instead of thinking of the evolution of modern media technology as a linear march towards a more precise or more authentic representation of reality, we may want to think of a number of distinct aesthetics, particular techniques of representing reality, that keep re-emerging throughout modern media history. I do not want to suggest that there is no change and that these aesthetics have some kind of metaphysical status. In fact, it would be an important project to trace the history of these aesthetics, to see which ones had already appeared in the nineteenth century and which ones only made their appearance later. However, for my purposes here, it is sufficient to assume that the major technological shifts in media, such as the present shift towards computer and network-based technologies, not only lead to the creation of new aesthetic techniques, but also activate certain aesthetic impulses already established in the past.

I will focus on two different aesthetics that, at first sight, may appear to be unique to the current digital revolution, but in fact accompany moving image media throughout the twentieth century. The two aesthetics are opposite of each other. The first treats a film as a sequence of big-budget special effects, which may take years to craft during post-production stage. The second gives up all effects in favour of 'authenticity' and 'immedi-acy', achieved with the help of inexpensive digital video equipment. I will trace these two aesthetics back to the origins of cinema. If Georges Méliès was the father of special effects film-making, then the Lumière brothers can be called the first *digital video realists*. To use contemporary terms, the Lumière brothers defined film-making as production (i.e. shoot-ing), while Méliès defined it as post-production (editing, compositing, special effects).

The fact that it is not only the theme of 'realism' itself, but also particular strategies for making media represent reality 'better' that keep reappearing in the history of media should not blind us to the radical innovations of new media. I do believe that new media reconfig-ure a moving image in a number of very important ways. I trace some of them in *The Language of New Media*: the shift from montage to compositing; the slow historical tran-sition from lens-based recording to 3D image synthesis; the new identity of cinema as a hybrid of cinematography and animation. For me, pointing out that some claims about the newness of new media are incorrect (such as tracing the historical heritage of certain real-ist aesthetics in this chapter) is the best way of establishing which claims are correct, as well as discovering the new features of new media which may have been overlooked. In short, the best way to see what is new is first to be clear about what is old. Dismissing the originality of digital special effects and digital 'immediacy' allows us to notice the unique capacity digital media has for representing the real, which I will address in the last section of this chapter.

DIGITAL SPECIAL EFFECTS

By the middle of the 1990s, producers and directors of feature and short films, television shows, music videos and other *visual fictions* had widely accepted digital tools, from digi-tal compositing to CGI to digital video cameras. According to the clichés used in Hollywood when discussing this digital revolution, film-makers are now able to 'to tell stories that were never possible to tell before', 'achieve new levels of realism' and 'impress the audiences with previously unseen effects'. But do these statements hold up under a closer scrutiny?

Let's begin by considering the first idea. Is it really true that Ridley Scott would not have been able to make *Gladiator* (2000) without computers? Of course, computer-generated shots of the Roman Coliseum are quite impressive, but the story could have been told with-out them. After all, in his 1916 film *Intolerance*, Griffith showed the audiences the fall of Babylon, the latter days of Christ's life and the St Bartholomew's Day Massacre, all without computers. Similarly, the 1959 classic *Ben-Hur* took viewers to ancient Rome, again with-out computers.

I do not accept the second idea that, armed with computers, film-makers can now get closer to reality than ever before either. More often than not, when you watch special effects shots in films, you are seeing something you never saw before, either in reality or in cinema. You have never before seen prehistoric dinosaurs (*Jurassic Park*). You have never before seen T2 morphing into a tiled floor (*Terminator 2: Judgment Day*). You have never before seen a man gradually become invisible (*Hollow Man*, 2000). So while in principle film-makers can use computers to show viewers ordinary, familiar reality, this almost never happens. Instead, they aim to show us something extraordinary: something we have never seen before.

What about situations when the special effects shots do not show a new kind of character, set or environment? In this case, the novelty involves showing familiar reality *in a new way* rather than simply *getting closer to it*. One example is a special effects shot of a mountain climber who, high up in the mountains, loses his balance and plummets to the ground. Before computers, such a sequence would probably involve cutting between a close-up of the climber and a wide shot of mountain scenery. Now the audience can follow the character as he flies down, positioned several inches from his face. In doing so, a new reality is created, a new visual fiction: imagining what it would be like to fall down together with the character, flying just a few inches from his face. The chances of somebody actually having this experience are about the same as seeing a prehistoric dinosaur come to life. Both are visual fictions, achieved through special effects.

DV REALISM

A special effects spectacle has not been the only result of the digital revolution in cinema. Unsurprisingly, the over-reliance of big budget film-making on lavish effects has led to a reality check. The film-makers who belong to what I will call the *DV realism* school purposely avoid special effects and other post-production tricks. Instead, they use multiple, often hand-held, inexpensive digital cameras to create films characterised by a documentary style. Examples of this include such US films as Mike Figgis's *Timecode* and *The Blair Witch Project* and the European films made by the Dogma 95 group, *Festen* (1998) and *Mifune* (1999). Rather than treating live action as raw material to be re-arranged later in post-production, these film-makers place most importance on the authenticity of the actors' performances. On the one hand, digital video equipment allows a film-maker to be very close to the actors, to be literally inside the action as it unfolds. In addition to a more intimate filmic approach, a film-maker can keep shooting for the whole duration of a 60- or 120-minute digital video tape as opposed to the standard ten-minute film roll. The increased quantity of much cheaper material gives the film-maker and the actors more freedom to improvise around a theme, rather than being shackled to the tightly scripted shots of traditional film-making. In fact, the length of *Timecode* exactly corresponds to the length of a standard digital video tape.

DV realism has a predecessor in an international film-making movement that began in the late 1950s and unfolded throughout the 1960s. Called 'direct cinema', 'candid' cinema, 'uncontrolled' cinema, 'observational' cinema or *cinéma vérité* ('cinema truth'), it also involved film-makers using lighter and more mobile equipment in comparison to what was available before. Like today's DV realists, the 1960s 'direct cinema' proponents avoided tight staging and scripting, preferring to let events unfold naturally. Both then and now, the film-makers used new film-making technology to rebel against the existing cinema conventions that were perceived as being too artificial. Both then and now, the key word of this revolution was the same: 'immediacy'.

During the same period in the 1960s, Hollywood also underwent a special effects revolution: wide-screen cinema. In order to compete with the new television medium, film-makers created lavish wide-screen spectacles such as the aforementioned *Ben-Hur*. Indeed, the relationship between television, Hollywood and 'direct' cinema looks remarkably like what is happening today. Then, in order to compete with a low-resolution television screen, Hollywood turned to a wide-screen format and lavish historical dramas. As a reaction, 'direct' cinema film-makers used new mobile and lightweight equipment to create more 'immediacy'. Today, the increasing reliance on special effects in Hollywood can be perceived as a reaction to the new competition of the Internet, and this new cycle of special effects film-making has found its own reaction: *DV realism.*

DIGITAL SPECIAL EFFECTS AND *DV REALISM*, HISTORICISED

The two ways in which film-makers use digital technology today to arrive at the two opposing aesthetics, special effects driven spectacle and documentary-style realism striving for 'immediacy', can be traced back to the origins of cinema. Film scholars often discuss the history of cinema in terms of two complementary creative impulses. Both originated at the turn of the twentieth century in France. The Lumière brothers established the idea of cinema as reportage. The camera covers events as they occur. The Lumières' first film, *Workers Leaving the Lumière Factory* (1895), is a single shot that records the movement of people outside their photographic factory. Another of the Lumières' early films, the famous *Arrival of a Train at a Station* (1895), shows another simple event: the arrival of a train at the Paris train station.

The second idea equates cinema with special effects, designed to surprise and even shock the viewer. According to this school of thought, the goal of cinema is not to record the ordinary, but to catch or construct the extraordinary. Georges Méliès was a magician in Paris who owned his own cinema. After seeing the Lumières' film presentation in 1895, Méliès started to produce his own films. His hundreds of short films established the notion of cinema as special effects. In his films, devils burst out of clouds of smoke, pretty women vanish, a space ships flies to the moon and a woman transforms into a skeleton (perhaps a predecessor to *Hollow Man*?). Méliès used stop motion, special sets, miniatures and other special effects to extend the aesthetics of the magician's performance into a longer narrative form.

The ways in which film-makers today use digital technology fits quite well with these two basic ideas of what cinema is, which began more than a century ago. The Lumières' idea of film as a record of reality, as a witness to events as they unfold, survives with *DV realism*. It also animates currently popular 'reality TV' shows (*Cops*, *Survivor*, *Big Brother*) where omnipresent cameras report on events as they unfold. Méliès' idea of cinema as a sequence of magician's tricks arranged as a narrative is realised anew in Hollywood's digital special effects spectacles, from *The Abyss* to *The Phantom Menace*.

Therefore it would be incorrect to think that the two aesthetics of computer-driven special effects and *DV realism* somehow are results of digital technology. Instead they are the new realisations of two basic creative impulses that have accompanied cinema from the beginning.

Such an analysis makes for a neat and simple scheme, in fact, too simple to be true. Things are actually more complicated. More recently film scholars such as Thomas Elsaesser revised their take on the Lumières.[2] They realised that even their first films were far from simple documentaries. The Lumières planned and scripted the events and staged actions both in space and in time. For instance, one of the films shown at the Lumières' first public screening in 1895, *The Waterer Watered*, was a staged comedy: a boy stepping on a hose causes a gardener to squirt himself. Moreover, even such supposedly pure example of 'reality film-making' as *Arrival of a Train at a Station* turned out to be 'tainted' with advance planning. Rather than being a direct recording of reality, *Arrival of a Train* was carefully put together, with the Lumières choosing and positioning passers-by seen in the shot.

Arrival of a Train can be even thought of as a quintessential special effects film. After all, it supposedly shocked the audiences so much they had to run out of the café where the screening was taking place. Indeed, they had never before seen a moving train presented with photographic fidelity, just as contemporary viewers have never before seen a man gradually being stripped of skin and then skeleton until he vanishes into the air (*Hollow Man*), or thousands of robot soldiers engaged in battle (*Star Wars Episode 1*).

If the Lumières were not the first documentarists, but rather the directors of *visual fictions*, what about their successors, the directors of *DV realism* films and 'reality TV' shows? They do not simply record reality either. According to the statement found on the official *Big Brother* Web site, '*Big Brother* is not scripted, but a result of the participants' reactions to their environments and interactions with each other on a day-to-day basis'.[3] Yet even the fact that what we are watching is not a continuous 24 hours a day recording but short episodes, each episode having a definite end (elimination of one of the house guests from the shows), testifies that the show is not just a window into life as it happens. Instead, it follows well-established conventions of film and television fictions: a narrative that unfolds within a specified period of time and results in a well-defined conclusion.

In the case of *DV realism* films, a number of them follow a distinct narrative style. Let us compare it with a traditional film narrative. A traditional film narrative usually takes place over months, years or even decades, for example, *Sunshine* (1999). We take it for granted that the film-maker chooses to show us the key events selected from this period, thus compressing many months, or years, or even decades, into a film which runs just for 90 or 120 minutes. In contrast, *DV realism* films often take place in close to real time and, in the case of *Timecode*, exactly in real time. Consequently, film-makers construct special narratives where lots of dramatic events happen in a short period. It is as though they are trying to compensate for the real time of the narrative.

So the time that we see is the real time, rather than the artificially compressed time of traditional film narrative. However, the narrative that unfolds during this time period is highly artificial, both by the standards of traditional film and television narrative, and our normal lives. Both in *Festen* and in *Timecode*, for example, we witness people betraying each other, falling in love, having sex, breaking up, revealing incest, making important deals, shooting at each other, and dying, all in the course of two hours.

THE ART OF SURVEILLANCE

The real time aspect of what can be called *reality film-making* – that is, film and television narratives that take place in real time or close to it, including 'reality TV' – has an important historical precedent. Although television as a mass medium became established only in the middle of the twentieth century, television research had already begun in the 1870s. During the first decades of this research, television was thought of as the technology that would allow people to see remotely what is happening in a distant place, hence its name, tele-vision (literally, 'distance seeing'). The television experiments were part of a whole set of other inventions which all took place in the nineteenth century around the idea of *tele-communication*: real-time transmission of information over a distance. Telegraph was transmitted text over a distance, telephone transmitted speech over a distance, and tele-vision transmitted images over a distance. It was not until the 1920s that television was redefined as the *broadcasting* medium, that is, as a technology for transmitting specially prepared programmes to a number of people at the same time. In other words, television became a means to *distribute content*, very much as the Internet does today, as opposed to the Internet before the mid-1990s, rather than the *telecommunication* technology.

The original idea of television has survived, however, and came to define one of the key uses of video technology in modern society: video surveillance. Today, for every television monitor receiving content, one can find a video camera which transmits surveillance images: from car parks, banks, lifts, street corners, supermarkets, office buildings, and so on. Along with video surveillance, which is usually limited to companies, the original mean-ing of television as seeing over distance in real time was realised again in computer culture: the Webcam, accessible to everybody. Like normal video surveillance cameras that track us everywhere, Webcams rarely show anything of interest. They simply show what is there: the waves on the beach, somebody staring at a computer terminal, an empty office or street. Webcams are the opposites of special effects films: feeding us the banality of the ordinary, rather than the excitement of the extraordinary.

Today's *reality media*, films that take place in real time (such as *Timecode*), 'reality TV' and Webcams, return us to the origins of television in the nineteenth century. Yet while his-tory repeats itself, it never does so in the same way. The new omnipresence and availability of cheap telecommunication technologies, from Webcams to online chat programs to cell phones, hold the promise of a new aesthetic which does not have any precursors: the aes-thetic which will combine fiction and telecommunication. How can telecommunication and fictional narrative join together? Is it possible to make art out of video surveillance, out of a real-time rather than pre-scripted signal?

Timecode can be seen as an experiment in this direction. In *Timecode*, the screen is broken into four frames, each frame corresponding to a separate camera. All four cameras track the events taking place in different parts of the same location (a production studio on

Sunset Boulevard in Hollywood), which is the typical video surveillance set-up (see plate 08). It is to Mike Figgis's credit that he was able to take such a set-up and turn it into a new way to present a fictional narrative. Here, telecommunication becomes a narrative art. Television in its original sense of telecommunication, seeing over distance in real time, becomes the means to present human experience in a new way.

Of course, *Timecode* is not exactly bare-bones telecommunication. It is not just a real-time recording of whatever happens to be in front of the cameras. The film is tightly scripted. We may think of it as an edited surveillance video: the parts where nothing happens have been taken out; the parts with action in them have been preserved. However, it is more accurate to think of *Timecode* as a conventional film that adopts visual and spatial strategies of video surveillance, such as multiple cameras tracking one location, while following the traditional dramatic conventions of narrative construction. In other words, the film uses a telecommunication-type interface to a traditional narrative, which means that it does not yet deal with the deeper implications of computer-based surveillance (we could also use other terms which have less negative connotations such as 'monitoring' or 'recording').

What would it mean for cinema, and narrative arts in general, to address these implications? One of the most basic principles of narrative arts is what in computer culture is called 'compression'. A drama, a novel, a film, a narrative painting or a photograph compresses weeks, years, decades and even centuries of human existence into a number of essential scenes or, in the case of narrative images, even a single scene. The non-essential is stripped away; the essential is recorded. Why? Narrative arts have been always limited by the capacities of the receiver (a human being) and of storage media. Throughout history, the first capacity has remained more or less the same: today the time we will devote to the reception of a single narrative may range from 15 seconds (a television commercial) to two hours (a feature film) to a number of short segments distributed over a large period of time (following a television series or reading a novel). However, the capacity of storage media recently changed dramatically. Instead of the ten minutes that can fit on a standard roll of film or the two hours that can fit on a digital video tape, a digital server can hold a practically unlimited amount of audiovisual recordings. The same applies for audio only, or for text.

This revolution in the scale of available storage has been accompanied by the new ideas about how such media recording may function. Working within the paradigms of Computer Augmented Reality, Ubiquitous Computing, and Software Agents at places such as MIT Media Lab and Xerox Park, computer scientists advanced the notion of the computer as an unobtrusive but omnipresent device which automatically records and indexes all inter-personal communications and other users' activities. A typical scenario involves microphones and video cameras situated in the business office which record everything taking place, along with indexing software which makes possible a quick search through years of recordings. (Given that a regular e-mail program already automatically keeps a copy of all sent and received e-mails, and allows us to sort and search through these e-mails, we can see that in the course of text communication this paradigm has already been realised.) The difficulty of segmenting and indexing audio and visual media is what delays realising these ideas in practice. However, mass recording can already be easily achieved: all it takes is an inexpensive Webcam and a large drive array (a number of hard drives connected together).

What is important in this paradigm, and this applies for computer media in general, is that storage media become active. That is, the operations of searching, sorting, filtering, indexing and classifying which before were within the strict domain of human intelligence become automated. A human viewer no longer needs to go through hundreds of hours of video surveillance to locate the part where something happens – a software program can do this automatically and much more quickly. Similarly, a human listener no longer needs to go through years of audio recordings to locate the important conversation with a particular person – software can do this quickly. It can also locate all other conversations with the same person, or other conversations where his or her name was mentioned, and so on.

For me, the new aesthetic possibilities offered by computer recording are immense and unprecedented, in contrast to the aesthetics of special effects and *DV realism*, which as I have suggested, are not new in cinema history. What may be truly unique about new media's capacity to represent reality is the new scale of reality maps it makes possible. Instead of compressing reality to what the author considers the essential moments, very large chunks of everyday life can be recorded, then put under the control of software. Imagine, for instance, a 'novel' that consists of complete e-mail archives of thousand of characters, plus a special interface that the reader uses to interact with this information. Or a narrative 'film' which a computer program assembles shot-by-shot in real time, pulling material from the huge archive of surveillance video, old digitised films, Webcam transmissions and other media sources. From this perspective, Godard's *History of Cinema* (1998) represents an important step towards such *database cinema*. Godard treats the whole history of cinema as his source material, traversing this database back and forth, like a virtual camera flying over a landscape made from old media.

In conclusion, let me once again evoke *Timecode*. Its very name reveals its allegiance to the logic of the old media of video: a linear recording of reality on a very limited scale. The film is over when the time code on the videocassette reaches two hours. Although it adopts some of the visual conventions of computer culture, it does not yet deal with the underlying logic of a computer code.

Contemporary creators of digital *visual fictions* need to find new ways to reflect the particular reality of our own time, beyond embracing digital special effects or digital 'immediacy'. As I have suggested, the computer's new capacities for automatically indexing massive scale recordings do offer one new direction beyond those that cinema has explored to date. Rather than seeing reality in new ways, the trick may be simply to pour all of it onto a hard drive, then find out what kind of interface the user needs to work with all the recorded media. In short, a film-maker needs to become an interface designer. Only then will *cinema* truly become *new media*.

Notes

1. Lev Manovich, *The Language of New Media* (Cambridge, MA: MIT Press, 2001).

2. See Thomas Elsaesser, 'Louis Lumière – The Cinema's First Virtualist?', in Thomas Elsaesser and Kay Hoffmann (eds), *Cinema Futures: Cain, Abel or Cable?: The Screen Arts in the Digital Age* (Amsterdam: Amsterdam University Press, 1998).

3. *Big Brother* Web site, <www.cbs.com/primetime/bigbrother>.

5.2

Old Media as New Media: Television

William Uricchio

Television, like other 'old' media such as film and telephony, is in the process of a digital transformation. Long before the much-touted transition to full digital television service took place, guests in most major hotels enjoyed access to televisions that provided wake-up, messaging and check-out services, movies-on-demand and video games, in addition to the usual offerings of cable. These were but a taste of things to come. Television's developers have since been doing their best to redefine the medium for the new age, expanding the services that it delivers and changing the notion of its audience interface (TiVo, DirecTV, and embedded directory systems), partly in a bid to lay claim to 'The Next Big Thing' and partly to hold their ground against incursions from newcomers. The threat, of course, comes from competing computer-based systems that also make use of video display technologies. More than a few cases of dotcom fever can be attributed to the idea that the Internet would displace television as the dominant provider of audiovisual information and entertainment. A radical sense of interactivity combined with customised programming possibilities, unparalleled access to the world 'out there' and a potentially rich data-stream of information on consumer behaviour all combined to make the idea of the Internet as a worthy successor to television credible in some circles. While it is too early to know which of the many new initiatives will survive, historical precedent teaches that the old medium may be repositioned, but it will not be replaced by the new. Having said that, the relationship between the old and new is likely to remain contentious, as both struggle for definition in a fast-changing media landscape.

Now more than ever, the questions of what television is, or whether video and computer games are autonomous media, or how we might consider the media status of the Internet, have significant discursive and financial implications. These same challenges face film, or radio, or recorded music, as new digital technologies transform (and compete with) existing processes of production, distribution and exhibition. The dynamic is not new. Indeed, it is endemic to the ongoing process of media redefinition particularly at those moments when a challenger appears on the horizon. A new medium, the challenger, must of necessity refer itself to existing needs, which are usually well covered by existing media, while at the same time demonstrating the condition of its newness, thus destabilising the status quo. At the same time, new technological capacities achieve (new) media status through a series of struggles over identity, representational capacity, business model, mode of production, regulatory frameworks, and so on. Historically, such struggles have been profoundly social, resulting in cultural and institutional consensus around a particular set of constructions, the new medium of the moment, effectively marginalising many viable alternatives. These alternatives remain interesting as indicators both of unexploited potentials (what the medium in question might have been) and often of recurrent desires that sometimes emerge as drivers for yet other media systems. This chapter will explore aspects of this process as they have affected television's development when it was a new medium, hope-fully shedding light on a developmental process common to today's new media. At the same time, I would like briefly to reflect on the process of 'doing' media history, as I believe that this paradox weighs heavily upon our sense of the past, highlighting certain devel-opments and rendering others marginal. In this sense, it is useful to keep in mind the continuing re-articulation of the medium and its capacities in both marketing discourse and the popular imagination. These developments have helped to undermine certain aspects of television's 'taken-for-grantedness', in part helping to account for reappraisals of the medium's history like the one that follows.

PARADOX

Television embodies one of the paradoxes central to distributed media technologies.[1] On one hand, if we take technology to be a culturally constructed process,[2] we know that it has myriad dimensions, that it is contested and subject to change as constantly and inevitably as culture itself. On the other hand, we know that system requirements and the demands of compatibility bring with them the tendency for stabilisation, centralisation and (in both technological and, one might argue, programming senses) conservatism. Distributed media technologies constitute something of an extreme case. Their status as media underlines the cultural, a dynamic area if ever there were one, and is compounded by the rapid changes in the media landscape that have taken place over the past 150 years, changes that have profoundly resituated existing media forms. However, the very fact of their distribution renders these media highly dependent upon compatibility and thus standardisation. This paradox helps to explain a great deal about television's historical development and its pat-tern of response in the current moment of redefinition.

The dominant popular notion of television owes much to the stability of the past 50 or so years, that is, a period of regulatory stability regarding the medium's technological stan-dards, broadcast operations and even programming. Most nations conceived of television largely within a conceptual framework that evolved, sometimes painfully, from radio. Radio, of course, initially experienced the remarkable freedom that accompanies a low technolog-ical threshold, an absence of determining precedents and no clear institutional consensus regarding medium capacity and form. Susan Douglas offers a portrait of the remarkable plu-rality of radio concepts and deployments that circulated in the US during the first decades of the twentieth century before the convergence of state and corporate interests defined the medium in something like the broadcast form that we have today.[3] Unfortunately, that plurality was short-lived. Television took its contemporary form while the learning curve of radio's transformation from a grassroots, two-way medium into a centrally controlled broadcast medium was still fresh in the corporate mind. To paraphrase RCA's Sarnoff, the corporation would not repeat its mistake of nearly 'losing' radio with the new medium of television. Thanks to the intersecting interests of the state and large-scale electronics corporations, one might easily have the idea of a medium frozen in time. Image quality, mode of production and programme conception differ little today from the 1950s' norm. In fact, the 525 scanning line standard in the US today can be traced directly back to early 1940s' technology and many programme forms can be traced back even earlier to radio precedents.[4] The pressures of limited broadcast spectrum resulted in various discourses about 'public' or 'state' ownership (and therefore accountability) and the need for co-ordination of broadcast signals and technical compatibility (and thus regulation and centralisation), cementing relations between the state and both hardware and software producers in most national contexts.[5] Not surprisingly, the fit between these mutual interests was sufficiently close as to result in nearly a half century of stability.

True, one could certainly point to technological shifts from tube, to transistor, to chip, or to increases in available programming from a handful of broadcast stations per market to many more narrowcast cable and/or satellite stations, or even to the ability to time-shift and reach outside broadcast and cable environments for programme material (the video revolution and, more recently, TiVo). However, the popular image of the television, its dominant applications, cultural status and most importantly our assumptions regarding the medium have changed remarkably little over the past half century. Yet despite the medium's 'taken-for-grantedness', despite the suppression of its radical potentials,[6] I would argue that television is one of the more extreme examples of the instability endemic to media forms. If we frame our understanding of television by looking further back than the medium's post-war configuration, a very different picture emerges.

PROTOTYPES

As a concept, the 'televisual' has from its inception contained many of the same ambitions that we see expressed today in the latest generation of interactive new media: the desire for immersion, extension and communication, to see and be a part of the world outside our physical reach. It has at times literally been inscribed with much of the same functionality that we today associate with computer-based media. Television's imminent digital future has led to a reiteration of these promises in an explicit manner, targeted directly at contemporary developments in digital media. The result of this discursive strategy has been to render vague the boundaries between otherwise distinct media. Although this posturing merits serious consideration, the future-oriented claims of television are complicated by the double quandary of omnipresent hype (even the most stable periods of the medium's history have been accompanied by constant claims of 'newer, bigger, better . . .'), and by the attempts of emerging new media systems to meet old needs in new ways, leading to frequent conflations of claims and struggles for identity. Both dynamics cloud the water sufficiently that fishing here for signs of the medium's radical potential is a tricky business indeed. However, if we look back to television's first decades, before it achieved its conceptual and institutional stability and its cultural 'taken-for-grantedness', we might be much more successful in assessing what 'might have been' and thus be in a better position to learn from, to paraphrase Carolyn Marvin, this old medium when it was new.[7]

Locating an appropriate entry point to a medium's history is a task complicated by the problem of determinacy.[8] If we work backwards from a fully developed medium to its point of origin, we risk replicating a dominant and frequently told success story and missing the many alternatives and dead-ends from which the winning construction emerged. On the other hand, if we begin with a wide spectrum of approaches to a particular problem (in television's case, as loose a definition as 'seeing at a distance'), then our conceptual framing of the problem becomes determining. Scholars of early film history have for some time been concerned with these issues, framing and reframing the genealogy of their medium and the processes by which a bundle of possibilities gave way to a dominant construction.[9] In the case of television, historical efforts have been considerably less energetic, providing only the weakest of orthodoxies and an even weaker set of alternative constructions.[10] Fortunately, there seems to be a relatively clear moment at which something like the televisual enters both the patent record and the popular imagination, giving us at least a reasonable starting place.[11]

As I have suggested, we must reach back considerably further than the birth of commercial or national broadcasting efforts in the postwar period. Television, which has long been seen as a fusion of film (the visual component) and radio (the broadcasting component), might profitably be repositioned within a trajectory of technologies which sought to connect two distant points in real time, that is, with technologies such as the telephone and the telegraph before it.[12] I would locate the earliest full-blown descriptions of a medium that could transmit live moving images from one point to another in 1877, the year after Bell's telephone was publicly demonstrated. The telephone's ability to send the ephemeral character of sound, as if live, over space seems to have encouraged any number of people to consider the possibility of doing the same with visuals. In June 1877, *L'année scientifique et industrielle* included a description of the 'telectroscope', a device attributed to Alexander Graham Bell that sent live images over a distance. Within two years of the telephone's invention, a now famous cartoon appeared in *Punch* which showed a girl in Ceylon speaking with her parents in London by way of a wide-screen 'electric camera-obscura' attributed to Edison and a telephone.[13] By the end of the century, Albert Robida would provide his detailed vision of television as an apparatus of simultaneity capable of entertainment, communication and surveillance.

The clustering of these anticipations (or insights) around the introduction of the telephone should not be terribly surprising. Already, by the mid-nineteenth century, the telegraph, which missed the liveness of the voice, but could transmit in near real time the alphabet upon which spoken language was based, joined forces with visual forms. Image telegraphy (for example, Belin's 1856 device), like a fax in its scanning and transmission of graphic form point-by-point, line-by-line, was relatively widespread and clearly established a link between a near live, electrical, word-based communication technology and visual images. The telephone, with its capacity to extend the grain of the voice in real time, was simply imagined as continuing the good work, conceptually extending its acoustical abilities to the ephemeral qualities of live motion. The surprise is rather more that, despite their admirable methodological reflexivity, historians of the moving image have missed this link thanks to their fixation with visual culture for the construction of a media genealogy that culminated in film. In tracing pre-cinematic developments, these historians almost never mention telegraphy, telephony or television. Yet television, both as a fully imagined moving image medium and as a (incompletely) patented technology, can be argued to have established the horizon of expectations for film itself some ten to 15 years before the Lumières' first 1895 projection, rendering film (motion without liveness) as something of a compromise to a world awaiting television. Such a view brings with it the need to rethink many of our assumptions about the early days of the film medium.[14]

What can we learn from these early visions of the new medium of television? Let's briefly examine two examples, one literary and one technological. In 1883, Albert Robida published *La Vingtième Siècle*, a science-fiction text full of remarkably prescient forecasting and marvellous illustrations. Robida's text elaborates a variety of scenarios for the telephonoscope, a display device that uses a large, oval-shaped flat glass screen to show distant live events. A cousin of the telephone both nominally and mechanically, for it can facilitate two-way communications together with the telephone as well as offering one-way audiovisual access, the telephonoscope, in one scenario, permits a Frenchman posted in the Far East to talk with and see his family back home (a function that Robida entitles '*la suppression d'absence*'). In another scenario, we read of the difficulties of attending the theatre, from coach-hiring, to inclement weather, to the poor sight-lines of nineteenth-century theatre boxes. The telephonoscope permits theatre-lovers to stay at home and, from the comfort of their living rooms, have front-row access to the stage action as it unfolds. Robida also elaborates the informational function of the device (world news, shown live as it happens); its role in the public sphere (billboard-sized public television displaying the day's events); and its potential for surveillance and voyeurism (as a 'mistake' offers a group of men a televisual view of women undressing).

Robida's description includes an array of televisual functionalities that we have either seen deployed (live entertainment and CNN-style live global news coverage, surveillance) or have long been promised (television-telephone service, most recently promised in next-generation cell phones). He understands the medium both as a one-to-one communication system and as a broadcasting system; and he situates reception both in the privacy of the home and in public settings. The defining elements of his imagined audiovisual medium are liveness, movement and the capacities for interaction and (apparently) immersion.[15] Many of these notions would be drawn upon by the following waves of new media. In articulating his ideas, Robida made use of existing media, the then six-year-old telephone, of course, but also a notion of visual display partially derived from the magic lantern or, perhaps more appropriately, the camera obscura.

The year following the publication of Robida's book (1884), Paul Nipkow, working in Germany, patented the disk that would be the heart of mechanical-optical television systems into the 1940s, the *elektrisches teleskop*. Although the name for Nipkow's device is also intermedially referenced to an existing technology[16] – this time visual instead of audio – in fact his mechanical reference is to an audio technology. Nipkow's disk is remarkably similar to the Polyphone system developed in Leipzig in the 1880s, a pre-gramophone music box system in which the software consisted of perforated metal disks. Nipkow created his image dissector by perforating a metal disk in a spiral pattern, standing it on end and giving it a spin, in the process effectively transforming the Polyphone's musical software into television hardware.[17] Like Robida, Nipkow described his new medium in terms of existing technologies, a verbal reference to extension in real time (the telescope) and a mechanical homage to an audio storage medium. In later years, Nipkow also circulated a creation myth, recalling his student days, when far from home and wanting to be with his family for the Christmas holidays, he came up with the idea for 'television'. Like the 1877 *Punch* cartoon, Nipkow sought to develop a medium capable of extension, interaction, virtual presence, communication . . .

PLURALITY

Robida's musings and Nipkow's patent helped to shape early thinking about television's possibilities, with other developers contributing to the discussion along the way. Although most of the components for what would emerge as working television were in place by the turn of the century, the medium remained largely a tinkerer's fantasy until the late 1920s when technologies such as radio, capitalisation from government and industry, and demand in the form of cinema sound systems, among other things, all converged. The late 1920s and early 1930s are notable as much for the battles between individual inventors and corporations (Farnsworth vs. RCA; Baird vs. EMI) as for the struggle over technological norms (optical–mechanical; electronic) and the developmental plurality of television's very conception. It is a period during which, in nearly every country with a developed television industry, these conflicts played out with roughly similar results.

The clearest examples can be found in Germany, which first introduced daily public television service in Berlin in March 1935.[18] By this point, independent British inventor John Logie Baird, finding little enthusiasm for his ideas from the BBC, formed an alliance with German partners and joined the Fernseh Company. However, Baird and partners faced parallel difficulties in Germany. The 1936 Olympics were the unlikely testing ground for the nation's two competing television systems: Fernseh's interfilm system and Telefunken's iconoscope system. Telefunken, part of a global RCA licensing network that included Baird's British competitor EMI, won the standards battle in Germany just as EMI triumphed in Britain and RCA dominated in America. There seemed to be a distinct pattern to the reduction of television's technological plurality, matching the technological need for stan-dardisation together with corporate might.

Television's conceptual contest played out with greater variation, again with Germany providing an excellent example. Thanks to a series of sometimes bitter struggles among political factions, government ministries and interested corporations, television found itself pulled in at least four different directions. The electronics industry, in the midst of a national campaign to put a radio in every German home, unsurprisingly backed a radio-like notion of television: a household appliance that could bring the events of the outside world into the living room and that, like radio, would thrive on live information and mixed-form enter-tainment broadcasts. To this end, a relatively inexpensive 'people's television receiver' was developed by the electronics companies, replicating the successful principle of the 'people's radio'. This view was contested by Goebbels and Hadamovsky of the Propaganda Ministry together with the socialist wing of the Nazi Party, all of whom felt (for very different reasons) that television should be seen outside the home in collective, public settings, serving as something of a surrogate for film with the added capacity to show live sports or political events. The Propaganda Ministry felt collective settings were more per-suasive; and the socialist wing believed that television should be free for all until receivers were so cheap that anyone could afford them. A third notion of television saw it as a two-way communication medium linked to the telephone, harking back to the earliest visions of the medium. Accordingly, a nationwide television–telephone network was established with facilities in major city post offices. Finally, the Air Ministry developed television for the pur-poses of both reconnaissance (using high-definition prototypes of up to 2000 scanning lines) and telepresence (visual guidance systems for bombs, rockets and torpedoes in the form of mini-television cameras and remote controls).

Each of these systems was deployed, and each gave form to a distinctive definition of television's capacities, whether representational or functional. Moreover, each was embed-ded in particular technological prototypes and medial *dispositifs*, with radio, film, telephone and telepresence in turn constructing distinctive notions of interface, audience and notions of effects. The point is that in this stage of its development, television as a new medium enjoyed considerable conceptual flexibility and was highly responsive to its media environ-ment. It was a medium that could have taken very different directions from that which we today take for granted. True, in national contexts such as the US where corporations such as RCA (NBC) and Columbia (CBS) enjoyed a particularly influential position, television was promoted almost exclusively within the radio paradigm, and in this sense it is indeed ironic to find such plurality in a totalitarian state. Nevertheless, the medium's potential to be con-figured in many different ways was explored even there, if primarily in research laboratories. The ultimate dominance of the radio model had far-reaching consequences. On one hand, television was in some circles conceived of as the 'completion' of radio, the next step in a teleologically driven evolution process by which the senses were extended, allowing wireless participation and a modicum of control in distant places. On the other hand, media-conceptual issues such as a state and corporate preference for one-way rather than two-way communication; regulatory issues such as the division and allocation of broadcast spectrum; content issues such as programme formats; and economic models, whether commercial, state or public, were all derived from the model radio provided in the late 1920s. The period was crucial for the suppression of the medium's plurality and the consolidation of its modelling, and for revealing the nature of the pressures that forged this new medium as it was prepared for public consumption.

Despite the top-down imposition of conformity in this period, and despite the medium's ensuing conceptual stasis, the eventual public release of the medium in the decade following World War II generated more than a few intermedial pressures. Long-standing rivalries generated some of these, as evidenced in the US where the telephone company, long the nemesis of the broadcasting world, attempted to stimulate a market for videophones and later lay claim to alternative (cable) distribution. Also in the US, independents attempted to break into what amounted to a network broadcasting monopoly by renting cinemas and providing live big-screen television special event coverage, for example, boxing championships, to collective audiences. However, the notion of television agreed upon by governments and large corporate players alike was not threatened by such peripheral activities. Other media, however, felt television's pressure far more directly. Radio, despite maintaining the cultural high ground relative to television, found its programmes from sports to drama not only copied, but also challenged by the addition of visual information. Cinema, experiencing a significant drop in its audiences and income in the postwar years, misdiagnosed the cause of its problems as television. As a result, it sought to bolster its identity as a medium and distinguish itself from the intruder: cinerama, increased colour productions, 3D films and even smell-o-rama were among its claims to an experience of scale and intensity specific to the medium against which television, it was hoped, would fade into obscurity.

CONTINUITIES

The cartoon record is rich with dreams of television, some hopeful and some anxious, serving as a barometer of popular sentiment regarding the medium and its possibilities. In the course of the 1936 Olympics, a German newspaper ran a cartoon looking forward to television during the year 2000 Olympics. From his bed, a man is shown watching a large, flat-screen television mounted to the ceiling above him. He has a remote control device that allows him to move the camera around the various Olympic events. If we read this as a prediction of things to come, the timing is about right; however, the more important point regards the recurrence of a desire for individually controlled programming, a sense of extension and the ability to interact with the world viewed. As such, it is part of a long tradition of popular utterances that seek to exploit television's visual contact with the world around it. No matter that television as we know it has long since turned from a medium of liveness to a videotape-facilitated time machine, recycling the past and simulating the present; historically, its dominant trope has been a recurrent obsession with liveness, with sensory extension, with the world of the present.

Certain specific manifestations of liveness and extension have helped to shape the (even imagined) medium of television, recurring throughout its history in both discursive and technologised form. As we saw with the *Punch* cartoon about Edison's supposed 'tele-phonoscope', or with Robida's related notion, or with the German deployment of a telephone–television system, or with today's news leaks about next-generation Nokia television-equipped telephones, the notion of two-way communication and interaction has been fundamental to the medium from the start. Although until recently there have been considerable technological challenges to the widespread use of such a system, the cartoon record also suggests that, despite this vision's centrality, it also harbours a darker side. Adding visual information to the telephone, it seems, also makes unwanted information available to the caller, generating the sorts of awkward social situations that cartoonists thrive on. Nevertheless, if both television and the telephone have been reluctant to join forces, the development of the Webcam would seem to address this long-term desire through the potential of another medium; it remains to be seen just how widespread its use will be. This development suggests that certain long-term, even formative, desires are not necessarily fulfilled. However, they can still be seen as hyperbolising aspects of medium identity. On the other hand, if fundamental needs are thwarted – for example, the early sup-pression of two-way communication initially available with the radio – we might have reason to think that one medium can find a ready market in the under-represented capacities of another (the recent rise of wireless telephony comes to mind).

A number of other continuities seems to accompany the development of new media. Brian Winston has offered a comprehensive developmental scheme for the pattern of recurrences, which I shall not repeat here,[19] but I would like to call attention to several social rituals that accompanied television's development, as well as that of other distributed media. These mainly have to do with moral panics, as well as with the threat of redistributing social power, shaping popular imagination and the right of representation. Whether tele-vision, film, comic books, recorded music or video games, the embrace of a new medium by a socially marginal cohort (marked by age, ethnicity, educational level, and so on) seems to provoke the critical attention of socially dominant groups. As a new medium struggles for acceptance, it usually finds its first large wave of adapters from outside entrenched and socially integrated media systems. Popularity combined with outsider status provoke con-cern, usually moral in nature, which in turn leads to calls for regulation and a consequent politicising of medium identity and participation. This is not to argue that content or tech-nologies or exhibition sites are necessarily free from social dangers, but rather that the medium itself is flattened in an equation with danger.

The moral issue might also be seen as masking larger ideological concerns with the distribution of knowledge, social power and the ability to control representation. A new medium disrupts not only the status quo of the existing media ecosystem, but it can poten-tially destabilise the economy of signs and the flow of information as well, thus posing a threat to those vested social interests charged with maintaining a particular world view. In most national contexts, this challenge was precluded by mandating that television, like radio before it, fall under the control of the state, either directly or via regulatory frameworks. The anxieties of established social cohorts may, in this sense, work towards the containment of a new medium's potential every bit as much as the technological demands of standardisation.

CONCLUSION

The pressures and process through which television transformed from a bundle of desires, dreams and technological possibilities into the taken-for-grantedness of the box sitting quietly in the corner are revealing. Although directly related to the particularities of historical moment and cultural context, they also share much with the historical development of other media systems. The tensions between innovation and standardisation, the determining potentials of various intermedially situated prototypes, the struggles to find a place in (and thus redefine) the media landscape and the threats to existing patterns of social organisation are all factors that each new medium has faced. The results have necessarily entailed compromise and the abandoning of the many rich possibilities of which each medium has been capable. Sometimes this takes the form of simple redefinition (do we consider television as the medium behind industrial or medical telepresence systems, or surveillance systems, or non-visible light spectrum imaging?). In television's case, we have generally chosen to distinguish between a particular cultural manifestation and more broadly manifest (functional) applications, but the distinction is largely a rhetorical one. At other times, it takes the form of repressing certain possibilities, leaving them open to other (new) media to pick up and address.

Reflections on media identity and developmental perspectives have much to gain from media history, although an exclusive preoccupation with the future of new media also seems to be a historically recurrent pattern. Having said that, we also need to consider the many environmental factors that have changed. For example, in today's media environment, convergence has accelerated significantly and altered the position of 'free-standing' media. Whether we consider economic organisation (where media conglomerates and crossownership are now standard), technology (where digital platforms are effacing older photochemical and magnetic media boundaries and providing a unified base), regional specificity (where satellite transmissions and global flows have penetrated to most areas) or, indeed, textual specificity (where increasing numbers of narratives and characters exist as elements in carefully sequenced transmedia networks), the concept of media interdependence is stronger than ever. These environmental factors do not weaken the insights available from the consideration of old media when they were new, but instead help to position them and selectively activate them.

The television medium, as noted at the outset, is in a state of rapid change. The planned use of adaptive agents, so that programming choices or personalised (interactive) narratives can be generated for individual viewers, the availability of video-on-demand, increased twoway service (currently limited to the 'buy now' variety) – all are either available or about to reach the market. Potentially interesting developments in cross-platform productions, whereby elements of a particular text appear on television, online and in other media are increasingly manifest. As we witness and contribute to this process of media (re-)definition, history may provide both the perspective and insight needed to read and learn from this transformation.

Notes

1. I use this (hopefully not too convoluted) construction in order to bypass the term 'mass media', both because the latter term is overladen with pejorative associations and because it fails accurately to describe media such as the telephone and computer.

2. And for the purposes of this paper, I do! See Raymond Williams, *Television: Technology and Cultural Form* (New York: Schocken Books, 1974).

3. Susan Douglas, *Inventing American Broadcasting, 1899–1922* (Baltimore, MD: The Johns Hopkins University Press, 1987).

4. William Boddy, *Fifties Television: The Industry and Its Critics* (Urbana: University of Illinois Press, 1990); Michele Hilmes, *Hollywood and Broadcasting: From Radio to Cable* (Urbana: University of Illinois Press, 1990).

5. Major national variations from the 1950s through the early 1980s included systems oriented towards commerce (US), the state (France), public/pluriform (Netherlands) and public service (UK).

6. I take the term from Brian Winston, *Misunderstanding Media* (New York: Routledge, 1986).

7. Carolyn Marvin, *When Old Technologies Were New: Thinking about Electric Communication In the Late Nineteenth Century* (New York: Oxford University Press, 1988).

8. Hayden White has perhaps most elegantly called attention to the implications of where we choose to begin and end our historical narratives in his *Metahistory: The Historical Imagination in Nineteenth-Century Europe* (Baltimore, MD: The Johns Hopkins University Press, 1973). Television in this regard is exemplary. Seen from the perspective of the dawn of the broadcast era in the years following World War II, the medium's history might be read as a textbook case of collaborative efforts between industry and government stabilising a 'new' technology, with an earlier medium, radio, providing the main organisational and programming parameters for its deployment. The intervening years would then be positioned as both a confirmation of the wisdom of this original model and as a testament to the slow but steady refinements of media technology (tubes to chips), interface (dial to remote control) and synergetic potential (ranging from delivery and storage systems to programming sources). If we begin our story at a different point, the historical trajectory leads to quite another set of insights.

9. I refer here to the post-Brighton turn in early film studies, a development that has proven remarkably productive over the past 20 years.

10. With the notable exceptions of Albert Abramson, *The History of Television, 1880–1941* (London: McFarland, 1987); Herman Hecht, *Pre-Cinema History: An Encyclopaedia and Annotated Bibliography of the Moving Image before 1896* (London: BFI/Bowker/Saur, 1993); George Shires, *Early Television: A Bibliographic Guide to 1940* (London: Garland Publishing, Inc., 1997).

11. At least one commentator traces the story of television back to the ancient Egyptians; others, such as Brian Winston, have made a strong case for considering the deep history of the many chemical

and engineering developments that television (as we know it) eventually would call upon. This historical frame reaches much farther back than my own; the distinction is that my argument centres on the concept of the medium, rather than on the history of its component parts.

12. Conceptually, I see the sixteenth-century development of the camera obscura as a direct conceptual predecessor to television, but, for the purposes of this chapter, I take the televisual in a more literal sense. See William Uricchio, 'Technologies of Time', in J. Olsson (ed.), *Allegories of Communication: Intermedial Concerns from Cinema to the Digital* (Berkeley: University of California Press, 2001).

13. George Dumaurier, 'Edison's Telephonoscope (Transmits Light as Well as Sound)', Almanac for 1879, *Punch* 75 (9 December 1878).

14. William Uricchio, 'Cinema as Detour?: Towards a Reconsideration of Moving Image Technology in the Late 19th Century', in K. Hickethier, E. Muller and R. Rother, (Hg.), *Der Film in der Geschichte* (Berlin: Edition Sigma, 1997), pp. 19–25.

15. Robida's illustrations repeatedly depict a look of astonishment on the faces of audience members, particularly those engaged in watching news; viewers of entertainment programming, by contrast, usually look relaxed.

16. In fact, Nipkow's linguistic reference would take root in the German language. An alternative and now archaic term for the telescope is the *Fernseher* (literally, far-seer), and this is the term by which television is known in contemporary Germany.

17. Although there is a circumstantial case to be made for Polyphone's relationship to Nipkow's discovery, I have found no direct evidence linking the two systems.

18. The claim is complicated by the fact that Germany's initial efforts differed little from what was being broadcast in the US, England and other countries on an experimental basis. Nevertheless, the Reichs Broadcasting Service represented a collaboration between industry and the state that continued largely unbroken until the last months of the war and was responsible for significant innovation on both programming and technological fronts. For an overview, see William Uricchio, 'Television as History: Representations of German Television Broadcasting, 1935–1944', in Bruce Murray and Christopher Wickham (eds), *Framing the Past: The Historiography of German Cinema and Television* (Carbondale: Southern Illinois University Press, 1992), pp. 167–96.

19. See Brian Winston, *Misunderstanding Media*.

5.3

New Media as Old Media: Cinema

Jan Simons

WHAT'S IN A NAME?

If anything, the term 'new media' has an unequivocally ambiguous status. Since any 'old medium' can be digitalised and integrated into a new media object, the term 'new media' virtually encompasses all media once all difference between media has been dissolved 'into a pulsing stream of bits and bytes'.[1] In this sense, the term 'new media' is a generic term which indicates the commonality between digitalised objects, like the terms 'fruit' and 'furniture' do for the objects that they categorise. On the other hand, the term 'new media' also functions as a plural, because it refers to a vast variety of genuinely new, digital media such as CD-ROMs, Web sites, DVDs, kiosks, 3D virtual reality environments, game consoles, and so on, provided, of course, that they are digital, multimedial and interactive, the features commonly ascribed to 'new media.' However, does this actually mean that, when a film such as *Harry Potter and the Sorcerer's Stone* (2001) is screened in the cinema, released on video or broadcast on television, it is part of the 'old media', but when released on DVD it is a 'new media object'? The answer is 'yes' if we follow Marshall McLuhan's dictum that the 'content' of a medium is another medium. However, it becomes less obvious when one realises that the adaptation from the novel to the film involves a more radical transformation of the 'content' and the way this content is accessed and perceived than the 'transformation', if any, from the film or video to the DVD, in spite of the latter being digital, interactive and multimedial.

In this sense, the term 'new media' is a bit like postmodernism: everybody seems to know what is meant by these composites, but nobody knows exactly what they mean. To say that a medium or media are 'new' or that a work of art is 'postmodern' is not saying very much except that the media designated by that term are different from the media we are familiar with or that the work of art under consideration comes 'after' modernism. Both terms have more in common than their minimal informative meanings. On the one hand, they carry with them the very justification for the vagueness of their meanings: the 'new' being by definition 'unknown', and the 'post' indicating that we are leaving familiar ground and entering one that is as yet unexplored. On the other hand, both terms have been over-used in the worlds of fashion, advertising and art criticism, where everything is always 'new', and 'post', 'neo', or 'retro', to raise more than a sceptical eyebrow. Just as the term 'postmodern' has gradually gone out of fashion, so, too, will the term 'new media'. For whatever both terms might mean, they also define the state of the objects the nouns they are combined with refer to as transitory and temporary: nothing can stay 'new' or 'post' forever. The industry already prefers to use the term 'information and communication technologies', the meaning of which is at the same time broader than that of new media; it encompasses objects such as mobile telephones which are generally not referred to as new media, as well as what have now become 'old media'. More precisely, it points towards the technological basis of media and the purposes for which they are put to use.

The three features that are commonly attributed to new media, namely digital, interactive and multimedia, seem to form a 'folk theory' of new media. Whatever their usefulness for practical everyday purposes may be, folk theories are often based on intuition and phenomenological experience rather than on analysis and precisely defined terms, and they give rise to mystifications and confused understandings. The words 'digital', 'interactive' and 'multimedia' may serve well to explain to a prospective buyer the differences between a computer and a television set, or a CD-ROM and an audiotape, but they hardly suffice to explain theoretically the differences between 'old' and 'new' media. In fact, the very terms 'old' and 'new' media risk misleading theoreticians.

REMEDIATION REVISITED

The distinction between 'old' and 'new' media underlies the concept of 'remediation', which was introduced by Jay David Bolter and Richard Grusin in their influential book *Remediation: Understanding New Media*. Remediation, in its most general and simple sense, means 'the representation of one medium in another medium', but in the context of digital media remediation means more specifically digital media's representation of their predecessors. That new media 'remediate' old media is in itself hardly surprising, given that data from all other media can be digitised. However, by describing the relationship between 'old' and 'new' media in terms of 'remediation', Bolter and Grusin not only explicitly accept this distinction as a sound theoretical basis for their enterprise, but they are also forced to frame their concept in an art historical schema that is derived from theoretical models of the old media, rather than from empirical observations and analysis of the new media. According to Bolter and Grusin, the history of media in general and the history of painting, photography and film in particular are driven by the search to satisfy the desire of what they call 'immediacy', the desire of being immediately in touch with the represented objects without being obstructed by the medium which represents the representation. This theory of artistic evolution echoes André Bazin's account of the history of art, which, according to him, originated in a 'mummy complex', the wish to defend the appearances of the dead against the passage of time. The psychological need to overcome death and the destructive working of time made the search of optimal resemblance with the real art's natural destiny.[2] Cinema was, for André Bazin, the latest and most perfect achievement in the search to 'embalm time', whereas for Bolter and Grusin, immersive virtual reality is the latest medium 'whose purpose is to disappear'.[3] In their view, 'new media' in general try to achieve the same goals as their predecessors, but in better and superior ways (after all, new media attempt to 'remediate' their predecessors).

Like Bazin, Bolter and Grusin are also well aware that there is yet another strand in the history of art in which artists tried to emphasise the stylistic, material and formal dimensions of their work. Bazin, however, calls the latter 'pseudo-realism' which satisfies itself 'with the illusion of form', whereas Bolter and Grusin acknowledge the 'reality' of what they call 'hypermediacy', but then describe modern and postmodern hypermediacy as another form of immediacy because modernism 'emphasised the reality of both the act of painting and its product'. Ultimately, hypermediacy is just another form of rendering the sense of the unmediated presence of the work of art or the new 'hypermedia' themselves.[4]

Lev Manovich observes in his book *The Language of New Media* an 'anti-montage' tendency in computer culture. Montage can thus be seen as a form of 'hypermediacy', because it 'aims to create visual, stylistic, semantic, and emotional dissonance between different elements' and, by doing so, attracts the spectator's attention towards the construction that sets bounds to and separates these elements at the same time.[5] On the other hand, digital compositing 'in which different spaces are combined into a single seamless virtual space, is a good example of the aesthetics of continuity; moreover, compositing in general can be understood as a counterpart to montage aesthetics'.[6] This story is quite different from a previously claimed return of digital cinema and new media to 'the cinema of attractions', which tended to emphasise the discontinuity and conflicts among its heterogeneous compounds. It also contrasts with the multimedial dimension of new media, because multimedia almost by definition draws the user's attention to the differences of the media and to the dissimilarities of the 'information environment' of which they are part. Whatever their other merits may be, the newly coined terms 'immediacy' and 'hypermediacy' seem to transfer the typical 'old media' debate between realistic and anti-realistic tendencies into the realm of 'new media', rather than throwing a new light on both old and new media from the more advanced stance of the latter.

DIGITAL, ANALOGOUS, CONTINUOUS

It is not only the usually very loosely defined terms 'old' and 'new' media that are sources of confusion. So, too, are the terms that specify their features. 'Digital' is one such example. Lev Manovich, for instance, rightly criticises the frequently made equation of digital with discrete and analogue with continuous. He points out that cinema is based on the sampling of time and thus accomplished a 'conceptual break from the continuous to the discrete'.[7] However, for film semioticians from the pre-digital era, the form of a sign was either motivated by its referent or not.[8] For these theorists, the opposite of analogue was not digital, but arbitrary. Moreover, as Christian Metz pointed out, the distinction 'discrete–continuous' did not make much sense in cinema because film lacked a finite inventory of discrete units comparable with the phonemes and morphemes of a natural language. Raymond Bellour observed that film frames or 'photogrammes', now relabelled by Manovich as 'samples', could not serve as points of departure for film analysis because they do not display cinema's most characteristic feature: movement.[9] These film theorists did not regard 'discreteness' as one of cinema's major features because cinema managed to overcome the discreteness of film frames in a seamless, continuous 'flow' of movement. This difference of opinion between Manovich and film semiologists obviously follows from the different levels at which they define the cinematic 'sign': Manovich defines it in technical terms (the material support of the cinematic image), whereas film semioticians defined the film image phenomenologically in terms of the way it was perceived and experienced by the spectator. From this perspective, cinema was not considered as discrete at all, and presumably film semioticians would argue in exactly the same manner against the presumed 'discreteness' of digital cinema.

Nor were 'old' media such as film, photography or figurative paintings unequivocally considered as 'analogue'. Umberto Eco argued that photographs can be digitally analysed, which is what happens when they are printed through a raster or scanned by a computer.[10] The Belgian philosopher Henri Vanlier even argued that photographs are inherently digital because they are obtained by the conversion of silver grains into 'darkened/not-darkened, that is the choice yes/no or 0/1: they are also digital'.[11] Avant-garde artists in the early twentieth century claimed to lay bare the 'discrete units' of the language of all painting (for example, the horizontal and vertical lines and primary colours in Mondrian's paintings).[12] Whether one considers a medium as 'digital' or 'analogue' thus seems to depend on one's theoretical stance and preferred level of analysis, rather than on the technological properties of a medium itself.

The equation of analogue with motivated and digital with arbitrary is equally problematic. Eco points out that smoke is 'motivated' by fire, but not analogous to it, just as the length of a mercury column in a thermometer is what Greg Currie calls 'naturally dependent' on but not analogous to the amount of ambient heat.[13] Webcam pictures, on the other hand, can be as unmanipulated and 'naturally dependent' on their models as any good old photograph.[14] Analogous and motivated representations of independently existing models remain an option within the range of possibilities of computer-based imagery. Is not 'photo realism' one of the main objectives software programmers and practitioners of digital imagery try to achieve?

The equation *digital:analogue = discrete:continuous = arbitrary:motivated* gives rise to yet another, often surreptitiously introduced folk theoretical distinction. According to this, digital signs are arbitrary and manipulated (or 'construed'), and thus unreliable as far as their veracity is concerned, whereas mechanically produced analogous signs are caused by, and by that very fact true to, their models. However, truth-telling and truthfulness are not functions of machines, codes and technologies, but of the intentions, purposes and ethics of the people who use them. One notices that the set of distinctions that started off as an endeavour to come to terms with new media ends up in the domains of ethics and ideology. This is a clear indication that we are dealing with folk theoretical rather than scientific notions of new media. In the contexts of these folk theoretical notions, the terms 'digital' and 'analogous' are not only often used to refer to different aspects and different levels of semiotic artifacts, but the meanings of these terms also tend to shift when they are applied to one aspect or level rather than another.

The terms 'digital' and 'analogous', then, only seem to have a clear meaning when applied to clear-cut examples such as numbers, phonemes and digits on the one hand, or photographs, film images, drawings or music records which bear some obvious similarity to their models on the other. As we have seen, however, even these 'good examples' do not stand a closer inspection. Most problems with the digital–analogous distinction arise from a systematically made category mistake that takes the ingredients for the recipe. The fact that computerised objects consist of pixels, bits and bytes does not seem to be of much interest to the user, who is simply interested in the texts, images, films or sounds he or she retrieves from the computer's hard disk or from a Web site on the Internet. From the user's point of view, a text remains a linguistic object and images remain iconic objects. Texts and images will still be categorised as belonging to different classes of symbolic objects, which require different cognitive competences and skills for their processing and understanding, regardless of the elementary similarity of their shared 'digital codes'.

Moreover, in spite of differences in size, quality and resolution, a painting will not be processed in an essentially different way whether it is presented in its original form, by a photographic reproduction in a catalogue, or by a digital copy on a museum's Web site. Indeed, one can translate content from one medium to another (films to video and DVD, music from records to tapes to CDs, photographs from paper to computer screens, from family albums to publicly accessible Web sites, paintings from canvas to photographs to digital copies, from museums to place mats, cups, ties, posters, toys, kitchen utensils, and so on) without essentially changing its status as a cultural artifact.[15] Depending on the level of analysis, the material or technological basis of a symbolic object does not necessarily decide its semiotic and cognitive status. This, together with the difficulties of giving a precise meaning to the terms 'digital' and 'analogous', makes the whole digital–analogue distinction a non-starter.[16] Manovich, therefore, rightly tries to avoid the word 'digital' in his book *The Language of New Media*.

ATTRACTIONS OF NEW MEDIA

One of the most remarkable effects of new media on film that theorists and critics have observed is a return of cinema to its origins and early forms. Without claiming a direct influence of new media, Bolter and Grusin notice that 'today the typical 35mm or 70mm Hollywood film is closer in spirit to the cinema of attractions than it has been in decades'.[17] This cinema of attraction predated the narrative cinema and as Tom Gunning, who is responsible for introducing this term in film history, writes, instead of being a non-narrative cinema, it treated a story simply 'as a frame upon which to string a demonstration of the magical possibilities of the cinema'.[18] The same has indeed been said about New Hollywood Cinema, in which the story often provides a thin thread that holds together a series of spectacular, mostly computer-generated special effects.[19]

Lev Manovich goes even further by claiming that pre-cinematographic and early cinema techniques that had been marginalised by the classical narrative Hollywood cinema are brought back to the centre by digital cinema.[20] These techniques include animation, the manual construction of images and the discrete character of both space and movement in moving images. In digital cinema, live-action footage has become raw material for further compositing, animating and morphing, and film scenes can even be generated directly in a computer with the help of 3D animation software. In spite of the popular association of computers with automation, digital cinema film frames are 'hand-painted' frame by frame. Due to hardware limitations such as insufficient bandwidth and memory, digital film-makers were forced to use 'loops'. Through these developments, digital cinema severs the so-called indexical bond that tied film images and photographs to their models and has again made cinema 'a particular branch of painting–painting in time'.[21] However, Manovich does not explain how this relates to a previously signalled anti-montage tendency in new media productions. In Manovich's approach to new media, early cinema techniques and digital compositing seem to represent Bolter & Grusin's opposing tendencies of 'immediacy' and 'hypermediacy'. New media seem to be not only capable of integrating all previous media in a single information environment, but they also combine, integrate, resolve or even transcend contradictions and oppositions manifest in those old media. Digital cinema seems to encompass early cinema, classical cinema, art cinema, experimental cinema and immersive virtual realities all at the same time. Or might it be that some unresolved problems of classical and contemporary film theories reemerges in the context of new media?

MULTIMEDIA

What is said about 'digital' also applies to the notion of 'multimediality', which is usually taken to refer to the 'seamless integration of data, text, sound and images of all kinds within a single, digital information environment'.[22] The use of the term 'multimedia' has indeed, as this definition suggests, been restricted to refer to digital, computer-based environments. However, as Manovich again rightly points out, multimediality is not a feature unique to new media. Cinema, television and the theatre already combine images, texts, sounds and often slide projections, rear projections and other sorts of special effects obtained by the inclusion of one or more 'other' media. The 'multimediality' of the theatre in fact inspired Eisenstein's concept of 'montage of attractions'.[23] Even the computer screen's capacity to display a number of co-existing windows is not entirely unique to new media, as films have often treated the screen as simultaneously being a two-dimensional 'textual' surface and a three-dimensional narrative space, as in the opening sequence of Star Wars (1977), where a scrolling text presents an 'expositio'.[24]

Expressions such as 'seamless' combined with 'digital', however, suggest that the boundaries between the different contributing media begin to blur because all sorts of media have been 'transcoded' into the digital codes of the computer language. Again, the technological basis of a medium does not necessarily decide its semiotic and cognitive status, and it seems hard even to try to imagine an information environment in which no differences could be detected between texts, sounds and images. We are, after all, perfectly capable of making such distinctions in the seamlessly integrated information environment of our everyday surroundings, and there is no reason to assume that we should lose this capacity even in a 3D–VR environment. As Manovich observes, the computer screen usually reserves separate windows for each different media object and the user switches from one to the other.[25]

'Multimedia', then, actually means that a single information environment offers the user simultaneous access to different sorts of media. The novelty of new media, therefore, primarily consists of the computer's capacity to give access to different types of media at the same time, and this basically boils down to a capacity to present 'old media' in new ways and to suggest new uses for these old media. Multimediality in itself is, however, neither unique nor new, and the novelty of new media mainly and most importantly consists of a repositioning and redefinition of old media: what Jay David Bolter and Richard Grusin call 'remediation'.[26]

One of the effects of this remediation is that 'old media', and in particular cinema, are being re-described from the point of view of the 'new media'. Manovich's use of the term 'sample' for a film frame is just one example. Redefined as part of an information environment, cinema becomes one among several information and communication technologies. A film's content can be redefined as 'information' that can be conceived of as a collection of data that can be organised in various ways, out of which a film's particular narrative is just one possible choice. A film, then, 'can be thought of as an interface to events taking place in 3D space'.[27]

This idea of cinema as an 'information space' is not dependent on computer databases in itself. Edward Branigan, for example, distinguished six ways of organising data, all of which can play some role in a narrative and all of which can be understood as alternative ways to present the same collection of data.[28] His point of reference was cognitive science, rather than computer science, although both are, of course, intimately related to each other. Marsha Kinder coined the term 'database narratives' for films that follow a particular narrative path, but also allow the spectator to see that 'many other alternatives are equally possible'.[29] She mentions Buñuel, Marker, Resnais, Ruiz, Greenaway, Akerman and Tarantino as her favourite film-makers, most of whom created 'database narratives' long before the advent of the computer. Some of the short stories of Jorge Luis Borges have become classical explorations of such alternative virtual spaces. More generally, the notion of film as a particular interface to information stored in a database fits nicely with the post-modern notion of narrative as a contingent projection of a narrative structure onto a more or less random selection of events. In this view, the narrative chain of causes and effects as well as the selection of events itself might very well have been otherwise.

CINEMA AS A THEORETICAL MODEL

In theories of new media such as these, cinema becomes the model that has to be emu-lated and the limit that has to be overcome at the same time. It becomes a model because cinema has been and still is the medium that most successfully has achieved what Christian Metz once called 'the impression of reality' and what Bolter and Grusin rebaptised as 'immediacy'. It succeeded in transporting the spectator into the virtual reality of a fully fledged fictional world, but this success came with a price. The physical space of the spec-tator and the virtual space of the film's diegesis remained 'ontologically' separate. Immersive virtual 3D reality promises to overcome this limit, and, by subscribing to this goal, media theorists adopt Bazin's Utopian hope for a 'cinéma total'.[30] This search for a more or less perfect immediacy, however, conflicts with another part of the history of film practices and film theory, which has always stressed the illusionary and artificial nature of cinematic worlds. It looks as if in new media theories these two tendencies result in an unresolved hesitation, if not conflict, between new media's 'immediacy' and 'hypermediacy'.

These contradictions are first the result of attributing to cinema a central position in theories of new media and, second, the heritage of some unresolved problems of 'classical' and 'contemporary' film theory. To start with the latter, to say that 'immediacy' is the main aesthetic and psychological goal of cinema means accepting a folk theoretical notion of cinema, according to which film provides the spectator with 'a window on the world'. As with all folk theories, this is a useful description of film in several ways, but limited. André Bazin acknowledged this when he concluded his essay on 'The Ontology of the Photographic Image' with the enigmatic sentence: 'D'autre part, le cinéma est un langage.'[31] The unresolved and barely acknowledged problem with film theory is that there is no single, unified, literal concept of film. Our concepts of film, whether populist or academic, are essentially a mixture, or what cognitivist linguists Gilles Fauconnier and Mark Turner call a 'blend' of two metaphorically structured concepts of film: the notion that 'film is a window on the world' and the notion that 'film is a language'.[32]

The first metaphorical concept is the result of the projection of perceived similarities between human visual perception onto the cinematic apparatus, as it is conceived of in commonsensical knowledge. The human eye is mapped onto the camera, the eye's lens is mapped onto the camera's lens, and the retina is mapped onto the filmstrip. The relationship that normally exists between the object of perception and the percept is mapped onto the relationship between the object in front of the film or photo camera and the 'imprint' of that object on the film. As the percept of visual perception, the image registered on the filmstrip is said to be 'caused' by the perceived object. The immediacy, 'presence' and veracity that are usually ascribed to film images and photographs follow from this metaphorical projection because the spatial and causal connections between the perceiving subject and the perceived object give rise to what George Lakoff calls the 'idealised cognitive model' (or ICM) of seeing. According to this ICM, '1. You see things as they are. 2. You are aware of what you see. 3. You see what's in front of your eyes.'[33] This ICM entails that if you see an event, then it really happened, that if you see something, then there is something real you have seen, and that to see something means you notice it and know it, and that if something is in front of your eyes, you see it. As Lakoff notices, this folk theoretical notion of visual perception does not accurately fit the experience of seeing, but as it works most of the time, it is taken as defining the representative cases of seeing. This ICM and its underlying spatial configuration have been projected onto film and photography wholesale and have given rise to realist film theories that elevated the 'indexical' bond between the filmed object and its filmic representation to the ontological basis that grounds 'realism' as the specificity of cinema and photography.

These often highly sophisticated film theories that inspired an equally highly sophisticated film aesthetics are, however, nothing but the explicitly elaborated assumptions of commonly understood folk theories. As with most metaphorical conceptualisations, the metaphor 'film is a window on the world' only partially captures its desired meaning. Contrary to normal human visual perception which evolves continuously in 'real time', films consist of deliberately selected and arranged 'pieces' of space and time, and, moreover, are projected at times and places other than the time and place where the sounds and images were recorded. The 'film is a window on the world' metaphor conveniently downplays the complexity of the cinematographic processes before, during and after shooting, and crucially misses the representational and symbolic dimension of film as a cultural artifact that nevertheless is an important part of the filmic experience.

It is this part that is captured by the 'film is a language' metaphor, that is apparently the exact opposite of the 'film is a window on the world' metaphor, as it emphasises the symbolic rather than the indexical relationship between film images and the objects they represent. Rather than stressing the resemblances of film images and their models, film practitioners and film theorists who took the 'film is a language' metaphor as their point of departure emphasised film's capacity to marvel with the unknown, the unexpected and the metaphysically impossible. It should be noticed, however, that the concept of language that this metaphor projects onto film is not a scientific linguistic theory but, once again, a folk theory of language, which emphasises not only the symbolic, formal and systemic dimensions of language, but also its intentional and communicative aspects.[34] In this metaphorical concept, film is simultaneously conceptualised as a 'channel' through which 'messages' are transmitted and as a 'grammar' or a set of conventions that governs a film's intelligibility. It is precisely in this very loose and rather metaphorical sense that Lev Manovich uses the word 'language' in the title of his latest book, *The Language of New Media*, to signal 'the emergent conventions, recurrent design patterns, and key forms of new media'.[35]

These metaphors are certainly not unique to film and photography, as Alberti's famous description of a painting as a *finestra aperta* and scores of studies of 'the language of . . .' quite convincingly demonstrate. They also continue to play a role in efforts to come to theoretical terms with new media, as the aforementioned title of Lev Manovich's latest book makes clear. The focus on the dialectics of 'immediacy' and 'hypermediacy' seems to result from the metaphors inherited from folk theoretical conceptions of cinema, rather than from a rigorous empirical investigation of the practices and needs that are emerging around new media. Both of these terms highlight the extremities between which most film theories and film aesthetics oscillate, depending on the metaphor they select for their conceptualisation of film. Even for film, it is not clear whether the term 'immediacy' captures a genuine desire among film spectators or whether it refers to an a priori assumption which derives from the metaphor 'film is a window on the world'.[36]

It is, however, far from clear that metaphors that more or less usefully capture some important aspects of one domain are as illuminative in other domains, even if the latter are closely related to the former. Many new media theorists tend, for instance, to highlight the audiovisual and spatial components of the information environment created by new media. The information environment provided by the computer is, however, not only a screen or 3D virtual reality that offers the user a simulated space to navigate, it is also still a 'desk' that provides the user with tools to work with. After all, the computer is still also a calculator, a typewriter, a notebook, a post office, an archive, a diary, a newspaper and so on. That is, it still performs a lot of functions for which terms such as 'immediacy' and 'hypermediacy' hardly seem to make any sense. As film images, digital images may be either 'records' of a pre-existing reality or depictions of a fictitious, imaginary reality; unlike most film images, however, digital images can be both representations of an existing real world and depictions of an imaginary world at the same time, or neither. The 'film is a window on the world' or 'film is a language' metaphors do not seem be very useful when one tries to come to terms with a 3D virtual environment, whatever it may simulate. In retrospect, new media may help us to realise that these metaphors are maybe not the most suitable tools for describing and understanding many aspects of cinema either.

If there is one thing to be learned from the history of film theory, it is that even sophisticated theories turn out on closer inspection to be elaborations of metaphor-based folk theories. If cinema provides us with a model for theorising new media, this model must be meta-theoretical: beware of widely accepted but, more often than not, ill-defined commonly held notions ('new media', 'digital', 'interactive', 'multimedia'). Do not take widely accepted beliefs at face value (such as the presumed eternal struggle in the arts between the 'representation of reality' and the 'reality of representation', however these may be cast), and do not take it for granted that every new medium 'remediates' its predecessors. New media may simply not have been designed with such a purpose in mind in the first place. However, do not foster the illusion that you can do without metaphors. The trouble with metaphors is that you cannot live with them, but you cannot live without them either.

Notes

1. Peter Lunenfeld, 'Unfinished Introduction', in Peter Lunenfeld (ed.), *The Digital Dialectic: New Essays on New Media* (Cambridge, MA: MIT Press), p. 7.
2. André Bazin, *Qu'est-ce que le Cinéma?* (Paris: Éditions du Cerf, 1975), pp. 9–10.
3. Jay David Bolter and Richard Grusin, *Remediation: Understanding New Media* (Cambridge, MA: MIT Press, 1999), p. 21.
4. Ibid., p. 58.
5. Lev Manovich, *The Language of New Media* (Cambridge, MA: MIT Press, 2000), p. 144.
6. Ibid.
7. Lev Manovich, *The Language of New Media*, p. 28.
8. Christian Metz, *Essais sur la Signification au cinéma, Tome I* (Paris: Klincksieck, 1983), p. 113.
9. Raymond Bellour, *L'Analyse du film* (Paris: Éditions Albatros, 1979).
10. Umberto Eco, *A Theory of Semiotics* (Bloomington: Indiana University Press, 1979), p. 190.
11. Henri Vanlier, *Philosophie de la Photographie* (Laplume: ACCP, 1983), p. 20.
12. See also Malcolm le Grice, 'Digital Cinema and Experimental Film Continuities and Discontinuities', in Yvonne Spielmann and Gundolf Winter (eds), *Bild-Medium – Kunst* (Munich: Fink, 1999), pp. 207–17.
13. Gregory Currie, *Image and Mind: Film, Philosophy, and Cognitive Science* (Cambridge: Cambridge University Press, 1995), p. 63.

14. See W. J. Mitchell, *The Reconfigured Eye: Visual Truth in the Post-Photographic Era* (Cambridge, MA: MIT Press, 1994), p. 161.

15. Lev Manovich, *The Language of New Media*, p. 331.

16. See Jan Simons, 'What's a Digital Image?', in Yvonne Spielmann and Gundolf Winter (eds), *Bild-Medium – Kunst*, pp. 107–22.

17. Jay David Bolter and Richard Grusin, *Remediation*, p. 157.

18. Tom Gunning, 'The Cinema of Attractions: Early Film, Its Spectator and the Avant-Garde', in Thomas Elsaesser (ed.), *Early Cinema: Space, Frame, Narrative* (London: BFI Publishing, 1990), p. 58.

19. Not everybody agrees with this description of New Hollywood Cinema. David Bordwell argued that a typical New Hollywood film such as *Die Hard* (1988) was constructed along similar strategies as the classical Hollywood film, and Warren Buckland made a similar point about *Jurassic Park* (1993), another paradigm example of the New Hollywood film. See David Bordwell, 'Die Hard und die Rückkehr des klassischen Hollywood-Kinos', in Andreas Rost (Hrsg.), *Der schöne Schein der Kunstlichkeit* (Frankfurt: Verlag der Autoren, 1995), pp. 151–202; Warren Buckland, 'A Close Encounter with *Raiders of The Lost Ark*: Notes on Narrative Aspects of the New Hollywood Blockbuster', in Steve Neale and Murray Smith (eds), *Contemporary Hollywood Cinema* (London: Routledge, 1998), pp. 166–77.

20. Lev Manovich, 'What is Digital Cinema?', in Peter Lunenfeld (ed.), *The Digital Dialectic*, pp. 172–92.

21. Ibid., p. 192.

22. Tony Feldman, *An Introduction to Digital Media* (London: Routledge, 1997), p. 24.

23. Sergei Eisenstein, *The Film Sense* (London: Faber and Faber, 1977), pp. 181–3.

24. See also Roger Odin's analysis of the opening sequence of Jean Renoir's *Partie de Campagne* (1936) in 'L'Entrée du spectateur dans la fiction', in J. Aumont and J. L. Leutrat (eds), *Théorie du Film* (Paris: Éditions Albatros, 1980), pp. 198–213.

25. Lev Manovich, *The Language of New Media*, p. 97.

26. Jay David Bolter and Richard Grusin, *Remediation*.

27. Lev Manovich, *The Language of New Media*, p. 326–7.

28. Edward Branigan, *Narrative Comprehension and Film* (London: Routledge, 1992), pp. 19–20.

29. Marsha Kinder, 'Designing Interactive Frictions with Nina Menkes, Pat O'Neill, and John Rechy', *Style*, Summer, 1999, < www.findarticles.com/cf_0/m2342/2_33/59586987/p3/article.jhtml?term=>, p. 3.

30. André Bazin, *Qu'est-ce que le Cinéma?*, p. 19.

31. Ibid., p. 17.

32. Gilles Fauconnier, *Mappings in Thought and Language* (Cambridge: Cambridge University Press, 1997); Mark Turner and G. Fauconnier, 'Conceptual Integration and Formal Expression', *Journal of Metaphor and Symbolic Activity*, 10.3, pp. 183–204.

33. George Lakoff, *Women, Fire, and Dangerous Things: What Categories Reveal about the Mind* (Chicago: University of Chicago Press, 1987), p. 128.

34. See Jan Simons, Metaphors We Watch by. Forthcoming.

35. Lev Manovich, *The Language of New Media*, p. 12.

36. Noël Carroll once spelled out what this desire for immediacy would entail for spectators of horror films. See Noël Carroll, *The Philosophy of Horror or Paradoxes of the Heart* (London: Routledge, 1990).

5.4

New Media as Old Media: Television

William Boddy

The transition from analogue to digital television in the US and elsewhere since 1998 has provoked widespread predictions of fundamental change in moving-image culture, including forecasts of the slow death not only of commercially supported network television, but also of the entire economic and cultural logic of mass marketing that has supported commercial broadcasting for half a century.[1] The technological promise of digital television, in the form of higher-definition images, greater bandwidth and interactive services, has thrown into crisis, or at least historiographic relief, long-established industry practices, business relationships and textual forms. The uneven adoption of digital technologies across the fields of consumer electronics, programme production and delivery systems has exposed new fissures among sectors of the television industry and brought new economic players into the business, in the form of both start-ups and well-established firms, with significant amounts of venture capital being raised even in the wake of the collapse of dotcom share prices on Wall Street.[2]

The current uncertainty has also put into question traditional industry and popular accounts of the medium's role as signifier of national identity (and public service broadcasting's political rationale in the UK and elsewhere), its ontology of liveness and photographic realism and its place as a consumer product within the gendered household. One place where these shifting scenarios of identity and utility are enacted is the ephemeral 30- and 60-second commercials for a range of emerging digital television products and services, including high-definition television receivers, personal video recorders and interactive television services. While some of the recent digital television consumer products and technologies, like the hugely successful DVD player, fit comfortably within already-established business models and viewing practices, others, notably the personal video recorder and virtual advertising, are seen by many within the industry as potentially disruptive of the medium's established textual and economic practices. In the eyes of at least some observers, who evoke the full convergence of the television set and home computer, digital technology will thoroughly transform the television industry, its programming and advertising practices, and the position and function of the apparatus in the home.

The network television industry has reacted with ambivalence to the transition to digital television and to the wider reconfiguration of the medium's role in American society. While the modest fortunes of high-definition television since its public launch at the end of 1998 have underlined the distinct interests of consumer electronics manufacturers, broadcasters and cable operators, it has been the prospect of the wide diffusion of hard drive-based personal video recorders that has provoked the greatest anxiety among broadcasters and advertisers, and the most extravagant visions of a moving-image landscape altered almost beyond recognition by smart television sets and empowered viewers.[3] I would like to address some of the early, often highly speculative, responses to digital television and to identify the ways in which the move to digital technologies has already altered some widely shared cultural and economic assumptions about the medium.

THE CONTEXT FOR THE TRANSITION TO DIGITAL TELEVISION

It is important first to note the unusual historical circumstances in which the US television industry is confronting the transition to digital television. The long-term decline in network audience share as the result of an increasingly fragmented television audience (a decline mitigated in the 1990s by a strong advertising economy and more recently by the spectacular success of a few prime-time network programmes, including *Who Wants to Be A Millionaire?* and *Survivor*), has thrown into crisis the perennially disputatious economic relations between networks and their affiliates, advertisers and programme producers. The continuing consolidation of television station ownership into ever-larger chains, fuelled by permissive federal regulators, has alarmed network leaders who have long envied the more stable and substantial profit levels of station owners. On the other hand, affiliates, facing networks that are increasingly merely parts of larger media conglomerates with interests in cable, satellite and Internet platforms, worry that their status as the dominant delivery vehicle for television programming is in jeopardy. The economic foundation of the network–affiliate relationship, the networks' payment of compensation to stations in return for affiliate airtime, is under concerted network attack; these efforts have provoked a number of group owners to launch a regulatory challenge to network business practices, provoking in turn two networks to withdraw from the National Association of Broadcasters in retaliation. The uncertainty about the long-term viability of the fundamental economic premises of a half-century of American commercial television has made the networks extremely sensitive to the perceived threat of the personal video recorder, which, they worry, would allow massive numbers of households to avoid exposure to television commercials.

Other, more short-term developments within the industry have also affected the way in which new digital technologies have been perceived. At the end of the 1990s, the US networks, faced with escalating programme licence fees for star- and writer-producer driven prime-time dramatic programming, have embraced a range of inexpensive 'reality TV' formats, often with spectacular short-term financial results. In addition, the threatened Hollywood talent strikes in the middle of 2001 encouraged a substantial stockpiling of such scriptless and actor-free programming before the 2001–2 season. Coincidentally, it is precisely these non-traditional entertainment formats that have been viewed as best suited for the design of integrated interactive features and intensive product placement, encouraging networks to explore these applications of digital technology.

Meanwhile, the bursting of the dotcom speculative bubble and the precipitous cooling of the national advertising market at the beginning of 2001 brought the first decline since 1974 in the so-called up-front network television market, where networks solicit spring commitments from advertisers for the forthcoming autumn television season. The decline in network advertising has made the networks fearful of any erosion of their audience figures at the hands of the television-commercial evading personal video recorder and extremely eager to work with advertisers on forms of advertising which would be impervious to such technological agents, including sponsorship, product placement and other forms of 'embedded commerce'.

Finally, events in the US computer and consumer electronics industries have also shaped the short-term economic prospects for enhanced digital television products and services. The *New York Times* in late May 2001 reported the first ever *decline* in the number of residential Internet customers, following the extinction of several free ISPs; the same newspaper reported that US personal computer sales actually *shrank* in the previous two quarters.[4] Meanwhile, prospects for continued high levels of spending in the consumer electronics and computer technology sectors appear dim; as one observer put it in the spring of 2001: 'It's a truly disquieting moment for the sellers of technology. They're in the difficult position of trying to unload a trunk full of cheesecakes in the parking lot of an all-you-can-eat restaurant.'[5] Previous growth forecasts of the entire range of interactive and digital television products and services will need to be put in a new context of falling consumer confidence and technology share prices, restricted access to venture capital for start-ups and a slowing advertising market.

THE BUSINESS FORTUNES OF THE PERSONAL VIDEO RECORDER

Notwithstanding the early optimistic predictions of personal video recorder sales and the alarmist claims of the destabilising effect of the device's ability to evade commercials, sales of the devices were modest throughout most of 2001. As the *Washington Post* noted in April 2001: 'In 1999, Boston-based Forrester Research predicted that 50 million homes would have DVRs by 2005. Fewer than 300,000 have sold so far.'[6] By October 2000, weak sales forced ReplayTV, whose earlier plans for a $119 million initial public offering were abandoned by the sell-off in technology stocks, to withdraw from manufacturing stand-alone personal video recorders altogether, in favour of attempting to license its technology for integration into other consumer devices, from cable boxes to DVD players and television sets.[7] In February 2001, after failing to attract additional private capital, ReplayTV was acquired by Sonicblue, the maker of the Rio MP3 player, in a stock swap valued at $120 million; as ReplayTV's vice president for marketing confessed to the *Washington Post*: 'It certainly is not the billions of dollars we were calculating a year ago.'[8] In April 2001, ReplayTV's rival TiVo announced that it intended to lay off 25 per cent of its staff and pare its marketing expenditures in order to cut overall expenses by 35 per cent; at the same time, TiVo also raised its lifetime subscription fee by 25 per cent.[9] Meanwhile, by the spring of 2001, TiVo stock was trading as low as $4, down from its previous high of $78 in June 2000; as TiVo's chief technology officer admitted in April 2001: 'As we ramped up our distribution and marketing, we all came to the realization that it is going to be harder than we thought.'[10] The *Washington Post* quoted one stock analyst of the personal video recorder business: 'We've switched from this euphoria surrounding the potential to a lot of doubt,' and one April 2001 survey of six financial analysts following TiVo noted that only one of them 'is rating the company higher than a "hold"'.[11] A senior vice president at Thomson electronics told a journalist in December 2000 that 'we still have a lot of questions about that [stand-alone PVR] category because the business model is very, very difficult. . . . All of those [stand-alone] products are subsidised to some extent, and it is still pretty open as to whether the revenue streams would really be out there long term to maintain that business model.'[12]

With personal video recorder sales much slower than earlier optimistic predictions, the device's anticipated effect in depressing the viewing of television commercials has been small to non-existent through the middle of 2001. While Forrester Research in January 1999 predicted that within ten years personal video recorders would be in 82 million homes and that the number of television commercials actually watched by viewers would be cut in half, many in the field are skeptical of the device's impact on advertising practices.[13] One media sale executive told *Broadcasting and Cable* in February 2001: 'The impact right now is negligible. There are hardly enough boxes out there now to start a trend. It's really not even enough to experiment with.'[14] In January 2001, the *Financial Times* noted that TiVo executives, faced with slow personal video recorder sales, were now 'keen to pull back from the dire predictions that were being made about TiVo's impact on commercial broadcasting. Now the stress is very much on what the machines can offer broadcasters . . .', including fuller use of late-night time slots.[15] In fact, TiVo's accommodation to broadcasters and advertisers began with the original design of the unit's remote control features; unlike its rival ReplayTV, according to TiVo Entertainment Group's publicity material aimed at potential advertising partners, 'TiVo chose not to offer a skip button, which would eliminate the informative value of advertising. We will work with you to create advertising content that is most effective in a fast-forward environment.'[16]

This ambivalence on the part of TiVo is also expressed in the company's own television advertising. As one journalist noted, 'the problem facing the industry goes to the core of the clever, yet ambiguous, TiVo television ads that seem to encourage viewers to zap ads that they don't want to see. TiVo touts its value to the advertising community, while pitching itself as a way for TV viewers to skip those same commercials.'[17] On the one hand, the eight 30-second national television commercials made in 2000 and 2001 by TiVo's advertising agency, Goodby, Silverstein and Partners, offer a series of humorous, sometimes edgy vignettes illustrating life with TiVo, including a controversial commercial, 'Network Programmers', which the CBS network refused to run on its hit programme *Survivor* in July 2000. The commercial's single-take tracking shot follows two silent, well-muscled men sweeping past network high-rise offices and secretaries' desks calmly to throw a 30-something network executive through his corner office window, while a sardonic voice-over intones: 'Look at these guys. Network TV programmers. They decide what we watch and when we watch it. Who needs them. TiVo. TV your way.'[18] The other TiVo commercials similarly evoke the viewer-liberating, anti-commercial ethos of the product, using everything from fake 'masculine itching' ads with ex-football heroes on a golf fairway to sober-sounding public service appeals for an end to an epidemic of 'people hurting TVs and TVs hurting people' staged in a hospital emergency room filled with human and television-set casualties (see plate 10).

However, the anti-commercial inflection of TiVo's own commercials belies the company's more ambivalent business model. TiVo has a dizzying array of equity partners from cable and satellite companies, consumer electronics manufacturers, and programme producers and networks, and the company has tried very hard to present the personal video recorder as a technology which will aid television advertisers, not put them out of business.[19] Current efforts include four so-called 'branded areas' where TiVo turns over screen space and hard disk storage areas directly to advertisers. These include TiVo Direct, 30 minutes of direct response video programming pre-installed in the personal video recorder; *TiVo Takes*, a TiVo Studios-produced weekly programme magazine, with interactive-encoded previews of upcoming programmes; Network Showcases, an on-screen menu of branded network partners; IPreview, interactive television promos; and *TiVolution Magazine*, a weekly-updated branded on-screen text preview of forthcoming programmes.

'HOW GOD WATCHES TELEVISION': LIFE WITH THE PERSONAL VIDEO RECORDER[20]

With only 154,000 TiVo units sold by January 2001 (and less than half of US consumers reporting to have heard of the product), substantive research is scant on how the personal video recorder alters audience viewing habits.[21] Furthermore, it may be misleading to extrapolate from the experience of so-called 'early adopters', who are likely not to be representative of the eventual mass market, if any, for the device. However, in its promise of viewer sovereignty over the programme schedule, the personal video recorder has already provoked a revision of the cultural value of the entire television medium for some observers. Writing in opposition to 'TV Turnoff Week', an annual event organised by the TV Turnoff Network (formerly TV-Free America, with media scholars George Gerbner, Todd Gitlin, Mark Crispin Miller and Neil Postman on its board of directors) and endorsed by the American Medical Association, the National Education Association and the American Academy of Pediatrics, one American journalist admonished readers instead to record 'absolutely everything for future viewing', and cited TiVo's suitability to this task. After all, she argued, 'we'd never walk into a library or bookstore, spin around blindfolded and decide to read whatever our hand fell on. We wouldn't tell our kids, "It's time for your bedtime story. Here's this month's *Playboy*".'[22] The ability of the personal video recorder to tailor the flood of programming to individual tastes and schedules has had the effect of elevating the cultural prestige of the medium as a whole, at least among some trade observers.

What the company's own market research has suggested is that TiVo purchasers are 'decisively male', high status, primarily between the ages of 25 and 44, with high levels of disposable income and leisure spending, likely to have computer skills and homes already filled with DVD players, personal computers with Internet access, and young children.[23] Proprietary ethnographic research data presented at the Association of National Advertisers annual Television Advertising Forum in March 2001 indicated that 75 per cent of TiVo users still begin their viewing sessions with live television, turning to recorded material on their hard drives only if they find nothing that interests them.[24] The researcher also reported that while almost all TiVo users report using the device to avoid commercials, actual observation indicated that commercials were still being watched, although more selectively; the video recorder works as a commercial filter, not a commercial eliminator, according to the researcher.[25] In any event, it is likely that viewers highly averse to watching commercials before TiVo were already using other means to avoid watching them. The research also indicated that the recorded programming least likely to contain commercials which were skipped upon playback were children's shows, and men were more likely to avoid commercials than women.[26] A TiVo executive more recently estimated that 50 to 80 per cent of owners scanned through at least some commercials.[27]

The implied gender issues in the preliminary audience research have found resonance in the trade discussions of the personal video recorder. One industry journalist in January 2001 wrote: 'I think pausing live TV is largely "a guy thing", another way that men can use the remote to prove we are the masters of our universe'.[28] While it is premature to describe the 're-masculinisation' of the domestic television set with the introduction of the personal video recorder and other interactive television devices, the position of the television set within the larger masculinist subculture of home theatre technophilia and connoisseurship has already affected the medium's position within both the household and wider cultural life. One attempt literally to reposition the emerging 'Technographics segment' that Forrester Research calls the 'Mouse Potato' ('Technology-accepting, entertainment-focused, and with above-average incomes')[29] was a partnership announced in January 2001 between Microsoft and the US furniture manufacturer La-Z-Boy Inc. to market a $1,500 WebTV-equipped recliner, named 'The Explorer', complete with a WebTV wireless keyboard, two months' free WebTV service, a fused, surge-protected 110V power outlet and AC adapter for laptop use, a DSL port, and a standard modem line; concealed within the other armrest is storage for remote controls and a cupholder. One Internet news site began its announcement of the product launch with 'Internet junkies and couch potatoes unite!', and the rhetorical and literal condensation of the figures of Web surfer and television viewer, fixed in discursive opposition in the trade and popular press over the past decade, suggests the wider stakes of the putative merging of computer and television set via digital technologies.[30] Another commentator on the new recliner evoked the incongruity of the imagined merger of Web surfer and television viewer in a characteristically comic and condescending tone endemic to such discussions: 'Middle America, lie back and meet the Internet. . . . Plug in, log on and veg out'.[31]

In addition to Microsoft's attempts to revive the oxymoronic advertising appeals of early television-set manufacturer DuMont to the male viewer as an 'armchair Columbus', the current re-gendering of the television apparatus in the home can also be seen in the thriving subculture of TiVo hackers, sustained through a number of unofficial Web sites which thus far have generally been tolerated by TiVo. TiVo's Linux-based operating software has attracted a relatively large number of hackers who seem chiefly interested in installing higher-capacity standard computer hard drives, although hackers have also reportedly succeeded in changing the compression algorithms of the TiVo software.[32] In May 2001, the *New York Times* quoted TiVo's customer relations director's estimate that about 1 per cent of the company's 150,000 customers have altered their machines, thereby invalidating their machines' warranties; he told the paper that the company had rewarded some hackers with gifts of free service for telling the company about hacks they had accomplished.[33] After quoting a number of male TiVo hackers, the *Washington Post* concluded: 'The "hackability" of a product can be appealing in its own right to some customers – the ones who are curious, technically minded or cheap. To a hacker, a modification doesn't even have to be particularly useful – just elegant.'[34] A full account of the meeting of the prosaic television set with the gendered subculture of computer hackers would need to consider the ways in which the individual artifact of domestic technology may constitute, in Sherry Turkle's words, an 'evocative object, an object that fascinates, disturbs equanimity, and precipitates thought'.[35] Both the television set and personal computer can become powerful constructive and projective media, consolidating personal and social identities, and the diffusion of the personal video recorder promises to reconfigure the psychological and social meanings of these familiar domestic technologies.

While TiVo buyers are 'decisively male', the device's ambivalent position between the gendered technologies of domestic television, on the one hand, and the personal computer and home cinema, on the other, highlights tensions within the consumer electronics market going back to the development of high-fidelity audio as a male subculture in the late 1940s and 1950s, tensions enacted in quotidian battles over household spending, domestic space and viewing and listening habits.[36] TiVo's Web site, for example, contains a number of testimonials from male customers related to such micro domestic battles across the US, including 'my wife normally cringes when I bring home a new gadget, but she LOVES TiVo, and calls it "hers"'; 'the only audio/electronic component that my girlfriend actually doesn't want to disconnect the moment it enters the system'; and '. . . even my wife, who is not quite the gadget nut I am, is thrilled with TiVo'.[37] Another TiVo promotional page, 'Celebrity Quotes', includes a quotation from retired football quarterback Steve Young which indicates how TiVo's entrance into the household may or may not disturb traditionally gendered household routines:

> I thought once I stopped playing football, things would be quieter. But with a new baby in the
> family, I'm more busy than ever. With TiVo, I can record all the games and watch them
> whenever I want. And with the ability to pause live TV for a diaper change, my wife may love
> TiVo even more than I do![38]

It is clear that the personal video recorder, itself a marriage of television and computer technologies, has evoked a range of complex consumer responses enmeshed with larger cultural figurations of the television viewer and computer hobbyist. TiVo's Web site quotes one journalist:

> TiVo is like a drug. It enhances humdrum parts of your world, eats up your time, taps your wallet and is extremely difficult to explain to anyone who hasn't used it before. Fortunately, personal digital video recorders don't have the downsides of most drugs, and they're a lot cheaper than most illicit habits. But after using TiVo for a while, I'm finding it very hard to conceive of going back to plain old TV.[39]

While the rhetoric of addiction and time-wasting here evokes the traditional figure of the disreputable television viewer, the appeal to an exclusive subculture of initiated users also suggests the more elevated fraternity of the male hi-fi hobbyist and computer enthusiast, which since the 1950s has been rhetorically constructed as the antipode to the commercially debased, passive and lowest-common-denominator activity of television viewing. Significantly, in addition to retired football players and mid-tier showbusiness celebrities, TiVo's 'Celebrity Quotes' Web page also features a prominent endorsement from legendary personal computer pioneer Steve Wozniak, co-founder of Apple Computer, and one of TiVo's customer testimonials includes the simple endorsement, 'best invention since the PC'.[40] In a different context, TiVo's national television advertising attempts to link the personal video recorder to the heroic cultural narrative of the personal computer industry in a 30-second commercial, entitled *Earl*, which features a physically unprepossessing 20-something male driving his dilapidated automobile the wrong way up a freeway entrance, gleefully decapitating a parking meter, interrupting a graveside service with the 'Hallelujah' chorus and demanding (successfully) that he bring home a giant live tiger from a bewildered zoo employee. 'Now that I have TiVo, and I can watch whatever I want, I want to *do* whatever I want.... Not everyone understands.... Then again, not everyone's got TiVo,' he explains over the assorted incidents. The cultural fantasy of technologically delivered social mastery by interpersonally-challenged male technophiles, the 'revenge of the nerds', has been a powerful mythic scenario of the personal computer industry in the US.[41]

CONCLUSION

Beyond the ways in which the introduction of the personal video recorder may alter long-held, everyday understandings of the television medium, the mere threat of the personal video recorder has already encouraged a range of new technological and advertising countermeasures to the digital recorder's ability to evade standard television commercials. In the spring of 2001, the contracting advertising market for network television and the technological threat of the personal video recorder with its ability to ignore advertisements together created a climate of increased network accommodation to advertiser wishes in prime-time programming. In addition to the still rather exotic use of virtual imaging technologies to insert branded sports enhancements (including branded virtual first-down markers in the foreign feeds of the January 2001 Super Bowl), virtual signage at sporting and other live events, and virtual products placed into network or syndicated program-ming, the advertising and television trade presses over the past few years have been filled with calls for sponsors and broadcasters to develop advertising vehicles that would rebuff the expected loss of advertising viewers armed with digital recorders. This would happen through the development of what TiVo calls 'embedded commerce', impossible even for technologically enhanced viewers to avoid, including on-screen banner ads, intensive use of conventional product placement and the move to single-sponsor infomercials and entertainment programming.[42] The growing use of such 'embedded commerce' in the forms of intrusive product placement, star-talent product pitches and sponsor-designed programmes represents an eerie echo of some of the earliest business practices in the US television industry, with important implications for a range of issues from the creative freedom of television writers and producers to the design of programme formats them-selves. Despite, or perhaps because of, the networks' increasingly desperate efforts to retain advertisers through increased product placement and branding opportunities, some in the industry have expressed fears that, in the words of Forrester Research's Josh Bernoff, 'broadcast networks [will] lose their reputation for quality', as viewers increasingly evade commercials, advertising revenues fall and audiences rebel against intrusive product placement.[43]

At the same time, it is important to keep in mind that the commercial prospects for inter-active television generally and the success of any specific personal video recorder service such as TiVo or Ultimate TV are by no means assured in the US or elsewhere. Indeed, the question of which domestic device will serve as portal and recorder for digital television is still unsettled; contending platforms include satellite and cable decoder boxes, DVD players, video game consoles, and television sets themselves. Similarly unsettled are the contentious financial agreements among hardware makers, content providers and delivery system operators to share prospective interactive television revenues, leading one analyst quoted in *Advertising Age* in December 2000 to lament that 'there are too many pigs at the trough'.[44]

In any event, the current instability and contention within the US television industry has at least had the salutary effect of making it clear that 'television' as we have so long known it has always been historically and ideologically contingent. The social meanings of tele-vision are complex and deep-seated, and may not be exclusively, or even especially, driven by changes in technology. As the present turmoil demonstrates, technological change affects distinct interests within the industry in very different ways, provoking revealing clashes among the competing actors and public constructions of the medium. At the same time, television as an informal nexus of textual practices, commercial and regulatory institutions, popular attitudes, and audience practices may prove to be more robust and long-lived than the current ubiquitous prophets of the medium's imminent demise imagine.

Notes

1. See, for example, Michael Lewis, 'Boom Box', *New York Times Magazine*, 20 August 2000, pp. 36–41.

2. May Wong, 'Digital Television Gold Rush Is Starting', *Toronto Star*, 1 May 2001.

3. For a discussion of the HDTV issues, see William Boddy, 'Weather Porn and the Battle for Eyeballs: Promoting Digital Television in the USA and UK', in John Fullerton and Astrid Soderbergh-Widding, (eds), *Moving Images: From Edison to the Webcam* (Sydney: John Libbey, 2000), pp. 133–47.

4. Bob Tedeschi, 'The Rush to the Web Appears to be Slowing, But Has the Audience Peaked or Will It Keep Growing?', *New York Times*, 21 May 2001, p. C9.

5. Scott Kirsner, 'Diminished Appetites', *Boston Globe*, 30 April 2001, p. C1.

6. Christopher Stern, 'DVR, Stuck on Pause: Digital Video Has Lowered Makers' Stock, Staff, Hopes', *Washington Post*, 6 April 2001, p. E1; for similarly optimistic predictions from Forrester, see Tobi Elkin and Hillary Chura, 'PVRs Revolutionizing TV Ad Buys', *Advertising Age*, 18 September 2000, p. 16; Josh Bernoff, *TV Viewers Take Charge* (Cambridge: Forrester Research Inc. 1999).

7. Steve Gelsi, 'ReplayTV Clicks IPO Off for Now', *CBS.MarketWatch.com*, 22 August 2000; Tobi Elkin and Richard Linnett, 'Replay Strategic Shift Marks Victory for TiVo', *Advertising Age*, 4 December 2000, p. 6. In May 2001, Replay announced a deal to supply its personal video recorder software to Motorola, the US's largest manufacturer of cable set-top boxes; see Jon Healey, 'Company Town; ReplayTV to Supply Video-recording Software for Motorola Converter Boxes', *Los Angeles Times*, 1 May 2001, part 3, p. 7.

8. Jon Healey, 'Sonicblue to Buy ReplayTV for $120 Million', *Los Angeles Times*, 2 February 2001, p. C1; Christopher Stern, 'DVR, Stuck on Pause: Digital Video Has Lowered Makers' Stock, Staff, Hopes'.

9. See the TiVo press release, <www.tivo.com/news/pr_detail.asp?article=10968&frames=no>.

10. Christopher Stern, 'DVR, Stuck on Pause: Digital Video Has Lowered Makers' Stock, Staff, Hopes'.

11. Rick Aristotle Munarriz, 'Fool Plate Special: Theory of TiVo-lution', *MotleyFool.com*, 6 April 2001, <biz.yahoo.com/mf/010406/plate_010406.html>

12. 'Thomson Puts TiVo on Hold', *Consumer Electronics*, 30 October 2000.

13. Josh Bernoff, *TV Viewers Take Charge*, p. 11.

14. Lee Hall, 'Coming Soon to a PVR Near You; TiVo to Provide Uploadable Advertisements, While Giving Customers the Means to Skip Them', *Broadcasting and Cable*, 26 February 2001, p. 40.

15. 'Creative Business: TiVo', *Financial Times* (London), 23 January 2001, p. 40.

16. TiVo Entertainment Group publicity material.

17. Lee Hall, 'Coming Soon to a PVR Near You', p. 40.

18. 'Short Take: CBS Scraps TiVo commercial', *Bloomberg News*, 6 July 2000.

19. The list includes AOL Time Warner (13 per cent, with an option to buy 30 per cent), Advance/Newhouse, CBS, Comcast Corporation, Cox Communications, DirecTV, Discovery Communications, Encore Media Group, Liberty Media subsidiaries, Liberty Digital, NBC, Philips Electronics, Showtime Networks, SONY, TV Guide Interactive and The Walt Disney Company; see TiVo's Web site, <www.tivo.com/tivo_inc/partners.asp?frames=no>.

20. Andy Ihnatko, 'TiVo Revolutionizes TV', *Chicago Sun-Times*, 8 May 2001, p. 50.

21. The percentage of Americans aware of the product was reported by Tim Spengler, Initiative Media, North America, at the personal video recorder panel of the 2001 Association of National Advertisers Television Advertising Forum, 29 March 2001, Plaza Hotel, New York City.

22. Gail Pennington, 'TV Is Just Too Valuable to Turn Off', *St. Louis Post-Dispatch*, 15 April 2001, p. F9.

23. Personal interview with Ken Ripley, National Director, Advertising Sales, TiVo, New York City, 27 March 2001.

24. John Carey, Greystone Communications, at the personal video recorder panel of the 2001 Association of National Advertisers Television Advertising Forum, 29 March 2001, Plaza Hotel, New York City.

25. Ibid.

26. On the other hand, some TiVo users expressed the desire to be able to use TiVo to search for commercials as well as for programming for viewing. According to TiVo's behavioural research on TiVo users, Saturday is the most popular day for video playback; the most popular time of day for viewing recorded material is early fringe time and late night; the heaviest taping target time is prime time; and the average interval between recording and playback is two days. According to TiVo, personal video recorder households watch an extra three hours of television per week: Ken Ripley, National Director, Advertising Sales, TiVo, at the personal video recorder panel of the 2001 Association of National Advertisers Television Advertising Forum, 29 March 2001, Plaza Hotel, New York City.

27. Michael McCarthy, 'Ads Are Here, There, Everywhere: Agencies Seek Creative Ways to Expand Product Placement', *USA Today*, 19 June 2001, p. 1B.

28. Craig Leddy, 'TiVo Hard Drives Raise Hard Questions', *Multichannel News*, 15 January 2001, p. 54.

29. Josh Bernoff, *TV Viewers Take Charge*, p. 12.

30. Jay Steinberg, 'For the Lazy Boy', 12 January 2001, <www.edgereview.com/ataglance.cfm?category=edge&ID=162>.

31. Dan Richman, 'Microsoft, La-Z-Boy Team up for World's First "E-cliner"', <stacks.msnbc.com/local/pisea/M7203.asp?cp1=1>.

32. Amy Vickers, 'Digital tv uk: TiVo Deal Fuels Questions over BSkyB Set-Top Choice', *New Media Markets*, 7 July 2000.

33. David J. Wallace, 'You Will Be Reprogrammed. Your Toaster, Too', *New York Times*, 3 May 2001, p. G1.

34. Kevin Savetz, 'Breaking It Open, Making It Better', *Washington Post*, 2 March 2001, p. E1.

35. Sherry Turkle, *The Second Self: Computers and the Human Spirit* (New York: Simon and Schuster, 1984), p. 12.

36. See Keir Kightley, '"Turn it down!" She Shrieked: Gender, Domestic Space, and High Fidelity, 1948–59', *Popular Music*, 15: 2.

37. See <www.tivo.com/entertain/talk/testimonial_category.asp?category=A&page=4&frames=no>.

38. See <www.tivo.com/entertain/celeb_quotes_p2.asp>.

39. Sascha Segan, 'A New View on TV: Digital Video Recorders Go Way beyond VCRs', *abcnews.go.com*, 11 December 2000. The TiVo link is at <www.tivo.com/news/product_reviews.asp?year=2000&frames=no>.

40. <www.tivo.com/entertain/talk/testimonial_category.asp?category=A&page=7&frames=no>.

41. See, for example, Stephen Segaller, *Nerds 2.0.1: A Brief History of the Internet* (New York: TV Books Inc., 1999).

42. TiVo press release; for an account of increased interest among advertising-supported cable networks in advertiser-supplied programming, see Jim Forkan, 'On Some Cable Shows, the Sponsors Take Charge; Advertiser-supplied Programming Trend Focuses on Outdoorsy and Family Genres', *Multichannel News*, 4 June 2001, p. 53; on the growth of product placement, see Wayne Friedman, 'Eagle-Eye Marketers Find Right Spot, Right Time; Product Placements Increase as Part of Syndication Deals', *Advertising Age*, 22 January 2001, p. S2.

43. Josh Bernoff, *TV Viewers Take Charge*, p. 14.

44. David Card, senior analyst, interactive TV, Jupiter Research, quoted in Tobi Elkin and Richard Linnett, 'Replay Strategic Shift Marks Victory for TiVo', p. 6.

Further Reading

Agre, Philip E. and Marc Rotenberg (eds), *Technology and Privacy* (Cambridge, MA: MIT Press, 1998).

Baym, Nancy, *Tune In, Log On: Soaps, Fandom and Online Community* (New York: Corwin, 1999).

Bolter, Jay David and Richard Grusin, *Remediation: Understanding New Media* (Cambridge, MA: MIT Press, 1999).

Bukatman, Scott, *Terminal Identity: The Virtual Subject in Postmodern Science Fiction* (Durham, NC: Duke University Press, 1993).

Caldwell, John (ed.), *Electronic Media and Technoculture* (New Brunswick, NJ: Rutgers University Press, 2000).

Carroll, Noël, *Theorizing the Moving Image* (Cambridge: Cambridge University Press, 1996).

Cassell, Justine and Henry Jenkins, *From Barbie® to Mortal Kombat: Gender and Computer Games* (Cambridge, MA: MIT Press, 2000).

Cherny, Lynn and Elizabeth Reba Weise (eds), *Wired Women: Gender and New Realities in Cyberspace* (Seattle: Seal Press, 1996).

Cubitt, Sean, *Digital Aesthetics* (London: Sage, 1998).

Cubitt, Sean, *Simulation and Social Theory* (London: Sage, 2000).

Darley, Andrew, *Visual Digital Culture: Surface Play and Spectacle in New Media Genres* (London: Routledge, 2000).

Deivert, Bert and Dan Harries, *Film & Video on the Internet: The Top 500 Sites* (Los Angeles: Michael Wiese Productions, 1996).

Druckrey, Timothy (ed.), *Ars Electronica: Facing the Future* (Cambridge, MA: MIT Press, 1999).

Elsaesser, Thomas and Kay Hoffmann (eds), *Cinema Futures: Cain, Abel or Cable? The Screen Arts in the Digital Age* (Amsterdam: Amsterdam University Press, 1998).

Feldman, Tony, *An Introduction to Digital Media* (London: Routledge, 1997).

Fullerton, John and Astrid Soderbergh-Widding (eds), *Moving Images: From Edison to the Webcam* (Sydney: John Libbey, 2000).

Gauntlett, David (ed.), *Web.Studies: Rewiring Media Studies for the Digital Age* (London: Arnold, 2000).

Gledhill, Christine and Linda Williams (eds), *Reinventing Film Studies* (London: Arnold, 2000).

Hilmes, Michele, *Only Connect: A Cultural History of Broadcasting in the US* (Belmont, CA: Wadsworth, 2001).

Kinder, Marsha, *Playing with Power in Movies, Television, and Video Games: From Muppet Babies to Teenage Mutant NinjaTurtles* (Berkeley: University of California Press, 1993).

Kolko, Beth, Lisa Nakamura and Gilbert B. Rodman (eds), *Race in Cyberspace* (New York: Routledge, 2000).

Lancaster, Kurt and Henry Jenkins, *Interacting with Babylon 5: Fan Performances in a Media Universe* (Austin: University of Texas Press, 2001).

Landow, George, *Hypertext 2.0: The Convergence of Contemporary Critical Theory and Technology* (Baltimore, MO: Johns Hopkins University Press, 1997).

Laurel, Brenda, *Utopian Entrepreneur* (Cambridge, MA: MIT Press, 2001).

Le Grice, Malcolm, *Experimental Cinema in the Digital Age* (London: BFI Publishing, 2001).

Lessig, Lawrence, *Code and Other Laws of Cyberspace* (New York: Basic Books, 1999).

Levy, Pierre, *Collective Intelligence: Mankind's Emerging World in Cyberspace* (Cambridge, MA: Perseus Press, 2000).

Lister, Martin (ed.), *The Photographic Image in Digital Culture* (London: Routledge, 1995).

Loader, Brian and Douglas Thomas, *Cybercrime: Law Enforcement, Security and Surveillance in the Information Age* (New York: Routledge, 2000).

Lunenfeld, Peter (ed.), *The Digital Dialectic* (Cambridge, MA: MIT Press, 1999).

Lunenfeld, Peter, *Snap to Grid: A User's Guide to Digital Arts, Media, and Cultures* (Cambridge, MA: MIT Press, 2000).

Manovich, Lev, *The Language of New Media* (Cambridge, MA: MIT Press, 2001).

Mitchell, William J., *The Reconfigured Eye: Visual Truth in the Post-Photographic Era* (Cambridge, MA: MIT Press, 1992).

Morse, Margaret, *Virtualities: Television, Media Art, And Cyberculture* (Bloomington, IN: Indiana University Press, 1998).

Murray, Janet H., *Hamlet on the Holodeck: The Future of Narrative in Cyberspace* (Cambridge, MA: MIT Press, 1997).

Negroponte, Nicholas, *Being Digital* (New York: Alfred Knopf, 1995).

Poster, Mark, *The Second Media Age* (London: Blackwell, 1995).

Poster, Mark, *What's the Matter with the Internet?* (Minneapolis: University of Minnesota Press, 2001).

Rieser, Martin and Andrea Zapp, *New Screen Media: Cinema/Art/Narrative* (London: BFI Publishing, 2001).

Rutsky, R. L., *High Techne: Art and Technology from the Machine Aesthetic to the Posthuman* (Minneapolis: University of Minnesota Press, 1999).

Seiter, Ellen, *Television and New Media Audiences* (Oxford: Oxford University Press, 1999).

Sobchack, Vivian (ed.), *Meta-morphing: Visual Transformation and the Culture of Quick-Change* (Minneapolis: University of Minnesota Press, 2000).

Spielmann, Yvonne and Gundolf Winter (eds), *Bild-Medium – Kunst* (Munich: Fink, 1999).

Stone, Allucquère Rosanne, *The War of Desire and Technology at the Close of the Mechanical Age* (Cambridge, MA: MIT Press, 1995).

Tapscott, Don, *Growing up Digital: The Rise of the Net Generation* (New York: McGraw-Hill, 1999).

Turkle, Sherry, *Life on the Screen: Identity in the Age of the Internet* (New York: Simon and Schuster, 1995).

Wasko, Janet, *Hollywood in the Information Age* (Cambridge: Polity Press, 1994).

Weibel, Peter and Timothy Druckrey (eds), *Net Condition: Art and Global Media* (Cambridge, MA: MIT Press, 2001).

Index